FOURTH EDITION

The **Principal's Companion**

To Bonnie, with love you've made it all possible
And to Rebecca, our role model

To David J. Robbins, a teacher
and leader whose message about
the power of relationships continues
to influence who we are and our work
To Muriel Robbins, a teacher,
counselor, and musician who inspires us with
her wisdom, commitment to serving others,
spirit, and personal example
To Ray, your love and encouragement
remind us of the important things in life
and to
Lydia and Alex, your dedication
to make a difference in the world matters

FOURTH EDITION

The **Principal's Companion**

Strategies to Lead Schools for Student and Teacher Success

PAM ROBBINS | HARVEY B. ALVY

Foreword by Kent D. Peterson

CORWIN
A SAGE Company

CORWIN
A SAGE Company

FOR INFORMATION:

Corwin

A SAGE Company

2455 Teller Road

Thousand Oaks, California 91320

(800) 233-9936

www.corwin.com

SAGE Publications Ltd.

1 Oliver's Yard

55 City Road

London EC1Y 1SP

United Kingdom

SAGE Publications India Pvt. Ltd.

B 1/I 1 Mohan Cooperative Industrial Area

Mathura Road, New Delhi 110 044

India

SAGE Publications Asia-Pacific Pte. Ltd.

3 Church Street

#10-04 Samsung Hub

Singapore 049483

Acquisitions Editor: Arnis Burvikovs

Associate Editor: Desirée A. Bartlett

Editorial Assistant: Ariel Price

Production Editor: Amy Joy Schroller

Copy Editor: Amy Rosenstein

Typesetter: C&M Digitals (P) Ltd.

Proofreader: Dennis W. Webb

Indexer: Rick Hurd

Cover Designer: Karine Hovsepian

Copyright © 2014 by Corwin

Printed in the United States of America

A catalog record of this book is available from the Library of Congress.

ISBN 978-1-4522-8759-1

This book is printed on acid-free paper.

SFI® Certified Sourcing
www.sfiprogram.org
SFI-00453

16 17 18 10 9 8 7 6 5 4 3 2

Contents

Foreword

Kent D. Peterson

Professor Emeritus
University of Wisconsin–Madison

The fourth edition of *The Principal's Companion* maintains the relevance, quality, and usefulness of the earlier editions. Continuing the clear and cogent writing and thinking of the first three editions, this volume provides an enormous wealth of ideas, information, and conceptual models that will be important to aspiring principals, new principals, and experienced principals as well.

In addition to updating new knowledge about leadership, curriculum and instruction, the change process, working with the community, and many other topics, this edition adds considerably to our understanding and concerns about bullying, the use of data for decision making, and student differences. Both the updating and the new topics make this a very contemporary look at how to be an excellent principal in the 21st century.

While the number of chapters may seem a little daunting, all work well together. The organization of the ideas makes the book highly useful whether read through or delved into topically. The chapters cover all the major tasks, responsibilities, and roles of school principals. These can be read as stand-alone sections, when the reader wishes to dig deeply into that topic such as working with parents or faculty meetings. Or they can be read as a well-sequenced look at the principalship overall.

The Contents section offers an excellent overview of the broad and well thought out set of ideas found in this book. The set of topics and the organization of sections, chapter titles, and section headings are themselves a useful tool for an aspiring or new principal. The ideas and issues addressed and described in the Contents provide a useful organizer for thinking about the principalship. But to gain the full benefit of the book, a close read of the chapters is needed.

Some chapters attend to specific aspects of the school year, the roles one takes, the nature of a principal's relationships, and the personal side of leading. Some focus on particular aspects of the principal's year—such as the first days of school—and provide thoughtful and useful ideas on that time period. Other chapters look at various roles of the principal—shaping the school's culture, developing the vision and mission of the school, or engaging parents—and detail concrete and specific ways of taking on these roles effectively. Several chapters speak to the nature of a principal's relationships with teachers, parents, and central office. These are definitely a must-read, for these relationships often make or break a school. A set of chapters address the importance of attending to the emotional and personal needs of a leader, which, if ignored, will affect the quality of relationships and even one's health. These chapters are rich with insight.

The fourth edition comes to us from two highly reflective practitioners and thinkers who have brought a wealth of useful ideas and knowledge from a wide array of sources. The book is conceptual and practical, readable and complex, as well as useful and applicable.

Books for principals and aspiring principals should foster careful thinking and relevant skills in an easily accessible format. *The Principal's Companion,* fourth edition, accomplishes these things in a highly usable format. The richness of ideas, breadth of examples, and thoughtful questioning make this book applicable for the development of more successful leaders as well.

Effective principals should not be a luxury that schools only occasionally enjoy. Rather, effective leadership is needed and required in *all* schools. This fourth edition provides an enhanced array of the most current ideas and research for achieving this important end.

Preface

Alone, the principal often wonders, "Am I doing the right thing? Have I demonstrated a commitment to the success of each teacher and student? Have I taken a moral stand to represent the voiceless?" Although she is surrounded by hundreds of individuals on a daily basis, the school principal ironically often feels isolated when key decisions need to be made, for there is no colleague on-site with the same role. For example, alone in her office, a high school principal wonders about the subtle and not-so-subtle remarks students are making about ethnicity. Having 54 nationalities represented in the school could make it a potential tinderbox or an incredible context for teaching tolerance, social justice, valuing diversity, and building understanding. Her leadership actions will have a profound affect in determining which of these possibilities becomes reality.

Many principals reflect on the nature of their work and describe it as characterized by paradox. Some say that they feel like they are alone and in the spotlight at the same time. Alone, in the privacy of his office, a middle school principal, having heard from teachers about several students being bullied, wonders why the school's commitment to address this issue has not succeeded. The secretary then informs the principal that several concerned parents have called asking to see him and an assistant principal concerning the issue. A local reporter has also called to ask for an interview with the principal on cyberbullying in the school.

Principals feel alone when asked to lead an effort in an area in which they have received little formal training. One district sent out an August memo to all principals indicating that they will be using the new teacher evaluation system this school year. The principals have received two days of training on the new system and instruments. Upon reading this memo, an elementary principal reflects, "I'm pleased that we are taking evaluation seriously, but I do not have enough training. Shouldn't we first pilot the instrument? How am I going to build trust with the faculty? This is a big part of my job, yet I have never really had any guidance on how to do this."

Creating a learning environment that promotes college and career readiness, teacher accountability, raising student achievement, 21st century skills, diversity, tolerance, and social justice, as well as academics, school safety, environmental guidelines that protect the health and general welfare of staff and students, developing and maintaining a green focus, social and emotional learning, and with diminished resources . . . never before has the principal's role as a public figure been so demanding. What's more, there is pressure to perform in a context where others frequently offer "expert" advice. After all, everyone's been to school! But what is the best decision? How can the principal ensure what is in the best interest of students and staff? Because of questions like these, we wrote *The Principal's Companion*.

WHY A FOURTH EDITION?

Although some educational issues remain constant, practitioners, researchers, the daily news, and the Internet remind us that much of the educational landscape has changed since the 2009 third edition of *The Principal's Companion*. In response to these changes, the fourth edition includes more than 200 new references and examines the principal's role in relation to various topics, including the following:

- Shifts in curriculum, instruction, assessment, and professional development
- Federal legislation that affects practice—from No Child Left Behind to Race to the Top
- Principal standards and expectations for the 21st century
- Common Core State Standards
- Moral leadership, social justice, and committing to students without privilege
- Addressing the achievement, opportunity, and discipline gaps
- Supporting lesbian, gay, bisexual, and transgender students
- Accountability and state testing
- Assessment and data-driven decisions
- Teacher supervision and evaluation process that enhances the quality of student work and achievement
- Updated instructional implications of brain research
- Walk-through supervisory approaches and instructional rounds guided by the concept of visible learning and feedback from students
- Strategies to enhance teacher conferencing and observations
- Approaches to improve graduation rates
- Crisis management after Sandy Hook Elementary School
- Trust and leadership
- Classroom management strategies that address system inequities
- Bullying, cyberbullying, and social and community responsibility
- Strategies to work with all parent communities
- Teacher leadership and leadership teams
- A model to promote student learning (a revised graphic: the student learning nexus) reflecting current trends to support supervisors and teacher leaders

- Structures for professional development that build individual and schoolwide capacity to address differentiated staff and student needs in ways that leave their mark on policy and practice
- Faculty meetings and a faculty meeting planning template
- Shaping school cultures to promote professional learning communities and the expanded role of teacher leadership teams
- Storytelling as a powerful culture-shaping leadership tool
- Social and emotional learning
- The Individuals With Disabilities Education Improvement Act of 2004 and Response to Intervention
- Technology as a leadership, teaching, and professional development resource
- Tips on budgeting during tough times
- Superintendent expectations for principals
- Websites on leadership topics

Some of these issues have historically been part of the administrator's work life, but many are new or are being spotlighted more emphatically now than in the past. As authors, we continue to feel compelled to explore both research and practice to support principals in their quest to effectively address important issues. However, we are quite cautious about taking on topics simply because they are in vogue. Our focus in *The Principal's Companion* is steered by a continuing commitment to promoting those actions that best serve all students and a belief that relationship building and communication skills represent critical leadership abilities. For example, high test scores on challenging state and national performance measures are certainly important. But equally important is developing within students a reverence for learning and those social and emotional skills that enable them to become contributing citizens in a democratic society. Although these attitudes and skills often are not measured formally, research shows that they are essential to leading a satisfying life and fostering a healthy 21st century society.

ENDURING FEATURES OF THE BOOK

The Principal's Companion seeks to explore both classical and current leadership issues that are likely to impact student learning for many years to come. The primary purposes of this book remain the same—to provide ideas, approaches, strategies, resources, tools, techniques, and reflective opportunities for practicing and aspiring principals and to facilitate educational improvement when and where it counts, in every classroom and school, each and every day.

There are countless theories and ideas about leadership, but there is no one secret formula for success. Effective leaders invent creative solutions as they face challenges associated with new demands on their role or new situations and examine the consequences of their actions, often making midcourse corrections. As one principal put it, "I try to make thoughtful decisions. Operating by the seat of one's pants is not the best way 'to do' the principalship. Yet the work demands that one address issues as they emerge. The bottom line is you try to do what is best for students and staff." Although principals cannot succeed without a fundamental understanding of theory, because of the immediacy of workplace demands, they often hunger for tried-and-true practices. Both theory and practice are essential for effective leadership.

Experience tells us that many principals have discovered strategies to tackle problems similar to those faced by their colleagues. However, because of the isolation that characterizes the principalship, there are seldom avenues to tap this tremendous potential treasure. *The Principal's Companion* mines multiple sources to provide practical strategies for principals who often operate alone. School principals need to know that they are part of a learning community of educational companions working together to help colleagues be the best they can be. This combined collegial effort will help principals create the kind of teaching and learning environment that supports teachers' efforts to bring about successful student performance. The interactive nature of the book, with reflective questions at the end of each chapter, is intended to help principals feel as if there is a colleague out there with whom to interact. The reader also will "hear" the voices of many practitioners who are quoted throughout the text. This will give current and aspiring principals a perspective of what it is like in the field and different contexts to help them connect with others. Ultimately, newcomers and seasoned principals will learn that all of us make mistakes, meet challenges, and succeed.

Although this book is written primarily for current and aspiring principals, it will also be of interest to principal mentors, central office leaders, professional developers, university professors, school board members, directors of national and international principals' centers and associations, and leadership consultants.

Recognizing that principals are quite busy and have little time to waste, the chapters in this book have been kept short and to the point. Each one reflects a topic that principals have indicated is important. The ideas, experiences, strategies, and techniques described in each chapter are grounded in research and practice. Each chapter concludes with a set of questions so that the reader can write reflections inspired by the chapter or note strategies that he or she wants to try. This is an invitation to write between the lines, to add to one's collective knowledge base, thus enhancing the value of the book for the reader. Each chapter is designed to stand on its own and can be read in one sitting.

Success in the principalship depends on many factors. This book addresses these factors in seven parts, with chapters included under umbrella themes:

Part I: The Principal's Many Roles describes the roles of learner, manager, communicator, and leader during a crisis, co-creator of the learning organization, and shaper of school culture. This section makes a strong case for recognizing that effective principals and assistant principals play a variety of roles—all of which are necessary for instructional leadership and the essential role of teacher leadership teams. Fulfilling the roles that create a climate for growth, making sure schedules work, and setting a personal example of learning from successes and mistakes are some of the issues we address in this section.

Part II: Critical Skills for Effective Leadership examines and makes many suggestions regarding effective human relations strategies characterized by emotional intelligence and the vitally important function of time management and working effectively with the central office. We emphasize that these are critical areas because one cannot get the job done without succeeding in cultivating, practicing, and maintaining collegial relationships at the school site and central office and without taking control of one's time.

Part III: Honoring the School's Mission concentrates on the importance and process of mission building as a guiding force in the organization. We examine how to implement change in a way that provides meaning and constant renewal of the school's mission and generates commitment to the change among organizational members with an emphasis on the critical role of trust and how school leaders cultivate and sustain trust.

Part IV: Working Together to Build a Learning Community links a variety of components that must interact synergistically if a school is to truly be a learning community. These components include building a collaborative environment; promoting teacher leadership; addressing critical issues in instruction, curriculum, and assessment that relate to classroom decisions that enhance student work; effectively using faculty meetings as a tool for capacity building; and meeting a variety of professional growth needs focused on building teachers' collective capacity to promote student learning. Additional components include supervision and evaluation of teachers to promote quality teacher decision making based on student learning and strategies to maximize feedback to teachers regarding their performance in meeting professional goals and student needs.

Part V: Starting Effectively and Staying the Course looks at the importance of providing meaning to traditional events such as the first days of school or the opening of a new school. Often principals miss opportunities to see how these events can serve as key tools for shaping the school's culture and providing a foundation for continuous growth. We also include an expanded section on tips to enhance a principal's effectiveness. Here, the reader will find ideas about organizing time, budgeting when resources are scarce, planning for a new school, using technology efficiently, and incorporating helpful strategies to stay on task.

Part VI: Embracing Your Constituencies provides strategies to enhance one's interactions with students, parents, and the greater community, including businesses, emergency service personnel, social services, senior citizens, politicians, and the media. This section takes a holistic approach, viewing parents and the greater community as an integral part of the school, and examines social justice issues and efforts to improve graduation rates.

Part VII: The Principal's Professional and Personal Worlds looks at the individual principal. The focus here is to examine ways for the principal to grow, personally and professionally, and to remain vibrant, healthy, and continuously engaged in the pursuit of best practice regarding teaching, learning, and ethical school leadership.

The individual chapters serve as a menu of options from which the reader can select to meet pressing needs, assist in planning, or use as a resource. Many readers of the earlier editions commented that *The Principal's Companion* validated their existing practices, foreshadowed situations that needed to be addressed, and raised the bar for professional practice. In lonely moments of reflection, it also served as a companion. As professional colleagues, we welcome you in joining a continuous conversation about the principalship and wish you much success in what we believe is a sacred profession.

Pam Robbins
Staunton, VA, and Napa, CA

Harvey B. Alvy
Cheney, WA

Acknowledgments

arvey Alvy's first principal while teaching at the Frederick Douglass School in Harlem, the late Lionel McMurren, will always be remembered as an ethical leader whose support for new teachers inspired them to reach great heights. Harvey is especially indebted to other administrators, mentors, teachers, school secretaries, and friends who have shared ideas, provided constructive criticism, and supported him as a teacher, elementary and secondary principal, and Professor of Educational Administration at Eastern Washington University. These include Ted Coladarci, Forrest Broman, David Chojnacki, Bob Gibson, Richard Shustrin, Alan Siegel, Drew Alexander, Steve Kapner, Elaine Levy, Jane Liu, Don Bergman, Rob Beck, Betty Bicksler, Nelson and Lisa File, Casey and Chris Tuckerman, Ken Karcinell, Bob Connor, Bob Stockton, Paul Schmidt, Konni deGoeij, Uma Maholtra, Abby Chill, Nili Sadovnik, Sandy Bensky, Les Portner, Joan Dickerson, Alan Coelho, Lynn Briggs, Chris Valeo, Chris Steward, Ted Otto, Kathy Clayton, Mike Dunn, Deb Clemens, Becky Berg, Sean Dotson, Josh Garcia, Troy Heuett, Billie Gehres, Sharon Jayne, Steve Smedley, Tammy Campbell, Jim Howard, Larry Keller, Leonie Brickman, and the late Boni Rahaman, Tom Overholt, Phil Snowdon, William C. Shreeve, and Len Foster. In addition, I would like to acknowledge the wonderful administrators, teachers, and support staff of the American Embassy School in New Delhi, India, the American International School in Israel, the Singapore American School, and Eastern Washington University. To Norman Alvy and Vicki Alvy, as mom said, and dad believed, "You're the best." Harvey's wife, Bonnie, and daughter Rebecca, as always, deserve a degree of recognition that cannot be measured; their love is sustaining.

Pam Robbins would like to acknowledge Percy Haugen and Ernie Moretti, principals who provided inspiring induction experiences for her as a teacher, modeled the role of learning leaders, and created a sense of meaning and enthusiasm for her work as well as a commitment to helping every student achieve. Pam would like to express deep appreciation and gratitude to the many educators who continue to influence her work, offering guidance, valuable insights, feedback, and professional learning. Special thanks are due to Margaret Arbuckle, Roland Barth, Ginni Bauguess, Cindy Bevevino, Mike Bossi, Debbie Brown, Ginny Connelly,

Lee and Debbie Cooke, Ann Cunningham Morris, D. D. Dawson, Terry Deal, Betsy Dunnenberger, Karen Dyer, Dot Earle, Maurice Elias, Carl Glickman, Gayle Gregory, Tom Guskey, Doug Guynn, Leah Hanger Roadcap, Mark Hansen, Allen Haymon, DeWitt House, Stephanie Hirsh, Tara Kidwell, Karen Steinbrink Koch, Lou Martin, George Manthey, Kathleen McElroy, Ray McNulty, Jay McTighe, Patrice Newnam, Kent Peterson, Leslie and Mike Rowland, Jane Scott, Dennis Sparks, Judith Warren Little, and Pat Wolfe. The late Claudia Gallant, Gene Broderson, Jane Bailey, Gracia Alkema, Judy Arin Krupp, Susan Loucks-Horsley, Frank Gomez, and Pat Schettini are gratefully remembered for their professional colleagueship, wisdom, and the profound difference they made in my life and in the field of education.

Heartfelt thanks are due to Ray Cubbage for his love, sage advice, companionship, patience, and inspiration.

Finally, special thanks are due to Kim Gray for the countless hours she spent processing this manuscript, for her perseverance, friendship, and her positive spirit.

PUBLISHER'S ACKNOWLEDGMENTS

Corwin would like to thank the following individuals for taking the time to provide their editorial insight and guidance:

Dr. Phillip F. Diller, Associate Professor Educational Leadership
Shippensburg University of Pennsylvania
Shippensburg, PA

Dr. Maria C. Guilott, Consultant
Retired in 2011 from the University of Southern Mississippi
Retired in 2007 from St. Tammany Parish Schools, LA

Dr. Roseanne Lopez, Executive Director of Elementary Education
Amphitheater Public Schools
Tucson, AZ

About the Authors

 **Pam Robbins** is an independent educational consultant who serves school districts, educational service centers, professional associations, state departments of education, leadership academies, universities, and corporations throughout the United States, Canada, Europe, Great Britain, the Far East, and South America. Pam's professional interests include leadership, supervision and evaluation, the leadership practices of Abraham Lincoln, developing learning communities, brain research and effective teaching, instructional strategies for the block schedule, peer coaching, mentoring, and presentation skills.

Pam began her teaching career in special education. Later, she taught in the intermediate grades and coached high school basketball. As an administrator, she served as Director of Special Projects and Research for the Napa (CA) County Office of Education, and Director of Training for the North Bay California School Leadership Academy. Pam also provides national and international professional learning sessions for the Department of Defense Education Equity Division, the Ministry of Education in Singapore, Ford Motor Company, the Association for Supervision and Curriculum Development (ASCD), the American Society for Training and Development (ASTD), Learning Forward, Phi Delta Kappa (PDK), the National Association of Elementary Principals (NAESP), National Association of Secondary School Principals (NASSP), and the National School Boards Association.

Pam earned her doctorate from the University of California, Berkeley. Her doctoral studies focused on the leadership and development of learning communities. She was awarded the Best Dissertation Award by the National Staff Development Council.

Pam can be contacted at probbins@shentel.net.

Harvey B. Alvy served as a practicing principal for 14 years in both elementary and secondary schools. His teaching career began at the Frederick Douglass School in New York City, and he later taught in middle and high

schools in the United States and abroad. Overseas experiences included the American School in Kinshasa, Zaire; the American International School in Israel; the American Embassy School in New Delhi, India; and Singapore American School. Harvey is a founding board member of the Principals' Training Center for International Schools and was selected as a National Distinguished Principal for American Overseas Schools by the National Association of Elementary School Principals. In 2004 he received the Eastern Washington University (EWU) CenturyTel Faculty Achievement Award for Teaching Excellence.

Harvey earned his doctorate in educational administration from the University of Montana, focusing on the problems of new principals. He has conducted seminars, workshops, and presentations both nationally and internationally on the newcomer to the principalship, moral leadership, instructional leadership, effective supervision of teachers, characteristics of great teachers, educational change, and the leadership of Abraham Lincoln.

Harvey held the William C. Shreeve Endowed Professorship in Educational Administration until 2012 when he became Professor Emeritus at EWU. He can be reached at halvy@ewu.edu.

PART I

The Principal's Many Roles

Leader as Learner

It's a new experience every day.

—A principal's voice[1]

PRINCIPAL AS LIFELONG LEARNER

There is no setting in which the concept of the lifelong learner is more important than a school. In fact, many professionals now conceptualize the school as a professional learning community (DuFour, DuFour, & Eaker, 2008) that nurtures a culture of learning not only for students but also for administrators, teachers, support staff, and parents. This is a powerful notion that can impact student success. As Barth (2001b) notes, "More than anything else, it is the culture of the school that determines the achievement of teacher and student alike" (p. 33).

Bennis and Nanus (1985) remind us that successful leaders take responsibility for their own development and are *perpetual learners.* Schlechty (2001) stresses, "If the principal is to help teachers improve what they do, the principal must continuously be learning to improve what he or she is doing" (p. 145). Senge (1990) suggests that a characteristic of the successful leader is the ability to instill in others the desire to learn what is necessary to help the organization reach its mission. And George (2007) reflects, "Authentic leadership is empowering others on their journeys. This shift is the transformation from 'I' to 'We.' It is the most important process learners go through in becoming authentic" (p. 44). Applying this notion to the principal of a school, the leader can model for everyone in the workplace what lifelong learning means. For modeling to be effective, though, it should be sincere, consistent, purposeful, and empowering. Thus modeling authentic and empowering leadership begins with the character of the leader—and character is destiny. Zenger and Folkman, in their research based on ratings of 25,000 leaders, remind us, "Everything about great leadership radiates from character" (2002, p. ix). It is no surprise that the 2013 National Association of Elementary School Principals (NAESP) and the National Association of Secondary School Principals (NASSP) report, *Leadership Matters,* notes, "Great schools do not exist apart from great leaders" (NAESP & NASSP, 2013, p. 1). There are several ways to model effectively.

LEARNING IN MANY CONTEXTS

One way the principal can model lifelong learning is by continuing to participate in the development and demonstration of effective teaching practices. For example, a principal collaborating with teacher leaders can help create faculty meetings in which conversations about teaching, learning, and assessment become institutionalized through various activities. During these conversations, principals should purposefully support the remarks of both new and veteran teachers to model a high regard for the contributions of all faculty. Another context in which the principal can function as learner is during the supervision process. The following scenario demonstrates how the leader-as-learner theme is played out in two ways: learning about behaviors and activities that facilitate student and teacher learning, and also behaviors and strategies that enhance the principal's effectiveness in the supervisory process.

An effective and common supervisory technique includes a preobservation conference in which the principal and a teacher, through a questioning process, work together to "unpack" the teacher's thinking about the lesson to be taught. Together they discuss learning objectives, planned teaching behaviors, student activities, evidence of student learning, and data the principal will be collecting. They discuss potential problems and fine-tune the lesson plan. During the observation, the principal, steered primarily by the teacher's request for information, collects data. Collectively, teacher and principal learn about curricular, instructional, and assessment practices that produce desired student outcomes. In the postobservation conference, the principal and the teacher often examine student work and ask questions that foster reflection on and analysis of the lesson. Together they discuss what worked to facilitate student learning. At the conclusion of these reflections, they analyze what would be done the same and what would be done differently if the lesson were to be taught again.

Additionally, the principal asks, "Thinking about this conferencing process, what strategies and techniques did I use that facilitated your thinking as a teacher?" The principal might also ask, "What might I have done differently?" Thus the principal and the teacher collaboratively analyze the conferencing practices that enhance or hinder teacher thinking and learning about curriculum and instruction. Together they find ways to make the conferencing experience worthwhile for both.

Principal-as-student experiences can be an innovative way to provide a new perspective and important insights about a school. The principal can spend time in classrooms taking on the student role as a participant in a discussion, a team member in a cooperative group, or a reader or teacher. A particularly successful principal-as-student strategy is "Principal for the Day." One high school principal holds an essay contest each year that results in a student exchanging roles with the principal for one day. The principal takes on the class schedule of the student selected as principal and completes the student's homework assignments, attends classes, and takes examinations. This is a wonderful way to celebrate learning, remain visible, attend classes, and build relationships with students. It also increases the principal's awareness of the quality of classroom learning. These experiences can be shared on a schoolwide basis, in faculty meetings, or with the school's parent-teacher organization. Students and teachers appreciate the interest in them and enjoy the novelty of the situation. If a principal has not functioned in these roles before, it is critical to let teachers know ahead of time "what you're up to."

The principal can teach demonstration lessons; possibly on critical thinking skills stressed with the English Language Arts (ELA) Common Core State Standards (CCSS), and record the lessons to use at a faculty meeting. This provides an opportunity to apply new ideas and practices. Then the principal can talk with staff about experiences in teaching and learning associated with presenting lessons. If the principal's lesson is only fair, and the "rough edges are showing," this can be comforting to staff. It is nice to know that leaders are not flawless. This builds trust because teachers realize that the principal has walked in their shoes, is willing to accept feedback from the faculty, and has an understanding of classroom conditions.

The principal can also function as a learner by reading and sharing research with teachers and parents. By writing or speaking about new learnings, the principal can pass on knowledge of recent research while modeling a love of learning.

Still another way that the principal functions in the learner role is by participating in professional development sessions. Too often principals introduce speakers and run off to another meeting. Principal participation emphasizes the importance of these professional development opportunities and validates the teachers' time spent in these sessions.

When the principal attends a conference, there are frequently opportunities to purchase DVDs, podcasts, or download sessions. Teachers should be encouraged to do the same, possibly even watching a live streaming video during the conference or on demand at a later date. Try picking out the best sessions and starting a digital collection in the staff room, teachers' center, or library. These resources should be available for staff or parents. The principal can also send a follow-up report on the conference to staff or sponsor a volunteer brown-bag lunch on key conference ideas. If there is sufficient interest in a topic, wikis or blogs can be initiated to engage in a discussion forum on the school district Web site.

Principals can help encourage Action Research projects by individuals or groups of teachers on educational ideas of interest to the staff. To illustrate, in one school district several elementary and high school teachers engaged in an Action Research project exploring the use of student portfolios. The teachers met periodically to discuss their experiences and student reactions, and the principal facilitated the process by helping to gather articles on portfolios, keeping a record of the project, and helping to develop an Action Research report with the staff. Staff who were planning to pursue the project during the following school year used several recommendations from this report:

- Continuing the project on a voluntary basis
- Developing portfolio partners among the faculty to compare notes every couple of weeks during the year
- Having students in one class share portfolios with other classes
- Collecting more nuts-and-bolts ideas on portfolios
- Recording oral readings or presentations of student work
- Refining ways to help students reflect on and evaluate their progress through self-assessment and use of rubrics
- Helping teachers fine-tune their conferencing skills with students
- Providing strategies to help teachers structure classes to engage in frequent conversations with individual or cooperative groups of students promoting higher level questions based on close reading of nonfictional texts
- Considering strategies to present portfolios to parents during an evening or afternoon of student-led conferences

These suggestions by teachers assisted both the principal and the teachers in their quest to continually learn. By encouraging teachers to network and use the resources of a principal's office, including secretarial services, and maintaining a database on portfolio progress, principals send a clear message of support for professional development and can be a great help to teachers engaged in learning activities designed to enhance students' classroom experiences.

Another strategy to support learning includes organizing book study groups or clubs among teachers and parents. When principals are involved in these groups as facilitators or participants, the learning leader role is strengthened and modeled. In one high school a successful book study group read *Focus,* by Mike Schmoker (2011b), and *Drive,* by Daniel Pink (2009).

Principals who solicit comments about their job performance from staff members at the end of the year send a strong message that they seek and appreciate staff input as another resource to promote learning. Furthermore, asking for staff feedback models trust building, a stance of openness, and a commitment to ongoing learning. The following form was used for several years by one of the authors to gain faculty input on a principal's performance:

Dear Faculty,

Over the years I have asked each faculty member with whom I have worked to give me helpful hints to improve my job performance. I know that you are all very busy, but I would appreciate it if you could take a few minutes to answer the questions below and help me evaluate my performance so I can do a better job next year. Obviously, your comments will remain confidential. If you would like to remain anonymous, please word process your comments. Please put your comments in the "Harvey" envelope on Prema's desk. I would appreciate your comments by the last faculty day, May 27.

Thanks, Harvey

1. What are some of the things that I am currently doing that you would like to see me continue?

2. What am I currently doing that you would like to see me discontinue next year?

3. What suggestions do you have to help me improve my job performance (e.g., Is there a particular area that I should pursue for additional training? Is there a book or article that you suggest I read?)?

4. Do you have any additional comments?

This procedure is simple to execute and often yields constructive feedback and helpful ideas. It also provides an opportunity for the principal to assess the perceptions of staff in relation to his or her self-perception. Feedback can be enhanced when the perspectives of students, classified staff, parents, assistant principals, and community members are solicited. This type of feedback, often referred to as *360-degree feedback,* can offer multiple perspectives for consideration.

Principals who keep reflective journals often share insights derived from this activity with staff, which sometimes encourages staff members to become reflective about their own craft experiences and practices. Supporting the notion of leader as learner, Barth (1990) emphasizes principals' tremendous capacity to release energy in a school by becoming sustained, visible learners. Barth also describes the phenomenon of an "at-risk" principal as any educator who leaves school at the end of the day with little possibility of continuing learning about the work that he or she does (cited in Sparks, 1993, p. 19). Rolf P. Lynton of the World Health Organization has also offered some powerful insights about reflection by noting that we all go through events on a daily basis. What distinguishes an *event* from an *experience* is that an event only becomes an experience after you have time to reflect.[2] Each experience offers an opportunity to learn. When teachers, students, and parents see a principal's desire to learn and share ideas, norms and expectations that celebrate learning can develop within a school. Moreover, the *learning leader* model transfers to the classroom, where teachers demonstrate for students that they, too, are both leaders and learners.

THE EXPANDING ROLE OF THE PRINCIPAL

Researchers with The Wallace Foundation (2013), after conducting several studies on student achievement and school leadership, reflected, "Ten years ago, school leadership was noticeably absent from most school reform agendas, and even the people who saw leadership as important to turning around failing schools expressed uncertainty about how to proceed. What a difference a decade makes" (p. 5). With the advent of President Bush's initiative, No Child Left Behind in 2001, and President Obama's Race to the Top grant program, operating since 2009, researchers and school leaders have been looking for a formula to achieve student success. Not surprisingly, the research consensus is that teachers have the greatest impact on students, while the principal's impact is indirect. "Principal's work through other leaders in schools to influence what goes on inside of classrooms" (Supovitz, Sirinides, & May, 2010, p. 47) and, through their leadership work, "have the potential to unleash latent capacities in organizations" (Louis, Leithwood, Wahlstrom, & Anderson, 2010, p. 6).

How can principals influence others? The fundamental leadership responsibilities are as important as ever and remain the same: principals are expected to help create and strengthen the mission and vision, shape the culture, take responsibility for instructional leadership, keep the school safe and orderly, work with faculty and the community, act with integrity, and respond to contextual influences outside of the school (Educational Leadership Policy Standards, 2008). But the principalship has expanded.

Today principals are expected to

- advocate for all students advantaged and disadvantaged, including those facing challenges because of racial, ethnic, religious, economic, exceptionality, gender, LGBT, or homeless issues (Darling-Hammond, 2010; Johnson, 2013);
- facilitate the use of data-based decision making schoolwide and in individual classrooms;
- support small nested and schoolwide professional learning communities to expand and celebrate teacher leadership (NAESP, 2008);
- lead the effort to implement the CCSS aligned with coherent and specific curriculum plans, instructional strategies, assessment measures, and focused staff development initiatives (Jenkins & Pfeifer, 2012);
- recognize that workplace factors, such as building trust, are critical to new and veteran teacher success and desire to stay at a specific school (Johnson, 2012);
- seize the advantages of communicating through advanced social networking technologies, yet respecting the importance of traditional personal interaction with students, teachers, families, and the community (Smith, 2013); and

- recognize that success as an instructional leader depends on management skills to coordinate human and material resources focused on the school mission. Management skills are particularly vital during this tough fiscal period with limited resources (The Wallace Foundation, 2013).

A GLOBAL PERSPECTIVE

A leader's commitment to promoting lifelong learning throughout an organization is simply a smart strategy and an ethically wise decision when contemplating the world from a global perspective. In his influential book *The World Is Flat*, Thomas Friedman (2005) discusses the fact that successful corporations are cross-training their workers to develop multiple skills because future employment will depend on a worker's ability to be flexible and mobile: "The whole mind-set of a flat world is one in which the individual worker is going to become more and more responsible for managing his or her own career, risks, and economic security" (p. 284). Based on his observations of India and China as well as the instrumental role that technology and initiative play, Friedman stresses that, in recent years, "the global competitive playing field was being leveled. The world was being flattened" (p. 8). Not surprisingly, he supports emphasizing math and science education as well as technology and critical thinking for both women and men. Yet at the same time, Friedman stresses the importance of generalists, those who specialize in integrating subject areas and have "a renaissance view of the world" (Friedman, 2008, p. 2). Friedman, interviewed by Daniel Pink, maintains that school leaders need to recognize "why the liberal arts are more important than ever. It's not that I don't think math and science are important. They still are. But more than ever our secret sauce comes from our ability to integrate art, science, music and literature with the hard sciences. That's what produces an iPod revolution or a Google" (pp. 1–2).

School leaders who seek to understand the demographic changes in their own schools gain a greater perspective on the changes, and engage in lifelong learning, by recognizing the world as a dynamic, interdependent global community in which the "distance" between cultures and world issues is shrinking. In the United States today, there are more and more students who are nonnative English speakers from multicultural, immigrant, or migrant backgrounds. These students and their families have left their native countries to be a part of the U.S. historical narrative, the story of a nation of immigrants that has succeeded because of the ingenuity and hard work of its people.

School principals, as active and influential citizens, have a moral obligation to promote the success of each child in the school, regardless of race, class, ethnicity, gender, or country of origin. At the local school level, this commitment to the success of each child can be realized through the promotion of heterogeneous classes from prekindergarten through Grade 12. That local act sends a powerful message with global implications.

WHEN OLD AND NEW IDEAS CONVERGE

The Value of Repertoire and Celebrating the "Genius of the AND"

As principals' knowledge and experience increase, they are often faced with new ideas that appear to conflict with previous learning. Educators are expected to make either/or decisions regarding innovations that affect instructional practices and, consequently, students. To illustrate, in some quarters the CCSS are perceived as a total break from previous educational initiatives. However, an examination of the standards reveals goals that effective teachers and curriculum specialists have always considered when developing outcomes. To illustrate, McTighe and Wiggins (2012) connect their contemporary concept of backward design and framed curriculum "in terms of worthy *outputs*" (p. 7) to the classical work of Ralph Tyler in *Basic Principles of Curriculum and Instruction* (1949) and today's *Mathematical Standards* (National Governors Association, 2010). The first question that Tyler suggested more than 60 years ago was, "What educational purposes should the school seek to attain?" (p. 1). Most discussions of today's CCSS begin with a similar output question: What curriculum and instructional practices should be implemented so students are college and career ready? McTighe and Wiggins also note that Tyler emphasized the importance of content and skills, just as the *Mathematics Standards* stress "the need to connect the mathematical practices to mathematical content" (p. 8 in the Standards as cited in McTighe & Wiggins, 2012).

The mandate to teach content **and** skills is an important issue for learning leaders working to support both curriculum goals with faculty and students. Some educators lean toward the "more content camp," suggesting that teachers often ignore facts for frills, while "21st century proponents" maintain that students can quickly get their facts from the Internet while learning and leveraging their skills. Andrew Rotherham (2008) squarely addresses the issue:

> Schools, the 21st century skills argument goes, focus too much on teaching content at the expense of essential new skills such as communication and collaboration, critical thinking and problem solving, and concepts like media literacy and global awareness. . . . This view threatens to reopen a debate in American education that is not new either: content pitted against critical thinking rather than the two complementing each other. (pp. 1–2)

An effective strategy to manage this issue and countless other either/or challenges is to embrace the vision of Collins and Porras (2002) to celebrate the "Genius of the AND" while rejecting the limited "Tyranny of the OR" vision.

> Instead of being oppressed by the "Tyranny of the OR," highly visionary companies liberate themselves with the "Genius of the

AND"—the ability to embrace both extremes of a number of dimensions at the same time. Instead of choosing between A OR B, they figure out a way to have both A AND B. (p. 44)

As school leaders, we can easily fall into the either/or trap when working on contentious issues related to teaching, learning, and assessment. Often we are encouraged to discard one idea for another. The "Genius of the AND" reminds us to compromise, seek, and celebrate good ideas—and good people—across the spectrum. We will return to this strategy throughout the book.

From the Elementary and Secondary Education Act (ESEA) to the No Child Left Behind (NCLB) Act to Race to the Top (RTTT): Slow but Steady Progress

When studying the history of education in the United States, it is clear that the federal government initially had little intent of playing a major role in statewide education decisions. Remember, education is not mentioned in the U.S. Constitution. However, by the middle of the 20th century, the federal position had permanently changed because of three major acts. First, President Eisenhower decided to use National Guard troops in Little Rock, Arkansas, to enforce the Supreme Court's decision in *Brown v. Board of Education.* Second, in response to the Russian launch of Sputnik in 1957, U.S. leaders decided that this country was falling behind in math and science education, so in 1958 they passed the National Defense Education Act to upgrade schooling in the scientific fields. Third, passage of ESEA in 1965, as part of President Johnson's War on Poverty, directly involved the federal government in compensatory programs, from Title I to Head Start, to lift up the poor and help them succeed in schools. It is helpful to conceive of President Reagan's A Nation At Risk initiative (1983), President Bush's NCLB Act (2002), and President Obama's RTTT Program (2009) of competitive federal grants as part of the government's continued intervention in schools. Although many educators expected President Obama to replace NCLB with a new law, the gridlock in Washington has narrowed the President's action to RTTT grants and waivers related to aspects of NCLB.

NCLB and RTTT have both critics and supporters. Both initiatives have helped keep education a front-burner issue, not only for educators, students, and their parents or guardians, but for all stakeholders who believe that the future success of the United States depends on the quality of its schools. Educators will need to address the following components to meet legislative and public expectations (Alvy & Robbins, 2008; Boykin & Noguera, 2011; Darling-Hammond, 2010; National Governors Association, 2010; Noguera, 2011, 2012; Zhao, 2009):

- Each student, regardless of race, ethnicity, religion, socioeconomic status, gender, sexual orientation, homeless status or exceptionality, is entitled to a high-quality education. This commitment includes meeting the needs of traditionally voiceless underserved populations.

- Schools and teachers must be accountable for student learning.
- The achievement and opportunity gaps among different groups must be closed.
- As the CCSS are implemented, school principals must advocate for alignment of curriculum, instructional plans, teacher professional development, and individual state or consortium assessments (e.g., Smarter Balance and Partnership for Assessment of Readiness for College and Careers).
- High averages on statewide or CCSS consortium assessment tests will no longer be acceptable if students from minority, impoverished, or other underserved groups perform below standard. Disaggregating test scores will remain a critical first step to ensure that the needs of each group are addressed.
- Regardless of statewide or consortium assessments, school leaders will continue to fight for multiple measures of student progress (e.g., teacher observations and both traditional and alternative assessments, including portfolios, culminating projects, and formative tests) to gain a more accurate portrait of student success. Value-added data, although controversial, will likely be a component of the testing equation to assess student progress over time.
- School leaders will continue to struggle with the public's desire for testing accountability and transparency, with the educators' desire to personalize learning and address individual student needs, student voice, and authentic assessments.
- Although the pressure for successful assessment scores is considerable, it is obviously unethical to alter test results to comply with expectations. Principals must stand strong and set a personal example for district leaders and teachers to ensure this does not occur under their leadership.
- The commitment to students must include the teaching of both 21st century skills (e.g., problem solving, media literacy, global awareness, collaborative work) and meaningful content. This commitment must hold for traditionally disadvantaged students and schools where higher-level thinking skills are often neglected in lieu of "teaching to the test" and learning the "facts."
- Decisions related to curriculum, instruction, assessment, classroom management, and professional development should be grounded in evidence-based and Best Practice research.
- Hiring highly qualified teachers in each core subject area regardless of the economic base of the local school district will remain an important social justice objective. Statistically, less qualified teachers, based on certification status and college majors, have been hired disproportionally in schools with greater poverty.
- Supervisors charged with implementing the teacher and principal evaluation systems will need to confront the challenge of fairly weighing student test scores as part of the evaluation process (required by

RTTT) with other performance expectations and professional growth goals so talented individuals are retained and ineffective individuals are not.

- States, districts, and individual schools must provide transparent data to parents and the community, a "report card" that indicates how schools are doing in several categories, including test scores. Schools that do not achieve adequate progress will be expected to take corrective action. Parents will play a greater role in determining their children's educational setting within the realm of school choice.

- Districts and schools will continue to struggle with determining the best ways to assess exceptional students, including English language learners, students with disabilities, and all students with special talents. Response to Intervention (RTI) will be implemented as an important schoolwide early intervention strategy to help all students succeed and reduce the number recommended for special education.

- The alarming number of high school dropouts and underprepared graduates, especially in disadvantaged poor and urban areas, must remain a national focus. The combination of academic rigor and social support, especially related to personalization and trusting teacher student relationships (Boykin & Noguera, 2011, p. 70), is a promising strategy that should be pursued.

- Although the standards and assessment movement is presently emphasizing success in ELA and mathematics with increased interest in STEM subjects, the neglect of other core academic areas, and the visual and performing arts, social and emotional learning, physical education, and health-related schooling responsibilities is of great concern if we are committed to the needs of the whole child.

- Maintaining safe schools continues to be the top priority of all educators and interested stakeholders. Horrific school shootings; tragic weather-related incidents; and bullying, harassment, and intimidation events demand vigilance, better crisis management, and prevention strategies.

A final but important note: Learning leaders armed with essential understanding of how the old and new converge will find themselves equipped with the wisdom to effectively and confidently guide the school into the future.

NOTES

1. Authentic principal voices from interviews, workshops, writings, and informal conversations will be heard throughout the book.

2. We thank Dr. Steve Atwood of UNICEF for introducing us to Dr. Lynton's ideas.

REFLECTIONS

This space provides a place for you to write down ideas that have been generated by this chapter, things you want to try, or adaptations of ideas presented here.

1. What are some things you might do to model leader as learner?

2. What might be some observable indicators or artifacts of a school that is functioning as a professional learning community?

3. How can principals facilitate a learning environment for adults within a school?

4. What questions should principals or assistant principals ask to gain helpful feedback on their performance?

5. How do you think the CCSS and RTTT teacher and principal evaluation mandates will impact your role?

6. Why did you become a school principal, or why would you like to become a principal?

7. What insights or new questions do you have as a result of reflecting on the ideas presented in this chapter?

2

Leader as Manager

To facilitate learning, the instructional leader also makes sure that the classroom lights are working.

—A principal's voice

As practitioners, we need to ensure that schedules work, Smart Boards, and document cameras are in classrooms, and transition times run smoothly. Instructional leadership behaviors will have a greater impact on student success and often reflect effective long-range leadership planning, but teachers, students, parents, and the community are more likely to notice immediate problems due to management glitches (R. Grant, personal communication, October 2007). These problems include the less-than-glamorous flooding toilet, school bus breakdown, schoolwide computer server or Internet problem, scheduling error, and leaking ceiling. The long-range vision may make you a great leader tomorrow, but today the public notices the poorly lit hallway (which is interpreted by some as displaying minimal regard for safety and security). However, we should not be fooled into thinking that success as an educational leader ends with neat bookshelves, quiet hallways, or the latest software for student records. We must not forget that students should be the ultimate beneficiaries of all management actions. Yet much of the leadership literature contains a subtle disdain for management.

Although the concept of the principal has shifted from gatekeeper (Deal & Peterson, 1994) to instructional leader, collaborative decision maker, leader of leaders, and results-oriented instructional leader (Glickman, Gordon, & Ross-Gordon, 2010), any discussion of leadership can become a romantic abstraction if leadership is not discussed hand in hand with management. One has to secure and coordinate human and material resources to manage leadership. Part of management is paying attention to a school's physical environment; it is difficult to focus on learning if the physical environment does not promote it. For example, changing the contents of a display case outside of a high school office each month can send a strong message about student learning. If the display case includes work from various subjects and extracurricular activities, the school is honoring each discipline.

INSTRUCTIONAL LEADERSHIP REQUIRES EFFECTIVE MANAGEMENT

Effective principals are effective managers. They must communicate, develop relationships, and coordinate the efforts of teachers, assistant principals, custodians, secretaries, counselors, librarians, students, cafeteria workers, parents, transportation workers, central office, security personnel, social workers, and community partners. Although we have previously stressed the importance of leadership and management (Alvy & Robbins, 1998), the abundance of contemporary research supporting both elements is a significant shift in the literature. In a study sponsored by Stanford University, Grissom and Loeb (2009) concluded,

> Effective instructional leadership combines an understanding of the instructional needs of the school with an ability to target resources where they are needed, hire the best available teachers, provide teachers with the opportunities they need to improve, and keep the school running smoothly. (p. 23)

Grissom and Loeb identify "Organizational Management" as the complementary element to instructional leadership. This is similar to a key practice of effective principals identified by The Wallace Foundation (2013), "Managing people, data and processes to foster school improvement" (pp. 4–6). Chenoweth and Theokas (2013), drawing conclusions from eight years of research on how high-poverty schools turn around, state that effective principals, "put instruction at the center of their managerial duties. . . . Where once the job was primarily defined as a managerial one, principals are now expected not just to run a smooth operation, but also to be change leaders and improve achievement" (p. 58).

As instructional leaders and managers, it is critical to display respect for every individual who serves the school. When considering the primary purpose of schooling, principals should always remember that, although some employees may appear to be on the periphery, everyone contributes in his or her own way to a school's success. Principals must model in all their relationships the behavior that they expect throughout the school and the community. To illustrate, principals or assistant principals should work closely with classified staff, such as bus drivers, who appear on the fringe of the classroom experience because they can offer a valuable perspective. Principals, assistant principals, or district personnel should share with classified staff the school goals and advocate important programs (e.g., antibullying efforts). Because of their unusual schedule, bus drivers are in the community, the diners, the barbershops, hair salons, and other public places during part of the school day. What individuals say about the school in these venues can go a long way toward influencing how the school is perceived in the community.

Honoring these workers can have a very positive affect on them. To illustrate, Johnston (2001) relates the story of Ramon Curiel, who recruits and hires the 6,000 bus drivers, teacher aides, custodians, and other classified staff in Long Beach, California. Curiel gave credit to and celebrated their contribution to the overall improved grades of the students in the district because of the role they played in developing school climate. To the classified staff he said, "Look, you had something to do with this" (p. 18). As a bus driver in Harrisonburg, Virginia, reflected, "I am the first point of contact kids have with the school. A friendly greeting from me when they step on the bus brings a smile to their faces. My positive attitude influences what teachers experience on a daily basis."

A principal's work produces many additional management challenges involving policies, resources, behaviors, procedures, and data. These challenges can be classified into four categories that reflect the various arenas in which the leader must function as manager: classroom, school site, community, and support services.

MANAGEMENT RESPONSIBILITIES AND STRATEGIES

Classroom

Principals must help to maximize the availability of sufficient and high-quality classroom supplies and instructional resources to enable teachers to focus on student learning. Principals need to be on top of the classroom supply inventory so that key items are available during the year for teachers and students. Some principals delegate this job to a responsible individual or secretary. In small schools, principals retain this function for themselves. Although it is important to know how to delegate, one can never give up the responsibility for the task. When you delegate, you need to check for clear understanding, provide support, and follow up regularly. If the person to whom you have delegated comes up with an innovation, assure the person that you have confidence in him or her and encourage the resourcefulness.

The availability of classroom supplies and instructional resources for staff is heavily reliant on data relating to curricular needs. One must ask teachers whether the resources are serving their purposes. Does a particular instructional resource improve the quality of the educational program? Are the resources helpful for gathering assessment data to measure student progress? Is there enough money in the budget for a year's supply of computer paper? What classroom supplies were consumed completely last year? What instructional resources are in great demand at the start of the school year? What are some of the new resources available to make life easier for the staff (e.g., tablet devices)? How can the resources be distributed more efficiently? Is waste taking place, and if so, why?

Staff members' perceptions of resource availability are another important consideration. The policies for allocating classroom supplies and instructional resources reveal much about the values and beliefs of the organization. For example, is the supply room locked and materials strictly allocated? Are the veteran teachers in possession of the best resources; do they keep "a rainy day stash of supplies" (Marrs-Morford & Marshall, 2012, p. 38)? With your own school in mind, reflect on how "the system" works. Does it match the mission of the school? If your school promotes enrichment for all students, then you must have enrichment material and classroom options available for various instructional disciplines (e.g., novels, technology resources, online subscriptions, science kits, challenging math manipulatives) that can be used by all classroom teachers. A teachers' resource center in a school or district office can serve as a central area in which to keep instructional material to be used by all teachers, which may diminish greatly the desire to hoard the best instructional material.

With regard to the environment, is your school ecologically conscientious? Do the school office and each classroom collect paper to be reused or sent to a recycling plant? Are plastic containers, cans, and bottles collected for recycling? Helpful ideas about being more environmentally conscious can come from a variety of sources. One high school ecology club convinced the superintendent to purchase copier paper for the district that was ecologically superior to paper purchased previously. To save paper, handbooks and weekly newsletters can be posted online on school and district websites. Although papers savings will be substantial, copies need to be available for those who do not have Internet access (Marrs-Morford & Marshall, 2012, p. 38).

Some principals encourage staff input on the creation of policies and procedures related to resource requisition and allocation, which expands the leadership function of many staff members. These new roles build ownership of school-level practices and policies. If greater teacher involvement in resource allocation follows expanded teacher involvement in curricular and instructional decisions, then the resources will surely be used more efficiently and with greater meaning.

Although Web-based student information systems software enables schools to keep data for almost every important category (e.g., attendance, student demographics, schedules, grades, transportation, lunch data, budget, discipline), it's critical that selected systems address district needs, are user friendly, and include training and timely updates. These programs should make life easier for teachers so they can concentrate on teaching and use record-keeping to help personalize learning and address student needs.

School Site

A safe environment contributes to an effective school. Furthermore, the physical appearance of a school can contribute to and reflect positive or negative school climate or morale (Astor, Benbenishty, & Estrada, 2009). Graffiti and vandalism negatively affect the school and its administration, teachers, students, and community. Thus principals should inform school custodians to remove graffiti immediately and quickly repair broken lights and windows, loose banisters, or damaged lockers to ensure safety and maintain pride in the appearance of the school.

There are many ways to positively influence the physical environment of the school. For example, one school staff collectively designed a hallway mural that depicted key standards addressed in K–5 classrooms; images of the Nile River, pyramids, and Egyptian mummies underscored essential social studies learnings. Classes at some schools have donated benches, trees, and flower gardens as an indication of their commitment to the school. This has significantly decreased vandalism and enhanced social and emotional competence.

Principals and teachers need to recognize that a school's physical environment or indoor air quality (IAQ) may be contributing factors if students appear to be lethargic or are experiencing frequent nasal, throat, eye, skin, or lung problems. Asthma in particular is a problem because it is triggered by dampness and mold. As the primary cause of absenteeism in schools, students suffering from asthma often see their grades drop because of nonattendance (Environmental Protection Agency [EPA], 2012b). Further, "nearly half [of U. S. schools] have problems related to indoor air quality" (EPA, 2012b). Maintenance works. Increased maintenance leads to improved attendance, health, and academic performance. "In one study, students in classrooms with higher outdoor air ventilation rates scored 14 to 15 percent higher on standardized test scores than children in classrooms with lower outdoor air ventilation rates" (EPA, 2012a). Recommendations to improve IAQ include following scheduled maintenance inspections (thus avoiding backlogs) and reminding staff to report moisture, leakage, and signs of mold (EPA, n.d.). It is certainly counterproductive if school districts hire fewer janitorial staff or reduce their hours as a cost-cutting measure if IAQ problems persist—likely increasing student absenteeism (EPA, 2012a). The EPA has published on its website guidelines and resources to help schools with environmental concerns (www.epa.gov/iaq/schools).

A related responsibility is maintaining a litter-free environment. Principals have organized "trash patrols" and other activities to assure an attractive campus. One principal developed a program called The Eagle's Eyes. The eagle is the school's mascot, and anytime someone was observed doing something to enhance the campus—from picking up litter to planting a tree—that person would be acknowledged with a note written on stationery headed with "The eagle's eyes saw. . . ." These individuals could also be celebrated during assemblies.

Often overlooked as a principal management responsibility is the need to keep support personnel informed about student behavior and expectations. Principals find student behavior to be an essential topic, not only for teachers but also for parent volunteers, paraprofessionals, and support personnel such as school bus drivers, cafeteria workers, classroom aides, and library personnel. To address this topic, seminars can be planned to discuss issues related to student behavior as well as confidentiality issues and the Family Educational Rights and Privacy Act (U.S. Department of Education, 2013). When the emphasis is on organizing, teaching, and reinforcing students ("catching students being good") during the first three weeks of school, the staff and support personnel generally report fewer discipline referrals. These strategies will contribute to a safe, vibrant learning environment.

Leading and Learning by Wandering Around

In addition to physical appearance and air-quality issues, plant maintenance, and safety are also critical management dimensions. One way to ensure safety is through Leading and Learning by Wandering Around (LLBWA), which involves the principal purposefully getting out from behind the desk and walking around the school (Robbins & Alvy, 2004). Research by Marzano, Waters, and McNulty (2005) reveals that a key principalship responsibility correlated with student achievement is "Situational Awareness . . . leaders' awareness of the details and the undercurrents regarding the functioning of the school and their use of this information to address current and potential problems" (p. 61). It is our belief that LLBWA is a technique that uniquely enables a leader to monitor the pulse of a school by keeping abreast of the undercurrents and potential problems. Marzano et al. (2005) suggest that one should not be surprised that situational awareness is an important principalship responsibility because "it makes intuitive sense that a school leader must understand the innermost workings of the school at the nuts-and-bolts level to be effective. The more one knows about the inner workings of an organization, the more one is able to lead and manage that organization" (pp. 64–65).

In this chapter, the strategy of LLBWA refers primarily to maintenance concerns. However, LLBWA has an additional, powerful application: promoting instructional excellence (discussed in Chapter 9). A key attribute of this technique is that the principal must have a clear plan for where the "wandering" will occur. The goal is to visit these areas frequently, with classrooms being the top priority. Many principals create a checklist of key areas, from classrooms to storage sheds, with their smartphone or tablet using a spreadsheet app. Just customize the app for your school. Figure 2.1 provides an elementary school example.

Whenever the principals have a few minutes, they look down the checklist, determine where they have not visited during the month, and purposefully wander to one of those locations. In doing this, one principal discovered that an electrical outlet was located next to a sink in the boys' restroom. A call to the maintenance department quickly corrected this

Figure 2.1 Example of a Leading and Learning by Wandering Around Record

	September	October	November
Kitchen			
Cafeteria			
Custodian's office			
Girls' restroom			
Boys' restroom			
Library			
Storage shed			
Bike rack			
Kindergarten playground			
Regular playground			
Baseball diamond			
Classrooms—Wing A			
Room 1			
Room 2			
Room 3			
Room 4			
Room 5			
Room 6			
Classrooms—Wing B			
Room 7			
Room 8			
Room 9			
Room 10			
Room 11			
Room 12			
Kindergarten room			
Computer lab			

hazardous condition. A great way to visit classrooms and the rest of the school is to do so with the school custodian. A principal or assistant principal might meet with the custodian once a month, and they walk around the school. This enables them to see maintenance needs and communicate about school programs and activities as well as get input from teachers. On these walking tours the building "talks." A strong message is conveyed to students, teachers, parents, and visitors by what is on the hallway walls, on the walls of the cafeteria, in the display cases, or on the floor. A walk in one school revealed that the lawn was being watered five minutes before physical education classes were going to play on the field.

Usually, there are 5–10 maintenance requests that result from these walks. The walks provide maintenance personnel with undivided attention from an administrator and opportunities to receive treasured feedback. Also, these walks let the staff know that the principal is interested in the day-to-day running of the school.

Spending time in corridors, classrooms, stairwells, and other areas throughout the building gives the principal a chance to oversee plant safety and spread good news and caring words to staff, students, community members, and parents. Using this approach, the principal is able to communicate, plan proactively, and minimize interruptions. Interestingly, in a study of atypically low-violence and high-violence schools in Israel (Astor et al., 2009), principal visibility, similar to the LLBWA approach, made the difference in the low-violence schools. Consider these two contrasting descriptions: in a low-violence school: "The principal is seen by the school as having a central role in driving the school agenda. . . . He spends much of his time outside the office engaged with students and knows what occurs on campus" (p. 444); in a high-violence school: "The principal does not leave his room and does not visit the school grounds" (p. 444).

Another proactive management technique is to visit classrooms before or after school to see bulletin boards, special displays, learning centers, and student work. A principal can note, for example, whether a computer lab or journalism classroom is used actively during these times. When staff members receive a complimentary note from the principal about their rooms, it is a great way to start the day and reinforces the notion that the classroom is the center of the school.

LLBWA is also an excellent time management technique. The principal uses precious minutes in an efficient way to manage what is important. One principal talked of conducting "one-legged conferences" during her walks about campus. As an example, she cited talking with a custodian about his excellent care of the front lawn and simultaneously requesting that he mow the lawn by the primary wing at a time other than 12:45 p.m., when students were engaged in reading. She invited him to participate in the reading program at that time so that students could see him modeling reading as a lifelong skill. Another idea might be to invite the custodian into the classroom to talk about how he uses math in his daily work. Cafeteria staff, the nurse, librarians, teachers, parents, and community members could be asked to share how they have applied learnings from school.

Community

Principals manage the image of the school in the community and the communication flow between school and community by adopting a proactive stance. This can greatly affect the community perception of the school and support for school activities and funding, as well as students' perceptions of parental support for the school. Several examples that follow were shared at a job-alike session sponsored by the National Association of Elementary School Principals and held in Washington, D.C., for Nationally Distinguished Principals.

Principals can conduct a regular "Neighborhood Walk and Watch" designed to take the principal into the neighborhood that surrounds the school to talk with community members, spread good news about the school and students, find out about community developments, and lend an interested ear.

One principal organizes a late spring "Dinner on the Grounds." Each class prepares for this event by writing letters of invitation and sending them to family members and key civic leaders, all of whom must make reservations to attend this function. At a special assembly held during the evening, the school takes the opportunity to highlight its mission and important values by conducting a ceremony in which awards are given for the most improved student, student leadership, good citizenship, and academic excellence. Following the assembly, quilts and blankets are spread out, sack dinners are handed out, and the school band plays.

Many principals enhance the image of the school in the community by joining civic service clubs and regularly reporting on school affairs. Often these organizations provide grant opportunities for schools, so keeping them informed may benefit the school in several ways. In addition, administrators meet with education reporters and editors from the local newspaper and cultivate positive relationships with them.

One principal challenged the president of a large international seed company to trade places with him for a day. This joint get-acquainted venture resulted in a delightful school–business partnership. Scientists and other personnel from the company worked with the teachers to develop a project in which students formed greenhouse companies in their classrooms and produced plants for a Mother's Day plant sale.

Another principal initiated an e-mail pen-pal program between students and a local navy submarine unit. In one high school, students corresponded with scientists at the South Pole.

Recognizing the rising costs of feeding families, one school extended a hand to community members by organizing a bulk food purchase. This involved placing large orders for frozen foods to secure a substantial discount for community members. In a Bronx, New York, school, selected students were discreetly given backpacks of food to provide some nourishment during the weekend.

Still another example of managing the school in the community occurred when the principal and staff of a school in Hawaii realized that many parents of preschoolers had negative school experiences themselves and were therefore reluctant to come to school. So the principal and staff decided to go to the community. They set up blankets and provided refreshments in a local park and invited the parents to visit. On each blanket was a learning station for parents. This activity demonstrated to the community that the school was approachable and had much to offer.

In Rockingham County, Virginia, a school's staff volunteered to conduct parent conferences at a local chicken-processing plant where a large number of immigrant parents worked. The school administration provided Spanish and Russian interpreters to communicate with parents who didn't speak English. This increased parents' understanding of student learning and access to the school and greatly enhanced school–community relationships.

Support Services

Societal conditions and increased social service agency cooperation have made support services in the community still another facet of principals' management responsibilities. That is, to serve students, staff, and parents, principals need to know about the community resources available to support the local school. Many principals, especially in full-service schools, work with agencies that provide support, including Big Brothers and Big Sisters organizations, the community clothes closet, the county health department, mental health service agencies, child protective services, crisis lines, the community library, and services for the homeless. Most schools have resource files with the name, address, e-mail, and phone number of each agency. The files might also contain literature collected during get-acquainted visits to these organizations. Having well-organized files enables easy access to this information for parents and students in need. During Open House or Back to School Night, a directory of information regarding support services can be distributed and made available online to parents. This same information can also be provided to students. (For further discussion of community-based organizations that assist schools, see Chapter 17.)

CRISIS MANAGEMENT PLANNING

The American Academy of Experts in Traumatic Stress defines a crisis as "a traumatic event that seriously disrupts our coping and problem-solving abilities. It is typically unpredicted, volatile in nature and may even threaten our survival. A crisis can present a drastic and tragic change in our environment. This change is generally unwanted and frightening, and may leave us with a sense of vulnerability and helplessness" (Lerner, Volpe, & Lindell, 2003, p. 11). Each school faces the possibility of an emergency at any time. Weather emergencies may include tornadoes, hurricanes, excessive rain, windstorms, floods, or earthquakes. School, medical, or drug emergencies may include kidnappings, shootings, terrorist attacks, hate crimes, cyberbullying, a drug overdose, a severe allergic reaction, fires, traffic accidents, a sudden death of a classmate or teacher, or a tragedy in the community.

Tragic PreK–12 school shootings in the United States and abroad, and the horrific events of September 11, 2001, have been wake-up calls for everyone associated with schools to proactively develop crisis management plans. The Sandy Hook tragedy, Virginia Tech, and Northern Illinois

University have taught us that everyone is vulnerable, from PreK–12 to the university. An effective plan is the best opportunity to reduce the chance of a tragedy and to minimize injuries and save lives when a tragedy does occur.

Shortly after the tragedy of September 11, some of the nation's chief executives were asked to "offer a vision for tackling an overwhelming disaster. Their wisdom, distilled, came down to four basic truisms: be calm, tell the truth, put people before business, then get back to business as soon as possible" (Wayne & Kaufman, 2001, p. 1). Following this wisdom entails being prepared. If crisis management tactics and practices are well planned and in place, they provide the scaffolding for leadership action when an unexpected crisis occurs. Bill George (2007) reminds us that an important precursor to developing an effective crisis management plan is to be aware of one's values and their impact on action:

> It is under pressure—when your success, your career, or your life hangs in the balance—that you must decide what your values are. When you are forced to make trade-offs between your values under difficult circumstances, you learn what is most important in your life and what you are prepared to sacrifice for. Those who develop a clear sense of their values *before* they get into a crisis are better prepared to keep their bearings and navigate through difficult decisions and dilemmas when the pressure mounts. (p. 87)

Of course, when acts against students or staff occur, it is essential that the missing social and emotional ingredients that may have contributed to the alarming events are not lost, given the immediate need to respond to the crisis.

The Federal Response to Sandy Hook: Purposeful Emergency Planning

Every school must have a crisis management planning manual that includes appropriate steps for each type of emergency. Following the Sandy Hook events, President Obama asked several federal agencies, including the Departments of Education, Homeland Security, and the Federal Emergency Management Agency, to prepare a new federal document for school crisis planning that was titled the *Guide for Developing High-Quality School Emergency Operations Plans* (U.S. Department of Education, 2013). The Guide provides an excellent broad outline for districts and schools that want to review their present crisis plan or develop a new plan. Six general planning steps are recommended (pp. 5–23):

1. **Form a Collaborative Planning Team**—select team members, "lessons learned from experience indicate that operational planning is best performed by a team" (p. 5)

2. **Understand the Situation**—identification and assessment of threats, hazards, vulnerabilities, and risks

3. **Determine Goals and Objectives**—determination of which threats and hazards will be addressed, ranking the risk possibility and developing goals and objectives for each one

4. **Plan Development (Identifying Course of Action)**—based on threats, hazards, and determined objectives, an action plan is developed with scenarios addressing "the what, who, when, where, why and how for each threat and hazard" (p. 14)

5. **Plan Preparation, Review, and Approval**—draft plan reviewed by key stakeholders including "first responders, local emergency management officials and staff" (p. 16)

6. **Plan Implementation and Maintenance**—stakeholders hold meetings, train based on specific roles and responsibilities, executing drills, reviews, and continuous revisions with community partners. "Plans should evolve as the school and planning team learn lessons, obtain new information and insights and update priorities" (p. 22). Download the complete Guide at: rems.ed.gov/docs/REMS_K-12_Guide_508.pdf

Crisis Planning: The Nuts and Bolts

Although the preceding Guide provides general planning steps, very specific practical elements of a good plan need to be considered. The following "nuts-and-bolts" suggestions were adapted from several excellent sources (Bagin & Gallagher, 2001; Dwyer, Osher, & Warger, 1998; Lawton, 2002; Lerner et al., 2003; National Mental Health Association, 2006; National School Public Relations Association, 1996; U.S. Department of Education, 2013; Warner, 2000). An effective plan should include the following practical elements:

- The rationale for the plan (e.g., zero tolerance for bullying, supervising hallways), noting that prevention is the first step to avoiding a crisis
- A list of crisis team members; although the school will have a core team on campus for the initial crisis period, an expanded team should be included in all planning and used during the crisis (e.g., principal; assistant principals/deans; counselors; school psychologists; classified representatives such as secretaries, teacher aides, and custodians; central office personnel; school nurse; school security officers; appropriate safe and drug-free program coordinators; law enforcement, fire, and emergency service personnel; community social service and health service agency representatives; clergy; media representatives; parent and student representatives)
- A generic form to define and assess a crisis situation
- Generic procedures that go into effect for all crises

- A regularly updated emergency phone tree with chain-of-command information
- An updated list of faculty with current American Red Cross training certification
- A description of types of crises covered and specific procedures for each crisis, with clearly coded or separate colored pages for each type of crisis. For crises that demand lockdowns, a shelter in place, safe rooms, and escape routes, alternative routes and rooms should be part of the plan (e.g., an active shooter might be blocking a route)
- A list of crisis code signals for faculty; students; and fire, police, and emergency service personnel
- Maps of facilities with areas for a crisis control center, distributed to faculty and fire and police personnel
- Maps clearly delineating evacuation procedures, distributed to faculty and fire and police personnel
- A designated crisis spokesperson for faculty, media, and parent communication
- A description of communication procedures with emergency service personnel for immediate contact
- Information on faculty and community training procedures and school drill schedules (e.g., lockdown, tornado, fire drill, active shooter)
- A plan to ensure that all critical parties have received the crisis management planning manual
- Copies of brochures that have been distributed to parents relating to school crisis planning
- Templates of "backpack" letters that address specific crises
- Procedures to ensure that students, staff, parents, and community members are kept informed and comforted during the aftermath of the crisis
- An evaluation process to update plans each year or following a crisis; most recent updated plans should be available for downloading on district and school websites

Developing a School–Community Plan for the Prevention of Serious Violence

To be truly proactive, preventive measures relating to the possibility of serious violence should also be part of crisis management planning. The U.S. Department of Education report *Early Warning, Timely Response: A Guide to Safe Schools* (Dwyer et al., 1998) includes many excellent strategies to help schools prevent and deal with violent incidents. The difference that one individual can make in connecting with a potentially violent student is a primary theme of the report. All members of the community, administrators, teachers, families, fellow students, classified staff, and community stakeholders must collaborate to develop positive relations with students. The authors of this report make the following essential points:

- Safe and responsive schools are characterized by a focus on academic achievement; welcoming and involving families in the school; links to important community agencies, including the police, emergency and health services, and the faith-based community; an emphasis on positive relations among students and staff; an open school discussion concerning safety issues; fair and equal treatment by faculty, staff, and students in terms of racial groups, ethnic background, religious preference, and sexual orientations; eliminating targeting or bullying of students; creating safe and nonintimidating ways for students to share concerns with administration, faculty, counselors, or parents about potential violent acts; and disciplinary policies that include a code of conduct with specific consequences and clear policies concerning antiharassment, antiviolence, and due process rights.

- Early warning signs of possible violence include feelings of rejection, persecution, or social withdrawal and isolation; having been a victim of violence at home or in school; low interest in school and academics; expressions of violence in drawing, writings, or speech; impulsive, threatening, and bullying behavior; disciplinary and violent history; intolerance and prejudicial attitudes; drug or alcohol abuse; gang affiliation; and access to firearms.

- Imminent warning signs of serious violence include severe physical fighting at home or school, vandalism of property, rage for minor reasons, detailed threats and plans to harm or kill others, possession and use of firearms, sudden withdrawal, and self-injurious behaviors or threats of suicide.

- Intervention practices, depending on severity of threat, include contacting the principal, guidance counselor, school psychologist, family, health service, or law enforcement agency; persistent efforts to help a student and cut through the bureaucracy even when the threat is diminished; avoiding inappropriate labeling of a student because of profiling; and enforcement of the Gun Free School Act, requiring expulsion of students for a minimum of one year for bringing a firearm to school.

- Intervention practices to improve the behavior of violent students include access to a team of education specialists to assist students; parents and teachers sharing responsibility with child and family service agencies, law enforcement, the juvenile justice system, and other agencies; working closely with parents of troubled children; maintaining confidentiality when appropriate; developing the capacity of staff, students, and families to help; simplifying staff requests for assistance; implementing early intervention procedures; developing social skills programs; and referring children for special education evaluation.

- Action steps for students to create safe schools include participating in peer mediation and conflict resolution programs, listening to friends and encouraging them to seek out a trusted adult, joining organizations that oppose violence in schools, joining community youth-oriented activities, working with teachers and the administration to create a safe and nonbureaucratic process for reporting violence-related activities, knowing the school's code of conduct, working with law enforcement officials in the school on safety audits and safety tips, role modeling appropriate behavior when intensive feelings of anger arise, and seeking help from a trusted adult.

- Suggestions by experts to maintain a safe physical environment include maintaining supervised access to buildings and grounds; reducing class and school size; adjusting schedules to minimize time in hallways or other potentially dangerous locations; modifying traffic flow patterns to limit conflicts; conducting a safety audit; closing campuses during lunch; supervising key areas at critical times; prohibiting congregating students in at-risk areas; having adults, including parents, visible in the school; staggering dismissal and lunch periods; monitoring areas around the school; and coordinating safe routes to and from school with law enforcement officials (Dwyer et al., 1998).

After a series of school shootings in September and October of 2006, safety experts stressed three key points related especially to the tragedy of shootings by students or outsiders. First, it is critical that all students are "visible to others in meaningful, responsible ways" (Chaltain, 2006, p. 48) and that they are valued by adults in the school. Second, Gregory Thomas, New York City's former security chief of schools, states that "creating real and imagined barriers around schools is another way to deter intruders who are looking for a vulnerable target. 'Imagined' barriers are signs that tell visitors to report to the front office for a pass, or reminders that the school is in a 'gun-free, drug-free zone that tells people there will be more dramatic consequences for certain behaviors'" (quoted in Maxwell, 2006, p. 17). Third, Thomas emphasizes that adults and students must be sensitive to the environment, with students helping adults identify intruders who are strangers inside or outside of the immediate school area. Adults need to respond and challenge intruders if necessary, either personally or with the assistance of security personnel.

Responding to an Active Shooter Situation

(U.S. Department of Education, 2013, pp. 63–64):

1. Since law enforcement may not be immediately present, "making sure staff know how to respond and instruct their students can help prevent and reduce the loss of life" (p. 63).

2. "There is no single answer for what to do, but a survival mindset can increase the odds of surviving. As appropriate for your community, it may be valuable to schedule a time for an open conversation regarding this topic" (p. 63).

3. "During an *active shooter situation,* the natural human reaction, even if you are highly trained, is to be startled, feel fear and anxiety,

and even experience initial disbelief and denial. You can expect to hear noise from alarms, gunfire and explosions, and people shouting and screaming. . . . There are three basic options: run, hide, or fight. You can run away from the shooter, seek a secure place where you can hide and/or deny the shooter access, or incapacitate the shooter to survive and protect others from harm" (p. 63). Extensive details on training strategies related to running, hiding, and fighting can be found on the downloaded U.S. Department of Education Guide (2013).

4. It is critical to consider "that it is not uncommon for people confronted with a threat to first deny the possible danger rather than respond. . . . [During the World Trade Center tragedy], people close to the floors impacted waited longer to start evacuating than those on unaffected floors . . . Train staff to overcome denial and to respond immediately, including fulfilling their responsibilities for individuals in their charge. For example, train staff to recognize the sounds of danger, act, and forcibly communicate the danger and necessary action (e.g., "Gun! Get out!") (p. 64).

Final Thoughts on Crisis Management

Bringing in key community members involved in emergency work (e.g., firefighters, protective service workers, trauma unit personnel) to speak with students helps develop a respect for and awareness of emergency procedures. Furthermore, having a strong public relations program with the local police department, including officers speaking at the school about proactive crime prevention or automobile safety, could later prove very valuable if the police need to be called into the school's vicinity because of an emergency.

It is helpful to provide time for school student service teams (e.g., nurses, school counselors, social workers) to have regular contact with related community health professionals. Communication between school personnel and community professional groups can increase knowledge and significantly inform actions. In the most serious cases, this can lead to valuable coordination regarding potential teenage suicides or gang violence. The contact also keeps school personnel informed about current research to help students who are bulimic or anorexic. Child protective service personnel can offer useful information about child abuse—how to recognize it, how to raise teacher and student awareness, and how to work with abused students. Administrators and teachers are required by federal law to report suspected cases of child abuse. Indicators related to physical abuse, physical neglect, sexual abuse, and emotional abuse must be followed up on by school personnel (Morrison, 2009).

Although very rare, students have died from eating foods with ingredients to which they are extremely allergic. The ultimate tragedy for a family, school, and community is, of course, a child's death. Schools must ensure that they have updated information regarding students' health, medication, and psychological needs. Those who need to know should be informed. Health and emergency procedure data should be updated regularly. Student information systems that include student emergency information and photos are vital during a crisis. Key facts such as food allergies or medical/health problems, custody issues, and other important data should be highlighted and communicated to appropriate personnel, including the school secretary, the nurse, cafeteria workers, counselors, social workers, and teachers.

Many schools offer workshops for teachers, support staff, and administrators to prepare for emergencies. Medical preparedness can include training to cope with shock victims, people who are choking or having epileptic seizures, people who are bleeding severely, and those who need CPR. Areas where accidents might occur should be identified and procedures developed to address each possible accident. Obvious locations are playgrounds, hallways, locker rooms, cafeterias, and bus stops. An emergency crisis kit might include a flash drive with current student data, a crisis management manual, a bullhorn, a phone tree, permanent markers, wristbands, legal pads, pens, a fully charged smartphone, and a current yearbook, in addition to typical first-aid resources.

We have learned during the past 20 years that school leadership is much more than instructional leadership and management. School leaders are expected to stand strong in the face of tragedy whether caused by humans or nature. Our schools have been changed by Columbine, 9/11, and Sandy Hook; hurricanes Katrina and Sandy; and tornadoes in Missouri and Oklahoma. Some of these events took the lives of children in school, while other tragedies made attending school overwhelming, and in some cases impossible. Although it is accurate that schools experience fewer acts of violence than in the past, those who have lost children in school will not be comforted by that fact. Principals have learned some lessons, however, that can help us move forward. Here are a few:

• When tragedy strikes, the community needs the principal to stand strong. Part of leadership is having the courage to put one foot in front of another and rallying the community when circumstances are most dark. The courage of Dawn Hochsprung, principal of Sandy Hook Elementary School, and the other educators who lost their lives on December 14, 2012, will inspire a generation of school administrators to lead their schools and communities as passionate advocates for sound crisis management planning. These plans must be based on thoughtful prevention, protection, quick response and recovery strategies that "[restore] the learning environment" (U.S. Department of Education, 2013).

• We have learned that it is now more frightening not to talk about an act concerning crisis management than to ignore the topic even though active shooter and lockdown drills are part of the discussion. Nirvi Shah (2013) reported that one school was so out of compliance in 2013 that it was required to conduct eight drills in one day. Now that is frightening! Not surprisingly, following Sandy Hook in 2012 and the tornado tragedies in 2013, states are instituting new or additional laws requiring that drills or simulations begin earlier in the year, and that more active shooter, intruder, lockdown, and tornado drills occur.

- Crises are so complicated that having only one plan for a particular situation may not be sufficient. For example, on 9/11 part of the planned evacuation zone for some schools in the vicinity of the World Trade Center was "ground zero" (National School Safety Center, 2010). During the 2013 tornado in Moore, Oklahoma, the safe room did not prevent the tragedy. On the spot decisions may entail deviating from the original plan.

- A question first raised following Columbine and 9/11 and being raised again is, "How far must schools go to create a safe and welcoming environment without turning our nation's schools into armed camps" (National School Safety Center, 2010)? It is a complicated question to answer, even more so when one considers that during the 2009–2010 school year armed security staff were already in about 28 percent of U.S. schools, more than 50 percent in middle schools and 60 percent in high schools (Wieder, 2013). School leaders need to consider where they stand on this question and be prepared to discuss it with the district administration team, teachers, students, parents, and the community.

- Schools should not overpromise what they can guarantee about safety to their communities. Although "students are 99 times more likely to be victimized in the community," parents expect their schools to be 100 percent safe (National School Safety Center, 2010). Principals need to let parents know about the preventive measures being taken, announce drills and simulations in newsletters and during parent events, and ask parents to let their children know that they must take the drills very seriously. Posting crisis management plans on district and school websites and sharing information with community partners should also occur so the whole community takes an interest in school safety.

A FINAL OBSERVATION REGARDING SCHOOL MANAGEMENT

When considering the classroom, school site, community, and support service management responsibilities of the principal, it is interesting that the responsibilities seem to move from the inside of the school (the classroom) to the outside world (support services). The classroom, school site, community, and support services are linked, and the principal's ability to successfully take advantage of this linkage depend on his or her ability to see the linkage as based on relationships among people, not simply as structural entities that need to remain in communication with one another. Clearly, instructional leadership and management go hand in hand.

REFLECTIONS

This space provides a place for you to write down ideas that have been generated by this chapter, things you want to try, or adaptations of ideas presented here.

1. Separately, consider several characteristics of effective leaders and of effective managers. What conclusions can you draw about management or leadership from your selected characteristics?

2. Develop a key area checklist for LLBWA at your school.

3. Make a list of various types of crises that should be addressed in your school's crisis management plan. Are there some generic planning elements that would apply to most crises on your list? If so, what are these elements?

4. Explore and select online resources that would complement or enhance your crisis management plan.

5. Review a couple of school crisis management plans outside of your state, are there salient differences? If yes, consider why.

6. What insights or new questions do you have as a result of reflecting on the ideas presented in this chapter?

3

Leader as Shaper of School Culture

Culture either makes or breaks efforts to promote school success. As a veteran principal, new to a school, it influences my behavior and I work with staff colleagues to influence it!

—A principal's voice

School culture matters. Lasting school improvement efforts can always be traced to positive, collaborative, learning focused changes in the culture of the school. Relationships among professional colleagues in such schools are characterized by trust. There is "increasing evidence from both private and public organizations that organizations with stronger cultures are more adaptable, have higher member motivation and commitment, are more cooperative and better able to resolve conflicts, have greater capacity for innovation and are more effective in achieving their goals" (Seashore Louis and Wahlstrom, 2011, p. 52). Deal and Peterson (1999) write, "The culture of an enterprise plays the dominant role in exemplary performance" (p. 1). In the business world, culture is inextricably tied to financial results. We now know that culture is a profound predictor of success in schools. While the classroom teacher is the most powerful influence on student achievement, school culture is the next most influential factor. Furthermore, there are specific elements of culture that have a direct link to staff and student learning. The pages that follow present a definition of culture, examine how it influences daily practices, and explore its significance with respect to powerful leverage points for producing positive school change. Effective school leaders have the ability to promote learning focused, collaborative cultures that produce success. This chapter offers specific suggestions regarding how to develop, enrich, and sustain school cultures so that all members of the school community can achieve this success, learning and thriving in the process. It offers the bridge—from research to practice.

DEFINING CULTURE

As cited by Deal and Peterson in *Shaping School Culture* (2009, pp. 5–7), the concept of culture is certainly not new. Willard Waller wrote about it in 1932! Many definitions of culture exist:

> *"The web of significance in which we are all suspended"*
>
> —Geertz (1973)

> *"The way we do things around here"*
>
> —Bower (1966)

> *"The pattern of basic assumptions—invented, discovered, or developed by a given group as it learns to cope with problems . . . that has worked well enough to be considered valid and, therefore, to be taught to new members as the correct way to perceive, think and feel in relation to those problems"*
>
> —Schein (1985, p. 9)

> *"A subtle spirit that can be sensed the moment one walks into a school"*
>
> —California School Leadership Academy

We define school culture as the practices that stem from a set of core values and beliefs influencing norms, interactions, operating procedures, reward structures, celebrations, physical environment, written and unwritten rules, expectations, perceptions, and relationships. Culture is steeped in history and tradition. It is carried on by organizational members who convey the essence of the culture in their actions and interactions. Often it is communicated through story. The culture of the school carries deep meaning for its members. It influences daily life in the school—conversations, teaching practices, meetings, supervisory actions, hiring procedures, professional development, and student achievement. Even if a school is new, it will, in many cases, reflect the previous school cultures from which its staff members have come. It is essential that members of new organizations take time to explicitly describe the values and attributes of the ideal culture they would like to create in the new organization.

While the concept of culture is not new, what is new about culture is that specific cultural practices have been identified as having transformative power in achieving results. Culture is the meaning that individuals create in their world of work. Deal and Peterson (1993) remind us that "the inner, unspoken set of values and purposes that weave quality into the daily routine and motivate everyone to do his or her best" is equally if not more powerful in moving a school toward achieving a vision of quality. Because the way people interact daily or "do business" at a site dramatically influences its ultimate productivity for all members, culture is a powerful school improvement tool. For example, at Parkside Middle School in Prince William County, Virginia, the administrative team started a tradition that now influences interactions in every meeting that is conducted. At the end of each meeting, someone is assigned to ask the question, "What have we decided or done today to make the lives of Parkside students better?" A "backup person" is also assigned in case the question asker is absent. This simple tradition reminds everyone in the culture about the core value embedded in the vision of the school—our purpose here is to serve every student so that each one thrives. Goleman, Boyatzis, and McKee (2002) explain, "When people feel good, they work at their best" (p. 14). It is not surprising that if a culture is a negative or toxic one, it can serve as a hindering force to school improvement efforts. The pervasive influence of culture can also serve to protect a school from willy-nilly responses to passing fads. Because each element of culture has a potential to positively or negatively influence new practices, if any school improvement effort or federally, state, or locally mandated initiative is to be implemented well, the culture of the organization must first be studied to assess which cultural elements would support the implementation process, and which may need to be transformed.

Figure 3.1 illustrates the interactive elements of school culture. Each element is dynamic in nature; that is, it influences the current culture and is sensitive to competing elements that may threaten its existence and reshape the culture. If the culture is cohesive, all of the elements should reflect treasured core values and beliefs. In studying the elements in this figure, the leadership in one company realized that their "employee of the month" parking place award was inconsistent with the value they placed on teamwork. The CEO reflected, "Our reward structure is unraveling the very value of teamwork we are trying to instill in our employees." As a consequence of realizing this, the award was modified so that enough parking spaces were allocated for an entire team.

There are four types of culture in which these elements are found (Robbins & Alvy, 2004, pp. 24–29):

- Positive
- Negative
- Toxic
- Fragmented

In positive cultures, there is a pervasive climate of positivity. Staff members display an eagerness to do whatever it takes to serve students and to support one another as professional colleagues. The elements in

Figure 3.1 Interactive Elements of School Culture

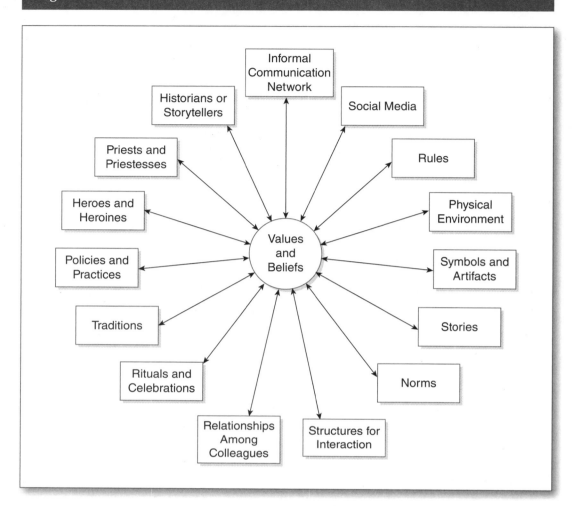

these school cultures are positive in nature. For instance, the norms and celebrations reflect values of "going the extra mile" and taking responsibility for every student.

In negative cultures, the elements convey teacher-centered practices rather than practices that support students. In these cultures, there are traditions such as the most tenured staff are assigned to the highest achieving students. The emphasis is on "if you put your time in, you will be rewarded." Staff members in negative cultures tend to do the bare minimum. A teacher from a negative culture explained it this way, "I do just good enough to get by, and not bad enough to be noticed. When 3:30 rolls around, I beat the buses out of the parking lot."

In toxic cultures, the elements often "poison" the environment. There are traditions of student bashing, staff bashing, parent bashing, or community bashing. The rumor mill "spilleth over" with toxic stories, defeated attitudes, and hopelessness. In these cultures, organizational members often feel smothered by doom and gloom. Energy is sapped by people who serve as toxic waste dispensers or "negaholics" (Carter-Scott, 1991; Peterson & Deal, 2009).

Fragmented cultures are made up of a variety of subcultures that can be positive, negative, or toxic. The physical environment usually conveys mixed messages. To illustrate, in one Pennsylvania high school, above a classroom door was a photo of a rainbow with the caption "Follow your dreams." Across the hall was a picture of an angry man pointing his finger with a caption warning, "Because I said so!" These physical artifacts portrayed the sense of fragmentation, as did the mix of interactions, celebrations, and traditions—some negative, some positive, and some toxic.

Of the four types of culture, each with their corresponding elements, the most difficult and time consuming to work with are the toxic and fragmented ones.

The sections that follow detail how the elements of culture can each serve as tools for transforming schools into positive, collaborative, learning-focused contexts. These elements can also be used to reinforce or enhance cultures where positive transformations have already occurred.

CORE VALUES AND BELIEFS ARE THE HEART OF CULTURE

A company can grow big without losing the passion and personality that built it, but only if it's driven not by profits but by values and by people. . . . The key is heart. . . . If you pour your heart into your work, or into any worthy enterprise, you can achieve dreams others may think impossible.

—Howard Schultz, CEO of Starbucks,
in Schultz and Yang (1997, p. 8)

Hattie (2012b) asserts that "the culture of the school is the essence of sustained success" (p. 170). At the core of every school culture is a set of treasured values and beliefs. These values and beliefs dramatically affect the behaviors of organizational members and ultimately, results. Values and beliefs serve as leverage points for change. For example, Hattie (2012b) described a large high school on a change journey. The principal took two to three years to build a climate of collegiality and trust, as well as create core values and beliefs that focused on student learning and improving every student in the school. The principal "provided a school-based reporting engine to help teachers keep track of their effects on individual students, provided resources to help teachers build graphs of the individual trajectories of all students . . . [he] created time for teachers to meet to prepare common assessments and then monitor their individual effects on students. This led to rich conversations . . . and the school is now renowned for the quality of evidence about its success in raising achievement" (p. 176). Hattie observed, "If there had been one whiff of accountability, the mood would have turned counterproductive" (p. 176). Taking the time to build the belief that emphasized the value of examining the impact of one's teaching practice on student learning, and using that data to monitor and adjust instructional strategies led to significant gains in student learning. This example illustrates the critical importance of aligning improvement efforts with core values and beliefs. If such alignment does not exist, it is essential to focus efforts on developing the requisite values and beliefs so that the change process will meet with less resistance. Elmore (2004) asserts that school leaders are responsible for cultural changes in schools. He points out that school leaders do not change schools by mandate, but rather by specific displacement of existing norms, structures, and processes by others—"the process of cultural change depends fundamentally on modeling the new values and behaviors that you expect to displace the existing ones" (p. 11).

Abundant research (Barber & Mourshed, 2009; Hattie, 2009; Odden & Archibald, 2009) suggests that when core values and beliefs focus on shared leadership, in which all members of the school community possess collective responsibility for student learning, higher levels of student achievement result. In collaborative, learning-focused cultures such values and beliefs flourish. They drive the creation of structures to examine student performance, schedules that maximize time for planning, problem solving, tutoring, and forums that herald the rich resources afforded by the unique perspectives and knowledge individual educators collectively amass.

THE PHYSICAL ENVIRONMENT REFLECTS CORE VALUES: PORTRAITS OF PRACTICE

In cohesive cultures, core values are reflected in the physical environment and interwoven with other cultural elements. Chime Charter Middle School (CCMS), for example, was founded with a vision to honor diversity and inclusion. At this urban middle school, located in the Los Angeles Unified School District, creating and sustaining a positive school climate was the number-one priority. The staff implemented three practical sets of strategies: environmental, interpersonal, and instructional (Murawski, Lockwood, Khalili, & Johnston, 2009/2010). As a consequence of these strategies, there was a decrease in bullying and an increase in positive behaviors visibly evident throughout the school.

Environmental strategies included the creation of *signs* that reflected a core value of promoting a safe environment. Members of the student council and school leadership committee made, posted, and enforced the signs. A typical sign read, "This is a violence-free, abuse-free, bully-free school. Please show kindness and respect in your words and actions" (p. 75).

In terms of interpersonal strategies, at the secondary level, *Lunch Clubs* were initiated by faculty to create opportunities for students to have choices for social interaction without losing class time. Students could choose a different activity every day! Choices included dance, karaoke, movies, origami, and art. Two additional options, *Friendship Circle* and *The Art of Giving*, were added to reinforce the school's vision of inclusion.

These options emphasized the principle of accepting others; positive friendships blossomed in these structured sessions.

Tolerance activities were also implemented. To reduce teasing, harassment, name-calling, and social isolation, an annual event called "No Name-Calling Week" was scheduled. Faculty used literature to communicate with students about how harmful name-calling directed at race, ethnicity, sexual orientation, or mental ability can be to students. They presented lessons from a website called www.nonamecalling.week.org. Of course the goal is to promote no name-calling throughout the year.

Instructionally, students at this school experienced the positive core values of the culture through messages communicated by the physical environment and reiterated by classroom curriculum experiences; speakers from diverse cultures; video discussion; staff modeling; and partnerships among the school, parents, and the larger community.

Kent Peterson and Terry Deal once told a group of new leaders at the Vanderbilt Principals' Academy, "The walls talk." In inclusive schools all students work is posted. Student work is celebrated and prominent on walls; in display cases; and on shelves in the office, library, and auditorium. The nature of the work reflects core values. In one school, an entire department conducted special projects about the value of diversity. Student writing, artwork, and photography adorned the common areas throughout the school. In addition, photos and displays from elective classes such as robotics, firefighting, health sciences, and music capture the attention of those who walk through the school. Anyone who spent time in this physical environment could clearly perceive what the core values of the school were.

One school in Israel displayed a bulletin board depicting a vineyard in the entry hall. Interspersed with the vines was every student's name. This symbolically communicated the importance of each student as well as their connection to each other and the learning community. Reflecting on the messages communicated by the physical environment, a principal commented, "You can tell what's important in a school by what you see when you walk in the front door. What's on the walls, what's in the trophy case, sends a strong message to all who enter the building."

In a culture that values learning, relationships, and quality, there are visible places in the building, where staff members spend time, that reflect these values. The teachers' workroom is one such example. A key aspect of this space at one elementary school is a professional library that includes current journals, books, notices about professional development, DVDs, computers, and a binder of helpful websites. It is a setting where ideas are exchanged and books, articles, lessons, and podcasts are discussed. Teachers find resources there to develop curriculum materials, plan instruction, or assess the impact of curriculum and instruction on students. The dialogue among colleagues often includes exchanges about useful blogs and other online resources. Activities are also in place to remind organizational members of the importance of learning, collaboration, and quality, and to provide avenues for such ends. Examples of this include a schedule for peer coaching or a time when, on a schoolwide basis, everyone reflects through journal writing, article exchanges, or book clubs.

At break times and lunch, professional colleagues often meet in this room to problem solve difficult situations related to student learning, plan units across the curriculum, discuss "test-prep" ideas, or swap stories about successful practice. Hanging on one wall is a sign that says "Help Wanted." Under the sign are several manila envelopes teachers have hung, each with visible requests written on the front. One reads, "Help Wanted! I have a ninth-grade student with fourth-grade reading skills in my class. Any ideas how to help this student develop skills, independence, and keep up with the pace of class?" Next to the envelopes are cups with pens and pencils and a shelf with index cards on which to write ideas. Teachers can often be seen writing ideas on the cards and placing them in the envelopes, as well as reaching into the envelopes and reading cards that others have written. One teacher commented, "This is the way we informally support each other, learn from one another, and improve the quality of learning for our students!"

RITUALS DISPLAY CORE VALUES AND CALL ATTENTION TO WHAT IS IMPORTANT

A ritual is defined as "any practice or pattern of behavior regularly performed in a set manner" (dictionary.reference.com, n.d.). Rituals embed purpose and meaning in the cultural fabric of the school. Formal and informal rituals exist throughout schools and organizations. They reflect cherished values and focus the attention of organizational members on what is important. A principal reflected, "We've created an informal ritual here of all staff members, taking turns of course, greeting the students as they get off the bus. We believe it's a powerful way to connect with students and for many kids it may be the first smile they see that day!"

In a large urban high school, staff members and students have articulated the value of staying physically fit. There is a ritual at this school of students walking the hallway in a clockwise manner five minutes before they go to their first period class. The music to which they walk is chosen by students (and okayed by class advisors). This ritual has had the added value of reducing tardies. Students revel with this structured opportunity for social interaction. Staff members supervise the halls and connect with students during this daily ritual.

Another familiar ritual is the faculty meeting. In a culture that values learning from one another, a faculty meeting can become a forum for learning. Meetings can be organized to have teachers share ideas that are working in their classrooms. For example, teachers who are experiencing success with implementing Common Core, differentiating instruction, or publishing student work can show samples and lead a discussion on their experiences. If an atmosphere of trust exists, ideas that were not successful can also be shared. The principal can share successes and failures.

This promotes the idea of leader as learner. How can one learn without making mistakes and taking risks? A CEO of a large corporation once stated, "Failure is the opportunity to begin again more intelligently." To promote this idea, the principal encourages teachers to try lessons that are experimental and demonstrates his or her support.

Another faculty meeting or professional development activity that can be used to foster learning and model a classroom instructional strategy is the jigsaw strategy. For example, in reviewing schoolwide test data, one leadership team analyzed that an achievement gap existed for several groups of students. The team planned a faculty meeting that would promote staff understanding of what an achievement gap is and provide practical strategies to close the gap. The meeting opened with the presentation of school-level data that revealed an achievement gap. The leadership team explained that in today's meeting a powerful cooperative learning strategy called a jigsaw would be used to convey the content of four articles on closing the achievement gap. Staff members formed "home groups." In each group, individuals counted off from one through four. "Ones" would read the first article, "twos" the second article, and so on (see Figure 3.2a). Following this, staff members who shared the same number met to become "expert" in the content of the article they read. This involved discussing key points, identifying helpful examples, and deciding how they would teach others what they read (see Figure 3.2b). Finally, home groups reconvened, and each member explained to the others what he or she had read (see Figure 3.2c) and the implications for their own teaching practices.

At the conclusion of the teaching episodes, groups synthesized their collective learnings and reported out to the total group. The principal functioned as a group member during the entire jigsaw process. The culminating task was one in which the jigsaw participants drafted a list of recommendations for how they would proceed in taking action to "close the gap" in the school.

Many principals use the jigsaw technique with different types of content. For instance, at the beginning of the year, some use it to review information contained in the faculty or school handbook. Others use it to share articles about implementing new initiatives for working with special education students and at-risk students, effective teaching practices, or strategies to develop common assessments. The strategy celebrates individual accountability and fosters collaboration and interdependence among faculty members. These attributes reflect the values that are being developed, celebrated, and reinforced in the culture. Another technique that calls attention to learning together is the "listening posts" activity. The faculty meeting facilitator asks group members to generate possible topics for discussion, such as differentiated instruction, working with English language learners, developing rubrics, and homework. Topics for discussion are then posted on chart paper in different locations of the room. Individuals gather around topics of interest and have a 15- to 20-minute discussion at these "listening posts." Each group's ideas are recorded on butcher paper posted around the room. These ideas are often

Figure 3.2 Jigsaw Activity

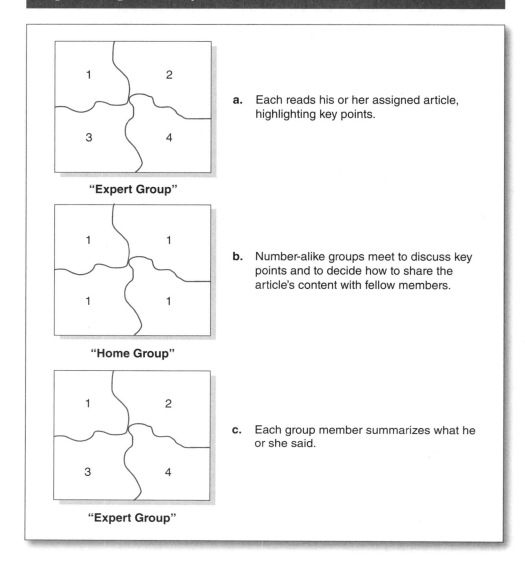

"Expert Group"

a.   Each reads his or her assigned article, highlighting key points.

"Home Group"

b.   Number-alike groups meet to discuss key points and to decide how to share the article's content with fellow members.

"Expert Group"

c.   Each group member summarizes what he or she said.

word-processed or images are captured with an iPad and later distributed to the faculty. Following the discussion, each group prepares a two-minute summary of its conversation and reports out. Many times the "reporting out" phase plants seeds of interest among other faculty members. A variation of this activity is the use of classrooms instead of areas of the room as listening posts. This has the added value of getting faculty members into classrooms other than their own. Strategically, it is important for staff members to examine how "listening posts" might also be used in the classroom to build readiness for topics about to be taught, extend, refine, or review content and provide practice in summarizing and public speaking.

The brown-bag lunch is another learning ritual. One high school staff member who attended several cooperative learning workshops shared her experiences with interested staff during lunch. Teachers followed up these sessions by experimenting with cooperative learning techniques in their classrooms. At the final session, teachers decided they wanted to support one another in their cooperative learning activities. As a consequence, they continued meeting once a month at lunch to exchange ideas. The principal supported this activity by publicizing the meetings and providing logistical support and refreshments. At another school, teachers held brown-bag lunches to discuss how they could use their Smart Boards as an interactive, integrated curriculum tool as they implemented Common Core State Standards.

CELEBRATIONS CALL ATTENTION TO WHAT IS IMPORTANT

In positive, learning-focused, collaborative cultures, learning is valued and celebrated publicly. At many schools, student recognition assemblies are held every six to eight weeks to celebrate student successes. Celebrations need to be strategically planned to reflect cherished core values. For example, in one school students are cited for helping out a new classmate, citizenship, improving attendance, making significant academic improvement, or teaching another student. Groups of students are complimented for excellent behavior in the cafeteria or keeping the campus clean. Whatever is celebrated reflects what is being emphasized in the culture. Following a recognition assembly, the principal sends notes home to parents, informing them of their child's accomplishments. The recognition program reflects the culture's values to parents and community members, as well as reinforces the values for organizational members. For example, if the school culture places value on teamwork, it is important to recognize teams or groups of students rather than a "student of the month."

Celebrations put the school's values on display. At one school, Martin Luther King Day was celebrated by faculty, parents, and students. First, a YouTube video excerpt from King's "I Have a Dream" speech was played and the principal and leadership team gave a presentation about what Martin Luther King Jr. stood for, emphasizing values such as the love of fellow human beings, nonviolence, and equal opportunity. Next, they pointed out how these same values were shared by the school and cited specific examples to which students could relate. As an example, the principal asked the students how they would feel if, because of their hair color, they had to use separate drinking fountains, restrooms, and cafeterias. Finally, students and faculty sang songs such as "Lift Every Voice and Sing" and "We Shall Overcome." The assembly provided some insight into what it was like to live through the 1960s. When the ceremony was over, many participants had tears in their eyes. One teacher remarked, "As a school, we're closer now, and have a feeling of what we're all about."

In the wake of September 11, one high school had an assembly around the themes of developing tolerance and acceptance, and valuing diversity. It is essential that all programs—even holiday programs—have meaning, are inclusive, and reflect the core values of the school. A valuable assessment is to make a list of the current celebrations at a school and then analyze those celebrations to determine which values they highlight. Then consider, are there any values not celebrated that should be?

HOW PEOPLE SPEND TIME REFLECTS CORE VALUES

In *It's Not Us Against Them* (2009), Ray McNulty characterizes Brockton (MA) High School as having a school culture that "centers on positive relationships" and where "students consider the school a safe haven." Brockton High serves a community that struggles with poverty, gangs, and drugs. Yet it is "the state's highest performing urban school" (p. 38). McNulty notes, "On any given afternoon, you find students throughout the building after classes have ended for the day, which is hardly surprising when you consider that about 3,500 of the school's 4,350 students participate in extracurricular activities" (p. 191). The afterschool presence of students is the norm, and students are often seen interacting with teachers and administrators. Clearly, the quality of the students' participation is a consequence of the relationships within the school. The relationships and sense of purpose students perceive dramatically influences how they choose to spend time. As Maya Angelou (2013) once said, "People will forget what you said, people will forget what you did, but people will never forget how you made them feel."

Schedules also reflect core values and how time is spent. One middle school's staff saw the value of providing an integrated course of study for its students. As a result, the schedule was reorganized so that teachers had 74 minutes of common planning time to develop rich learning experiences for students.

Many schools organize charity drives or send middle or high school students out to volunteer in the community for service credit; this sends a clear message that the school is concerned about others. Such activities also teach about empathy and develop a valuing of community service. The December holiday season is an excellent time to have a food, clothing, or toy drive for those in need. Student government can help organize these events, assisted by faculty advisors so that it becomes a collaborative enterprise among students and adults.

History reminds people about what an organization has stood for over time. On the 40th anniversary of the American Embassy School (AES) in New Delhi, India, a teacher received a stipend to write a history of the school. This went a long way toward building the idea of tradition. The middle school buried a time capsule with a video of the school and samples of schoolwork. The elementary school student council took the lead in renaming two school buildings after famous people who exemplified the values for which the school stood. In addition, the following school song was written by one of the teachers to reflect the core values, and there was a student contest to select the title:

The World of AES

To the city of New Delhi

We come from far and wide

Boys and girls of every nation

Standing side by side

In the beauty of the gardens

We learn to take good care

Of ourselves and of each other

And this world that we all share

At AES, AES the finest school we know

Where the boys and girls and grown-ups

All really like to show

That we're smart and "green" and friendly

And we lend a helping hand

In this very special school

In a very special land

Each day we try our very best

In everything we do

The school is like a sailing ship

And we are all the crew

We work and play together

As we sail upon the sea

There's no other place in India

That we would rather be than . . .

—by the students and faculty of AES, led by Marilyn Ferguson

NORMS ARE THE UNWRITTEN RULES OF CULTURE

Generally, individuals within an organization behave toward one another according to the expectations they perceive to exist within the culture. These group expectations are usually a function of an unwritten code for behavior called norms—or, as Terry Deal said, "the way we do things around here" (personal communication, 1989).

In some schools, for example, there are norms that encourage people to voice their opinions, even if those opinions go against the grain of the majority voice. As a teacher from Maine explained, "At our school, everyone has a right to disagree. No one must voice his or her opinion. But, if you don't take responsibility for voicing your opinion and a decision is made by the rest of the staff, you must agree not to stand in the way of the wheels of progress." In schools where this type of norm is strong, individuals who risk offering an opposing viewpoint have often become celebrated as heroes because they make others think about their attitudes and actions. One teacher noted, "At our school, we can always count on Andy. He has his feet planted firmly in concrete. . . but he reminds us, who often have our heads in the clouds, of brass tacks reality!"

When norms at a school encourage prospecting for internal resources, the activities reflect that stance. Peer-coaching programs are an example. At one school, a peer-coaching program has been operating successfully for three years. To keep the project going, teachers formed mixed newcomer and veteran groups. There are strong norms within this culture that emphasize the importance of teaching and learning from one another. When practices such as peer coaching support collegiality and cooperation in this way, they become embedded in the fabric of school life.

When new information or learning opportunities are needed in collaborative cultures, the norm has often become "Let's look within our own rich reservoir of talent to see what we might tap." When one school's professional development committee surveyed the teachers about what they were most interested in, it came to light that increasing rigor and improving questioning techniques was a major area of interest. The teachers organized some of the homegrown talent to put on a staff workshop. Topics such as developing questions, activities, and assessments based on Bloom's taxonomy, Socratic seminars, and using wait time became a schoolwide focus as a result of the workshop.

Sometimes new norms are needed to replace toxic ones. At one school, at the beginning of the year, an assistant principal found a stack of negative referrals, six inches high, on the desk of his predecessor. He reflected on the need to focus on positive as opposed to negative behavior. The assistant principal shared with staff members that if they referred a student to the office for misbehavior, he wanted them to refer that same student to his office for positive behavior within six weeks. Within the semester, he and the staff could see dramatic changes in the climate and culture of the school.

In schools that operate as Professional Learning Communities (PLCs), there is a shared norm: Each staff member will do whatever it takes to help every student in the school thrive.

POWERFUL STORIES COMMUNICATE AND REINFORCE CULTURAL VALUES

Stories appeal to reason and emotion. The use of story is one way to inform and remind new and existing members of a culture about its core values. Every school has stories that, as a matter of tradition, are passed on to new staff members. Generally, these stories signal important values or beliefs. For example, at one school, new teachers are told about a former teacher who always had special techniques for helping at-risk youth. Through the story, they learn that because the school did not at that time have a forum for staff sharing, when that teacher retired, a library of knowledge "burned." Hence that teacher left her mark on students, but not on the teaching profession. Because of this great loss, teachers at the school now take special care to make sure that quality time is set aside for professional dialogue and the sharing of ideas and practices. A ritual called "See Them Teach Before They Leave" is instituted each spring; returning faculty members are encouraged to visit classrooms of departing teachers. Following this ritual, an assembly is held at which the bronzed classroom doorknob of each departing teacher, affixed to a wooden plaque and inscribed, is presented to that teacher. The plaque inscription reads, "Thank you for opening your door and sharing your classroom secrets. You kept a library of knowledge from burning."

In addition to reminding organizational members about important values, stories can also provide a way of talking about sensitive issues with a more comfortable distance. The following story, related by a college student, could be used during a faculty meeting to remind teachers of the tremendous influence they have on students' lives beyond the academic arena—an influence that can last and alter life paths.

Katie's Story

I spent the first 14 years of my life living in what I understood to be a happy family of four. However, by the time I entered high school, the facade had begun to crumble and the profound dysfunction, substance and mental issues, and abuse poured out. My parents had an ugly divorce. As a result, my home life was troublesome and unstable. I was a living, breathing dichotomy—the outwardly successful student nominated for valedictorian, tennis captain, flautist, class president, and yet, I was simultaneously so confused and smothered by dysfunction that I quietly struggled with severe depression and bulimia. At 16, I moved out of my parents' homes and in with my best friend and her family. During this uncertain period, one of my teachers went so far as to give me the keys to her home to provide me with a backup plan and peace of mind. At 17, I was offered an incredible opportunity to leave high school a year early. While moving alone to a state I had never been to in order to participate in a dual-enrollment program at a college I had never heard of was difficult, it offered an escape from my current reality.

It is certain to say that I did not leapfrog from my dysfunctional home in New Jersey to my refuge in Virginia to my current institution in North Carolina by myself. Many kind souls helped me along the way. I have always counted several teachers among these influential people. I can recall every teacher from PreK

(Continued)

(Continued)

through my sophomore year of college. Many of them, from my gentle, golden-hearted second- and third-grade teachers to the inspiring and supportive professors I am lucky to learn and work with at my current university, have profoundly shaped my identity.

While there are many ways in which teachers have touched my life, one of the most unlikely yet incredibly powerful connections I made was with teachers in my high school's agricultural department. Like the outstanding teachers I already knew, they helped comfort and guide me throughout this decisive period of my life. I fondly remember these teachers pulling me into our school's FFA chapter, involving me in public speaking and other competitions. I recall the first day they hooked me into the organization.

I was the only sophomore girl in an introductory natural resources class, adrift in a sea of freshman boys. I was less than thrilled with this situation. During a lecture on the deer life cycle, an off-duty ag teacher pulled me out of class a few minutes early to discuss the department's hidden plans for me.

"Katie," the teacher began in his thick southern drawl, "you are one smart cookie. There's something special about you, girl; the universe has big plans for you. But, in the meantime, the ag department wants to invite you to try out to be our public speaker at this year's state convention." A few minutes later, the other two teachers joined us to reel me in.

In retrospect, there were a number of "countable" benefits to the kindness these teachers showed me: involvement in a tight-knit organization, valuable job preparation, and fabulous resume-building opportunities. However, their actions, like the efforts of other teachers before and after them, also yielded intangible benefits, the positive effects of which even I am uncertain. This single isolated invitation would bloom into important mentoring relationships for me. Each of these teachers would spend countless hours before, after, and during school sharing pleasant and difficult conversations; laughter as well as tears; and boundless empowerment. Throughout my three years of high school; their emotional support, positive energy, engagement, and recognition of my strengths helped me focus on the silver linings of my life and the brighter future that lay ahead.

It is pleasantly ironic that, today, I find myself at Elon University, immeasurably grateful to have received a full scholarship through the Watson Odyssey Scholars program. Like many of my peers, getting here has been quite an unusual odyssey. But, these days, I am independent, happy, healthy, and absolutely flourishing. I continue to enjoy close relationships with many of the former teachers who were so influential in my life and also cultivate new relationships with current professors, several of whom are becoming mentors to me.

In recognition of those who have and who continue to help me, I dedicate a significant portion of my time to "paying it forward" by participating in tutoring and mentoring programs. Sometimes, the work can be frustrating—as a college student straddling the poverty line, I am always broke. This often leaves me unable to buy extra supplies for the children with whom I work. When this frustrates me, I recall the amazing yet budget-strangled teachers from my public school background. The importance of teachers can never be equated with the crayons or textbooks they can or cannot buy. The most important resource they have is and has always been their engagement with students—from fostering innovative, critical thinking; laughing at a shy student's poorly timed joke; to investing love and effort into mentoring, teachers have incredible power with and responsibility to their students. I was lucky enough to have teachers who empowered me—if someone tells you that you are bright, capable, responsible, worthy, and promising, it is easier to believe that reality and to fulfill that destiny. On the other hand, it is also easy to inspire students to fail and to live negatively.

Growing up in a school district which I considered a home away from home helped me to succeed. Many teachers focus on measuring the academic impact they have on students' lives. However, for students like me, in addition to the knowledge and skills these teachers imparted, it was the immeasurable, intangible ripple effects from their positive, personal dedication that launched me on a continuing odyssey marked by high expectations and hope.

In many school cultures that function as PLCs, storytelling is a regular part of every PLC meeting. When staff members share stories of student success or transformation, it reinforces the notion that professional colleagues will do whatever it takes to assure that every student succeeds! The Carnegie Corporation (2013) sponsors StoryCorps on their website. Several school leaders have shared stories from this incredible resource to promote understanding, overcome adversity, or build and celebrate commitment to the profession of teaching.

Thus far, through anecdotal examples, we have discussed a framework of interactive elements for thinking about school culture. In the pages that follow, we consider how a culture might be transformed if it is not a positive one, or if it is not aligned with a school's vision.

READING, TRANSFORMING, OR SHAPING A CULTURE

School cultures vary tremendously. Schools that have positive, cohesive, healthy cultures perform better than those with weak, unhealthy cultures. The complexity of cultural transformation or shaping can be overwhelming. Because no two cultures are alike, what worked in one culture, may not work in another.

One of the most daunting tasks of school leaders is to first read, and then shape the culture to reflect treasured core values and beliefs. This is particularly difficult if the culture is entrenched and negative or toxic.

Deal and Peterson (2009) suggest that the principal shapes a culture through a variety of means. They believe that it begins with "reading" the existing culture and then progressively moving to actions that create or reinforce core values, norms or practices, consistent with the vision of the school. Reading a culture involves listening to stories told by staff, examining artifacts such as pictures or objects that have deep meaning for organizational members and reviewing operating procedures and communications. This "reading" is critical because, as Peterson and Deal (2002) remind us, "The past is truly never far away. People remember the past and the feelings it produces" (p. 49). Kent Peterson, speaking to a group of new and aspiring principals at a colloquium sponsored by the Association of California School Administrators cautioned, "If you don't read the culture first, it can rise up and bite you in the act!"

Examining what is celebrated, who are the informal power brokers, what the rituals are, what gets rewarded, and how time is used all provide a telling portrait of the culture of a school or organization. Prior efforts at school improvement, mandated initiatives, crises faced by the staff, traditions, and information about the former principal's leadership style also yield valuable data for constructing a profile of the existing culture. Once this information is garnered, the principal, in concert with the leadership team and staff, identify specifics related to the ideal vision of a school. In keeping with this vision, detailed plans are made to gradually transform the culture so that the rituals, rewards, routine activities, stories, and norms call attention to the values embedded in the new vision. Deal and Peterson (1990), in a series of case studies, noted that principals (and other leaders) shape culture in both formal and informal ways. They identified six major culture-shaping strategies:

1. Developing a sense of what the school should and could be

2. Recruiting and selecting staff whose values fit with the school's

3. Resolving conflicts, disputes, and problems directly as a way of shaping values

4. Communicating values and beliefs in daily routines and behaviors

5. Identifying and articulating stories that communicate shared values

6. Nurturing the traditions, ceremonies, rituals, and symbols that communicate and reinforce the school culture

What school leaders do will differ dramatically. One cultural transformation may take a year, whereas another may take five. What is essential is that the principal and leadership team hold the values and beliefs in focus as daily tasks are conducted and that these values and beliefs are articulated widely. Continuous growth and improvement must be emphasized.

Sharon Kruse and Karen Seashore Louis (2009) use the term *intensification of leadership* to describe an approach to changing the cultural conditions that affect teaching and learning. Specific cultural attributes are directly tied to student success. Thus, Kruse and Seashore Louis point out, "Improving culture is not an end in itself, but the means by which school leaders can address the goals of student progress and achievement" (p. 8). There are three features of school cultures that have been tied to student learning:

- Professional Community
- Organizational Learning
- Trust (Kruse and Seashore Louis)

One powerful leverage point for creating positive, learning focused *professional communities* is work that focuses on developing structures and processes to facilitate the sharing of successful practices, as well as mistakes, reflective dialogue, collaboration, and problem solving. Members of these professional communities take collective responsibility for all students and strongly value the expertise that each individual community member collectively brings to the community. In these communities, there are norms that "together we are better and more skillful than alone." As one teacher leader said, "We would never dream of taking on a difficult case without consulting a trusted colleague." Kruse and Seashore Louis (2009, p. 8) note, "The concept of *organizational learning* suggests that continuous improvement through collective engagement with new ideas will generate enhanced classroom practices and deeper understanding of how organizational improvement occurs."

Trust among professional colleagues is closely tied to cultural change. As Bryk and Schneider (2004) and Tschannen-Moran (2004) suggest, trust among and between teachers and other groups is linked to increased student achievement. When professional colleagues perceive that trusting relationships exist, they are more likely to share successful practices and be willing to acknowledge problems of practice. There is less concern about being judged or in competition with other faculty members. School leaders set the tone for building trust by modeling trusting relationships, aligning actions with words, and following through on commitments. Trust is a powerful building block for creating and sustaining professional community and organizational learning.

An essential strategy for building positive, professional learning communities is to expand the membership of the school leadership team. This provides expanded leadership responsibilities and opportunities for teachers as well as serves as a conduit for getting information about current initiatives affecting teaching and learning out to the faculty at large. As one principal reflected, "There's simply too much for any one person to do. Sharing leadership responsibilities builds trust among colleagues and increases ownership of initiatives. It gives momentum to our school improvement work."

Echoing this principal, Karen Seashore Louis and Kyla Wahlstrom (2011) write, "Involving the school community is critical . . . schools need to build strong cultures in which the many tasks of transforming schools require many leaders" (p. 52).

While shared leadership is essential, organizational members will always be focused on the formal leader's behavior. Hence, it is critical to be aware that small acts can speak volumes!

Be aware of the following:

- What you model
- How you greet people

- What you pay attention to when you visit classrooms, interact with faculty members, or students
- What's first and what's last on your meeting agendas
- How you spend time
- What you value in teachers, support personnel, classified staff
- How you use humor

The energy and vitality of the workplace climate plays a profound role in its productivity and organizational members' sense of well-being.

Shaping the Culture Through Storytelling

It is essential that the core values of the culture reflect beliefs about what is important. Often stories can be used to communicate these core values. To illustrate, in one high school the core values included the importance of considering the "whole child" and "matters of the heart." Faculty members often remarked, "Our school is a home for the heart and the mind." The following story illustrates how the core values of this school culture permeated the interactions of staff and students. The faculty reflected that it was often the high achievers or the students who got in trouble who received the most attention. Wanting to change this trend, they asked one another: "Who are the students who get ignored? Who are the students who are likely to slip through the cracks?" They decided on a plan of action. Each faculty member collected pictures of the students who often slipped through the cracks or were ignored. They published a compilation of each faculty member's students. The document was called "The Vanilla Kids." The name comes from the notion that vanilla is not as memorable a flavor as blueberry, cherry, or butter pecan. The expectation was that each faculty member was to reach out and communicate every time he or she saw a vanilla kid. "You could see a difference in the students and in the culture of the school within three weeks," one staff member reflected. Ordinary people can do extraordinary things to make a difference for students!

While the leader's behavior, leadership team behavior, team membership, rewards, celebrations, and rituals can be used to shape or transform culture, as these examples illustrate, stories provide still another valuable tool for shaping culture. As a reader, perhaps you were moved by the "vanilla kids" or Katie's story in this chapter. Certainly you have been moved by compelling stories told within your own culture. Hoar (quoted in Kouzes & Posner, 2006) asserts that "in the end it's all about the story that gives people meaning to not only what we're doing, but to what we're aspiring to achieve" (p. 63). This explains why stories are powerful tools for transforming cultures and changing behavior in organizations. After reading *It's Not Us Against Them—Creating the Schools We Need* (McNulty, 2009), a principal and leadership team, aspiring to get the entire faculty on board with respect to truly integrating technology in the learning experiences of students, presented the following excerpt from the book at a whole school planning day:

Kids long to be proud of their schools and of what they can accomplish there. But for too many learners, coming into school from the rich and dynamic world in which we live is like trekking into the desert or stepping back into history. For today's learners, the technologies introduced over the past twenty years—cell phones, iPods, [iPads], laptops, and more—have always been part of their experience. Yet rather than working to integrate these technologies seamlessly and productively in the classroom, many schools ban these items during school hours. It's as if these students are carpenters who must leave their power tools at the door and then build a large, intricate structure using hammers and handsaws.

Integrating technology into the educational experience . . . is vital. Technology already has changed the way we think and learn, work and play—indeed the ways we build and sustain relationships. The future of education isn't only sitting in the chairs in our classrooms, it's also nestled into the backpacks and back pockets of each learner. It's not good enough for us simply to acknowledge that all these technologies exist. We need to integrate them because we need to help our learners understand technology's role not just in their personal relationships, but also in their future professional success. After all, isn't adaptability an essential skill we need to model and teach to our children? Isn't the concept of adjusting to change essential for them to be successful in the 21st century? (pp. 39–40)

After sharing this excerpt, staff members worked in table groups to brainstorm ways in which technology could be integrated into daily learning experiences. Table groups posted the results of their dialogue on chart paper, then did a "wisdom walk" in which they walked around the room to view the work of other table groups. Many adults used their iPads to photograph ideas they wanted to use. One faculty member observing this reflected, "My students often use their cell phones to get assignments on the board." The excerpt from the book stimulated an awareness of the need to integrate technology and a conversation that still continues today!

Research documents the tremendous capacity of storytelling. Consider the following account from Kouzes and Posner (2006):

Stanford University organizational sociologists Joanne Martin and Melanie Powers studied the impact of stories on MBA students, an often numbers-driven, highly competitive, skeptical audience. Martin and Powers compared the persuasiveness of four methods of convincing the students that a particular company truly practiced a policy of avoiding layoffs. In one situation they used only a story to persuade people. In the second, they presented statistical data that showed that the company had significantly less involuntary turnover than its competitors. In the third, they used the statistics and the story, and in the fourth, they used a straightforward policy statement made by an executive of the company. . . . As you probably anticipated, the most believable was number 1, the story only. The students who were given only the story believed the claim about the policy more than any of the other groups and remembered it better several months later. The executive delivering the policy statement was the least convincing. (pp. 63–64)

Kouzes and Posner's (2002) landmark book *The Leadership Challenge,* underscores the use of storytelling as a leadership tool. The authors make the following insightful points:

- It is important to "lead by storytelling" and "put storytelling on your meeting agenda" (pp. 98–100).
- "Telling great stories is one of the most effective ways leaders can model the values and beliefs essential to organizational success" (p. 381).
- "Stories aren't meant to be kept private; they're meant to be told. And because they're public, they're tailor-made for celebrations. In fact, stories are celebrations and celebrations are stories" (p. 359).
- "Well-told stories reach inside us and pull us along" (p. 383).

How can the power of storytelling shape the culture of the schoolhouse (Alvy & Robbins, 2010a)? Consider the following scenario. In one school the principal became aware that the sixth-grade team was dysfunctional. Backbiting, bullying, and self-serving battles replaced the resource sharing, problem solving, and collaboration that benefited students whose teachers were on other teams. The principal was distressed that the human toll, in terms of student learning, would be great if the sixth-grade team members were unable to resolve their differences. In an effort to ameliorate the toxic energy that was rampant in this underperforming team, the principal shared the following story about President Abraham Lincoln:

Building a Team for the Nation's Greater Good

In 1855, Abraham Lincoln expected to be co-counsel with the well-known and respected Pennsylvania lawyer Edwin M. Stanton on the celebrated McCormick Reaper patent case in Cincinnati, Ohio. Lincoln, with a passion for inventions and new mechanical gadgets, prepared extensively for the case and looked forward to working with Stanton. Stanton, however, viewed Lincoln "as a Western hick and snubbed him throughout the trial. . . [and] supposedly referred to him as 'that giraffe' and that 'creature from Illinois'" (Oates, 1994, p. 103). Lincoln, always the lifetime learner, remained in the courtroom and learned much from Stanton's performance. Seven years later, on January 13, 1862, Lincoln appointed Stanton to the Secretary of War cabinet position. Stanton was

> Astonished that Lincoln had appointed him Secretary of War. After all, Stanton had humiliated Lincoln back in the McCormick Reaper case. And in Washington this past year, Stanton had vilified this "imbecilic" President, this "original gorilla." . . . But Lincoln made it clear that he bore Stanton no ill will. If the McCormick Reaper episode had been one of the most humiliating episodes of his life, Lincoln had put that aside now. He never carried a grudge, he said later, because it didn't pay. (p. 278)

Stanton's appointment was but another example of Lincoln's greatness; he did not let petty differences serve as obstacles to the greater good. As the nation's leader, Lincoln's objective was to fill the cabinet with those most able to carry out the national purpose: to serve as a democracy of, by, and for the people. In *Team of Rivals*, Doris Kearns Goodwin (2005) observes that "Lincoln's choice of Stanton would reveal. . . a singular ability to transcend personal vendetta, humiliation, or bitterness. As for Stanton . . . he would . . . come to respect and love Lincoln more than any person outside of his immediate family" (p. 175). When Lincoln died on April 15, 1865, at 7:22 a.m., it was Stanton who stated the immortal words, "Now he belongs to the ages" (p. 743).

In this example, the principal drew on a period of national crisis as a tool to resolve petty differences for the greater good: student learning.

FINAL THOUGHTS ON CULTURE

One principal noted, "Culture is really the stage on which leadership gets played out. If, for example, the shared vision for a school is to be a 21st century 'home' for the heart and mind, one has to ask, 'To bring this to reality, what will it take? What will be in the halls, on the walls, in the trophy case? What will the stories be like that are told to newcomers? What will be the traditions, celebrations? Who will be on the leadership team?' And, what's more, as a principal I always have to be aware of how my behavior—what I attend to, put last on my priority list, what I participate in, what I don't—shapes the culture of the school." As Kent Peterson once reflected, "Probably one of the most important things a leader does is to create, shape, and manage culture." The ideal school culture is positive, learning focused, cohesive, and dedicated to helping every student thrive. The collaborative learning-focused school will be explored further in Chapter 11.

REFLECTIONS

This space provides a place for you to write down ideas that have been generated by this chapter, things you want to try, or adaptations of ideas presented here.

1. Reflect on the school culture in your organization. What are the core values and beliefs? How are they depicted in traditional ceremonies, rituals, reward structures, artifacts, and stories? Are they consistent with the vision of the school? Why or why not?

2. Are there traditions or rituals in your school that are contrary to the values of the school? If so, why do you think this is the case? How might you transform them if need be?

3. Identify key behind-the-scenes staff members who play a major part in school culture. What parts do they play?

4. What are the stories that are told in your school? How do these stories shape the behavior of organizational members?

5. What insights or new questions do you have as a result of reflecting on the ideas presented in this chapter?

PART II

Critical Skills for
Effective Leadership

4

The Art of
Human Relations

Getting the Job Done

You simply can't build an effective learning community without relationships, communication, and trust.

—A principal's voice

Displaying effective and ethical human relations is a key to leadership on every level. It is a thread that runs throughout the organization and affects the culture, climate, personnel practices, and every individual who has contact with the school. It impacts the relationship between the school and the larger community.

Human relations skills include working with people, building trust, creating a climate for teachers to comfortably discuss their own classroom practice, and helping individuals become all they can be. When positive human relations skills are manifested, people feel comfortable taking risks, experimenting, collaborating, and communicating ideas and feelings. These behaviors enable students and staff to perform at high levels.

"Relationships are at the heart of what we do . . . relationship is our most valuable currency. If we don't connect with peoples' hearts as well as their heads, it's not likely we'll move forward collectively . . . I believe we either build a bridge or a wall with every person we meet" (Scott & McLain, 2011, p. 61), reflected Brian McLain, principal of Denton Creek Elementary School in Coppell, Texas.

To illustrate the importance of these words in action, let's examine what happened at a middle school in Illinois. Last year, the middle school's leadership team (of which the principal was a member) worked closely with the school's parent group and established a phone and e-mail tree that could be activated at a moment's notice if there was an emergency situation or weather alert. One day, law enforcement officials called the school and urged them to go into lockdown as there was an armed bank robber at large in the neighborhood. The school responded immediately, following the lockdown procedures they had received at a central office–police department partnership session. While this was happening, a parent who had access to a police scanner overheard the communication between the police captain and other officers about the lockdown. He called the school, furious that the phone tree had not been activated. The secretary responded to the call by saying, "Mr. Chapman, I will have the principal return your call as soon as possible." Stirred by her response, Mr. Chapman also called the local television station, which dispatched its camera crew to campus. Eventually, the robber was apprehended, the lockdown was lifted, the phone and e-mail tree was activated with an explanation of what had transpired, and students were dismissed according to their regular schedule. The principal called the parent, who was still seething over the incident. The parent said, "How dare you ask us to put in time to create the e-mail tree and then not use it!" The principal responded, "I understand your anger and frustration both with not being notified and not being able to speak with me when you called. To be honest, my first priority was to be sure students were safe and perceived that they had support and were cared for in a secure building. After this happened, my next priority was to notify the parents and return to business as usual as soon as possible. I value my relationship with parents and I take my obligation to serve their children, our students, seriously. I regret that I have disappointed you and I hope we can rebuild the bridges that this incident may have destroyed." The parent was silent. Then he responded, "You put my child before me, as well you should have. You have regained my trust." As this incident conveys, the time taken to build relationships, a crystal clear vision of one's leadership priorities, and a comfort with embracing conflict and communicating all contributed to the results this principal achieved: safe students, clarity about values, and communication that created building blocks for trust.

As leaders, our responses to challenging situations are critical; the approach we choose directly influences the outcomes we derive. The principal in the preceding scenario was logical and direct, which took the emotional charge out of the situation. He modeled empathy and perspective taking. Managing one's own emotions often creates a calming antidote when conflict occurs. Many positive things come from handling conflict effectively: change, problem-solving solutions, understanding, and personal growth.

Difficult conversations are a natural part of life in great schools. These conversations take place in a variety of contexts—during professional learning community meetings, grade-level or department meetings, faculty meetings, supervisory meetings, or evaluation meetings. They take place in hallways, classrooms—even the parking lot! During these conversations, individuals are brutally honest with one another as teaching practices, student progress, interpersonal skills, follow through, commitments, teamwork, or test scores are discussed. Reflecting on how difficult and delicate these conversations are, Deb Ganderton, principal of Rose Elementary School in Escondido, California said, "There was some significant trepidation surrounding those first forays into a [difficult conversation]. Being nice was what tethered us, one to the other, and there was little desire to risk the relationship. The primary concern our team members articulated was wrapped around fear—fear the relationship would not survive a confrontation and all that entailed. We came to recognize . . . that if we continued to choose to perpetuate this pattern of avoidance, we were, in essence, saying, 'Your feelings as an adult are more important than the needs of these students.' This epiphany was a call to action" (Scott & Ganderton, 2012, p. 50).

This principal's insights highlight the need for schools to maintain a laserlike focus on high-quality instruction that culminates in learning for every student. Staff collaboration is essential if schools are to succeed in realizing this vision. However, in order for collaboration and conversation to thrive, relational trust among professional colleagues must be developed and nurtured. Robin Totten, principal of Orting (WA) Primary School notes, "Unaddressed adult issues can take our focus off what's best for children" (Scott & Totten, 2013, p. 54). She explains further that until adults function as a team, schools will have a difficult time helping students to learn. Always maintaining a vision of we are in this for students will help. Stay the course and remind others daily of the purpose of our work.

Exposing topics such as lack of initiative, sarcasm, playing favorites, or not following through on commitments is difficult work. Expressing feelings about these topics is uncomfortable. Often leaders want to bolt during situations like these. Don't give up! Instead, gather the perspectives of those involved. Choose questions, rather than statements, to frame a dialogue about the situation. Then sit back and listen. The leader will gain insight and learn from this approach and those involved will become empowered to solve their own problems. Asking questions, rather than making statements, causes people to think and feel less threatened. They engage in conversation as a consequence.

During times of conflict or emotional turmoil, be mindful that beliefs and perceptions lead to self-fulfilling prophesies. If one believes her colleagues or administrative team members are not trustworthy and will not follow through, these beliefs and perceptions will influence one's behavior and ultimately the results one derives. Deli Moussavi-Bock, Director of Training for Fierce in the Schools explains, "I humanize or dehumanize those with whom I come in contact, one interaction at a time. . . . Our beliefs inform our practice. . . . Gaining perspective on a situation or a person can change everything about my conversations with that person and our collective outcomes" (Scott & Moussavi-Bock, 2012, p. 53).

One high school principal, reflecting on the impact of human relations skills in his work said, "You can't really change others. You can only change yourself. My responses to situations ultimately determine the outcomes I get! I must manage myself if I am to lead others!" Principals and other school leaders experience a wide array of emotions as a consequence of their interactions which they must manage on a daily basis through their human relations work. The sections that follow are designed to offer insights to support this human relations work.

TASK AND RELATIONSHIP BEHAVIORS

One of the difficult aspects of the principal's human relations role is that task and relationship behaviors must be addressed simultaneously. If too much weight is placed on task behaviors as a measure of success, organizational members may feel stressed or pressured. If too much emphasis is placed on relationship behaviors, people may feel as if it's all fluff, and no progress is being made. The dialogue regarding the tension between task and relationship responsibilities has been with us since the emergence of management literature. Frederic Taylor's industrial model stressed individual and bureaucratic efficiency, whereas Mary Parker Follett and Elton Mayo emphasized interpersonal dynamics and "change-oriented and informal structures" (Stewart, 2006, pp. 4–5). In fact, Stewart creatively (and humorously) reduces the history of task and relationship literature: "Between them, Taylor and Mayo carved up the world of management theory. According to my scientific sampling, you can save yourself from reading about 99 percent of all the management literature once you master this dialectic between rationalists and humanists. The Taylorite rationalist says: Be efficient! The Mayo-ist humanist replies: Hey, these are people we're talking about! And the debate goes on. Ultimately, it's just another installment in the ongoing saga of reason and passion" (p. 5).

It can be helpful to reflect on key routine events—faculty meetings, newsletters, daily bulletins and announcements, social media, meetings with the staff—and consider in planning for these how you might balance task and relationship behaviors. For example, one principal plans faculty meetings with a leadership team made up of teachers. This allows him to sense the staff's attitudes toward key issues on the agenda. The agenda is constructed with time allocations for each item. Then it is distributed to the staff ahead of time so that items may be added prior to the meeting. During the meeting, in between every few agenda items, drawings are held or jokes are swapped for a brief period of time. On items that require staff input, table group discussions occur and collective group summaries are shared. At the end of the meeting, feedback is requested. In these ways, attention to both task and relationship behaviors is modeled.

One principal brainstormed a list of things she could do to balance attention to task (getting the job done) with relationship-oriented behavior (taking care of people). Elements of this list follow:

Task Orientation	Relationship Orientation
Begin and end meetings on time.	Allocate time for collaborative activities.
When you ask for behavior change or products, give concrete examples of what you expect.	Plan interactive activities during faculty meetings.
	Protect faculty members from verbal attack when ideas are discussed.
Request feedback on agenda construction and coverage at the end of meetings.	Ask for input regarding decisions to be made; allocate time for discussion.
Take written notes on requests, and follow up.	Schedule time for faculty members to work together (sharing ideas, trading lessons, integrating curriculum, reviewing state curriculum standards, teaching one another instructional approaches, developing rubrics of student work).
Assign time limitations to agenda items. If additional discussion time is needed, ask the faculty for more time or for permission to continue the discussion at the next meeting.	Follow up on staff development experiences with opportunities for staff members to share how they have applied recent learnings, with an emphasis on student work.

DIFFERENTIATED SUPPORT

Another effective human relations skill is being sensitive to the individual needs of personnel. For example, teachers new to the profession may need very directive support as they struggle and triumph in the early stages of their careers. This assistance may begin with a tour of the school and a review of basic policies and procedures, with time to ask questions. Additional support can be provided by a variety of people: the principal; assistant principal; a group of teachers; a mentor, coach, or lead teacher; or a combination of these. Support might include consultation, modeling, feedback, and opportunities to visit other teachers or to talk with trusted colleagues. Online resources might also be provided.

Successful experienced teachers, on the other hand, may prefer reflective listening, online resources, and coaching as opposed to directive support. Opportunities to work with colleagues on professional growth topics may be a stimulating aspect of the support provided to experienced teachers (see Chapter 10).

PERSONALITY STYLES

Another tool for enhancing relationships among all members of the school community and extended community is based on personality style. Understanding one's own style(s) and the styles of those with whom one interacts can be tremendously helpful in collaborative work. Kise and

Russell raise the question, "How do you help independent teachers form professional learning communities when their natural inclination is to work alone?" (2008, p. 1). Approaching this question with style in mind can yield valuable foundational skills for collaborative work.

Several resources on style exist. For example, Gregorc (1985) identifies four basic mind or learning styles that affect how individuals think, what they value, and how they behave. These styles reveal preferences for ordering and perceiving information. Ordering preferences range from sequential to random. Perception preferences range from concrete to abstract. Thus, a principal who, because of style, relates and perceives in an organized, concrete manner may have difficulty communicating with or valuing the work of a staff member who operates through a more abstract, random approach. Providing a workshop on style can be a lively, informative, and enjoyable professional development activity. Silver and Hanson's work (1996) offers still another resource on style. Their work invites educators to consider style from three perspectives: self, teaching style, and students' learning styles. Faculties in many schools have found this resource transformative in how they plan, deliver, and assess instruction. After learning about style, one high school math teacher reflected, "This [session on style] made me aware that I was teaching to one quarter of my class—the fourth who learned like I did!"

Focusing on style with staff members impacts classroom practices, as teachers become more aware of how their styles influence the lessons and student work they design and, consequently, student learning. In addition, success in human relations may result as a consequence of interpreting how individuals are affected by the context of a particular situation and acting appropriately, with a style perspective in mind.

RECOMMENDATIONS FOR SKILLFUL HUMAN RELATIONS

Following are some commonsense suggestions for a principal and leadership team to consider in working to help staff and students reach their highest levels of performance. These recommendations emerged as a result of observing and talking with many principals.

1. *Project yourself as a person first, and as a principal (or school leader) second.* Show your human side. Let the staff know that you are approachable and genuine. This helps colleagues feel that they, too, can be themselves. When you show your "rough edges," it gives people permission to show theirs, and authentic relationships have a chance to flourish. Although the leader strives to do the right thing, mistakes happen. In a sense, the leader is saying, "We are all humans, we make mistakes, and through our humanness, we learn."

2. *Be consistent about what matters.* As a leader, consistency is a great asset. Be sure that words and actions are communicating the

important values of the school. Furthermore, matching actions with words helps create *credibility* and provides the staff with a sense of security about what can be expected of the leader. Also, trust develops when the staff knows what to expect—what can be predicted—in the leader's actions.

3. *Never lose sight of the vision and your role in fostering the vision.* Maintaining a focus on the vision while working with teachers, students, and parents in the workplace allows one to stay on course and create positive attitudes and perceptions among others in the workplace. Focus on the people as you work on the vision.

4. *Take time to look at people; smile, respond, and laugh.* Taking time to interact sincerely, with a smile or a meaningful "hello," shows others that you care. Moreover, the nonverbal gestures that you make, and respond to, really count. Your ability to read nonverbals can make the difference in communicating effectively with a staff member or student, parent or community member. The message may not always be obvious, but it is still there to be received. Check out what you perceive to be mixed messages. Be aware that different cultural groups may have unique ways of communicating that may differ from your norm.

5. *Use active listening so people sense that you are really listening and that you care.* Active listening demonstrates that you are hearing what is being communicated. People are more likely to be motivated when they feel heard and understood. Active listening tells the speaker that his or her time is important and can also benefit the listener's understanding. Active listening usually includes asking clarifying questions to enhance understanding as well as paraphrasing. Unfortunately, we often listen only to respond. This communicates a message that what we have to say is more important than the contribution of another.

6. *Dignify people and take the high road.* When you look for the best in people and communicate by dignifying them, you can expect that the best will come back to you. Dignifying people includes taking the high road in all relationships. If you embarrass or insult someone, it is difficult to build bridges, and you will likely regret your actions later. Dignifying people shows respect, which can foster trust, and trust is the most critical attribute in building relationships among professional colleagues and the learning organization.

7. *Walk a mile in your colleague's moccasins.* Taking another person's perspective often reveals insights to which we would not otherwise be privy. This provides a greater appreciation of the other's needs, viewpoints, and, possibly, an inside view of what that person considers when making important decisions. Considering another's perspective can provide a measure of empathy as well.

The ability to empathize is one of our most sophisticated and valuable human gifts. Also, appreciating another's point of view enhances our capacity to fine-tune communication as a result of greater understanding. As the world and the school become smaller and more global in their constituency bases, taking time for individuals to share the unique perspectives afforded by their cultures or experiences enriches understanding and adds a valuable dimension to the organization.

8. *Respect, nurture, and celebrate diversity of ideas and people.* Diversity brings richness to a school. Encouraging and nurturing the diverse ideas of individuals can tap a new level of creativity that enables the staff to collectively face challenges. Diversity reflected in different ideas and cultural perspectives can enable the leader to see with many different eyes. This enhances one's overall perspective. Moreover, the person who might not share the leader's viewpoint, or the viewpoint of the majority, may be offering an important idea or thought that has been overlooked.

9. *Seek feedback from multiple constituencies—take the 360-degree option.* One practice that capitalizes on the value of diverse perspectives is called *full-circle evaluation* or *360-degree feedback* (Dyer, 2001). This process involves soliciting feedback from multiple and diverse sources so that leaders can gather data about their performance from those who interact with them. Examples of data sources include teachers, parents, students, classified staff, central office personnel, and community members. Several organizations have excellent instruments that can be used to gather 360-degree data. For example, a first-rate instrument is the National Association of Secondary School Principals' (NASSP, 2008) Leadership Skills Assessment, which provides data on 4 skill areas that are divided into 10 skill dimensions. The instructional leadership area includes setting instructional direction; teamwork and sensitivity; the resolving complex problems area includes judgment, results orientation, and organizational ability; the communication area includes oral communication and written communication; and the developing self and others skill area includes understanding one's own strengths and weaknesses and developing the strengths of others. After one completes the self-assessment, NASSP encourages the principal to get feedback from up to 15 colleagues in order to compare perceptions (NASSP, 2008; www.principals.org).

Vanderbilt University and the University of Pennsylvania teamed up to develop and field-test a 360-degree instrument that measures behaviors associated with student achievement and is aligned with the Educational Leadership Policy Standards (Olson, 2008). Vanderbilt Assessment of Leadership in Education (VAL-ED) measures six components of student achievement:

high standards for student learning, rigorous curriculum, quality instruction, culture of learning and professional behavior, connections to external communities, and performance accountability.

10. *Be accessible, open, and supportive.* People have a need to connect with one another, especially during the change process when many people feel lost, needy, incompetent, vulnerable, and out of control. Be there for them. Support can help individuals make the transition from old to new practices. Support entails listening, problem solving, reflecting, clarifying, and helping people develop workable solutions. Support may also mean spending time with people when tragedy or medical emergencies occur. One's physical presence at difficult times is deeply valued. Research in intensive care units has shown that the comforting presence of another person not only lowers the patient's blood pressure but also slows secretion of fatty acids that block arteries (Goleman, Boyatzis, & McKee, 2002). Thus, one's presence not only provides emotional comfort but also has the impact of changing a physiological state!

11. *Know your authentic self.* Experts on ethical leadership stress that knowing one's authentic self is a first step to understanding others and displaying positive human relations skills (Starratt, 2004). Harvard Business Professor Bill George (2007) reflects, "First, you have to understand yourself, because *the hardest person you will ever have to lead is yourself.* . . . Second, to be an effective leader, *you must take responsibility for your own development*" (p. xxxiii, italics in original).

12. *Take time to smell—and water—the roses.* One superintendent took five minutes to play catch with a lonely boy, and two months later learned that it had meant a great deal to the student. A principal walked into a small class of students receiving special assistance and asked a boy, "Jonathan, how are you doing?" Later, the principal was told that after he left, the child smiled at the teacher and said, "Wow, the principal knows my name!" Remember that in small ways we can make a big difference in people's lives. Portraying interest in a student's or staff member's work, for example, can be invigorating to the principal as well as the recipient. It communicates care.

The Chinese characters for *ear, eyes, you, undivided attention,* and *heart,* when combined, make up the verb *to listen* and remind us of the critical components necessary for effective human relations. (See Figure 4.1.) Consider posting this symbol near your desk or near a table at which you frequently hold conferences. Share the figure with staff, students, parents, and community members. It can communicate the value of listening, as well as the power of human relations.

Figure 4.1

THE ROLE OF EMOTIONS IN THE ORGANIZATION: REMEMBERING THE HEART

Experience tells us that when organizational members perceive that they are genuinely valued, feel recognized for their efforts, and are seen as important because of the contribution they are making, climate is enhanced and productivity soars. Indeed, leaders have a profound role in affecting the emotions of individuals within the workplace; their commitment to work, school, and climate; and, ultimately, productivity!

All of us, at one time or another in our lives, have been inspired by a great leader who brought out the best in us. Daniel Goleman and his colleagues Richard Boyatzis and Annie McKee (2002) explain in *Primal Leadership* that "great leadership works through the emotions" and that "the best leaders have found effective ways to understand and improve the way they handle their own and other people's emotions. Understanding the powerful role of emotions in the workplace sets the best leaders apart from the rest—not just in tangibles such as better business results and the retention of talent, but also in the all-important intangibles, such as higher morale, motivation and commitment" (pp. 3–5).

The leader who is skillful in human relations has the power to influence organizational members' emotions in a variety of ways. Goleman et al. (2002) suggest that the leader acts as a group's emotional guide. The leader's behavior literally influences whether staff members' emotions will be driven in a positive or negative direction. Staff will look to the leader for guidance, especially during times of crisis. In times of tragedy, they will look to the leader for emotional support. Goleman et al. explain that "we rely on connections with other people for our own emotional stability" and "other people can change our very physiology" (pp. 6–7). They support this statement by citing Lewis, Amini, and Lannon's (2000) research that "one person transmits signals that can alter hormone levels, cardiovascular function, sleep rhythms and even immune function inside the body of another" (p. 7). Reflecting on this research, a principal noted, "So that's why when negative information is churned out through the rumor mill people often complain of losing sleep and feeling grumpy! And, conversely, that's why when I give positive feedback to staff about their efforts with students they seem to get all pumped up." Indeed, researchers have found that human beings tend to mirror the emotional states of one another—positive or negative—when they are together. For example, people who are in rapport during a conversation often even mirror one another's body language.

Using Emotions Intelligently

How skillfully and successfully a leader models human relations skills largely depends on his or her *Emotional Intelligence.* Goleman (1995) defines Emotional Intelligence as "a basic flair for living—being able to rein in emotional impulse; to read another's innermost feelings; to handle relationships smoothly." Goleman et al. (2002) identify four dimensions of Emotional Intelligence and divide these into two areas. The first area has to do with personal competence, how we manage ourselves; the second area has to do with social competence, managing relationships with others.

The **Personal Competence** component includes *Self-Awareness* and involves knowing one's own emotions and understanding their impact on others. Being able to find words to describe emotions is a facet of this area of competence. It also means knowing one's strengths and limitations and having a sense of one's self-worth. *Self-Management* involves emotional self-control, being trustworthy, and having the capacity to be flexible when the need presents itself. Having an internal performance drive, the capacity to take the initiative, and a spirit of optimism are also competencies related to self-management.

Social Competence involves *Social Awareness* and *Relationship Management. Social Awareness* areas include empathy for individuals and the organization, organizational awareness, and a service commitment to recognizing and meeting client needs. *Relationship Management* includes inspirational leadership, the kind that involves guiding and motivating others with a compelling vision. It also refers to the ability to influence others, which usually means possessing a wide range of strategies for persuasion. Another key area of relationship management is the capacity to develop others through feedback and guidance. The person who manages relationships well often functions as a change catalyst and is skilled in conflict management, building bonds with individuals and fostering teamwork and collaboration.

Being aware of the dimensions of Emotional Intelligence and striving to model them as well as reflect on them during and after daily interactions will enhance relationships with staff members, central office personnel, other professional colleagues, parents, community members, students, and one's own family. These competencies also will inform actions that will contribute to the well-being and productivity of the organization. When people feel good about their working relationships with others, they will be able to focus on the centerpiece of school activity: making a difference for students.

REFLECTIONS

This space provides for you a place to write in ideas that have been generated by this chapter, things you want to try, or adaptations of ideas presented herein.

1. Make a list of things you do that have a task focus. Then make a list of things you do that have a relationship focus. Examine the lists to determine which one is longer. Why do you think this is the case? State what you do to simultaneously "get the job done" and "take care of people."

2. After reviewing the Recommendations for Skillful Human Relations, consider these questions: Are there particular recommendations that you believe you should work on? What other recommendations would you add to the list?

3. Reflecting on the four dimensions of Emotional Intelligence, what are your areas of personal strength? What are areas that you would like to strengthen?

4. Reflecting on supervision and evaluation, how might the four dimensions of emotional intelligence influence your work?

5. What insights or new questions do you have as a result of reflecting on the ideas presented in this chapter?

Managing Time
Leading With Purpose

What you pay attention to, and spend time on, communicates what you value.

—Kent Peterson

Time is the one resource we all share. However, what we choose to do with the time we have, how we actually spend our time, differs widely across individuals. No one actually "manages time." However, we can try to manage our use of time by clearly identifying our personal and professional goals and scheduling our time to reflect those goals. Easier said than done! The discrepancy between the amount of time that principals want to spend on the area of curriculum and instruction and the time they actually spent on the area is considerable. This is true for new or veteran principals and has been a constant source of dissatisfaction among principals for decades (Alvy, 1983; Johnson, 2008). In a Public Agenda study, cosponsored with The Wallace Foundation, principals who wanted to spend time on "curriculum, teaching technique, mentoring and professional development" were quite discouraged in how their time was used: "Just 1 in 10 principals [was] satisfied" (Johnson, 2008, p. 75). However, in the Public Agenda study, the principals did feel like they were doing better than previously. An intriguing aspect of the study related to why some principals thought they were doing better than others as instructional leaders. Johnson stated that the principals fell into two categories, "transformers" or "copers" (p. 73). The transformers believed in their kids to a greater extent, focused on instructional leadership, and brought a "can do" attitude to their time-management responsibilities. The copers felt overwhelmed and "believed they didn't have the time or freedom to do much more than get through their day" (p. 73).

BREVITY, FRAGMENTATION, AND VARIETY

Part of the difficulty associated with principals' efficient use of time lies in the characteristics of their work lives. In a study of principals' work, Peterson (1982) notes three attributes of their work lives: brevity, fragmentation, and variety. Peterson found that 85 percent of the principals' tasks lasted nine minutes or less. Often there was a sense of fragmentation related to the work because frequently forces over which they had no control interrupted principals, and in many cases these interruptions were unexpected. Furthermore, there was tremendous variety in the nature of their tasks. This variety demanded a wide range of emotions and technical skills, some for which the administrator had no previous experience or preparation. With federal mandates, a constant demand for data, and the variety of state and local curricular and instructional initiatives, the demands on principals' time are greater than ever before. The reality of brevity, fragmentation, and variety accentuates the need for systematically and thoughtfully addressing the multitude of tasks that beg for the principal's attention.

Although brevity, variety, and fragmentation make planned work very difficult to get done, paradoxically these attributes present an opportunity to work more effectively. For example, when taking a morning walk through classrooms (an important professional goal), a principal may be interrupted by a parent who is picking up make-up work for a sick child. This brief encounter presents the principal with an opportunity to express concern for the child and share the purpose of the morning walk through classrooms. This simultaneously communicates an interest in students and the school's commitment to instructional excellence. As the principal continues walking, he or she collects information about individual classrooms' culture and climate. So, in a sense, the brevity, fragmentation, and variety often give the principal an opportunity to do two or more things at once, an authentic example of Leading and Learning by Wandering Around.

TECHNIQUES FOR TIME MANAGEMENT

One principal remarked, "It is important to take control of one's schedule. That means long-range scheduling. If you think something is important—like visiting classrooms—build it into your schedule. That's the only way it will happen. Take care of yourself, and don't shortchange yourself on personal goals. I know that may seem selfish, but if your personal life is 'together,' it will help your professional life." Another principal reflected, "If you don't build what's important to you into the schedule, it will never get done . . . unimportant events always are there to fill the void." So how do you get it done?

"What is important is seldom urgent and what is urgent is seldom important." This astute observation, made by General Eisenhower during World War II, led to a proliferation of time-management systems "to get it done" using the famous "Eisenhower Matrix," a four-quadrant square used to prioritize tasks using the variables "important," "unimportant," "urgent," and "not urgent." Using this matrix, Stephen Covey maintained that we get trapped with urgent but unimportant tasks and neglect important tasks that appear not to be urgent (Covey, 1989). Important activities such as long-range planning, building relationships, reflection, and self-renewal often receive little or no attention because of responsibilities that press one's time. To illustrate, daily interruptions that are difficult to avoid (e.g., telephone calls, drop-in sales visits, some administrative meetings) frequently overshadow essential responsibilities to the organization and to oneself (e.g., visiting students on the field or in the classroom, organizing a professional development session with a Professional Learning Community team, meeting with several new teachers about their first few weeks on the job, attending your child's soccer match). A key to making good decisions related to importance and urgency *is setting priorities based on your vision of teaching and learning.* Consider the difference between the attitudes of transforming and coping principals discussed previously.

> Making the time to invest in [instructional leadership] was one of the distinguishing characteristics of the 'transformer' principals . . . copers, in contrast often admitted that instructional leadership was the facet of their work that they often sacrificed to the distractions and emergencies of the day. (Johnson, 2008, p. 75)

Even when we know our priorities and have scheduled key events, it is still difficult to follow through when, for example, someone knocks on the office door and says, "Do you have a minute?" Paul Bambrick-Santoyo (2012) acknowledges that the principal's day is "designed for distraction" (p. 70). To overcome pleasing everyone who wants a minute, he recommends using a "check-ins" strategy in which the principal holds him or herself accountable "by committing to meet with teachers, administrators, or others at a consistent time every one or two weeks" (p. 70). Bambrick-Santoyo has seen this strategy succeed because we are social creatures, and thus less likely to cancel a planned "check-in" postobservation conference in order to complete some paper work or have a discussion about a new movie with the secretary.

Time-Study Strategy

An effective way for principals to determine whether they have been prioritizing their time effectively is through a time study. For example, important professional items might include spending time in classrooms, halls, and on school grounds; giving feedback; developing and conducting professional growth activities; and professional reading. After the lists of important things are developed, think about other mundane tasks that are required given your role. Make a list of these, too. For instance, this list might include double-checking sections and rooms matched on the high school master schedule, morning and afternoon bus procedures, or working with classified staff to update student contact data. Personal items of importance might include time with family; time for fly-fishing, walking, golf, or basketball; and time to weave, knit, putter, or read.

Then create three to four high-priority personal and professional goals. Think about the activities associated with each. For instance, activities associated with the goal of spending quality time with your family might include going out for a family game night, going to dinner, having discussions, reading together, or building something. After your goals are developed, put them aside temporarily and conduct a study of your use of time. Do this for two weeks. You may choose to do this reflectively, at the end of each day, or as you move from task to task. Some principals use time-management applications that categorize each scheduled event (and alerting you of the event) and unscheduled events based on your priorities, by recording the event on a smartphone or tablet device. Another, more traditional option is to look back at your calendar for the previous month, noting how you spent time and comparing the schedule with your priorities. Carefully analyzing your use of time will help you determine what you want to do more of and what you want to do less of. Moving forward, key strategies should include affirming your role as an instructional leader, keeping the top priorities to a precious few (e.g., developing scope and sequence for the Common Core State Standards, personalizing student needs), and eliminating the "time wasters."

MANAGING BIFOCALLY

One way to use interruptions as leverage points to get more done is to manage bifocally. Kent Peterson, noted researcher on principals' work lives, suggests that bifocal leadership and management actions can actually help a principal accomplish two things at once. Here is how it works. Suppose you are working with a school improvement team on a budget committee. At the same time that you are working on the budget, you may seize the moment to educate the committee about the school's reading program—one of the budget line items. Or suppose you receive a phone call from an angry parent. Use the call as an opportunity to build positive bridges between the school and this parent, collaboratively problem solve, and gather data about how this segment of the parent population views the school. This approach uses the call as a leverage point for changing the perception of the principal and the school from negative to positive. Another way to manage time with insight involves the use of a "*smart* pocket planner." The box that follows outlines how this process works.

Managing Time With Insight: The Smart Pocket Planner

The "smart pocket planner" can be used so that the barrage of demands become leverage points for accomplishing tasks. One may use a smartphone, iPad, or tablet. Customize the format so it works for your school. Here's how the planner works:

1. To track progress toward realizing the vision:

   • Post the school's vision.
   • Identify key goals.
   • For anything that relates to the vision, jot down the date, the event, and your perceptions regarding how it relates to accomplishing the vision. Consider student work, conversations with students, parents, teachers, community stakeholders, phone conversations, school or classroom displays, and so on.
   • When it comes time for report writing, review the data you've recorded, examine it, and draw conclusions based on the vision and goals.

2. As a management tool:

   • Anytime you see something that needs to be done, type or record the item on your device as a reminder.
   • Decide whether you need to delegate the task to someone or do the task yourself.
   • For those tasks not delegated or completed, when you have a few minutes, complete the task. You'll be surprised how you can use brevity, variety, and fragmentation to your advantage.

3. For keeping track of supervisory visits, with a goal of distributing one's proximity across staff members, gaining a sense of classroom work, increasing storytelling capacity, and building schoolwide norms of practice:

   • With a spreadsheet application list staff members' names down the left side of the screen on your device.
   • Write the months across the top—three or four on the screen.
   • Every time you visit a staff member, jot down the date, time, and what you did during your visit (e.g., IS—interviewed a student, ESW—examined student work, LN—left a note, WT—walk-through visit).
   • When you have a few minutes—perhaps due to a canceled appointment—take out your smart pocket planner and visit someone you have not seen in action this month.

MULTITASKING: A MODERN-DAY SOLUTION OR HAZARD?

Our modern, fast-paced society applauds the benefits of multitasking. We take pride in telling our colleagues that we can complete six tasks at the same time. However, many experts warn us to embrace multitasking with caution. Consider Walter Kirn's (2007) observation:

This is the great irony of multitasking—that its overall goal, getting more done in less time, turns out to be chimerical. In reality, multitasking slows our thinking. It forces us to chop competing tasks into pieces, set them in different piles, then hunt for the pile we're interested in, pick up its pieces, review the rules for putting the pieces back together, and then attempt to do so, often quite awkwardly. (. . . A brain attempting to perform two tasks simultaneously will, because of all the back-and-forth stress, exhibit a substantial lag in information processing.) (p. 72)

Kirn also warns us of the extreme hazard of multitasking: "For every driver who's ever died while talking on a cell phone (researchers at the Harvard Center for Risk Analysis estimate that some 2,600 deaths and 330,000 injuries may be caused by drivers on cell phones each year), there was someone on the other end who, chances are, was too distracted to notice" (p. 76).

Dean and Webb (2011) provide excellent insights and recommendations related to digital information overload and multitasking. Citing Peter Drucker, they remind readers that CEOs need reflective and uninterrupted time to make critical decisions. Sharing compelling research, they note that when engaging in technology overload, we risk losing an edge—the ability to be creative and innovative when competing against others who value reflective time and one-on-one collegial problem-solving. Dean and Webb recommend focusing, filtering, and forgetting as a self-disciplining leadership strategy. Focusing on the task at hand, learning to filter (through delegation—a competent secretary can help filter out unimportant distractions), and forgetting the smartphone, laptop, or tablet in order to reflect and relax.

Dean and Webb highlight the importance of leaders setting a personal example and not enslaving oneself to a device. This can certainly apply to school leaders. If during a meeting the principal looks at his phone every time it vibrates, what message is the team receiving? Recently, a principal mentor was working with two new administrators, sharing ideas about leadership and trying to address concerns about opening the school year smoothly. One of the new administrators was checking her smartphone about every other minute. Sure it was impolite, but the mentor was more concerned about how well the newcomer would convey empathy to a troubled student or stressed colleague. Finally, Dean and Webb suggest that we need to be less impulsive about technology. It may feel good to respond instantly to a message, but if that becomes one's operational style, then what happens to the organizational mission and the leader's ability to fulfill that mission through relationships?

The desire to multitask will not fade away. The nature of the principalship makes multitasking very seductive. Embrace this temptation with caution. It may be the simplest but not the best solution for every circumstance a principal may encounter. Heed H. L. Mencken's sage advice: "There is always a well-known solution to every human problem—neat, plausible, and wrong."

FINAL THOUGHTS ON USING TIME

"By the end of the afternoon the [new principal] had said, 'I'll take care of it' 17 times" during interactions with various individuals in the school. Joanne Rooney (2013), the principal mentor shadowing the new administrator during that day, thought it was very noble for the principal to take on so much responsibility. But, of course, the mentor felt it necessary to start a conversation with the principal about delegation and time management. One person cannot do it all, and that is a good thing. We know that motivation increases when individuals are involved in the decision-making process, so delegation is a natural way to strengthen the learning community, helping others to fine-tune their own leadership skills, and enabling the principal to accomplish important school goals. Also, by involving others in leadership work, the principal is sending out a strong signal about trust—I know you can do this, and together we are creating a better learning community.

Furthermore, principals must be sensitive to the demands of the day, week, or year that constrain the time of others in the organization. When scheduling personal appointments and all-school activities, principals need to consider how time can be most effectively used to acknowledge the important role that others play in the organization and to send the message that time does not revolve around the principal. For example, personally asking a teacher about the best time to schedule a professional appointment, or directing the secretary to do the same, can go a long way in setting the proper tone for the appointment. In one school, no faculty meetings are held on Friday, at the request of teachers, so they can take care of pressing professional needs before the weekend. Another example of respecting teachers' daily work lives is providing monthly and yearly calendars that identify important deadlines and events (e.g., report card due dates, Martin Luther King Jr. assembly, statewide testing dates). It is imperative to adhere to these deadlines, whenever possible, out of respect for teachers.

On a more personal note, all of us probably have recognized that our performance tends to peak at certain times during the day. Some refer to themselves as morning people. Others jokingly remark, "Don't even ask me to think before 10 a.m." (Actually not a good tactic for school principals!) However, there is a note of seriousness in all this talk. Sensitivity to one's most creative or best "thinking" time can help you schedule those tasks that require the greatest concentration at times when your performance is optimal. Of course, this will not always be possible. To support your time-management plan, communicate your priorities and philosophy to the secretary and the staff. This can enable them to assist and support you in sheltering peak performance time as well as provide a model for them. It might be appropriate to provide examples of how you would like the secretary to respond (e.g., "Mr. Smith is visiting classrooms now, may I schedule an appointment or have him call you back?").

One final thought: When your behavior aligns with your values and beliefs, you will feel comfortable with yourself, your colleagues, and your environment. Professionally, you will feel better about your day because you will know that you have made every minute count. (Additional time-management suggestions can be found in Chapter 16.)

REFLECTIONS

This space provides a place for you to write down ideas that have been generated by this chapter, things you want to try, or adaptations of ideas presented here.

1. Think about your goals. Conduct a time audit study.

2. Is your use of time aligned with your goals? Are any changes necessary?

3. What are some effective use-of-time strategies that you can implement on the job?

4. How have federal and state mandates impacted your use of time? What strategies have you used to effectively address these mandates?

5. Who needs to be aware of your time-management goals? How will you let them know?

6. How might you use the smart pocket planner?

7. What new insights do you now have about multitasking?

8. What insights or new questions do you have as a result of reflecting on the ideas presented in this chapter?

6

Effectively Working With the Central Office

Coordinating Teaching, Learning, and Professional Development

Principals have a lot of autonomy, but to be successful you need to understand the district, the mission, and the benefits to being part of a team and catch the wave of the support structure.

—A school superintendent's voice

Schools do not operate in isolation but as part of a school district with a broad philosophy and set of goals and values emanating from the central office (Fullan, 2007). Indeed the interactions "of the district and the school can have a powerful effect on student achievement" (Marzano & Waters, 2007). Forging a strong relationship between districts and principals is particularly essential today because of student accountability demands, teacher and principal evaluation mandates, the Common Core State Standards (CCSS) initiative, and college and career readiness expectations. As a result district offices are "re-culturing," and "focus[ing] less on administration and more on supporting principals to improve instruction" (The Wallace Foundation, 2013, p. 16). The largest district in Georgia,

Gwinnett County, sent out a powerful message to the community by renaming its district office the "Instructional Support Center," affirming the belief that either educators "teach or they *support* teaching and learning" (Mendels & Mitgang, 2013, pp. 23–24).

Sustained change will necessitate a strong district commitment and the availability of in-service training, funding, and instructional resources for students, teachers, principals, and other school-site educators. In fact, Fullan and Stiegelbauer (1991) have noted, "Individual schools can become highly innovative for a short period of time without the district, but they cannot stay innovative without district action to establish the conditions for continuous and long term improvement" (p. 209). Fullan (2007) has also stressed the critical nature of lateral capacity building. That is, other schools across the district, state, and nation provide an invaluable storehouse of human and instructional resources, including stories of successful innovations. Dwindling assets juxtaposed with federal and state mandates necessitate sharing ideas to build capacity, for if only some schools in a district or state are successful—and that success doesn't spread laterally—then a commitment to all students remains unfulfilled. Thus, lateral capacity is a moral imperative.

CAUGHT IN THE MIDDLE

Principals often find themselves caught in the middle between staff and the central office. Federal, state, and district policies and timelines must be followed while accomplishing the business of the school. This often involves sheltering teachers from outside interferences. This enables them to represent the needs of the school. Schlechty (2001) reminds principals, "Learn to see yourself as a member of the district-level team as well as the head of your own team at the building level. Recognize that your school is not the only system you need to consider; it is part of a larger system. Other schools and other principals are not—or should not be—your competition" (pp. 213–214).

HOW IS THE SCHOOL DISTRICT GOVERNED?

Understanding governance can considerably enhance a principal's work life. The relationship between a school and the central office will depend to some extent on the structure of governance and size of the district. Developing effective strategies to work with the central office will depend on understanding how the district works. Concerning governance, there are many traditional and experimental decision-making models. In one district critical decisions are made in the central office with little input from the school site. In another district, the school may be largely autonomous, with control of the purse strings in the hands of a site-based counsel that includes a principal, parents, teachers, and community members. What about the role of the elected school board? In most districts, school board members see their role as supporting and fine-tuning the broad policies of the district.

COMMUNICATION BETWEEN THE SCHOOLS AND THE CENTRAL OFFICE

Although gaining an understanding of the governance structure is important, a lot will depend on the personnel in the central office and schools and their mutual ability to communicate. Communication should be a two-way street, and the school principal can be the key to orchestrating an effective relationship with the district team. The central office views the principal as the primary contact person. Thus, from a practical viewpoint, it is easiest for a district office to say, "We need to get in touch with the Carver School; let's call the principal, Ms. Breyer." But the principal should not expect that it is the job of central office personnel to always initiate the contact. The principal's attitude must be, "It is my job to communicate proactively with the central office." Otherwise, the principal may hear from the central office only when something is wrong or when they have a new idea to be implemented without school input.

How can principals effectively initiate contact with the central office? Traditionally, central office personnel do not spend as much time in schools as they would like. Principals need to build occasions into the school calendar to bring central office personnel and school board members into schools. Invite them to major programs, and let them know when Senior Projects, Invention Week, or the Science Exhibition is taking place, or when the middle school is performing a play. Send them the dates of important events well in advance. Acknowledge their presence when they attend these events. Bring students to the central office to share their reports or math investigations. Coordinate live streaming of events and post videos of student activities on the school or district website, or on YouTube for later downloading by district office personnel.

Communication also depends on knowing how the informal organization works, how things really get done. Fair or unfair, the image of the central office is often one of a bureaucracy that moves slowly and is dominated by red tape. (It will be interesting to see if the accountability pressures and "reculturing" of the central office as a learning center changes these perceptions.) How does one cut the time and red tape necessary to communicate an idea or jump-start a potentially rich innovation? Principals should consider these questions: With whom should you really speak? Who are the power brokers in the central office? Who "hangs together"? The idea is not to beat the system but rather to institute effective programs for students and teachers as quickly as possible. Engaging veteran principals or others who have worked in the school district for a long time is the best way to discover how the informal organization operates.

Schlechty (2001) advises central office personnel to remember that their "most important job is to create and manage systems that will enable principals and teachers to concentrate on the core business of schools, the creation of intellectual activity that students find engaging and from which they learn. Only secondarily, if at all, should you [central office personnel] see yourself as a supervisor" (p. 212). The central office in Long Beach, California, cut the red tape by streamlining the process for employing qualified teacher applicants. The school district tries to complete applicant physical examinations, fingerprinting, and paperwork in one day—and in one building. The rationale for consolidating the process is simple: "If someone has a bad experience when they come in here, we may lose a good teacher" (Johnston, 2001, p. 18).

At times school leaders use thoughtful strategies to slow down or eliminate an idea from the central office that may offer little prospect for student success. Deal and Peterson (1994), in *The Leadership Paradox,* describe the "bifocal principal" who needs to follow the "central office directives [yet] be creatively insubordinate" (p. 49). On the other hand, it is important to build a relationship of mutual trust in which successes and failures are shared. Central office staff need to know that the school site values them and that they play an important role. Their efforts deserve to be validated. Central office personnel may not verbalize the idea, but they too often feel distant from schools. As one assistant superintendent noted, "How many articles and headlines have you read about central office leaders? I suspect you've read very few" (quoted in Grove, 2002, p. 45). When a school reaches out and recognizes the role of the central office, that act can greatly reduce the distance. Again, invite central office personnel to events that celebrate student and teacher success. They will remember. The next time an idea develops, in a school that has forged a warm and effective relationship with central office, implementation of a change just may come a little easier.

THE DISTRICT OFFICE AS A TEACHING AND LEARNING CENTER

To serve schools and teachers, central office personnel in the Arlington, Virginia, public schools take responsibility for assisting new teachers and teachers having difficulties, developing and implementing grants, meeting with citizen committees, organizing student art exhibitions and science fairs, conducting the textbook adoption and ordering process, and designing and conducting staff development (Grove, 2002). In Pittsburgh, Pennsylvania, central office supervisors work in schools to coach principals and principal trainees guided by the Educational Leadership Policy Standards. This initiative has invigorated central office leaders because "[this] newly flattened central office structure encourages midlevel supervisors to get out of the office and spend most of the week walking school halls and sitting in classrooms alongside the principals" (Samuels, 2008, p. 26).

According to Rorrer, Skrla, and Scheurich (2008), the role of the district office as a partner in the school reform effort has been overlooked since the movement began in 1983. But times are changing. Rorrer et al. surmise that district offices are now full partners, focusing on four areas: (1) providing instructional leadership, (2) reorienting the district office culture to support teaching and learning, (3) establishing policy coherence so resources and instructional needs match, and (4) maintaining an equity focus "to own past inequities" (p. 329). This fourth point is compelling: "Recent research on districts demonstrate progress in increasing achievement for all students and in narrowing achievement gaps in districts serving racially and economically diverse students" (p. 329).

Honig (2012) stresses that the "work practices" of executive-level district administrators had shifted "from mainly management, monitoring, or other hands-off principal support roles to central offices operating as main agents of principal learning. . . . teaching rather than monitoring or directing" (p. 767). Honig's research team observed district leadership in New York City, Atlanta, and Oakland. Although each city had different titles describing central office folks working with principals, the researchers called these individuals Instructional Leadership Directors (ILDs). "Taking responsibility for one's own development" and helping other principals to grow as leaders were essential outcomes that ILDs hoped principals would come away with as a result of the professional development work (Honig, Copland, Rainey, Lorton, & Newton, 2010). Beyond Honig's research some central office teams partner with principals and conduct walk-throughs in district schools; they share observations with staff or Professional Learning Community (PLC) teams at the end of the day.

As noted in Chapter 1, the impact that principals have on student learning is indirect, as compared to teachers, but is still considerable especially because of the importance of a trusting relationship between teachers and principals. Without trust the supervisory process cannot work successfully. Interestingly, when the district office shows confidence and trust in principals and provides them with autonomy, the principal–teacher relationship improves, "Principals with more autonomy have higher rates of satisfaction and commitment levels, form better relationships with staff, and improve school climate (Price, 2012, p. 70). The implications of these results go beyond a principal's commitment. There is always a shortage of excellent teachers and principals. If principals are thriving because of their relationship with the district office, teacher satisfaction increases and teacher attrition decreases—everyone wins, especially students.

THE DISTRICT OFFICE AND PRINCIPAL EVALUATIONS: PARTNERING FOR SUCCESS

The evaluation of principals is required as part of the Race to the Top competitive grant program and since 2009 legislation in 33 states and the District of Columbia has made evaluation the law (Education Update, 2013). This development comes at the same time that district office leaders are reconceptualizing their roles as full participants in the school reform effort—not as bureaucrats focused solely on policies, budgets, and maintenance—but to transform schools. In 2011 the National Association of Elementary School Principals (NAESP) and the National Association of Secondary School Principals (NASSP) created a joint Principal Evaluation Committee that developed a framework of six leadership domains to assist districts with the evaluation process:

1. Professional Growth and Learning

2. Student Growth and Achievement

3. School Planning and Progress

4. School Culture

5. Professional Qualities and Instructional Leadership

6. Stakeholder Support and Engagement

In the report *Rethinking Principal Evaluation* (Clifford & Ross, n.d.), the two associations describe in detail each domain and strongly suggest that the evaluation of school principals by the districts should include multiple measures, with student test scores one of many. For example, based on the domain of "School Planning and Progress," the Principal Evaluation Committee recommends rating principals on "school improvement efforts directly under their control" (p. 16). For the "Professional Qualities and Instructional Leadership" domain, the committee recommends rating principals based on "portfolio artifacts, professional growth plans, observations of principals in practice, 'actionable feedback' to teachers, 360° surveys, and self-reflections" (p. 20). The committee stressed that other principalship standards (e.g., Educational Leadership Policy Standards, 2008) should also be considered when developing evaluation criteria. Finally, the report addresses leadership capacity building by advocating for district "systemic support" through ongoing professional development, recognition for superior performance, and newcomer induction mentoring.

MANAGEMENT TIPS FOR WORKING WITH THE CENTRAL OFFICE

Based on the preceding ideas, the following tips gleaned from successful principals can be helpful in working with the central office:

1. *Be assertive and seek professional development* opportunities with the central office

2. *Request a district-level activities calendar* with key events identified by the district several months before a new school year begins. Post the appropriate dates in your office, on your calendar, online, on the school website, and in the staff room.

3. *Create district project files.* As you collect information or ideas, simply place them in the appropriate file.

4. *Keep the district informed.* Many principals send weekly e-mails containing information about activities at the school, with attached student work, to the central office.

5. *Invite central office personnel* to celebrations, assemblies, class activities, and other school events.

6. *Pay attention to e-mails from the district.* Save them electronically or as hard copies for one to two years. You never know when you will need them again! Back up all important electronic documents.

7. *Make presentations to the board of education* to keep its members informed about school-level activities. When appropriate, use students during presentations.

8. *Try to ensure that school-level personnel have representation on state or district committees* when the state or central office are going to make important curriculum decisions that affect your school.

Managing in these ways affords principals opportunities to stay visible and keenly aware of what is taking place in schools, the district, and the community. Networking in this way is a key skill of the effective leader.

MAINTAINING A STRONG RELATIONSHIP BETWEEN THE CENTRAL OFFICE AND THE SCHOOL

The central office and the school need each other. Beyond standardized test scores, the federal and state governments cannot know the culture and precise needs of individual schools. The central office, then, may serve as a buffer or conduit between the local school and the large governmental agencies. Local context is critical. As Fullan (2007) observes, "To know what works in some situations does not mean we can get it to work in other situations" (p. 17). Those closest to the client often have the most relevant data on which to base decisions. As noted earlier, the central office can assist schools in various ways, including disseminating important information concerning the CCSS, assessment features, student data; the hiring of administrators, teachers, and support staff; and setting policy for the district and schools.

District staff can link the ideas of the various schools to keep the schools in touch with one another. And the various school sites can offer the district answers to questions about what is working. In some districts leaders take Instructional Round walks (see Chapter 9) together and then discuss whether important curriculum standards and teaching strategies are being implemented. The school site is, of course, the laboratory in which important decisions can be judged as being on the right track or needing further work. In education, we often lament the fragmentation of the curriculum and the need for sustained coherence. The same point can be made regarding schools in a district. Hopefully we will see less fragmentation as districts focus on rigorous college and career standards.

FORGING A SCHOOL AND CENTRAL OFFICE PARTNERSHIP: PUTTING STAFF AND STUDENT LEARNING FIRST

The Fort Osage Story. In Independence, Missouri, at the beginning and end of each school year, building leadership teams from each school in the Fort Osage School District meet with a Central Office Team made up of the superintendent; assistant superintendents of educational services, personnel, and business services; and the director of special education. Together they discuss the School Improvement Plan that school site staff have developed. They dialogue about the following:

- Goals
- The data that were used to develop each goal
- Evidence that will be observable if the goal was accomplished
- Needed resources
- Responsible parties
- An Action Plan (steps to be taken to address each goal)
- How the goal will contribute to staff and student learning

This process creates an understanding of, and respect for, the unique needs and accomplishments of each school. It also provides a window into how the staff in each school conceptualizes the school improvement process in relation to their daily work. The beginning-of-the-year conversations create a foundation of insights for school-level visits that central office personnel make throughout the year. At the end of the year, the closing conversations between the central office team and the building leadership teams provide vivid qualitative data about each school's accomplishments and challenges. Jeff White, assistant superintendent for educational services, reflecting on an end-of-year visit, exclaimed, "I am so jazzed about the high level of conversation that I just witnessed. The school is really turning around. It is evident that staff and student learning are thriving."

REFLECTIONS

This space provides a place for you to write down ideas that have been generated by this chapter, things you want to try, or adaptations of ideas presented here.

1. How is your school district governed? What are the organizational and individual sources of influence that need to be addressed in order to implement change?

2. How would you characterize your school's relationship with the central office? What are some strengths and weaknesses? Are there particular things you would like to change? Does the central office serve as a buffer or conduit for federal mandates?

3. Does lateral capacity building exist in your district? What are the activities that schools engage in to share expertise and problem solve?

4. What efforts is your district office making to become a center of teaching and learning?

5. What insights or new questions do you have as a result of reflecting on the ideas presented in this chapter?

PART III

Honoring the School's Mission

7

Understanding, Planning, and Implementing Change

If we don't change our direction, we're likely to end up where we're headed.

—Chinese proverb

We live in a fast-paced, constantly changing world. In education, we must create school and district contexts that are responsive to and reflective of these changes. Our actions must be informed by situational awareness—the balance between understanding the demands of college, career, and workplace reality and creating the contexts of PreK–12 schools in which the readiness to fit into these worlds is being conceptualized, prepared, sculpted, or perhaps retrofitted. What's more, it is a future world about which we lack specifics—only anticipated trends regarding what will be needed. We do know for example, that there will be less of an emphasis on how one uses what he or she knows. In spite of the lack of specificity about this future world in which we are preparing students to operate and ultimately become community members, there is much we do know about guiding the change process. It is to this end that our chapter is dedicated.

GUIDING THE CHANGE JOURNEY: THREE QUESTIONS

To accomplish change in the context of schools is an enormous and intricate task. The International Center for Leadership in Education in McNulty (2009, p. 80) suggests that schools embarking upon a change journey ask three critical questions:

1. Why do we want to change?

2. What do we want to change?

3. How do we change?

The "why" question invites members of the school community to create a *shared vision* of what the school will become. Engaging all members of the school community in articulating their beliefs and developing this vision will create both an understanding of the direction of the change as well as generate a passion to see the change to its fruition. The future focused vision also should be informed by data, better practice (inferring that practice can always be improved), research, input from all members of the school community as well as representatives from post-secondary education, science, and the business world. Only after the vision is created, agreed upon, shared, and internalized by those who will be responsible for implementing it or be impacted by it can the process of implementation begin.

As the implementation process for realizing the vision unfolds, the second question, "What do we want to change?" must be carefully entertained. *Qualitative and quantitative data* must be examined. The *voices* of students, staff, parents, and administration who will be affected by the "what" must be sought after. Besides site-level data, consider, have similar visions been implemented in other schools? Investigate what these implementers have encountered as *stumbling blocks* or useful *guideposts*.

Of course in some cases, "the change" is a "mandated initiative" which dictates "the what." For example, in those states implementing Common Core State Standards (CCSS), "the what" would involve curriculum, instruction, and assessment practices. It would also impact working relationships among professional colleagues and structures for interacting so that the implementation process can be well planned, be interdisciplinary and clearly articulated across grade levels.

The third question "How do we change?" is perhaps the most difficult. Organizational members are often much more comfortable in the planning stages, but the "how" question moves people from reflective dialogue to action. To address the third question, an *action plan* must be developed with specific goals delineated, as well as observable success indicators that will signal when these goals are reached. In addition, individuals and teams responsible for implementation and monitoring the implementation process must be specified.

Throughout any change process, there are some essential understandings, many of them classic, not new, in nature that will help change leaders as they guide others on the change journey. Becoming familiar with the change literature will support change leaders in guiding the change journey.

UNDERSTANDING CHANGE

Robert Evans (1996, p. xiv) reminds us, "Innovations begin with content, the actual program for change, but their success depends heavily on the readiness of people, the organizational capacity of schools, and, crucially, the kind of leadership that is exerted." A crucial understanding relates to being able to identify the type of change in which an organization is engaged. Heifetz and Linsky (2002) offer an explanation of "technical and adaptive" challenges and Evans (1996) offers a description of "first and second-order change," which are both very helpful to those leading change efforts. As noted in *Learning From Lincoln* (Alvy & Robbins, 2010a, p. 93),

> The "technical challenges" Heifetz and Linsky are referring to involve the implementation of change efforts based on problems we have faced before and solutions in which we "have the necessary know-how and procedures" (p. 13). Adaptive challenges, on the other hand, "require experiments, new discoveries, and adjustments" (p. 13), not just from the leader but also from a host of individuals. Thinking in new ways must occur and must include "changing attitudes, values, and behaviors" (p. 13). Heifetz and Linsky stress that with adaptive change, internalization of a problem must occur; that is a personal commitment to make the change is critical. Moreover, "the single most common source of leadership failure we've been able to identify . . . is that people, especially those in positions of authority, treat adaptive challenges like technical problems." (p. 14)
>
> Evans (1996), citing the seminal 1974 work of Watzlawick, Weakland, and Fisch, notes that first-order change efforts strive "to improve the efficiency or effectiveness of what we are already doing" (p. 5). Second-order changes create a new world view "and modify the very way an organization is put together, altering its assumptions, goals, structures, roles and norms . . . [and require changing] beliefs and perceptions." (p. 5)

School leaders' work is complex, challenging, and multidimensional. School leaders work with both first-order change—merely tinkering with existing systems—and adaptive, second-order change, which requires a fundamental transformation of existing systems and processes with new ways of thinking, responding, and operating. It is essential to be able to distinguish between the two.

Change often requires both a technical and an emotional response—because change impacts people. The "structure of meaning is rooted in feelings and experiences that have great emotional significance . . . perceptions and purposes can rarely be altered by rational explanations alone" (Evans, 1996, p. 30). Swept up with "the urgency of a problem and the promise of a solution, school leaders often fail to realize that those who will have to adapt to a change may reel with agony as a consequence of its implementation . . . school leaders can proactively plan for change by inviting individuals who will be affected by it to be part of naming the problem and engaging in the process to address it" (Alvy & Robbins, 2010a, p. 98). Recognizing that change brings a sense of loss when new ways of thinking and operating displace familiar practices is another important understanding for change leaders.

CHANGE BRINGS LOSS AND RESISTANCE

We rarely recognize that changes in the nature of work also create losses that trigger powerful individual or collective reactions. The costs may not be immediately obvious nor reflected directly in tangible ways, but left unattended over time, pressure builds up and can become a silent killer in organizations—much like hypertension in the human body. The unresolved loss of title or office can cause personal maladjustments, such as depression or excessive drinking; the substitution of a computerized system for manual procedures can create uncertainty, confusion, and a loss of identity. Wholesale changes in an organization can dramatically affect overall morale, productivity, and turnover. Most often, however, we fail to link these effects to the real cause. We attribute the blame to personal or other intangible sources, rather than to changes in the work setting.

—Deal (1985, pp. 293–294)

The downside of change so eloquently described by Terry Deal (1985) is often neglected when school leaders present teachers with ideas that "must" be implemented. One's individual enthusiasm for the change may be quite tempered by the experiences of other faculty. Staff experiencing change may feel loss and insecurity and show resistance and confrontation. In fact, these behaviors should occur. Resistance, in particular, should be expected and can be very helpful in understanding the different responses people have to the change and can actually improve facilitating the change process. Resistance will bring questioning and the need to examine the direction of the changes being implemented. In the end, if real change is to occur, organizational members must feel that the change has been effective and meaningful for them. Because change challenges status quo and the meaning people attach to routines, it provokes a sense of loss, creates confusion, challenges competence, and invites conflict. Change always impacts individuals within the organization. The collective response of individuals influences the organizational response. Thus, school leaders must plan the change journey with these two dimensions in mind.

CHANGE INFLUENCES INDIVIDUALS AND THE ORGANIZATION

Facilitators of change must show sensitivity to the individuals affected by change and the organization that is transformed as a result of it.

Initially and throughout the process, it is important to view change simultaneously from both individual and institutional perspectives. If the change experience is made relevant, if individuals are involved, given a voice and supported, and if trust exists or is developed among professional colleagues, it is likely the change will be successfully implemented across the organization.

Principals should recognize the tremendous role they can play as change facilitators or obstructers. As Hall and Hord (1987) point out, "Throughout our years of research and experience, we have never seen a situation in which the principal was not a significant factor in the efforts of schools to improve" (p. 1). Fullan (2007) has stated that "today, no serious change effort would fail to emphasize the role of the principal" (p. 156). Principals, supported by assistant principals and leadership teams, can make or break a school's effort to foster collaborative decision making, implement a new schedule or initiative, or engage in a schoolwide professional development activity. A principal's willingness to listen and set up collaborative teams during faculty and parent meetings indicates a desire to share decisions and engage in change. Furthermore, if teachers indicate an interest in a professional development activity, such as peer coaching, the principal sends a clear message of support or opposition by how he or she responds to the initial idea and facilitates or obstructs the project. In subtle ways—such as where an item is placed on an agenda—as well as grand, explicit ways, a principal's actions influence change. Also, Fullan reminds us that change and progress do not always go hand in hand. In fact, rejecting change may be a bolder move for a school principal than pursuing what appears to be a "quick fix" solution.

Because change is holistic, every aspect of the organizational system has the potential to be affected. This underscores the importance of systemic thinking; that is, that changes in one part of the system have an impact on others. For instance, new graduation requirements or longer class periods may have profound effects on curriculum, teaching, and assessment practices. Principals have a key role in preparing an environment where potential change initiatives can be rigorously examined by all staff members and, if appropriate, implemented.

One major factor in creating an environment for change is building a climate of trust in which risk taking and experimentation can occur. In fact,

Anthony Bryk and Barbara Schneider (2004) say that school staffs with relational trust are more likely to take risks and make the kinds of changes that result in student achievement. In their study of Chicago schools, "Schools with strong levels of trust as they began change efforts had a one in two chance of successfully improving reading and math achievement, as opposed to a one in seven chance of making gains where trust was weak" (von Frank, 2010, p. 2). This is easier said than done, especially in cases where previously the norms in the building emphasized "playing it safe," rather than experimenting with new practices. Because change involves new ideas, new behaviors, new materials, and new ways of operating, people need a safe environment to feel comfortable embarking on a change journey. When implementing new ways of doing things, an individual's performance often gets worse before it gets better. We all have experienced this when learning a new move in a familiar sport, for example. Fullan and Miles (1992) describe this experience as the implementation dip: "Even in cases where reform eventually succeeds, things often go wrong before they go right" (p. 749). Therefore, trust—among individuals and within the culture of the school—is an essential ingredient in the change process.

In many change efforts, because the innovation requires new forms of working relationships among individuals (e.g., Professional Learning Communities, data teams), there has been greater attention devoted to building relationships versus focusing on a specific end, such as achievement, that performance actually decreases initially (Robbins, 1991a). Leaders build trust by promoting "a school culture that emphasizes cooperation and caring, rather than competition and favoritism" (Uebbing & Ford, 2011). Since new ways of thinking and new practices cause individuals and schools to learn or relearn, and since the initial practice of new ways of doing things often lacks perfection, failure, resistance, and disappointment are predictable. School leaders must understand that even negative responses can play a positive role in facilitating the change process.

FAILURE, RISK-TAKING, AND CONFLICT: INGREDIENTS FOR CHANGE

The context in which change occurs must permit individuals to take risks and express different points of view. At Ford Motor Company, employees often comment, "Failure is the opportunity to begin again more intelligently." Hence failure becomes a source of knowledge. In the same way that failure comes to be viewed positively, the emergence of conflicting viewpoints often associated with a change effort can be positive as well. When different points of view are voiced, conflict often emerges along with lots of energy. This can actually fuel a positive change effort if conflict is harnessed to support quality results rather than be swept under the carpet or viewed as a negative. Thus, conflict can raise awareness of some aspect of the change that had not been considered before. This may have an important influence on the implementation of an innovation. In one school's change effort to move to grade-level teams, staff members had not considered the impact of teaming on specialists' positions. Conflict provided a source of knowledge that revealed a blind spot in the planning for teams.

An important quality of the expression of conflicting viewpoints is that there needs to be an orientation toward resolution rather than merely expressing a gripe. Conflicting ideas should be welcomed as providing valuable sources of information and insight to assist in planning for change or enhancing a change effort once it has begun. It has been said that if a change is "deep enough," it should be accompanied by conflict because it upsets the status quo. Finally, another reason to accept conflict is that it brings differences of opinion out in the open. More damage is done when saboteurs operate beneath the surface through covert interactions to obstruct change efforts. This approach uses the unofficial or informal communication network in the school—the system through which information travels faster than the speed of e-mail (and holds more credibility!). Conflict brings resistance with it: "A review of change literature reveals four basic stages that help innovators preemptively reduce the amount of resistance encountered and provide ongoing frameworks for preventing and overcoming resistance: build trust, create a clear vision, ensure a strong and consistent implementation, and support the change with consistent follow-through" (Armstrong, 2011, Winter, p. 2). School leaders need a repertoire of strategies to create trust, develop a shared vision (see Chapter 8), ensure implementation success, and provide valued follow-through.

STRATEGIES TO PROMOTE TRUST

With Konni deGoeij, Associate Coordinator, Administrator Assistance,

from the Alberta Teachers' Association

Because risk taking, experimentation, voicing conflicting opinions, and resistance are essential ingredients for change and because they thrive in a safe, trusting environment, attending to how to create such an atmosphere for change is an important first step. Yet this step can bring good or bad news. The bad news is that there is no recipe for successful change. However, that is also good news because it provides the opportunity to create a plan of action tailored to one's school. "How change and trust building will be addressed at a school site depends on such issues as a school's history, student diversity, staff turnover, relationships among staff members, schedules and logistics, and degree of community support. . . . The role of principal is critical in establishing and maintaining trust. Indeed, the ability to trust in one's own working environment and to contribute in a trusting and open manner have emerged as important facets of healthy school environments" (deGoeij, 2013).

Principal actions play a profound role in cultivating and sustaining trust in schools. Transparent communication forms a foundation for building relationships. This is particularly important when information is shared. If staff members perceive that the principal is telling the truth, he or she will be regarded as trustworthy. Transparency in how decisions are made and how they are implemented within the school is another important facet of the principal's manner of communication. It is critical that the rationale, background, and thought processes underpinning decisions are shared. "When principals give lip service to shared and collaborative decision-making and then make arbitrary decisions, teachers feel betrayed . . . People will accept a decision that goes against their preferences if they feel that, in the process of reaching a decision, the principal took their concerns and insights into consideration" (deGoeij).

The following recommendations can help build and sustain trust:

Walk the talk and practice open, honest communication and decision making. Credibility will result.

☐ Consistency between a principal's practices and words enables teachers to predict how a principal will respond, and how reliable he or she is. When the principal is perceived as reliable, confidence that he or she will consistently do what is right and follow through sets standards for behavior essential for fostering a trusting workplace environment.

Lead by example with integrity. Perceptions of reliability and confidence in leadership will result.

☐ Creating environments where people can feel safe enough to contribute is essential. When this occurs, staff members will be willing to express opinions, participate in decision making, try new approaches, make mistakes, support innovation, and take risks.

Principals earn trust by making themselves available, engaging teachers in conversation, and modeling authentic listening.

☐ Honor professionalism. When teachers perceive that they are trusted by the principal, they will feel empowered to share instructional practices, engage in collaborative work, try harder to achieve goals, and develop strategies to overcome setbacks.

When principals trust staff members to carry out tasks in a professional way, increased teacher self-efficacy will follow.

☐ Noticing the accomplishments of organizational members and providing the type of recognition that is valued by individual staff members communicates that the principal is aware of individual differences as well as values the contributions of staff.

Principals communicate a respect for individual differences when they provide different types and levels of recognition. Celebrate large and small successes.

☐ Developing a sense of community instills a sense of belonging, self-worth, and a willingness to be vulnerable. Finding meaning in work compels organizational members to form powerful relationships that result in capacity building and learning throughout the organization.

The principal plays a critical role in creating a sense of team by "being present," inviting staff members to have input into the change process, building consensus, and keeping lines of communication open.

☐ Building trust is a complex venture that takes time, focus, nurturing, and energy. When it becomes a consistent characteristic of the workplace, however, there is no end to its positive influence. In addition to acquiring a repertoire of strategies to develop and sustain trust, Michael Fullan's classic work, *The New Meaning of Educational Change* (2007), offers important insights that can inform one's practice as the change journey unfolds.

CLASSICAL INSIGHTS REGARDING CHANGE AND CONTINUOUS IMPROVEMENT

Exploring the literature on change can build one's capacity to facilitate the change process because it affords new perspectives on conditions that enhance the change process. As you review the following points from Fullan, consider change efforts you have experienced. To what degree does each point explain the success or failure of the change effort?

1. Organizations must create the capacity for change and continuous improvement; the innovation is not the only goal.

2. Sustained change involves "lateral capacity building" (p. 56).

3. Successful leaders build teacher capacity, distribute leadership, and promote program coherence (e.g., specific learning goals, sustained over time).

4. Leaders set direction, "develop" people, and create collaborative communities; a key to change is that relationships improve.

5. Change is a journey in context—a process, not a destination.

6. Resisters have some good ideas.

7. Having a great passion for a change can get in the way if it means ignoring the ideas of others and the change process. Leaders need to be committed to the change process as well as the change.

8. Sometimes charismatic gurus hurt the process if they cultivate disciples rather than independent thinkers.

Finally, when one is intimately involved in a change effort, it is often easy to lose heart. Fullan (2007) reminds us that change is not neat, but rather messy, most of the time. Yet change is inevitable and is a vital part of organizational and personal growth.

The Rand study provides another classic understanding about the change process that dramatically illuminates factors that impact implementation success. By planning change efforts with three phases in mind, the probability of success has a better chance of being realized.

THREE PHASES OF CHANGE

In an ideal world, one would collaboratively plan prior to implementing change and consider the following question: Is the change consistent with the vision and mission of the school? Careful attention should be given to diagnosing needs, generating commitment, and developing an action plan prior to implementing change. One principal reflected, "I know that you can't walk in and change everything in one year. I found that out the hard way. You have to walk in and look things over critically and reflect on your priorities and what the data say." Another, commenting on how much time the planning process took, said, "You just have to face the fact, as frustrating as it might be, that sometimes you have to go slow to go fast." Unfortunately, reality often does not permit us to look things over critically or to go slow to go fast. Often, mandates thrust an organization into an implementation stage without regard for a needed readiness stage in which understanding and commitment to the change might be built. By examining research-based observations in the classic RAND study of the phases that an institution should go through for successful change implementation (Berman & McLaughlin, 1978), individuals responsible for the innovation can work to ensure that the needed stages of the change process occur, even when there has not been time to set the stage.

The RAND study "set out to characterize the process by which an innovation is translated into an operating reality within school districts" (Berman & McLaughlin, 1978, p. 13). The study uncovered an interesting phenomenon:

> Rather than a single process, several different ones could be observed for different innovations and also for the same innovation at different times in its evolution. Although all change agent projects evidently encountered a similar sequence of events and activities, three characteristic phases could be discerned within the overall process. . . . These phases roughly correspond to the project's beginning, middle, and end; but we did not use this simple terminology because neither beginning nor end makes sense in the context of a constantly evolving local educational system . . . and because instead of a chronological sequence "from beginning to end," the activities defining each phase overlapped one another. Instead, we call them *mobilization, implementation, and institutionalization.* (p. 13)

It is helpful to think about the change process associated with implementing an innovation in terms of these three phases. One example might serve to highlight some of the critical activities within each phase. Suppose a school was interested in examining block scheduling as a way to foster the development of students' academic and social skills and reduce behavioral problems.

In the mobilization phase, curriculum and assessment planning as well as types of instructional strategies for the block would be studied. This could include readings, DVDs, exploring online resources, and visits to sites where block scheduling is routinely used. Enthusiasm, commitment, dedication, and support for block scheduling would be rallied among stakeholders who would ultimately be affected by the decision to implement its use: teachers, parents, students, administration, and support staff. Planning efforts should include the development of a team of representative stakeholders. Plans would be made regarding needed resources such as professional development, follow-up, and implementation support.

In the implementation phase, professional development would be provided, follow-up would occur, and feedback would be solicited regarding the quality of training and support and the applicability of block scheduling to the classroom curriculum and student needs. Appropriate modifications would be made based on this feedback. "Review and refinement" sessions would be conducted. Typical follow-up sessions might include analysis of classroom observations, peer coaching, collaborative lesson development, and idea swapping, problem solving, and sharing.

The institutionalization phase is marked by acceptance or modification of the change project. Institutionalized change would occur if block scheduling became standard educational practice in the classroom and at the school level. Newcomers to the school would be taught block scheduling strategies, and these strategies would be modeled at faculty meetings and during professional development days. Student body leaders could coach new and incoming students in useful strategies for operating in the block. One English teacher invited her high school students to write essays for newcomers to the school that were titled "Success Strategies for Surviving in the Block Schedule."

Just as the organization goes through stages associated with the change process, so do individuals. The degree to which they receive support during this process will have a major impact on whether they will adopt a particular change.

A LOOK AT CHANGE FROM THE INDIVIDUAL'S PERSPECTIVE

Federal and state mandates, district goals, advances in technology, new curriculum standards, new evaluation approaches, and a number of other forces frequently require schools, and the individuals within them, to change. As noted earlier in this chapter, the invitation or, in some cases, the mandate to change often asks the organization and staff members to abandon long-standing, familiar practices in exchange for new ways of doing things. This phenomenon leaves people with a sense of loss, a longing to go back to the old ways of doing things, and a concern that being asked to do something differently implicitly means that what they had done before was not good. Frequently, a sense of denial emerges: "If we wait just long enough, this, too, will pass."

Individual responses to change differ. Some people welcome it; others greet it with fear or anger. Part of facilitating the change process involves understanding the individual's change experience. Organizations change only as the individuals within the organization change. Change is a highly personal experience. Essentially, it is an individual experience and takes place one person at a time. Personal meaning is one critical influence that ultimately determines whether a person is willing to change. If the change effort holds meaning for an individual, that person may be more likely to change. People are more likely to adopt new behaviors when their own values and beliefs are consistent with the values and beliefs that undergird the new behaviors implied by the change.

Often, people are asked to change behavior before they have developed the new beliefs or values implicit in the change. This generates a feeling of discomfort. For long-lasting change to occur, individuals must first be provided with experiences through which they will develop the values and beliefs that drive the desired behaviors. Experiences change beliefs. Beliefs do not usually change without experiences. Many teachers have to experience positive results with students before adopting a new way of doing something. Unfortunately, teachers usually are asked to move on to the "next great thing" before having a chance to experience positive results and confidently internalize a new idea. An expert sixth-grade teacher, pleased with his emerging success teaching reasoning and problem-solving skills (per the National Council of Teachers of Mathematics), lamented that "we need to let teachers dwell on new ideas for 3 years, instead of 2 months or a year" (S. Bachman, personal communication, April 2008).

To build interest and meaning for individuals who will be affected by change, the California School Leadership Academy, in Hayward, California, identified four factors that leaders can use to facilitate change. Each of the following factors in this framework should be considered before embarking on a change effort:

- Relevance—whether a change is relevant to one's life or work responsibilities
- Feasibility—whether people view the change as "doable" given other demands on their time, their skills, and their philosophical beliefs
- Involvement—whether the individual being affected by the change has input into what the change will look like, sound like, and be like
- Trust—whether there is trust between the person being asked to change and the facilitator or initiator of the change

If staff members have collaboratively developed a vision that promotes quality teaching and staff and student learning, and if the proposed change is consistent with the vision, chances are it will be greeted with greater enthusiasm. It will be viewed as relevant, people will perceive it as feasible, it will have meaning because of the members' previous involvement with developing the vision, and an atmosphere of trust usually will have been established. Another important understanding about how individuals experience change is afforded by considering predictable stages of concern that organizational members experience in relation to a change initiative.

STAGES OF CONCERN

In addition to facilitating change by paying attention to creating individual meaning for the change process, successful change facilitators pay attention to how individuals show their level of interest or concern for change. Hall, George, and Rutherford (1979) developed common characteristics that indicate one's interest or concern regarding innovative or change experiences. They emphasize that how people perceive and understand change will be dictated by their personality and experience. Some people may perceive a change as an outside threat, whereas others may view it as rewarding. The degree to which a concern may be assessed and responded to accordingly will facilitate one's understanding and experience of the change effort. Figure 7.1, based on Hall et al.'s groundbreaking work, portrays these stages of concern.

One principal developed the chart shown in Figure 7.2 after learning about these stages of concern to remind himself about how to respond to individuals' comments related to a change effort.

Figure 7.1 Stages of Concern: Typical Expressions of Concern About the Innovation

Stage of Concern	Expression of Concern
6. Refocusing	I have some ideas about something that would work even better.
5. Collaboration	I am concerned about relating what I am doing with what other instructors are doing.
4. Consequence	How is my use affecting kids?
3. Management	I seem to be spending all my time in getting material ready.
2. Personal	How will using it affect me?
1. Informational	I would like to know more about it.
0. Awareness	I am not concerned about it (the innovation).

SOURCE: Hord, S., Rutherford, W., Huling-Austin, L., & Hall, G. (1987). *Taking charge of change*. Alexandria, VA: ASCD.

Figure 7.2 A Principal's Responses to Concerns About Change

Stage of Concern	Response
6. Refocusing	Stimulate a discussion and provide a comfortable setting so teachers can discuss how this could be enhanced or improved.
5. Collaboration	Relate ways that individuals can collaborate and share ideas.
4. Consequence	Show how it might affect staff and students.
3. Management	Invite users to demonstrate how they manage the use of an innovation.
2. Personal	Share how it might affect student and staff learning.
1. Informational	Explain what "it" looks like in practice; provide examples.
0. Awareness	Provide information.

SOME FINAL THOUGHTS ON CHANGE

How change is perceived has a major impact on organizational response. Harold Storlien, former superintendent of the Medicine Hat School District in Alberta, Canada, advised us to look at all problems as challenges and opportunities. The principal can set a personal example by viewing change as an opportunity and encouraging risk taking and ownership on the part of teachers regarding the changes. This will create a climate of trust, which is essential for success. Key personnel in the process must constantly ask: Who do we need to inform? Who needs to know about what we are doing: Teachers? Parents? Principals? District personnel? Students? Community members? The media?

Inclusion of relevant groups is a critical factor in the change process. In many cases, for example, the central office can be involved and supply the professional development, resources, time needed, and monetary support to implement the change. The whole system must be involved for the project to succeed. Schools must revisit their mission and vision during the process and ask the following questions:

- Is the change on the right track?
- In what direction is the innovation going?
- If it appears to be going off track, is that okay? What can we learn from the diversion?
- Has reality shown, based on actual classroom use, that the original plan was unrealistic?
- Do the new changes that appear necessary as a result of the initial experiments align with the mission and vision?
- Should the mission and vision be altered?
- Have the recommendations of professional developmental staff or previous examples of success of the innovation proved to be unworkable for this school? For example, if there is a recommendation that

student-led conferences with portfolios be implemented and required school wide after the training. Will that work for the staff?

- Should volunteers be enlisted to set examples and "massage" the project?
- Will the change positively impact students? Staff?

The human relations skills, experience, and presentation strategies of professional development staff brought into the school can obviously make or break the change effort. When trainers are enlisted to start a program, are they operating on a level appropriate for the staff? Professional development staff often know the ins and outs of an innovation and must remember that a staff member may know nothing about the proposed change. Professional development staff must consider: If we listen, but respond at a higher level than is appropriate, then we are not addressing needs. The track record of the professional development trainers must be considered: Have they been involved previously with the school district? Have they talked with the key individuals such as the principal, assistant principals, teachers, district personnel, parents, and students who may be affected by the change? Eventually, plans should be put in place to develop teacher leaders as trainers, building capacity at the local site.

A phenomenon to be aware of, and plan proactively for, is a state of entropy or running out of steam that occurs about midcourse in a change effort. Many change agents plan ceremonies to acknowledge progress to date and to recall critical events along the way in order to generate enthusiasm and energy among organizational members to sustain progress in implementing the change. "Be aware of this reality, plan for it, but don't interpret it as losing the battle," commented one principal when discussing entropy. Rosabeth Moss Kanter (1997) offers a helpful insight with respect to the notion that if a change doesn't immediately produce results, it is tempting to move on to the next new thing: "The difference between success and failure is often just a matter of time: staying with the project long enough to overcome the unexpected developments, political problems, or fatigue that can come between a great-sounding plan and actual results. A basic truth of management—if not of life—is that nearly everything looks like a failure in the middle. At the same time, of course, the next project always looks more attractive (because it is all promise, fresh, and untried)" (p. 129).

If the process gets off to a smooth start, ironically, it may be an indicator that something is wrong. The change may have been implemented too fast. Or the staff members, in the beginning, may be holding back their opposition and just going along with a top-down directive. Phil Schlechty (2001) reminds us that "compared to sustaining change, starting change is relatively easy" (p. 39). He points out that this is why more changes are initiated in schools than are sustained. In writing about the challenge of sustaining change, he notes, "Two things sustain change: one is a leader or leadership group that acts as a change agent; the other is a system or group of systems that supports change" (p. 40). This explains why, when the school culture does not have the capacity to sustain a change effort, "the change rarely outlasts the tenure of the change agent" (p. 40). A key leadership task, then, is to study and then create those system conditions that will support and sustain a change.

One must provide rituals and ceremonies to dignify and deal with the loss of previously used methods when appropriate. Often, when a new program is being implemented, previous ways of doing things are discarded before time is taken to see how they may still have a function or perhaps be integrated with new practices. For example, if CCSS for ELA are implemented, are current approaches to writing just being junked and considered to be educational failures? How can the work of teachers who spent 20 years developing the writing program at the school be dignified? Can an innovation be brought into a school with an acknowledgment of the elements of success of past practice? Is there a possibility that the old can be combined with the new instructional or curriculum strategy? For example, one principal reflected: "There are some things that are working in that school and you need to work with people in the school who know what it has been like before. . . . If we did something last year that works, you need to inservice me. If it didn't work, we need to talk about how we can make it different."

For an innovation to succeed, the change and the mind-set for change must take hold in the workplace. If you want to know whether the innovation has occurred, do not just ask the superintendent or the principal, assistant principal, or the teachers—visit classrooms. Then visit the classrooms two years after the project was introduced. Are there now coaches in the school who can train new staff on the innovation? That is, has the change been institutionalized? How is the innovation working in other schools? How is the innovative practice (e.g., Common Assessments, Implementing Common Core, Differentiated Instruction) being modified and improved? Are high school teachers talking with elementary staff about the change at districtwide functions? All personnel should be learning together throughout the system.

If the change is successfully implemented, eventual satisfaction should be observed throughout the system. The teachers should display satisfaction with the change, students will know of the change and talk about what has taken place, and site and district administrators will be a part of the process, as will parents. A key characteristic should be more school-wide interaction. In the end, change must be systemic; all elements that are affected by the change must be involved.

Kurt Lewin (1951), the pioneer of Action Research, once said, "If you really want to understand something, try to change it!" Indeed, change is an all-encompassing experience that envelopes both the organization and its members, evoking a multitude of responses. The world is characterized by chaos, unpredictability, and change. The only way to keep up with the changes is by building change into the system. Guiding change so that it is successful is certainly an essential skill of an effective leader. On reflection, we should consider that the change process goes hand in hand with the notion of leader as learner. Indeed, the measure of a leader may well be his or her capacity to understand and work successfully with change—to stimulate it, shape it, nurture it, guide it, manage it, revise it, and keep the change journey going.

REFLECTIONS

This space provides a place for you to write down ideas that have been generated by this chapter, things you want to try, or adaptations of ideas presented here.

1. Think about a change effort that you are anticipating or in which you are currently involved. How might the three questions at the beginning of the chapter guide the change journey?

2. What does successful change look like? What does poorly conceived/implemented change look like?

3. Examine the strategies to promote trust, which of these do you currently model? Are there any you wish to add to your repertoire?

4. Practice listening to individuals as they express concerns about a change. See if you can determine the stage of concern and an appropriate response.

5. What do you see as the two or three easiest traps that a school leader can fall into when trying to implement change? In what ways might these traps be avoided?

6. What insights or new questions do you have as a result of reflecting on the ideas presented in this chapter?

8

Building a Vision and a Mission Together

Our shared vision for the school serves as a compass and helps us focus our energies, chart our course, and stay on that course.

—A principal's voice

REFLECTING ON VISION AND MISSION

After more than a decade of research on school leadership, The Wallace Foundation (2013) identified five key practices effective school leaders undertake:

- Shaping a vision of academic success for all students;
- Creating a climate hospitable to education;
- Cultivating leadership in others;
- Improving instruction; and
- Managing people, data, and processes to foster school improvement. (p. 4)

Despite the difficulty of coming to consensus on how we can measure successful leadership, there is almost universal agreement that *"success in carrying out the mission and vision of an endeavor—a cause—should be a primary gauge of leadership success"* (Alvy & Robbins, 2010a, p. 7). Jim Collins (2005) in *Good to Great and the Social Sectors* hails the qualities of what he describes as "Level 5 leaders." These leaders are "ambitious first and foremost for the cause, the movement, the mission, the work—not themselves—and they have the will to do (whatever it takes) to make good on that ambition" (p. 11, emphasis in original).

Successful school leaders realize that a compelling vision and mission should have meaning for every member of the school community—along with the extended community it serves. These school leaders possess an unwavering sense of responsibility and commitment to collaboratively developing and "carrying out a shared vision and mission, aligned with deeply held values and beliefs that focus on equity, social justice, democracy, and creating those conditions under which profound levels of human learning can flourish" (Alvy & Robbins, 2012a, p. 14).

Before developing a shared vision and mission or revitalizing one that already exists, it is imperative that school leaders first develop a personal leadership vision that encapsulates their core values and beliefs. This process builds an essential understanding of self and generates an awareness that informs thoughts, feelings, and actions. A veteran high school principal remarked after engaging in writing her personal vision, "This was so powerful. In my twenty-five years of service as a leader, no one has ever asked me to write a personal vision. It really made me clarify my beliefs and what I envision as the school's purpose and the commitment I expect from myself and others to foster staff and student learning."

As part of the process of developing a personal vision, school leaders may reflect upon these questions:

- Will my leadership vision transcend time?
- How will the vision and mission make the life and future of every child more promising?
- Who are significant players—formal and informal leaders—who might leverage the impact of a shared school vision?
- What leadership qualities or attributes do I possess that will galvanize staff energies in working to create a shared vision and mission and bring it to life?

After the leader has clarity about his or her personal vision, then the important work of building or revitalizing a shared vision begins.

WHY HAVE A SHARED SCHOOL VISION AND MISSION?

What does our school stand for? To answer this question with some clarity, a school must have a shared vision—a purpose that can be witnessed in the daily activities of the school. Stephanie Hirsh (1995/1996), executive director of Learning Forward, explains, "A school vision should be a descriptive statement of what the school will be like at a specified time in the future. It uses descriptive words or phrases and sometimes pictures to illustrate what one would expect to see, hear and experience in school at that time. It makes reference to the facility, the curriculum, instruction, assessment, the staff and the community." The vision should be collaboratively developed and reflective of the stakeholders it serves: staff, parents, students, and community members. Special care should be taken to ensure that all students—special and regular education students, students of *all* cultures—be remembered, represented, and included in the vision.

"In contrast to a vision," Hirsh explains, "a mission statement is a succinct, powerful statement on how the school will achieve its vision. It provides guidance for actions on a daily basis. The mission statement answers: What is our purpose? What do we care most about? What must we accomplish? What are the cornerstones of our operations?"

There are as many definitions and descriptions of vision and mission as there are authors writing about the topic and schools trying to define their purpose. Although at first this may seem problematic, this may not be the case because the process of creating a vision and building a mission, which encourages participants to think about a school's purpose, may be more significant than an actual definition. For a vision or mission to be alive, the process must be a participatory one. Being involved in the process brings both ownership and commitment to the vision. Furthermore, it provides the opportunity for faculty members to discuss their values and beliefs related to schooling. For instance, in one high school, teachers talked about the fact that although student performance on high-stakes testing was important, given world affairs it was also important to educate the heart as well as the mind and to develop competencies such as empathy, perspective taking, and self-management.

When considering the vision and mission building process, one should keep in mind several ideas that have emerged from the literature on the characteristics of a powerful vision, especially for a learning community. A vision must be shared by the organization, and the organizational members must personally believe in the power of the vision as a force for creative, continuous improvement and as a force that can give personal meaning to their lives (Senge, 1990; Wheatley, 1992). It should be shared by those who are served by the school.

A school vision helps students, teachers, administrators, and parents have a sense of what is important in their particular setting. Knowing what is important helps those involved with the school make choices. It helps administrators set priorities, teachers construct lessons, and students find meaning in their work. A vision brings commitment throughout the system as people work together to create a school in which they personally are stakeholders. They believe in their work. In a Professional Learning Community (PLC), the vision and mission galvanize staff to act when it becomes evident that the vision and mission are not being realized. To illustrate, when it becomes evident that a student is not learning, staff members committed to the question "How will we respond when a student experiences difficulty in learning?" will do "whatever it takes" to make a difference (DuFour, 2004, pp. 7–11).

The principal and leadership team should play a major role in transforming the values and beliefs of the school into a vision. In fact, Roland Barth (2001a) defines leadership as "making happen what you believe in" (p. 446). This is accomplished through both symbolic and expressive leadership behaviors. From the symbolic perspective, a principal and other school leaders model and focus individual attention on what is important. From the expressive side of leadership, principals, and other school leaders talking with teachers, help crystallize and communicate the rationale for a vision and mission and generate shared discussions about what is important in the school. This attention to the meaning of a school leads to the development of a mission statement grounded in the collective beliefs of the staff. The process creates a commitment to shared direction and the energy to pursue it. The shared meaning helps create a team orientation: "Yes, we are working together!" Teachers can be confident that colleagues are working on the same key principles with students related to academic or social goals on each grade level. Interestingly, when school beliefs and values are internalized, teachers function more freely and effectively—with less supervisory intervention—because they know what is important in that particular school setting (Grimmett, Rostad, & Ford, 1992).

Given the many external pressures and expectations put on schools, staff must remain focused on pursuing the vision lest they risk veering off in one direction after another. Unless staff members have a clear direction, they may be spinning their wheels under the false impression that they are productively moving ahead.

A vision helps members of an organization identify what is important and avoid spending time on what is not. In reviewing the history of management, Drucker (1992) notes that we fail to work "smarter" and only ask "*How* is it [the job] done?" instead of "*What* is the task?" and "*Why* do it?" (p. 97). When our mission is clear, we know what the task is and why we should do it. Thus a school leader, in a setting where a shared vision and mission exists, should be able to answer questions such as the following:

- What kinds of social skills are important to the culture of the school?
- Do the results of teaching and learning have meaning? Do schooling experiences prepare students to be college and/or career ready?
- What are the best curriculum approaches, teaching strategies, assessment practices, and schoolwide traditions to accomplish the intended outcomes?

Peters and Austin (1985) stress that effective principals are "obsessed" with outcomes that represent the beliefs and values of the school. They function as a galvanizing force that propels collective actions toward their accomplishment.

SCHOOL ACTIVITIES
THAT HIGHLIGHT THE MISSION

The mission should consistently emphasize commitment to students, demonstrated in both talk and actions. During the school day, effective principals discuss educational issues, not Saturday night's faculty party. Successful principals serve as models for teachers, work closely with them, and engage in conversations about teaching, learning, and students. Skillful principals build leadership capacity in others. Committed principals ask about students: "Is Manuel improving in math?" "Has Stacey's home situation settled down?" "How is Bobby functioning in response to his brother's jail sentence?" They ask teachers: "Is there something I should be doing that I am not?" "How might I support you in pursuing the mission of our school through classroom and school wide activities?" Bennis and Nanus (1985) emphasize that getting "the message across unequivocally at every level is an absolute key" (p. 43). The message—the school mission—should be reiterated as often as possible: orally, in e-mails, the school website, during faculty meetings, at parent gatherings, and when working in classrooms with students.

At one middle school, students take a homework folder home every evening. The mission is printed on the inside cover. Sixth and seventh graders must have signatures from parents indicating that homework has been completed. Students in the eighth grade carry the same folder but sign nightly for themselves. Often a slogan is developed that encapsulates the mission. This short version of the mission might appear on the school website, school marquis, stationery, binders, or T-shirts to remind everyone of the mission.

The most effective way to communicate the mission is by personal example. A principal should spend time with students (low, medium, and high achievers) when possible, know their names, and join in celebrating student achievement and good citizenship. To illustrate, principals should use their offices to hear third graders read and share lunch with the middle school student government, the high school National Honor Society, service clubs, or the varsity basketball team. Principals should also reach out to students who may be English language learners or have learning or physical challenges. Effective principals encourage all staff to connect with the students and model the essence of the mission and vision in their daily actions. Principals should spend time on the playground, in halls, and in classrooms. The vision or mission can be reiterated through student recognition assemblies, complimentary notes to teachers, parent nights, bulletin boards that display student work in prominent places, and positive calls home to parents.

When discussing school culture, Deal and Peterson (1990) provide additional examples of activities that can contribute to strengthening a school's mission:

School traditions such as alumni homecomings, holiday celebrations, end-of-year gatherings, and yearly recognitions of merit, when infused with core values of the school, can build a shared sense of community and purpose. Graduation ceremonies, retirement rituals, academic awards banquets, and ceremonies to celebrate the granting of tenure to teachers can solidify the values of teachers and others, signal school purposes, and provide a social event to tighten collegial bonds.

It is important to analyze whether these traditions match the school's mission or contradict it. For example, one principal noted, "We were emphasizing collaboration and teamwork. Yet I realized we still had a 'Staff Member of the Month' award! Obviously, this needs to be changed to align with our vision of collaboration."

MISSION-BUILDING ACTIVITY

Although there are several ways to acquire a mission statement—borrowing one, buying one, synthesizing one—the most powerful strategy is to create one. The following technique represents one approach to developing a mission based on the collective visions of the staff, students, and parents. This approach has been used successfully by leadership teams and faculty throughout the United States, Canada, Europe (including Great Britain), and Asia.

Materials needed:

- chart paper
- tape
- markers
- large sticky notes
- index cards

Steps:

1. Explain what a mission statement is. For example: "A mission statement describes the purpose and beliefs of an organization and communicates a vision of what the organization stands for, what its members believe, and what ends will be accomplished in keeping with the purpose and beliefs. It serves as a galvanizing force for action."

2. Build a rationale for a mission statement. This step might include explaining why mission statements are helpful (shared sense of purpose, common direction, and energizer) and examining mission statements from other organizations. During this examination, the staff could be asked to analyze the values that seem to be implicit in the mission statement. Identify how a mission statement influences a staff member's life.

3. Invite the staff to take part in the development of the mission statement. Explain that this is an opportunity to synthesize individual staff

members' dreams or visions into a statement reached through consensus. This statement will represent the ends to which all within the organization will strive for and commit to.

4. Ask staff members to think for a moment about the place where they would like to send their own very special child to school. How would the child be treated? What would his or her experiences be like? How would he or she feel? Have staff members describe their thoughts on sticky notes.

5. Now ask staff members to think about the place where they would like to go to work every day. What would it be like? How would they feel? How would people interact? Have them write these ideas on sticky notes.

6. Have staff members take the content of their two sticky notes and fuse the two visions into one. Write the combined thoughts on an index card.

7. Individuals then meet in table groups of four to six and share their index cards. After they are all read, each table group uses markers and chart paper to create a composite of the individual cards to which all in the group can agree.

8. Pairs of table groups meet and share their charts. They synthesize their two charts into one.

9. Continue the process until the entire group creates one chart that represents the shared visions for the mission of all in the room.

10. If parents and representative students have not been involved in this process, this same procedure may be repeated with them and the products of their work captured with iPads or phones brought to the faculty. The staff could incorporate the content of these charts captured with the pictures with the ones that they created. In large schools, this process may be completed by department, team, or grade level and then the final products combined.

11. At another time, a contest could be held and the staff could work together to create a slogan that would encapsulate the mission statement. A mission statement alone, however, will not stay alive unless specific goals are created to accomplish the essence of the mission.

DEVELOPING YEARLY SCHOOL IMPROVEMENT GOALS TO ACCOMPLISH THE MISSION

Another excellent exercise to keep the school vision and mission in mind is to develop annual goals, an essential component of School Improvement Plans. Although each state or school district may have specific guidelines, the following process, modified to address each context, can be used to successfully develop goals and/or School Improvement Plans.

The process starts in the spring of a school year, looking toward the following year's opening of school. The teaching staff look at the previous year's goals and divide into about five groups of teachers across grade levels, subject areas, and friendships. (For the first year, initial goals can be set up using the topic headings such as those listed in the example that follows.) Each group reviews the goals to get the ideas flowing and then answers three questions: What are our major successes this year based on the goals? What are some areas that we still need to improve? What are the recommendations for next year? When the groups reassemble, they listen for common points. (A recorder word processes the common points or posts these ideas on butcher paper.) When three or four groups make the same point (e.g., effectively using common assessments, integrating technology), the teachers know that they are on to something. This energizes and begins focusing the staff for the next year. The faculty fine-tunes the goals during the first month of school and receives individual copies of the final document. The goals should be revisited often during the year by sharing experiences during faculty meetings and professional development days.

Again, it is important to stress that the process of writing specific school goals helps keep the principal and staff accountable. The goals become the "checklist for success" for that year, and ultimately the entire staff is responsible for implementing the goals.

Elementary School Goals

A. Student Expectations

  1. Focus on student responsibility to promote academic and social independence and acceptance of consequences. Stress student courtesy, caring, and tolerance.

  Implementation:

  - Tailor the school rules to promote your classroom goals.
  - Hold recognition assemblies with special themes (e.g., proper nutritional habits).
  - Use "Citizens of the Week" awards to emphasize specific school goals.
  - Stress the importance of positive behavior on the school buses.
  - Emphasize social-emotional learning experiences.

  2. In the classroom, maintain high expectations and challenge each child.

  Implementation:

  - Stimulate independent, critical, and divergent student responses.
  - Encourage the use of learning centers and enrichment resources or strategies.
  - Emphasize rigor in the curriculum.

3. Raise faculty and student consciousness concerning environmental issues.

   Implementation:

   - Model recycling, energy conservation, and "less is more" themes.
   - Integrate disciplines in units that address environmental issues, for instance, global warming.

B. Curriculum and Instruction

1. Promote the Common Core State Standards (CCSS) English Language Arts standards.

   Implementation:

   - Build awareness of the standards.
   - Stress the integration of the language arts in other disciplines.
   - Emphasize content area writing.
   - Recognize the importance of public speaking.
   - Increase the use of on-line resources and other reference materials to complement classroom learning experiences.

2. Continue the curriculum review process.

   Implementation—Science Committee:

   - Principles adopted by the Science Committee emphasizing NGSS (Next Generation Science Standards) will be shared with the faculty to make appropriate curriculum decisions.

   Implementation—Reading Committee and Fine Arts Committee:

   - Committees review important curriculum standards and plans for implementation.

3. Mathematics: Further work with CCSS Math standards.

   Implementation:

   - Conduct a math investigation at each grade level.
   - Provide workshops for new staff on the Math standards.
   - Schedule sessions for staff to share successful practices.

4. Raise consciousness concerning curriculum connections in all subject areas.

5. Social Studies: Continue refinement of global studies curriculum.

   Implementation:

   - Increase communication for regular classroom lessons on global studies in Grades 2–4.
   - Curriculum resources should be easily available to all teachers.
   - Work on timeline for semester reports (in Grades 3–5) to avoid overload in library and end-of-year pressures.

(Continued)

(Continued)

6. Place special emphasis on importance of curriculum pacing in all subject areas.

7. Pilot digital texts and BYOD (Bring Your Own Device) strategies.

8. Continue to challenge students with appropriate teaching strategies.

   Implementation:

   - Refine questioning and feedback strategies to diagnose student needs and provide appropriate resources.
   - Explore models for the "flipped classroom."

C. Professional Development

1. Expand peer coaching activity to include a variety of reflective teaching activities.

2. Continue professional learning community work.

   Implementation:

   - With significant number of new staff, assist them to maximize PLC use.
   - Highlight professional journal articles with all staff.
   - Conduct data workshops with the goal of building skillfulness in the use of data.

3. Portfolios: Extend student options and teacher involvement.

   Implementation:

   - Develop a system to support teacher dialogue about portfolios.
   - Expand the portfolio project to include more science and math options.
   - Continue to develop core staff with portfolio expertise.

4. Teacher Professional Growth: Pursue a variety of ways for teachers to assess their growth (e.g., digital videos, teacher portfolios, various observation instruments) and implement Professional Growth Plans consistent with the new district teacher evaluation process. Encourage staff to participate in the National Board Certification Process.

5. Faculty meetings: Increase teacher input and participation.

   Implementation:

   - Encourage Teacher Leadership Team members to plan or co-plan meetings.
   - Provide time for teachers to share ideas and success stories.
   - Increase cross-grade-level exchanges.
   - Integrate PLC work with faculty meetings.

D. Assessment

1. Experiment with a variety of formative and summative assessments of reading and math.

2. Update report card categories to reflect standards based curriculum.

3. Early Childhood Education Center: Systematically use High Scope curriculum and assessment instruments to observe students and tailor the curriculum to individual needs.

4. Build capacity to use online assessments.

E. Parent–Teacher Relations

1. Increase communication with parents through the monthly coffees.

Implementation:

- Create an outreach program for non- or limited-English-speaking parents.
- Provide wider access to online resources by expanding resource center hours.

2. Emphasize effective proactive communications with all parents.

F. General

1. Increase communication between specialist and regular classroom teachers.

Implementation:

- Both groups of teachers should take initiative regarding communication.
- Use daily "Look Book" e-mail to inform specialists of field trips and other events impacting daily instruction.
- Increase involvement of specialists in grade-level meetings.

Leaders emphasize that what a school stands for should be celebrated and not become simply an idea that gets lost in electronic or physical files. Individuals working in a school should work to agree on what their school represents. In fact, to take the idea a step further, many educational professionals are now writing professional and personal mission statements to help them take greater ownership of their day-to-day school activities and personal lives. This also helps school leaders keep on track by fostering constant reflection about their personal and professional work and experiences.

Much of what we have stated is encapsulated in the words of Peter Drucker (1992), the giant of 20th-century management theory:

What distinguishes the leader from the misleader are his goals. Whether the compromise he makes with the constraints of reality—which may involve political, economic, financial, or people problems—are compatible with his mission and goals or lead away from them determines whether he is an effective leader. And whether he holds fast to a few basic standards (exemplifying them in his own conduct), or whether "standards" for him are what he can get away with, determines whether the leader has followers or only hypocritical time-servers. (p. 121)

REFLECTIONS

This space provides a place for you to write down ideas that have been generated by this chapter, things you want to try, or adaptations of ideas presented here.

1. Examine the vision and mission statement of the school in which you work. Are staff members' daily actions guided or informed by these documents? If they are, do they need to be "tweeked"? How so? If they are not, what steps need to be taken?

2. How do you model an awareness of the vision and mission in your work as a leader?

3. Write a brief mission statement that exemplifies your vision of the good school. Provide two or three examples (paint an image) that show how the vision is realized in the day-to-day school activities.

4. What insights or new questions do you have as a result of reflecting on the ideas presented in this chapter?

PART IV

Working Together to
Build a Learning Community

9

Enhancing Teacher Growth Through Supervision and Evaluation Practices Designed to Promote Student Learning

I ask teachers before observing, "What aspects of teaching and learning do you want me to observe? What outcomes do you hope to achieve? How will you know that all students are engaged?"

—A principal's voice

ISSUES AND DILEMMAS

If schools are to be regarded as learning communities, everyone in a school must engage in learning. Our vision of lifelong learning for students can hold greater meaning if teachers and administrators have an ongoing conversation to improve their performance. Yet in many schools, teachers feel intimidated when principals walk into their classrooms and are especially fearful of the observation and conferencing process. This is a clear indicator that the traditional teacher evaluation process has failed. Ideally, principals and assistant principals, as instructional leaders, should frequently visit classrooms to see, share, affirm, and celebrate the important work of schools. Interestingly, teachers often resent the glowing written recommendations from principals who never seriously observed in their classrooms. This tells us that teachers feel "cheated" about the assessment of their performance and the missed opportunities for professional growth. Fortunately this is changing. Principals, assistant principals, coaches, and teachers are observing classes, networking, and talking about teaching, learning, curriculum, and assessment. Principals see teachers in action. As noted in the opening of Chapter 8, this approach is supported by The Wallace Foundation (2013) in its report stressing the principal's role in supporting instructional effectiveness to impact student academic success and "cultivating leadership in others" (p. 4).

Research demonstrates that student achievement is related to intentional classroom visits by the principal and a principal's knowledge of and ability to assist teachers with regard to curriculum, instruction, and assessment. Kathleen Cotton's (2003) influential work, *Principals and Student Achievement*, concludes that successful schools employ instructional leaders who observe classes and provide feedback to teachers while monitoring student progress data in a collaborative culture that supports continuous improvement. Marzano, Waters, and McNulty's (2005, pp. 52–61) research on 21 responsibilities of school leaders reinforce Cotton's findings. Responsibilities directly relating to instructional leadership include the following:

- Intellectual stimulation (i.e., encouraging collaborative staff dialogue with cutting-edge ideas to support innovative change)
- Involvement in curriculum, instruction, and assessment (i.e., hands-on involvement with teachers in classrooms)
- Knowledge of curriculum, instruction, and assessment (i.e., an understanding of research and best practice to inform teachers)
- Monitoring/evaluating (i.e., providing feedback and guidance to teachers concerning data related to student achievement)
- Visibility (i.e., showing up in classrooms and other school venues on a daily basis to support teaching and learning)

This view of instructional leadership contrasts with the old administrative paradigm of intimidation and control which lent itself to *snoopervising*, obviously causing bitterness on the part of teachers as principals *told* teachers what they were "doing wrong." That model has no place in schools functioning as learning communities. We need to refrain from operating on fear so the notion of growth is built in from day one. Principals need to communicate to teachers that supervision and evaluation processes are intended to build their capacity to promote student learning. Risk-taking and trust cannot flourish in an environment of intimidation (Glickman, Gordon, & Ross-Gordon, 2010).

In this chapter, we discuss essential ingredients for successful supervision, effective instructional strategies, brain-compatible practices related to cognitive science, guidelines for supervising with instructional frameworks, reflective clinical supervision strategies, tips for conferencing and observing, the use of walk-throughs for generating authentic feedback, guidelines related to evaluation and legal concerns, and final thoughts on supervision and evaluation. Beginning with the Effective Schools Movement 40 years ago, the term "instructional leadership" has been a mainstay of textbooks and principalship training (Neumerski, 2012), yet educators constantly lament that the promise of instructional leadership has not been realized. As you read this chapter, consider your own commitment to instructional leadership and how you can make this commitment a reality.

Supervision is providing support for teachers so they become the best they can be. Implicit in this definition is the development and refinement of a knowledge base and craft practice regarding effective teaching and learning. Supervisors provide resources and promote informal and formal conversations with and among teachers to affect curriculum, teaching, assessment, student learning, and professional development. For example, recommending a professional journal to a math or science teacher on STEM developments or sharing an article with the staff to stimulate a faculty meeting discussion on 21st century skills can be important contributions to the learning community made by a school principal. Additionally, providing support for interdisciplinary planning, assisting teachers in developing an Advanced Placement high school course, or facilitating a professional forum on assessment based on the Common Core State Standards (CCSS) are all activities that can be supported directly or indirectly by the school leader in an effort to foster professional growth.

ESSENTIAL INGREDIENTS FOR SUCCESSFUL SUPERVISION

To maximize the impact of supervision, principals must develop an honest, caring, and trusting relationship with teachers. Implicit in the process of supervision is the notion that adults have innate needs and desires to improve, grow, and learn. These desires are essential characteristics in a healthy school culture. This collegial desire to grow as professionals is supported by a study of teacher working conditions in Massachusetts led by Susan Moore Johnson (2012) of Harvard University, "The working conditions that mattered most to teachers were those that shaped the social context of teaching and learning in their school, the school culture, the principal's leadership, and the teachers' relationships with their colleagues. . . . Notably, across all communities, schools with better work environments for teachers also achieved greater growth in student learning" (p. 4).

Glickman et al. (2010) add that personal teacher needs for assistance vary depending on one's life stage, teaching skills, gender, personal story and reflections, career expectations, and commitment to the job. Principals must honor and address these individual needs to help teachers develop professionally and personally.

As principals actively learn from the teachers and students around them, and acknowledge that learning, everyone in the school becomes empowered with the knowledge that his or her ideas are influential. This notion can help create a risk-taking climate in the school. If we really mean that the leader is a learner, then the principal should expect to learn a great deal through the supervision and evaluation process—especially related to the particular context of a teacher's classroom decisions (e.g., Why that decision, at that moment?).

The ideal dialogue between principals and teachers can, in some ways, be seen as analogous to the process of scientific discovery. When old ideas are found to be ineffective or "mistakes" are discovered, the scientific community celebrates because an advancement has occurred. We need to celebrate responsible risk taking and "mistakes." This notion certainly translates to the classroom. As John Hattie (2009) has noted, a key variable for student and teacher success is feedback that is enhanced when the culture values mistakes: "It is critical to ensure that 'errors' are welcomed, as they are key levers for enhancing learning" (p. 4).

A postobservation conference with an experienced kindergarten teacher effectively illustrated this point. The lesson objective was to help students identify a variety of animal coats (e.g., skin, fur, scales, feathers) and recognize how the coats protect the animals. The teacher opened the lesson by showing a variety of animal coats and had the students touch them. She then asked the following question: "What do you think the fur and feathers do in the rain?" The kindergartners answered: "Get wet!" The answer she expected was: "The coats or coverings protect the animals." The students did not see protection at all—they saw a lot of wet animals!

The principal listened carefully as the teacher expertly analyzed her lesson. This experienced teacher noted that regardless of how long one teaches, "we tend to focus in on the lesson objective from an adult's viewpoint instead of thinking about what a child might say." As a supervisor, the principal was fortunate to be on the listening end of this conference as the teacher expressed an insight of universal meaning for all teachers.

A discussion of supervision would be inadequate without addressing teacher evaluations, observations, and conferencing. However, an important issue should first be noted. Practitioners are constantly advised to separate supervision from evaluation. Although conceptually it may be ideal to separate the formative and summative process (e.g., supervision and evaluation), the political reality and the day-to-day interactions between teachers and principals make this an unrealistic aim. Reality, for the principal practitioner, is that you can never fully separate supervision and evaluation. (Which to some extent explains why teachers are often uneasy about the purpose of walk-throughs.) A helpful way to conceptualize the interrelationship between supervision and evaluation is to think of supervision as the formative process that allows for several "dress rehearsals." The evaluation is the summative process in which institutionalized state and district guidelines are used to assess teacher performance. Although most supervisory texts and published frameworks remind us that the formative process is descriptive and nonjudgmental, again, reality tells us that it is almost impossible to avoid a degree of summative interpretation; we all seek to know if we are successful when teaching. Figure 9.1 demonstrates the interrelationship between these two concepts.

Figure 9.1 Formative Assessment and Summative Evaluation Continuum

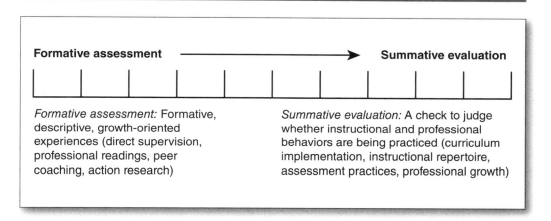

It is important that the supervision or evaluation process is nonintimidating and emphasizes growth. This idea should be shared with the entire faculty at the beginning of the year as well as during individual conferences with teachers. Most teachers are good to excellent, but we are often understandably consumed with the problems of firing the five percent who are not. Certainly, it is important to uphold standards of excellence. After assisting a marginal teacher, if no growth occurs within the allowed time period, the principal must document the teacher's lack of progress and seek nonrenewal using a legally defensible approach. (See Guidelines Related to Evaluation and Legal Concerns later in this chapter.) However, we cannot forget the other 95 percent; they need to know how important their success is to the students and that we support their professional growth efforts.

Even champions need coaches, and educators need to continually provide feedback to all teachers, including the best ones. As Blanchard and Johnson (1983) stress in *The One Minute Manager*, "Feedback is the Breakfast of Champions" (p. 67). Principals can model this notion by asking teachers for feedback regarding the effectiveness of the principals' supervisory practices and encouraging them to consider teacher leadership roles to impact the students even more.

By emphasizing the theme of growth, the supervisory climate is enhanced and the entire school takes great strides toward becoming a community of learners. One principal reported:

> One of my most productive conferences was with an expert teacher who was trying a particular cooperative learning technique for the first time. My job with her was just as important as with the marginal teacher. I needed to do what I could to provide meaningful data, ask questions to foster reflection and analysis, and to keep her motivation high. What she gained in her experiment with cooperative learning was a clinic for both of us on what should be included in a good cooperative learning lesson. We watched students taking ownership of their learning, assisting classmates who were having difficulty, and self-assessing their own progress during the lesson. I gained insight into what supervisory approaches were helpful. I won't have to worry about burnout with that teacher because she was engaged and motivated by the cooperative learning process and the opportunity to reflect and analyze the lesson and its effects.

Furthermore, her enthusiasm will hopefully stimulate other members of the staff, and her students!

It is a principal's responsibility to facilitate and expose teachers to a variety of useful, relevant instructional ideas. In this role, principals can foster teachers' reflective practices to help them analyze their teaching and interactions with students. At other times, teachers may request direct intervention from the principal. One teacher noted: "What if I am missing something that is really a problem in my teaching? How will I know if I cannot determine that as an area of weakness in myself?" The principal should also encourage and logistically provide for learning community discussions about curriculum and instruction led by grade level leaders, department chairs, coaches, and other teacher leaders.

Beyond the classroom, establishing a digital library of effective techniques, teaching episodes, and important topics for discussion (possibly generated by teacher resource sites such as TeacherTube, TeachingChannel, or Edutopia) can also help. Showing episodes during faculty meetings or encouraging individuals or groups of teachers to view and share ideas can help professionals reflect on their decisions. Finally, if principals are implementing a new state or district evaluation framework, reviewing the philosophy and rationale for the system will reduce anxiety among new and seasoned staff. Soliciting frank questions will help everyone gain a greater understanding of the instrument and process. Constantly emphasizing the critical relationship between teacher learning and student learning should be a part of the dialogue.

EFFECTIVE INSTRUCTIONAL STRATEGIES

The link between supervision and effective instruction should be an inextricable one based on solid research. That is, an understanding of cognitive science should drive the supervision and evaluation process, how the brain processes information, and the necessary elements that contribute to learning. This focus on brain-compatible learning also broadens traditional notions of supervision and evaluation by including an affective dimension. Research on brain functioning seems to indicate, for instance, that when learners feel at risk, their capacity to learn is reduced considerably because much of the mind's focus is turned to the task of establishing a sense of well being (interestingly, teachers often shut down when they feel at risk as well). Therefore, the learning environment and the attitudes and perceptions of teachers and students toward learning tasks should be included in any supervisory or evaluation focus.

Although many teaching strategies exist, it is helpful to examine some general themes that often characterize core elements of effective instruction. Cognitive science, enriched by research related to "the social and cultural contexts of learning" (Bransford, Brown, & Cocking, 2000, p. 8), has enabled educators to gain a greater understanding of important principles that can lead to enhanced student learning. Constructivist learning is certainly an essential feature of the science of learning, but Bransford et al. caution educators to take a balanced position, considering the complexity of teaching:

> A common misconception regarding "constructivist" theories of knowing (that existing knowledge is used to build new knowledge) is that teachers should never tell students anything directly but, instead, should always allow them to construct knowledge for themselves. This perspective confuses a theory of pedagogy (teaching) with a theory of knowing. . . . [However] there are times, usually after people have first grappled with issues on their own, that "teaching by telling" can work extremely well. (p. 11)

Hattie (2009) insightfully adds, "Educating is more than teaching people to think—it is also teaching people things that are worth knowing" (p. 27). Based on a balanced approach to teaching and learning, Bransford et al. (2000) suggest that three major principles have far reaching implications for teaching:

1. Students come to the classroom with preconceptions about how the world works. If their initial understanding is not engaged, they may fail to grasp the new concepts and information that are taught, or they may learn them for purposes of a test but revert to their preconceptions outside the classroom.

2. To develop competence in an area of inquiry, students must: (a) have a deep foundation of factual knowledge, (b) understand facts and ideas in the context of a conceptual framework, and (c) organize knowledge in ways that facilitate retrieval and application.

3. A "metacognitive" approach to instruction can help students learn to take control of their own learning by defining learning goals and monitoring their progress in achieving them. (pp. 14–18)

The practical application of these important findings is demonstrated below by considering how teachers prepare students for learning and use brain-compatible teaching strategies to maximize student learning. These concepts and strategies are essential tools for supervisors who serve as instructional leaders.

Preparing the Student's Mind for Learning

The minds of the learners first need to be prepared for the learning that is about to occur. This requires a meaningful focus of the learners' attention. Once this happens, it is important that an outcome be stated so that students will know where the lesson is headed. Even with a discovery lesson, a general outcome can be stated (e.g., "By the end of this lesson, you will be able to solve this mystery!"). Doing this creates an "Advanced Organizer" for the student. To begin instruction at the appropriate level of difficulty and resolve any preconceived misconceptions about what is to be taught, it is helpful to assess what students already know about the topic of the lesson and what they would like to know ("nothing" is not an acceptable answer!). Dr. Judy Willis, noted neurologist and educator explains, "Memory hinges on prior knowledge activation. Related memories are sent to the hippocampus to meet new input . . . we must activate prior knowledge every time we need to form a new memory" (August 10, 2011, ASCD webinar).

Since the mind stores information according to whether it perceives that there is a future purpose, it is helpful either to provide a meaningful purpose or to engage students in identifying the possible reasons for the lesson. Furthermore, if there are prior learnings that may assist the students in this lesson, they should be recalled as well.

Instruction

Instruction usually consists of three parts: input, modeling or demonstration, and active engagement or rehearsal. Input can be provided in several ways. The teacher may ask the students to explore online resources, videos, or readings prior to a lesson (as in a "flipped classroom"). Or, the teacher or groups of students may provide information, perform an experiment, show a video, model a process, or construct a model. Input may be provided by students, such as explaining a math investigation to the class. Following this, it is helpful to provide a demonstration or model so that the learners can see what was introduced during the input phase. Finally, students should be provided with an opportunity to think critically about what has been taught or experienced, and to rehearse what has just been taught and modeled. The key to rehearsal is that students should be able to demonstrate to the teacher that they comprehend the intended input and, as appropriate, that they can either recall the information or perform the task. This provides feedback from the students to the teacher regarding if students understand that which has been taught, or if reteaching is necessary.

Practice

To develop fluency and accuracy and to promote long-term remembering, students should practice the new learning under the teacher's guidance in the same manner that the skill ultimately will be assessed. When students have demonstrated that they can perform the skill independently, they should be encouraged to practice in a way that can be retrieved and recalled during assessment. Teacher guidance is essential to ensure perfect practice. (Errors practiced are difficult to eliminate.) This increases the likelihood that students will store or internalize correctly the content and skills that have been taught. Students need opportunities to revisit previously taught content so that this content remains vibrant and accessible over time. If you don't use it, it's easy to lose it!

Assessment

It is essential to determine if what has been taught has been internalized or mastered by the student. Therefore, informal and formal assessments are an important ingredient of the lesson design process. Even a simple observation of student performance can yield rich data about where instruction should go next. As one teacher leader remarked, "Today's assessment drives my instruction tomorrow."

These core elements can be helpful as part of the framework for discussing lesson plans, observing a lesson, and assessing the extent to which the teacher accomplished his or her desired goals, based on student understanding, using work samples as evidence of understanding.

Using Learning to Drive Teaching

The teacher's challenge is to identify *learning goals* and corresponding *criteria for success*. With these in mind, the teacher selects *instructional strategies* that she believes will be both *effective* and *efficient* to help every student accomplish those learning goals. As the lesson unfolds, by *observing students*, the teacher is provided with *feedback* about the *effect of her instructional strategies on student outcomes*. Based on the feedback, the teacher modifies the instructional strategies to assure that all students achieve at high levels (adapted from Hattie, 2012a).

BRAIN-COMPATIBLE TEACHING PRACTICES

"Neuroscience and education have successfully worked together to build knowledge that's applicable to the classroom" (Worden, Hinton, & Fischer, 2011, p. 10). The following 21 brain-compatible teaching practices offer teachers specific strategies to maximize student learning:

- Immediately engage the attention of learners when they come into the classroom. The activities need to be of high interest and anchored in benchmarks or standards. They can be used to build readiness for a lesson about to be taught or to review a previously taught concept. The brain remembers best what comes first, and next best what comes last. Information lingers in the sensory memory only three-fourths of a second. Then information is either forgotten or sent to short-term memory. If the teacher doesn't engage the attention of the learners, something else will!

- Routinely post lesson outcomes, benchmarks, or standards in a specific place on the Smart Board or whiteboard so students can refer to them. An agenda for the day and homework assignments should also have a regular place in the classroom. Advance organizers trigger attention and are linked to promoting memory.

- Use national or state standards to design curriculum and instruction and assess student work. Research indicates that high-performing, high-poverty schools implemented this practice with notable results. Making the brain aware of performance targets increases attention.

- Involve students in active learning experiences that engage a variety of learning channels: auditory, visual, kinesthetic. Seek ways to structure activities so that students may have an opportunity to use a variety of intelligences (visual-spatial, mathematical-logical, verbal-linguistic, musical, bodily-kinesthetic, interpersonal, intrapersonal, naturalist; Gardner, 2006). Individuals remember only 10–20 percent of what they hear. Active involvement focuses attention and increases the probability that students will remember what they have "rehearsed."

- Engage students in learning tasks such as experiments or experiential activities that require them to actively construct meaning. The brain actually forms new neural connections when it is actively engaged in "meaning making" based on experiences.

- Chunk curriculum content appropriate to the developmental age of the learner. The capacity of short-term memory appears to develop with developmental age. This has major implications for the design and delivery of curriculum.

- Change activities at least four or five times within the context of a lesson. For example, students may first be actively engaged in a warm-up activity, report out, experience direct instruction, create a graphic organizer to summarize learnings, stand, pair and share their work with other students, and respond to a prompt in their learning journals. The more firsts and lasts within a lesson, the more memorable its content.

- Provide opportunities for meaningful "rehearsal" or practice after initial content has been introduced. Periodically provide review activities to distribute rehearsal opportunities over time. The more opportunities a student has to meaningfully rehearse, the greater the chance that information will move from short-term to long-term memory. Providing rehearsal opportunities using a variety of learning channels will maximize the probability that long-term retention will occur.

- Structure opportunities for movement during learning experiences. Movement provides oxygen to the brain and increases attention.

- Seek opportunities to integrate the curriculum. For example, in the well-known *Dear America* series, students read autobiographical accounts written by fictional characters based on actual historical events. So history comes alive in a language arts context. Subjects are not found in isolation in the real world. Long-term memory stores information in networks of association. The more associations or connections a student has with a particular fact or concept, the more easily that information can be recalled.

- Use humor related to content. For example, concepts may be taught using a cartoon lecture. Humor increases retention up to 15 percent!

- Engage students in a variety of tasks that require higher-order thinking skills. Analysis, evaluation, and synthesis tasks require students to access and use remembered information to foster new neural connections in the brain.

- Provide for a variety of flexible grouping contexts that engage students in working with different classmates. Much learning occurs through social interaction. Students can receive instruction appropriate to their learning needs and pace in small-group settings. As students master academic content, they simultaneously develop skills in working with and appreciating others. For many students, a small-group setting reduces anxiety. According to brain researchers Caine and Caine (1991), the brain functions optimally in a state of *relaxed alertness.*

- Assign and grade relevant homework that extends rehearsal opportunities and reflects how content will ultimately be assessed. Students learn more when they complete homework that is graded, commented on, and discussed by their teachers. Be sure that homework is meaningful, represents perfect practice, and is focused on a few key critical attributes. Whenever possible, engage students in developing rubrics to assess their work. This increases their awareness of key attributes of quality work and lends credibility and authenticity to the grading process.

- Match instruction and assessment practices that are consistent with how standards and benchmarks ultimately will be assessed and the setting in which assessment will occur. Research on state dependence indicates that content will be most easily recalled when it is assessed under the same conditions as when it was originally learned.

- Use authentic assessment measures. Engage students in applying new and recent learnings in a real-world context. The brain remembers based on what is embedded in a particular context. For example, to remember what they had for dinner last Saturday night, most people will have to first remember where they were.

- Provide opportunities for students to summarize their learnings in written or verbal form and communicate them to others. Summarizing strengthens neural connections. When students rehearse through reciprocal teaching, retention is enhanced 65–90 percent!

- Monitor and invite students to monitor their own progress. Self-monitoring and feedback regarding recognition of efforts can be sources of intrinsic motivation and may increase attention and focus.

- Select assignments that are challenging and interesting. Provide a support structure to help students achieve success in a psychologically safe environment. The brain learns best in an atmosphere of *high challenge and low threat* (Caine & Caine, 1991).

- Create a learning environment where students perceive that they are (1) safe from physical, verbal, or psychological harm; (2) free to experiment and take risks when learning; (3) connected in their relationships with others, including the teacher and other students; and (4) valued members of the class. Sylwester (1995) notes that "emotion drives attention which drives learning and memory" (p. 72). If students feel safe and cared for, if teachers and others are responsive to their needs, students' ability to focus and learn will be enhanced.

- Encourage parents and guardians to stimulate their children's intellectual development and to provide a caring, responsive climate in the home. For instance, teachers can ask parents to help their children rehearse a presentation to be given in class or discuss the results of a recent class science experiment or play a student designed technology game. Environment plays a key role in brain development and intelligence. Verbal interaction with children, for example, has a direct impact on language and vocabulary development. A caring, responsive climate contributes to the development of a child's sense of self-esteem.

In addition to these 21 practices, Marzano, Pickering, and Pollock (2001) have identified nine powerful research-based instructional strategies. These strategies can make a significant difference for students if employed effectively. The nine strategies apply to all subject areas, all grade levels, and all socioeconomic groups. These strategies include comparing and contrasting, summarizing and note taking, reinforcing effort and providing recognition, homework and practice, nonlinguistic representations, cooperative learning, setting objectives and providing feedback, generating and testing hypotheses, and questions, cues, and advance organizers. These strategies could be reviewed during the supervisory process to support teachers in planning instruction, or as part of a small-group, Professional Learning Community, or faculty-wide professional development initiative.

GUIDELINES TO SUCCESSFULLY NAVIGATE THROUGH REQUIRED STATE AND DISTRICT TEACHER EVALUATION FRAMEWORKS

The Race to the Top (RTTT) grant competition and other efforts to increase teacher and principalship accountability have "sped up" the efforts of states to develop and implement teacher evaluation frameworks based on state teaching standards. Additionally, RTTT specifically requires states to use multiple measures and "significantly" weigh teacher success based on student growth data. Considering this challenge, Stumbo and McWalters (2010) note, "Although there is no clear definition of 'significance' some of the winning Race to the Top states set the weight of student performance at 50 percent or more of a teacher's evaluation score" (p. 10). There is a lot going on here. On the one hand, states, top down, are deciding on how much weight student tests will have on the teacher evaluation process. On the other hand, instructional leaders, bottom up, have the opportunity to make a difference in their own schools by successfully working with teachers using the instructional frameworks as a professional growth opportunity. Along with the CCSS (accompanied by thoughtful curriculum scope and sequence, sound lessons, and relevant professional development), the evidence-based teacher instructional frameworks offer the potential to truly raise the standards for students and teachers (Danielson, 2007; Marzano, Frontier, & Livingston, 2011). These guidelines will help with the process:

- *Embrace the Template.* Although each state's selected teacher evaluation framework may differ to some extent, the templates are usually similar. To begin, RTTT stipulates that the teacher evaluation systems must use "rigorous teacher performance standards" (Department of Education, 2013, p. 22460). Thus, each selected framework must include broad areas that relate to performance standards (e.g., domains) with levels of subheadings (e.g., components, categories, segments) that describe in some detail the landscape of teacher expectations. The broad areas directly relate to instructional strategies, content, assessment and classroom management, lesson preparation, and professionalism. State selected frameworks must include rubrics. Why? The RTTT requirements include, "meaningfully differentiat[ing] performance using at least three performance levels [rubrics]" (Department of Education, p. 22460). So that is the big picture. Instructional leaders then need to dive in and study the framework details, the weeds, selected by your district.

- *Clarity Is Helpful.* Danielson (2010) makes two excellent points about effective teacher evaluation frameworks. One, the frameworks provide "a consistent definition of good teaching" and two, they offer teachers and supervisors "a common language to practice" (p. 36). Teaching is complicated; it's a craft and science. But having a common vocabulary that relates to effective teaching really helps bring clarity to the teaching and learning conversation. This is critical. As we note later in greater detail Costa and Garmston (1991) stress that quality conversations about teaching and learning are rare. A common vocabulary, and rubrics that describe performance range, can bring clarity to the conversation. Use the framework as a springboard for dialogue!

- *Collaboration and Process Build Trust—and It Takes Time.* As instructional leaders learn about each component of the instructional frameworks, it is easy to forget that first we need to build trust through a collaborative relationship, then a serious discussion can take place about teaching and learning. Showing respect for teachers by conducting instructional conferences and conversations—in which they take the lead—will go a long way toward building rapport so the content of a framework can be discussed thoughtfully. Instructional leaders earn respect during conversations with teachers by authentically and visibly modeling learning about learning. Be patient. There is time to learn the content. As Zig Zigler said, "People don't care what you know until they know that you care." As a long-time principal, co-author Harvey Alvy found himself in this dilemma each time he began a new principalship since each school had a different evaluation system. It is much more important to build **trust** with teachers (through conversations and modeling). At a measured pace, increase one's content knowledge of the framework. Trust will lead to risk-taking and a willingness on the part of teachers to try something new. That's exciting!

• *The Goal Is Continuous Growth.* Teacher evaluation systems can become box canyons. Although evaluation is critical for most teachers it should be only part of a broader range of professional development activities. New and at-risk teachers will certainly be challenged by the process but for the vast majority of teachers it should be seen as one of many ways to grow.

• *Going Beyond the Frameworks.* Madeline Hunter used to lament that although she clearly stated that her seven steps of lesson design were essential, she never implied that all seven should be used for each lesson. Yet district evaluation expectations based on her model often required teachers to use all seven steps during lessons. Marzano (2009) makes a similar point noting with frustration that some districts have few expectations for teachers to go beyond the nine teaching strategies described in *Classroom Instruction That Works* (Marzano et al., 2001). What does that say about believing in the expertise of teachers and their capacity to go the extra mile or make sound instructional decisions based on student learning? Rubrics cannot "measure" the difference a teacher can make in the life of a student who may be experiencing bullying at school or abuse at home.

• *Stick to the Essentials.* In *Focus* (2011b), Mike Schmoker strongly suggests that educators are constantly engaged in elegant and complicated reform initiatives that rarely work. And, truth be told, we do not know at this point whether the CCSS and Teacher Evaluation Reforms will make a difference. In the meantime Schmoker reminds us not to lose sight of the essentials. What are they? "Three simple things: reasonably coherent curriculum (*what* we teach); sound lessons (*how* we teach); and far more purposeful reading and writing in every discipline, or authentic literacy (integral to both what and how we teach)" (p. 2). The takeaway is that when instructional leaders are engaged in conversations with teachers about their work, or observing them in action, it's important to focus on teaching and learning. We know a principal who, in addition to concentrating on the agreed upon preobservation teacher goals, always reminds himself just before an observation to focus on the lesson objective, discern how the teacher is accomplishing the objective, and consider whether student engagement is demonstrating that the objective is being mastered.

• *Mastering the Framework Is Not the Destination—It Is Student Success.* We create narratives. A school principal concentrating on understanding and applying an instructional framework can easily get lost in details and forget to look up and see the big picture. For instructional leaders a primary professional narrative should be to embrace and celebrate our work with teachers. Even teachers who are perceived as experts based on rubrics should still be defined by who they are and what they stand for. We should never confuse a piece of paper with a person's worth. We need to remember that accomplishing the professional development goals tied to a framework is just *one* aspect of a teacher's life. The much bigger prize is what they do to ensure student success.

INCREASING TEACHER AND ADMINISTRATIVE UNDERSTANDING THROUGH REFLECTIVE CLINICAL SUPERVISION

A four-step variation on the clinical supervision model can be used to implement the instructional framework and the previously reviewed teaching and learning strategies. With this model, the emphasis moves from the sole concentration on observable teacher behaviors to more important conversations and reflections about planning, teaching, learning, student work, and assessment. Thus the model serves as a catalyst for talking about teaching and learning. Again, the trust-building process is more important than the content. A critical part of this model is the preobservation conference that precedes the teaching. As Costa and Garmston (1991) have stated, "A good preobservation conference is worth six observations." The preobservation conference provides an opportunity for the teacher to talk, engage in a conversation, and unpack one's thinking behind the planning process. It also provides a reference point to compare expected and actual outcomes in the postobservation conference.

1. The Preobservation Conference

Usually the teacher will choose a lesson, the key points to be observed, expected student learning, and the desired type of data-gathering method. There needs to be a focus on building rapport, trust, and self-esteem. Listening to the teacher during the conference is a key supervisory objective. If the teacher talks more during the conference than the principal, declare the conference a success. Why? Because the teacher is talking and thinking about the teaching, learning, and assessment processes. Principals have to get away from the notion that it is their role to "run" the conference. However, this does not preclude asking effective questions to stimulate discussion. Possible questioning topics may relate to student work samples, CCSS, brain-compatible learning, diversity, equity, students with disabilities,

English language learners, problem solving, engaging all students, the complexity of group work, and valuing teacher decision making. One experienced principal often tells teachers during preobservation conferences, "I value your ability to make instructional decisions on the spot." Depending on the context, specific questions may include: What are your expectations for students? What evidence will you look for that indicates the student outcomes are in sight? When teaching, how do you know that students are engaged? How do you know they are progressing? How do you know that the standards are being achieved? How are you coping with the CCSS and specific challenges of special needs students? The more specific the preobservation conference discussion, the more fine-tuned the lesson and observation are likely to be. On the other hand, let the teacher know that you recognize the lesson can go in various directions. As the lesson unfolds, data are gathered based on the focus identified in the preobservation conference. This provides feedback for analysis that will occur in the postobservation conference. If a specific teacher instructional framework is being used, then Danielson's (2012) recommendation makes sense, "Precisely what the observer (supervisor, mentor, or coach) looks for in an observation is a function of the instructional framework that the school district or state has adopted" (p. 34). Figure 9.2 is an example of a preobservation form that teachers can use to focus the preobservation conference and lesson.

2. Observation

Traditionally, this has been the key step. However, the supervisor must work to reduce a teacher's anxiety about this step and stress that the primary purpose of the observation is to provide data from instructional episodes and student work samples for reflection following the lesson and for discussion during the postobservation conference. *The conversation about the observation may actually be more important than the observation.* Students may be informed about the observation so that they can see that adults also continue to grow. For example, "Mrs. Johnson will be coming in to watch our class today. She'll be interested in discovering what helps us learn." With the popularity of principal and teacher walk-throughs, a visit from the principal is no longer an unusual event in many schools. During this step it is crucial to observe teacher behaviors, students, and student work samples. Schlechty (2001) advises, "Rather than observing the classroom to see how the teacher is performing, the principal observes the classroom (and perhaps interviews students and reviews assignments as well) to determine the extent to which students are engaged, persist, and experience a sense of accomplishment and satisfaction as a result of what they are asked to do" (p. 144).

3. Reflections on the Observation

With this four-step model, solitary reflection is essential and critical to the success of this process. If a supervision model is used that includes

Figure 9.2   Preobservation Conference Form

Teacher's Name _____   Today's Date _____

Subject _____

1. Lesson Objective: What do you want the students to know and be able to do as a result of this lesson? What evidence would indicate that the lesson objective was met? What lesson/unit outcomes have guided the steps of the lesson? (If appropriate, please bring student work samples that emerged during the lesson to our postobservation conference to support the lesson objective and expected outcomes.)

2. How does this lesson "fit" into the subject curriculum? Are there particular CCSS and district curriculum goals that will be addressed by this lesson?

3. What background knowledge/skills do the students have for this specific lesson or the major topic/unit that includes this lesson?

4. Do you anticipate any particular difficulties that the class in general, or ELL, or special needs students, may encounter during this lesson?

5. Would you like me to observe any particular students during the lesson or ask students specific questions about their learning?

6. What will be the key aspects/steps of this lesson? What activities will the students engage in during the lesson to meet the outcomes and your expectations? Let's remember that the lesson may include surprises that we could not have anticipated that may alter the sequenced steps of the lesson. (If you prefer attach the lesson to this form.)

7. What evidence will you look for during the lesson to assess whether the expected lesson/unit outcomes are being reached?

(Continued)

(Continued)

8. What teaching strategies/techniques/issues and student learnings do you want me to concentrate on during the observation for discussion during the postobservation conference? Suggested areas for feedback include: teacher decision making, motivation, student work evidence, accomplishing outcomes, use of rubrics, student voice, providing feedback to students, reinforcing students, student participation, equity in the classroom, respecting diversity, tapping into preexisting knowledge, constructivists techniques, addressing standards, domain-specific concepts, lesson sequence/logic, scope and sequence, questioning strategies, traditional and alternative assessment strategies, opening or lesson closure, logic or difficulty of ideas, pacing, checking for understanding, atmosphere in the classroom, classroom management, clarity, higher-level thinking, problem solving, modeling new learning, use of technology, variety of activities, "out of the box" teaching techniques, organization of the lesson, creativity and imagination in the classroom, risk taking, student discovery of ideas, lab procedures, engaging all students, cooperative learning, peer support, use of instructional resources, teacher-centered behaviors, student-centered lessons, brain-compatible learning, multiple intelligences, blended learning strategies, social-emotional learning competencies, self-regulated or reflective learning, global awareness, other 21st century skills, and addressing special needs students. What have I missed that you would like feedback on? (It is recommended that only two or three strategies, techniques, or issues are selected for the observation and for discussion during the postobservation conference.)

9. What else do we need to discuss?

Date, room, and time of lesson _____

Please fill out this preobservation form before or, if necessary, during our conference. Your comments on the form will provide the basis for the preobservation conference, the observation, and the postobservation conference. I look forward to visiting your class and to our discussions!

pre- and postobservation conferences, then it is vitally important that the teacher has an adequate opportunity to analyze the lesson before the postobservation conference.

Along with student work, the principal should provide the type of data requested by the teacher. The teacher may then review the principal's notes based on the district instructional framework, script-tape (e.g., written play-by-play of the lesson) or the principal's summary of the lesson. Depending on the level of trust the lesson might be recorded. The principal will need time to write up the observational notes for teachers if both descriptive and interpretive data are needed. Another approach is to provide the descriptive data to the teacher immediately following the lesson without any interpretive supervisory comments so that the teacher may analyze it before the postobservation conference. The teacher, however, should be invited to reflect on the lesson and make observations before examining the data. The teacher analysis of the lesson may include a wide range of comments, such as why spur-of-the-moment decisions were made, patterns noted while checking for understanding, or what surprises occurred during the lesson.

4. The Postobservation Conference

The primary goal of the postobservation conference is to encourage the teacher to reflect on his or her decisions related to student learning (e.g., What happened as expected? What happened differently?). The teacher should have an opportunity to verbalize a comparison between his or her recollections of the lesson and the actual data from the observation.

Again, the teacher should dominate the discussion and, in most cases, decide where to go next. Interestingly, when trust is established, teachers prefer to take the initiative in stating that a lesson was successful or did not go well. When the teacher spots a problem, he or she takes ownership and is in the driver's seat in recommending ways to fine-tune a teaching strategy. As a conference facilitator, it is critical that the supervisor remain focused on the topics agreed upon during the preobservation conference unless behaviors occurred during the lesson that were unacceptable. Moreover, the conference can provide the opening for the next observation or another professional growth activity.

TIPS FOR CONFERENCING AND OBSERVING

Obviously, the preceding supervision model has many variations and depends greatly on the experience of the teacher, the experience of the principal, the context of the school and students, and the relationship between the supervisor and the teacher. The tips that follow are intended to generate additional ideas to enhance the supervisory process.

Using the Student Learning Nexus Model. It is always helpful for supervisors to have a model related to teaching and learning to help them see the global complexities of a lesson or series of lessons. The Student Learning Nexus Model (Figure 9.3) can be used as a compact framework for principals, assistant principals, coaches, teacher leaders, and central office personnel when considering aspects of instruction, curriculum, assessment, and the classroom environment as they relate to student learning. The model also can facilitate dialogue between supervisors and teachers during a reflective clinical supervision conference or among teachers using walk-throughs, instructional rounds, or peer coaching strategies. Note that each component of the model is interrelated and aligned with the other

Figure 9.3 Student Learning Nexus Model: Balancing Instruction, Curriculum, and Assessment in a Healthy Environment

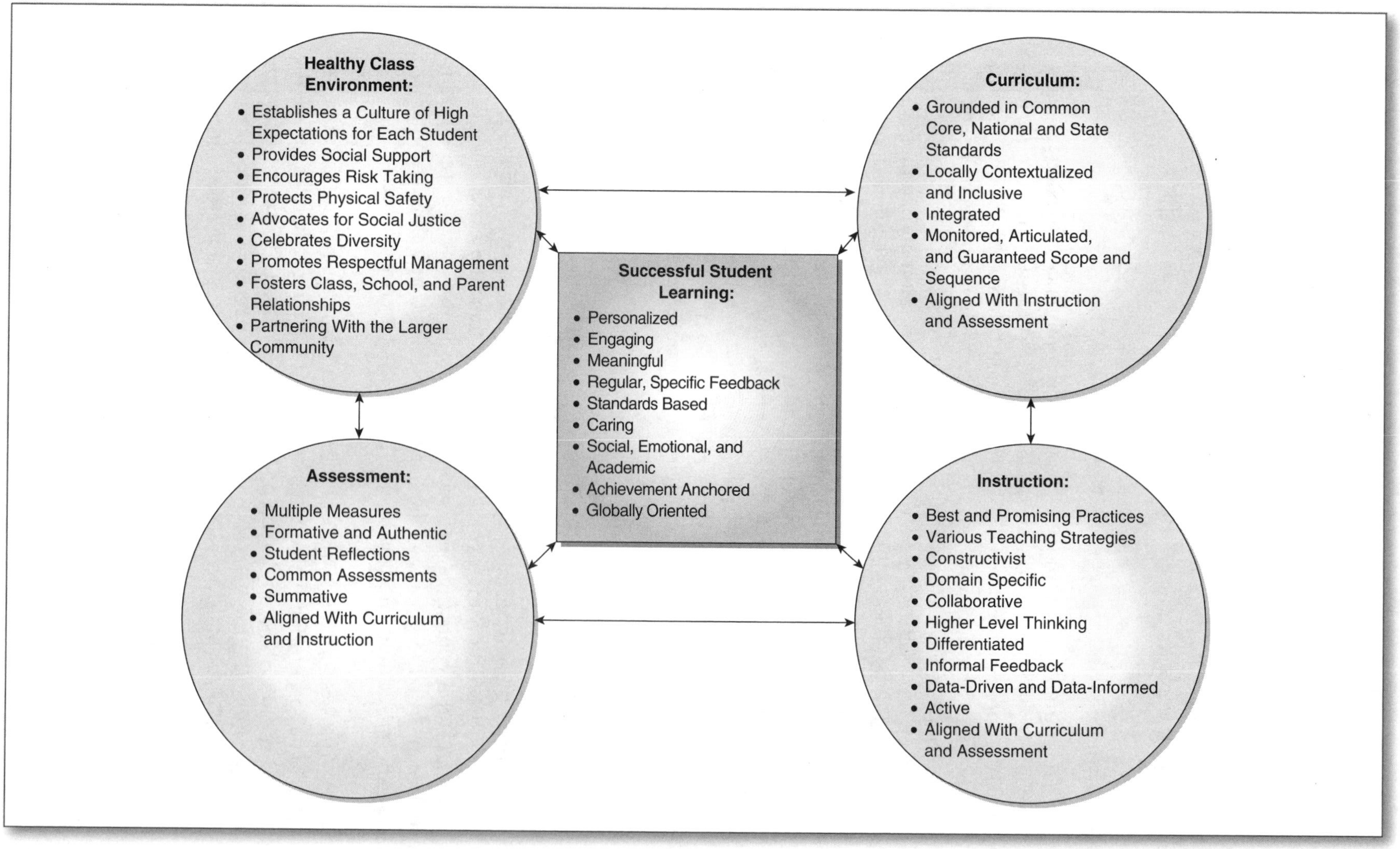

Curriculum:

- Grounded in Common Core, National and State Standards
- Locally Contextualized and Inclusive
- Integrated
- Monitored, Articulated, and Guaranteed Scope and Sequence
- Aligned With Instruction and Assessment

Instruction:

- Best and Promising Practices
- Various Teaching Strategies
- Constructivist
- Domain Specific
- Collaborative
- Higher Level Thinking
- Differentiated
- Informal Feedback
- Data-Driven and Data-Informed
- Active
- Aligned With Curriculum and Assessment

Successful Student Learning:

- Personalized
- Engaging
- Meaningful
- Regular, Specific Feedback
- Standards Based
- Caring
- Social, Emotional, and Academic
- Achievement Anchored
- Globally Oriented

Healthy Class Environment:

- Establishes a Culture of High Expectations for Each Student
- Provides Social Support
- Encourages Risk Taking
- Protects Physical Safety
- Advocates for Social Justice
- Celebrates Diversity
- Promotes Respectful Management
- Fosters Class, School, and Parent Relationships
- Partnering With the Larger Community

Assessment:

- Multiple Measures
- Formative and Authentic
- Student Reflections
- Common Assessments
- Summative
- Aligned With Curriculum and Instruction

components. Thus, if a district has a first-rate group of teachers but a curriculum that lacks coherence, then meaningful and successful student learning may be compromised. Supervisors, teachers, and district administrators should feel free to add components to the Student Learning Nexus Model to meet local contextual needs (e.g., as a tool for brainstorming about the School Improvement Plan). In essence, this model is intended to enrich the conversation about teaching and learning.

Feedback From Students Helps Teachers With Visible Learning. John Hattie's (2009) book *Visible Learning* has struck a chord with many educators. A key research finding on feedback is particularly honest, poignant, and exciting:

> The mistake I was making was seeing feedback as something *teachers provided to students*—they typically did not, although they made the claim that they did it all the time, and most of the feedback they did provide was social and behavioral. It was only when I discovered that feedback was most powerful when it is from the *student to the teacher* that I started to understand it better. . . . Feedback to teachers helps make learning visible. (p. 172)

What makes this finding so exciting for instructional leaders and teachers is that it invites educators to have a *conversation* about how to create classroom cultures that thrive on student "mistakes" and verbal reflections, recognizing that some of those mistakes and reflections (i.e., feedback) provide the fuel for improving one's teaching. It's a conversation with endless possibilities related to teacher and student growth because honest and thoughtful feedback empowers both students and teachers. Student feedback (if we are paying attention!) becomes a gift because it challenges teachers to constantly make midcourse adjustments to fine-tune their repertoire of teaching strategies—always searching for the best ways to help students understand difficult concepts and content.

The Digital Transformation and the Classroom. Supervisors expect to see teachers using various devices and online resources with students to enhance teaching and learning. Thus, when observing, supervisors should consider the following questions: Are best teaching practices and technology integrated to maximize teaching and learning possibilities—or is technology driving the lesson? Are the digital devices and online resources enhancing student feedback? Is technology empowering students as self-directed learners and empowering teachers as guides and coaches (Fairbanks, 2013)? How are teachers and students taking advantage of full access to information? Is digital content being used effectively? If blended learning is used, how are students without access to devices or the Internet at home expected to achieve success? As a leader, how can I level the playing field by creating opportunities for Internet access for those who don't have it? As a supervisor am I doing all I should to support technology savvy effective teachers and teachers who need more technology support to promote student success?

Use Student Work. Using student work during supervisory conferences helps teachers connect their planning, teaching efforts, and expected outcomes with the evidence students produce. Invite teachers to bring student work from the lesson when discussing the lesson outcomes. This provides evidence to discuss: What did the students do? What did they accomplish? Were the objectives and outcomes reached? Were students engaged in meaningful work? In most cases, this is very satisfying for the teacher and gives the principal a feeling for what is taking place in class. One experienced principal recommended considering the following issues and questions during a postobservation conference related to student work:

> Remember, all those wonderful activities may not show meaningful work. Prudently ask, during appropriate conferences: What is the point of the lesson? What are the "learnings"? Do the student products reflect the lesson objectives? Let's look at a range of products, exemplary products, average products, and unsatisfactory products. What are the rubrics? Are aspects of the student work reflective of standards? Keep in mind that the products at the postconference will show if quality work has been going on all year, not just during the two or three conferences.

Build Trust With Evidence. It's easy to draw opinions and conclusions while observing a class, but what really helps a teacher is evidence and description. This is just as true when we are trying to separate fact from fiction in our daily interactions with others. In *Crucial Conversations* (2002), Patterson, Grenny, McMillan, and Switzler advise us to "Separate fact from story by focusing on behavior. . . . Can you *see* or *hear* this thing you're calling a fact? What was the actual behavior" (p. 105)? To illustrate, what is a teacher to make of a supervisory remark such as, "Your lesson just clicked! I liked it!" It may feel good to hear the compliment, but it does not tell a teacher anything about his or her practice and its impact. When talking with teachers following an observation or when writing a lesson evaluation supervisors should just stick to descriptions of behaviors and what they actually saw and heard—the evidence. For example, consider the following description of a classroom math episode: "Four teams of students shared their problem-solving strategies and answered each assigned math problem. Then they shared their team results with other groups. Each student explained one problem and solution to members of the other group. While sharing results, the students manipulated images on their tablets to demonstrate two different solutions to each question. In one paired group four different solutions worked. The students expressed their enthusiasm for the results by asking to extend the time of the lesson so they could share some of their solutions with the whole class. Ms. Fernandez smiled and said, 'Okay, but the solutions better be good ones!' All of the students applauded her response." (Now I understand why the lesson clicked!)

Digital Videos. If a teacher records a lesson for an observation, consider recording only part of the lesson: the opening, the student group work, the teacher modeling, the questioning, or the closure. A 10-minute video will easily lead to a 45-minute conversation. Many teachers record themselves with flip cameras and select excerpts about which to dialogue.

Using Digital Devices: Collecting Observation Data With Smartphones, Tablets, or Laptops. Technology has enabled supervisors to conveniently gather classroom observation data and quickly share the information with teachers by using various digital devices. These devices can be used during traditional observations or during walk-throughs, and teachers and students expect to see them. Of course, teachers need to be informed during faculty, department, or grade-level meetings about any new observation and data-gathering systems that will be implemented. Applications have been developed for the major instructional frameworks and specific teaching or management topics such as student responses, Bloom's taxonomy, cooperative learning, time on task, teacher patterns of movement, wait time, inappropriate student behavior, quality of teacher directions, and specific observed behaviors for walk-throughs. Companies supporting these technologies stress that state and district terminology and evaluation criteria can be entered into the programs to customize the resources for local use. As with any new educational product, it is important that school leaders first pilot techniques to minimize glitches before the instruments are used on a regular basis. Also, some products that immediately summarize observation data (e.g., bar or pie graphs based on walk-throughs) appear to simplify the process. However, be cautious, interpreting the teaching and learning process before describing and having a conversation about these complex events can be misleading. Kim Marshall (2012b) has expressed strong reservations about personal interaction and how these devices are being used,

> It saddens me that so few school leaders take the time to talk to teachers after classroom visits. One of the more dubious practices in U.S. schools these days is administrators dropping into classrooms with clipboards, laptops or tablets, filling out checklists or rubrics, and sending them to teachers. This kind of one-way feedback is superficial, bureaucratic, annoying, and highly unlikely to make a difference. (p. 21)

Include Student Voice. Students can add an important dimension to the evaluation process. One principal recorded the preobservation conference, lesson, and postobservation conference with an experienced member of the staff. The teacher was helping the principal refine his conferencing techniques as he provided feedback on her teaching. The lesson was on dividing fractions. The teacher was very disappointed with how she began the lesson, and she shared this sentiment with the principal and her students after the lesson. She felt that their difficulty during the lesson was due to a lack of clarity on her part. The students told her that she was "way off" regarding her feelings about the lesson; in fact this particular lesson was one of the most challenging and interesting lessons of the school year. The students explained that the lesson really made them think, helped them actually see how to get the answers, and made them realize that more than one correct answer was possible. That experience helped the teacher and supervisor reflect on how difficult it is to assess lesson success. Thank goodness for student voice!

WALK-THROUGHS, INSTRUCTIONAL ROUNDS, SNAPSHOTS, OR DRIVE-BYS

In our book *If I Only Knew: Success Strategies for Navigating the Principalship* (Alvy & Robbins, 1998), we suggest using brief classroom visits as an excellent strategy to celebrate student and teacher success and affirm that the classroom is the center of a school. The popularity of walk-throughs is a welcome addition to the supervisory landscape, as the strategy has helped to reduce teacher isolation while also providing leaders with an opportunity to celebrate classroom success and monitor whether school-wide initiatives are being implemented. As noted earlier in the chapter, research strongly supports the notion that intentional principal visibility is related to student success.

A benefit of walk-throughs is that the technique can be used in several ways. The following options should be considered:

- Supervisors conducting walk-throughs should plan visits at different times during the day to see a variety of subjects taught and to get a feel for how the school "rhythm" may change during the course of a day. It is important that walk-throughs are scheduled on the supervisor's calendar, otherwise they will likely not occur.
- Principals should consider conducting walk-throughs with teachers. Together they can observe classes and discuss important student and teacher behaviors.
- Consider using walk-throughs to support schoolwide initiatives. Thus, if higher-level thinking techniques are being emphasized, the walk-through participants can look for related strategies.
- Teacher leaders and coaches can conduct walk-throughs with new or student teachers to point out effective strategies.
- Middle or high school departments and elementary grade-level teams can schedule walk-throughs to observe department or grade-level techniques or new strategies being piloted. Skretta (2007) recommends "leveraging the strengths of individual teachers for professional development of the entire faculty" (p. 21). Principals can encourage these activities by offering to substitute teach or hire a substitute teacher if funding permits the option.

The long-range potency of the walk-through is described by Granada and Vriesenga (2008) as they reflect on the success of the technique at East Jessamine High School in Nicholasville, Kentucky:

> [The] teachers and students had to adjust to having an administrator in their classrooms frequently. The administrators wondered how instruction would be affected. Within about six weeks, that question was answered as their presence in the classrooms became the norm. Before the walk throughs were implemented, instruction stopped any time an administrator entered a classroom so that the teacher could see what the administrator needed. Now when an administrator enters a classroom at East Jessamine, he or she rarely even gets a glance. A student may look over occasionally and smile or wave, but instruction and learning flow smoothly. Often students are unaware of the administrators' entry or exit. Some freshmen students told their teacher, "The principals are like ninjas, in and out silently." The administrators, in essence, had faded into the background. (p. 26)

Some cautionary notes are worth mentioning concerning walk-throughs. First, many teachers are uneasy about walk-throughs and see the event as a "drive-by" visit that might be used during the evaluation process. Quite rightly, teachers are concerned about a "bad teaching moment" having far-reaching implications. Thus, it is critical that district and school leaders explain to teachers the rationale for walk-throughs and how the process can be used effectively as another way of gathering information about classroom episodes and the culture of a school. Skretta (2007) suggests talking "with teachers beforehand about the importance of informal observations so they are not alarmed by your presence and do not assume that your visit is for student disciplinary reasons" (p. 21). Second, supervisors need to keep in mind that a walk-through is a snapshot of a classroom moment. Supervisors do not remain in the classroom for an extended period, thus they are likely to miss the ebb and flow of a lesson, a teacher's pacing and sequencing, and a student's deliberate understanding of a concept. Third, if districts are using walk-throughs as an evaluative strategy the administrators must be committed to frequent visit during a year, with 20 being a good target. Fourth, Gary Kipp (2012) worries that with principals determined to visit as many classrooms as possible (a good thing), they might be losing "sight of the critical role conversations play in improving professional practice" (p. 38). Kipp suggests adding the term "talk-through" to our supervisory lexicon to remind leaders how important it is to maintain that one-on-one contact. These cautionary points do not diminish the power of a walk-through, but like any technique walk-throughs have benefits and flaws.

Instructional rounds are a variation of walk-throughs. City (2011) states, "The model we've developed to improve practice is based on medical rounds, the primary way that doctors learn and improve their practice." Rounds are intended to be formative, "descriptive and analytic, not evaluative" (p. 37). The basic Instructional Rounds steps include: (1) networking with a small group of teacher or administrative colleagues (four is recommended) or a combination of the two groups, (2) discussing a "problem of practice" that relates to a school or districtwide core teaching and learning issue, (3) visiting three or four classrooms together in small groups usually for about 20–25 minutes (thus longer than walk-throughs), (4) debriefing, usually after all the rounds are completed, (5) "identifying the next level of work" (pp. 38–39). City stresses that a problem of practice (e.g., "Are students able to transfer learning from one content area or grade level to another," p. 40) serves as a filter, enabling the group to focus on one aspect of the classroom.

GUIDELINES RELATED TO EVALUATION AND LEGAL CONCERNS[1]

The legal guidelines related to evaluation are really for only 2 percent of the faculty, but 100 percent of the headaches.

—A principal's voice

Although this chapter certainly emphasizes the professional growth component of supervision and evaluation, there are times when quality assurance necessitates nonrenewal of faculty who, based on their teacher performance, are not meeting the needs of students. Although it is impossible to provide specific legal guidelines that will meet the particular expectations for each state concerning work with marginal teachers and possible nonrenewal, the following broad guidelines can serve as a starting point for principals:

• Pay attention to deadlines! Keep track of observation dates, due dates for written summaries of observations, and employment status deadlines. Concerning dates, know whether the deadlines relate to specific schoolwork days or all calendar days, including weekends, holidays, and other nonteaching days. Deadlines will likely be different for new teachers, tenured teachers, and marginal teachers on probation engaged in an assistance/improvement plan.

• Know the union contract inside and out. For example, are there restrictions on how you can use announced and unannounced observations? Are short observations, walk-throughs, or drop-ins permitted as part of the documented evaluation process?

• Know the state-selected or district instruments for evaluation and observation. Sophisticated teacher evaluation frameworks with performance standards and rubrics demand greater understanding than the more traditional forms. There may be different instruments for new teachers and experienced teachers, for successful teachers on professional growth plans, and for marginal teachers on assistance/improvement plans. Find out whether your own customized observation instruments or forms are acceptable or if district guidelines mandate specific instruments and forms based on district and union agreements.

- Document, document, and document. A paper trail must be maintained if nonrenewal may result based on classroom performance. The documentation should be tied to specific state or district expectations for teacher competency. Make sure the documentation is specific, professional, and includes dates and responses. Assume that notes (anecdotal records) and related e-mails could be made public. These records must be descriptive and factual, not judgmental.

- If it looks like a marginal teacher will be placed on a timeline for improvement with possible nonrenewal of a contract, then the specific teaching problem should be: (a) documented (described) with precise language that provides, (b) a rationale concerning why the behavior is detrimental to student learning, (c) a clear and explicit explanation of instructional performance expectations, and (d) specific recommendations or suggestions for improvement. Although this process is very challenging, school leaders have a moral obligation to students to pursue dismissal of marginal teachers if their performance remains unsatisfactory after following appropriate supervisory procedures.

- A plan for improvement and/or assistance should be based on state laws, providing an adequate warning and timeline for improvement (e.g., 90 days on probation). Although the union contract must be in compliance with state law, it may be more restrictive than state law. Again, know the state laws and the union contract. The improvement plan should clearly indicate the problematic behavior and suggested remediation interventions (e.g., mentoring, workshops, exemplary teaching strategy videos, observations of colleagues, conferences). Of course, the principal must follow up and document whether progress has occurred.

- Often, school district lawyers offer state legal workshops for principals concerning working with marginal teachers and legal issues related to nonrenewal. Although it is critical to attend these workshops, they do not substitute for quality supervision and professional development. Always stay in touch with district administration and legal counsel when nonrenewal is an issue.

- Because of state and federal mandates and new technologies we are in a **transitional period** concerning teacher evaluations. When events move quickly, growing pains are natural and mistakes are inevitable. Not every great idea works in the real world. Since we do not know how the present changes will play out, it is risky to make firm predictions. However, we can call attention to some of the issues and dilemmas that need to be addressed:

  □ Fairly weighing the multiple measures involved in teacher evaluation, including student test scores, observations, and possibly teacher portfolios, parent surveys, and other 360° evaluation alternatives
  □ Aligning state teaching standards with the selected state evaluation framework

> ☐ Providing supervisors with professional development and school-site "rehearsals" to gain knowledge of, and comfort with, the instructional (evaluation) frameworks
>
> ☐ Helping teachers gain knowledge of the frameworks and bringing them on board (while they are also implementing CCSS)
>
> ☐ Selecting the best devices and software applications for implementing evaluation procedures, considering validity, reliability, and user friendly aspects, of the applications; the complexity of teaching and the importance of personal and respectful feedback
>
> ☐ Working with unions and implementing the evaluation systems so all sides focus on meeting the needs of students and thoughtfully addressing teacher professional growth. For the short term, unions are likely to suggest that the evaluation frameworks have been rushed forward too quickly. Questions will include: Are the frameworks valid? Do supervisors have enough knowledge and experience to use the new systems effectively? What will constitute a "below standard" rating on the rubrics, possibly resulting in dismissal?

Finally, it is important to note that even when working with marginal teachers, one must always hope that the result will be successful for both students and teachers. As Tucker (2001) notes,

> Every administrator committed to taking his or her school to the next level of excellence should provide assistance to struggling teachers. They have an ethical obligation to do so because successful remediation affects many people. Students and their parents benefit because it ensures a quality educational experience. For teachers, remediation reflects the school system's concern for its teachers' professional development. Dedicated administrators know that whole-school improvement won't happen unless everyone performs well, and helping each teacher do so is an integral part of an instructional leader's role. (p. 53)

FINAL THOUGHTS ON SUPERVISION AND EVALUATION

Certainly, an effective supervisory process makes a principal a better evaluator when summative evaluations are required. With a good process, there are fewer surprises. Teachers most often respect the process because the principal is familiar with their teaching style, has engaged in conversations with them on teaching, and has seen student performance and work in their classrooms. Probably the most valuable part of the process of helping the principal reflect for the summative evaluation is the teacher's verbal or written analysis of his or her own performance and assessment of student progress, because the analysis reveals much about one's desire and ability to understand the classroom and grow as a professional. Although the evaluation instrument may be selected based on state expectations, in the past these were minimal standards for quality assurance. The new frameworks with evidence-based standards and performance rubrics have raised the bar. Together, the supervision and evaluation processes work to focus both the teacher and the principal in an examination of what contributes to learning for both students and staff. Collectively, these processes can and should support the school's vision of professional growth and student learning.

NOTE

1. The authors wish to thank Les Portner, Sharon Jayne, and Billie Gehres, three recently retired Washington state school administrators, for their assistance concerning these legal guidelines.

REFLECTIONS

This space provides a place for you to write down ideas that have been generated by this chapter, things you want to try, or adaptations of ideas presented here.

1. What are your thoughts regarding the broad definition of supervision provided in this chapter? For example, do you think the definition is realistic?

2. What would be the various considerations when observing and conferencing with the new teacher? The experienced teacher? What other teacher profiles should be considered?

3. What is your philosophy about supervising teachers?

4. What are two or three of your individual goals as a supervisor?

5. For the veteran principal, how have you grown as a supervisor? What areas do you need to strengthen?

6. What are we doing for our best teachers to keep them at the top of their game?

(Continued)

(Continued)

7. What instructional framework has your school district or school selected? What are the strengths and weaknesses of the instruments? What "growing pains" is the district experiencing concerning process and content?

8. If walk-throughs or instructional rounds are used in your district or school, do you think the strategy is being used effectively? Why or why not? Do you have other ideas for maximizing the use of walk-throughs or instructional rounds?

9. What are your predictions concerning the future of the teacher evaluation process?

10. What insights or new questions do you have as a result of reflecting on the ideas presented in this chapter?

Maximizing Feedback About Teaching

Differentiated Professional Growth Options

Without high-quality feedback, people will stagnate—there will be no growth. When people engage in rich conversations, it changes the culture to one of collective efficacy. Shining spots of distinguished practice are not enough to produce rich learning for all kids. Teachers and administrators need to talk with each other, learn, be willing to learn, and see each other as resources so that we are all moving forward in improving practice.

—Laura Lipton (in Armstrong, 2012, p. 5)

REFLECTIONS ON FEEDBACK

Research and practice make it clear that valued feedback and opportunities to use that feedback enhance performance and achievement. John Hattie's (2009) research conducted over several decades revealed that feedback was among the most powerful influences on achievement. But what exactly is feedback that leads to enhanced growth? Grant Wiggins explains that "helpful feedback is goal referenced; tangible and transparent;

actionable; user-friendly (specific and personalized); timely; ongoing; and consistent" (2012, p. 11). Laura Lipton adds, "Feedback that leads to growth and improvement is data-driven, is based on shared definitions and understandings between parties, acts as a foundation for conversation, and sets goals and improves practice by naming strengths and gaps in relation to a clear set of standards" (Armstrong, 2012, pp. 1, 4).

While feedback's value is well established, to have maximum impact, it must be high quality, consistent, and frequent. "The relentless loop of feedback, corrections, and improvement that builds true talent can't happen once every six months" (Bambrick-Santoyo, 2012, p. 29). A principal's worklife, however, makes frequent observations for every staff member an unrealistic goal. Yet, it is clear that teacher development and student achievement are two critical role responsibilities of the instructional leader. So how can this paradox be reconciled? To maximize feedback about teaching and learning in a way that leaves its mark on practice, it is essential to harness the collective knowledge of administrators, teachers, instructional coaches, students, and parents. In addition, feedback to improve practice should be differentiated so that it is perceived as credible, meaningful, valuable, and usable to the receiver. "Education leaders do well to model that which they commend" notes Carol Ann Tomlinson (2012, p. 89), reminding us of the inherent need to model those practices of differentiation of feedback for teachers in the same way we ask teachers to use differentiation of instruction in the classroom.

CREATING THE ENVIRONMENT FOR MAXIMIZING FEEDBACK

To create an environment that supports maximizing feedback about teaching, there must be a shared belief in the culture of the school that every person has the capacity to grow professionally. There must be a sense of both psychological and emotional safety. Genuine trust among professional colleagues is essential. Hattie cautions, "Feedback thrives in conditions of error or not knowing—not in environments where we already know and understand . . . teachers need to welcome error and misunderstanding in their classrooms. This attitude builds trust . . . the simple act of giving feedback won't result in improved student learning—the feedback has to be effective" (2012b, p. 23). Sadler (cited in Hattie, 2012b, p. 153) adds, "In order for feedback to be effective and useful, three conditions have to be met: the learner needs the feedback; the learner receives the feedback and has time to use it; and the learner is willing and is able to use the feedback."

How the feedback is received is influenced by how it is communicated. Consider the difference between, "Can you think of . . . the question itself expresses the potential doubt that the receiver can think of something . . . [and] What might be some ways to . . . which invites exploration of the topic" (Lipton, in Armstrong, 2012, p. 4).

BUILDING A FOUNDATION: GETTING STARTED

Invited feedback about teaching provides teachers with data about the use of particular curricular, instructional, assessment, social and emotional, and classroom management practices and their consequences. The data provide a lens through which teachers can reflect and examine their own behaviors in relation to their impact on student learning. It also provides the basis for a dialogue among colleagues about the thinking involved in planning and delivering instruction as well as assessing the impact on learning. Through the process of receiving feedback, teachers determine what they might do differently if they taught the lesson again. This analysis fosters professional growth, instructional excellence, and, ultimately, student learning.

Traditionally, other than from student to teacher, feedback about instruction has occurred during infrequent supervisory visits. Glickman et al. (2010), when addressing the topic of supervision, referred to a "super vision" of effective instruction. This play on words provides a helpful perspective on supervision and its ultimate capacity-building capability. What is critical is that there is a shared understanding among staff of what effective instruction means—the evidence for which is anchored firmly in student learning. Supervision is a growth-oriented process designed to enhance instruction, curriculum delivery, and assessment practices, primarily as a result of feedback based on classroom observation. Over time, it contributes to developing the teacher's thought process about teaching. Ultimately, it should result in enhanced learning for students.

MOVING TOWARD COLLABORATIVE FEEDBACK

In the past, the supervisory process has been conceptualized as occurring between a principal or supervisor and a teacher. However, with the focus on the school as a Professional Learning Community, many have raised the question about whether the supervisory process should be collaborative as well, to complement the cooperative goal structure of the school. The notion here is that teachers, working closely with students on a daily basis, have the capacity to provide one another with meaningful feedback that ultimately impacts student learning.

Proponents of this belief point to the fact that, in some settings, the individualistic nature of supervision occurring only between principal and teacher is inconsistent with the conceptualization of the school as a learning community where shared discussion and analysis of teaching and its consequences are a treasured part of daily life. As stated earlier, there is much evidence to show that, given the numerous demands on the principal's role, there is limited time for supervisory visits. Hence, with the exception of classroom visits that may occur during Leading and Learning by

Wandering Around, or walk-throughs, in many settings meaningful feedback about teaching becomes rather sparse. If teachers have the option of seeking feedback from other sources—colleagues, students, parents, and self, in addition to the principal—the process of continuous improvement based on frequent opportunities to receive feedback will be enhanced. Student as well as staff learning will flourish. Furthermore, a collaborative process provides an avenue through which to tap the rich knowledge base about teaching that exists in individual classrooms.

However, in spite of the powerful argument for a collaborative approach, some teachers express a desire to maintain the option of receiving the more traditional form of supervisory feedback from one's immediate supervisor.

Together, these points of view about traditional and collaborative practices have led to the accommodation of both in the development of a system of differentiated professional growth options. This approach is timely. Since most principals are requesting that teachers differentiate learning experiences for students, it is important for modeling's sake as mentioned previously, that principals offer teachers differentiated learning experiences rather than one-size-fits-all professional development.

DIFFERENTIATED PROFESSIONAL GROWTH OPTIONS: HOW THE SYSTEM WORKS

The process of providing differentiated professional growth options involves teachers and administrative staff developing professional growth goals for themselves and determining, from a menu of options, how they wish to pursue these goals. The ultimate outcome of this process should be to enhance individual staff members' collective capacity to foster high levels of student learning. The menu might include the following options:

- Reflective clinical supervision
- 360-degree feedback
- Cognitive coaching
- Conversations about student work
- Audio or video analysis
- Drop-in visit
- Student feedback
- Data talk
- Job-embedded learning
- Reflective journals
- Portfolios
- Peer coaching
- Problem solving
- Action research
- Study groups and online discussions
- Lesson study

- Professional book or video talks
- Individual professional growth plans
- Online learning and social networking

In some settings where a high degree of trust exists, these professional growth goals are shared so that staff members become aware of others' interest areas and can support one another. This can become the basis for shared work and networking. In other settings, principals may share their goals with the staff and then meet individually with teachers. Depending on the system and its policies, principals usually have the final decision-making power in the process of determining how goals might be met. In the instance when a staff member needs more direct guidance, this should be provided, especially for nontenured or at-risk, struggling staff.

The differentiated approach fosters positive attitudes and perceptions about teacher-initiated professional growth and creates a schoolwide focus on what contributes to cognition and the development of affective skills. As faculty members experience an environment where reflection, professional dialogue, collaborative study of teaching, and self-analysis become treasured values of the occupational culture, they experience learning about learning and learning about themselves. Collectively, these insights help sensitize staff to the need to replicate, in the classroom for students, those same conditions they have personally experienced. The ultimate goal is student learning.

SOURCES OF FEEDBACK: CATEGORIES AND APPROACHES

There are several sources of feedback: supervisor, principal, assistant principals, peers, self, consultants, parents, and students. To address professional growth goals, one may select from a combination of these. The following paragraphs detail a variety of approaches to providing feedback. Who engages in each of these is largely a decision of the person defining how his or her professional goals will be addressed. The professional growth goals should be grounded in how one's current skill set impacts student learning. It may also include the degree to which one's professional practice reflects the implementation of current initiatives such as the Common Core.

Reflective clinical supervision. This approach, described in detail in Chapter 9, involves a preobservation conference, observation, reflections, and postobservation conference. Discussion and analysis of teaching should be based on a common framework of language, such as the brain research, using the information-processing model. The goal of this process is to assist and support teachers as reflective classroom decision makers.

360-degree feedback. This type of feedback allows staff members "to gather data about themselves from multiple sources in their circles of influence. The fundamental premise is that data gathered from multiple perspectives are more comprehensive and objective than data gathered from only one source" (Dyer, 2001, p. 35). The raters might include superiors, subordinates, peers, parents, students, and community members. The individuals being rated by others also rate themselves. With 360-degree feedback, staff members have the opportunity to compare their views of themselves with the views that others have of them. Karen Dyer, manager of the education sector of the Center for Creative Leadership in Greensboro, North Carolina, writes, "The feedback is powerful because these data identify behaviors that leaders (and other staff members) can work either to strengthen or to diminish. In addition, 360-degree feedback assists them in comparing their performance to stakeholder expectations. The school district can also measure behaviors and characteristics that relate to the values, beliefs, goals, and strategies of the organization. . . . Crucial to using the 360-degree process is trust." Hence, to ensure overall quality, effectiveness, and integrity, Dyer suggests that five key factors be addressed in the 360-degree feedback process:

- Feedback is developmental, not evaluative.
- A coaching or mentoring session accompanies feedback.
- The development of a goal or action plan follows feedback.
- Feedback data belong to the receiver.
- The process is confidential. (p. 36)

One teacher who chose this approach reported that the data she received from students, regarding which of her instructional behaviors helped them learn best, provided a compelling case for her to continue differentiating instruction.

Cognitive coaching. This is a nonjudgmental process built around a planning conference, an observation, and a reflecting conference. It is not dependent on a common language. Rather, it involves using clarifying questions, pressing for specificity, reframing, and other communication tools so that colleagues who don't share a common language can still communicate. Anyone in the educational setting can become a cognitive coach—teachers, administrators, department chairs, or support personnel. A coaching relationship may be established among teachers, administrators and teachers, and/or administrators and fellow administrators (Costa & Garmston, 1994, p. 2).

In some districts, cognitive coaching skills are being used by school secretaries, counselors, bus drivers, aides, students, parents, playground supervisors, and cafeteria workers to enhance communication and establish trusting relationships. The goals of cognitive coaching, according to Costa and Garmston (1994), are "establishing and maintaining trust, facilitating mutual learning and enhancing growth toward holonomy [which is defined as] individuals acting autonomously while simultaneously acting interdependently with the group" (p. 13).

Conversations about student work. Conversations about student work engage small groups of teachers in examining the work they design for students and the results of that work. Phil Schlechty (2001), noted author of *Shaking Up the Schoolhouse,* states, "Teachers do not cause learning. . . . Rather, they design activities for students from which students will learn" (p. 83). Schlechty believes that when work is "designed right" and when the "right content" is addressed in the work offered to students, students learn. Hence, he says, "The primary source of variance in student learning is the quality of the work the teachers and the schools provide to students" (p. 84).

In conversing about student work, teachers usually follow a protocol. There are a variety available. Schlechty (2001) presents 10 design qualities that are likely to make schoolwork more meaningful and engaging. The design qualities are Content and Substance, Organization of Knowledge, Product Focus, Clear and Compelling Standards, Protection from Adverse Consequences for Initial Failure, Affirmation of the Significance of Performance, Affiliation, Novelty and Variety, Choice, and Authenticity (p. 107). Teachers in one district used these qualities as the basis for collaborative planning of student assignments and reflection after the assignments were given and student work collected. They noted the positive impact this process had on staff and student learning.

Audio or video analysis. This involves an individual recording him or herself (e.g., with a flip camera or smartphone), reviewing the recording either alone or with colleagues, and reflecting on the thinking, behavior, and outcomes derived from the performance.

Drop-in visit. This activity usually occurs when an individual drops in to a classroom meeting or presentation and leaves a note containing an observation or probing question.

Student feedback. "Harvard professor Ronald Ferguson and his Tripod Project colleagues have found that students are quite astute at sizing up teachers' instructional competence when they are asked about observable classroom behaviors in kid friendly language" (Marshall, 2012a, p. 52).

Data talk. This activity engages the teacher and teacher-chosen colleagues in analyzing disaggregated data and dialogue about which instructional and curricular practices are working well and which need to be changed. The goal is to help every student thrive.

Job-embedded learning. Teachers coplan and share professional learning with colleagues. Topics are based on current initiatives such as CCSS and student needs.

Reflective journals. Time for reflection fosters analysis. Writing about thoughts and perceptions after experiences causes one to think about behaviors and consequences. For example, when a teacher or principal thinks about instructional and curricular planning in relation to student learning, this activity promotes an analysis that adds to his or her own knowledge base about what promotes learning. The ability to think critically about one's professional performance is a cultivated skill that enables one to grow. This also entails exposing one's inadequacies and reaching out to other sources of knowledge (if journals are shared) within and outside of the school to solve instructional dilemmas. Journal formats may include a variety of forms: free writing, mapping, interactive journals, reaction, contemplation, elaboration, or cause-and-effect. Journals may be in traditional form or electronic. Once journal writing becomes a regular professional practice, reflection will become habit. Looking through past writings, one is often able to note growth and insights that become cause for celebration!

Portfolios. The portfolio approach is designed to promote reflection and analysis as well as demonstrate professional growth. Portfolios are generally a collection of artifacts that represent growth in thinking, planning, delivering, and assessing teaching. They may be in physical or electronic form. The goal of these endeavors is to promote student learning. They might also demonstrate growth in a particular area (e.g., integrating technology, interdisciplinary planning). Portfolios should not simply be scrapbooks of lesson plans and student work, but rather they should demonstrate progress.

Many teachers who use this approach elect to designate a portfolio focus such as literacy or implementing a specific initiative such as CCSS or Response to Intervention. Typical contents of a portfolio may be audio or video, student work, lesson plans, samples of tasks, and snapshots. Sometimes student or parent letters or graduate work related to the portfolio theme are included.

Peer coaching. Peer coaching occurs when two or three colleagues with similar role status join together to preconference, observe, and postconference with one another. Often, the cognitive coaching model is employed. It is critical that the inviting teacher, who requests feedback, steer the focus of the observation and determine the parameters of the discussion. The content of peer coaching activities should be confidential—shared only between the colleagues engaged in the process. Many schools hire math and literacy coaches who serve as experts within a school setting and add to teachers' repertoires. Models vary, but typically coaches, who may be full or part-time, instruct and conduct demonstration lessons as well. Two critical components of the peer coaching process are communication and trust.

Problem solving. Sessions are designed to encourage staff to share problems and collaboratively problem solve in a way that fosters learning. A variety of problem-solving approaches may be used. Not only do staff members learn as a result of this process, but they also use the problem-solving tools in their classrooms and meetings.

Action Research. Staff members who elect to participate in Action Research select an area of focus, develop a research question, identify a data collection plan, and create a data analysis plan. They identify who will assist in data collection and analysis as well as how findings will be posted and used. Data are collected and analyzed. Findings are described, summarized, and reported. The goal of Action Research should be to identify essential understandings about what contributes to student learning.

Study groups and online discussions (e.g., wikis, blogs). This structure provides staff with the opportunity to select a topic or theme and identify ways that they will study it. For example, one study group identified the theme of working with at-risk youth. Their mechanisms for studying included discussions of current practice, analysis of case studies, selected journal readings, a field trip to a local prison and dialogue with prisoners, and readings from books. Members of the group kept journals about insights and experiences. As they learned and applied ideas and practices in the classroom, they frequently met to share experiences. Some teachers and administrators decided to begin student study groups as a result of their experiences as adult learners. Some groups enrich their study group experiences with online discussions using wikis or blogs.

Lesson study. Lesson study engages teachers in codeveloping lessons. After a lesson is taught, professional colleagues reflect on teaching practices that foster student learning. Catherine Lewis (2002), writing about lesson study conducted in Japanese classrooms, describes five characteristics of this process. "They are lessons:

- observed by other teachers
- planned collaboratively
- designed to bring to life in a lesson a particular goal or vision of education
- recorded
- discussed with co-teachers or planners and sometimes an outside educator or researcher." (pp. 59–60)

Teachers report that this ongoing process is meaningful, helps them see their teaching, and fosters learning.

Professional book or video talks. These talks center on a particular book or article series in which staff members voluntarily indicate interest. At one school, for example, a weekly book talk was organized using John Hattie's (2012b) *Visible Learning for Teachers* as a focus for discussion. At another school, a book talk was organized to address *Understanding by Design Guide to Creating High-Quality Units* by Grant Wiggins and Jay McTighe (2013). At another, Charlotte Danielson and colleagues' (2009) *Implementing the Framework for Teaching in Enhancing Professional Practice: An ASCD Action Tool* was the focus of the book talk. A leadership team at a high school chose *Learning from Lincoln: Leadership Practices for School Success* (Alvy & Robbins, 2010a) for their book talk focus. What is essential when implementing book talks is that there are specific plans to use the content of the sessions in the classroom. This is often missing in the implementation process. Several schools conduct video talks. For example, they may watch videos of lessons from the Teaching Channel and then dialogue about their implications for practice.

Individual professional growth plans. This growth option accommodates the individual who prefers to pursue independent study. For example, one teacher wanted to increase his instructional repertoire. He chose to study Project Based Learning and Socratic Seminars. He read books and articles as well as watched videos and visited classrooms where these practices were being used. With this background, he began writing lesson plans to employ these models in his daily teaching. He kept samples of his plans and student work associated with these lessons in a portfolio.

Online learning and social networking (e.g., webinars, podcasts, courses, Facebook, Twitter, wikis, and blogs). These professional development activities enable individuals to engage in a range of online learning experiences from personal learning networks to options sponsored by major professional organizations and universities. Social networking options include blogs, wikis, Facebook, and Twitter. Universities and professional organizations offer online courses, webinars, and virtual conferences. A cautionary note: although online networking is enticing, designers are still grappling with how to replicate the value of face-to-face interaction. How do you replicate the spontaneous laughter that bursts out in a session? Or that moment in time when the presenter looks out at an audience and observes they are visibly moved by an experience?

SELF-ASSESSMENT: ESTABLISHING BENCHMARKS OF PROGRESS

In addition to developing professional growth goals and identifying which approaches will be used to address them, it is important that each staff member who participates in a differentiated professional growth options program identifies benchmarks of progress with projected dates of completion. For example, an early portfolio benchmark might be the decision about identifying categories into which items will be organized. Another might be the creation of a portfolio theme or goal. In addition to benchmarks, resources needed—human and material—should be noted. The benchmark target dates should be reviewed quarterly and progress celebrated. The final benchmark, no matter which approach is taken, needs to be evidence that teacher learning is impacting student learning.

INDIVIDUAL REFLECTION AND INSTITUTIONAL RENEWAL

It has been said that an event does not become an experience until one has time to reflect. Reflection is a precious resource in settings where most activities are characterized as fast paced, involving a constant stream of decision making. The tools for differentiated professional growth options are many. They provide choice for different types of adult learners who have a variety of interests and are at a variety of stages in their careers. What they have in common is the capacity to foster reflection and, potentially, an enduring desire to learn more about educational craft. Ultimately, the result of these activities should be an increased capacity to serve students and foster high levels of learning.

Implementing a system of professional growth options provides recognition of the need to nourish the professional growth of every individual in the school and to stimulate a collaborative effort to pursue learning about learning. Through this process, the entire institution becomes a richer knowledge source with increased capacity to serve its adult and student learners.

REFLECTIONS

This space provides a place for you to write down ideas that have been generated by this chapter, things you want to try, or adaptations of ideas presented here.

1. What opportunities exist for teachers and students to receive feedback at the school in which you work?

2. How does the concept of differentiated professional growth options fit with your philosophy regarding professional growth?

3. What might be some advantages and disadvantages of differentiated professional growth options?

4. What professional growth options do you prefer? Would you add any?

5. How might differentiated professional growth options support teachers in their efforts to help students address challenging state and national standards?

6. What insights or new questions do you have as a result of reflecting on the ideas presented in this chapter?

11

Building a Collaborative School

The Power of Teacher Leadership and Community

If you want to go quickly, go alone; if you want to go far, go together.

—African proverb

Each student's opportunity to thrive increases when the context in which he or she learns is characterized by genuine collaboration. Collaborative work among professional colleagues who enjoy trusting relationships increases the organizational capacity to solve problems, provides for skill based and emotional support, and creates opportunities for teacher leadership. The end result? Staff and student learning. While abundant research substantiates the inherent relationship between collaborative cultures and student achievement, and many working models exist, authentic examples of schools that truly function as collaborative communities of learners are sparse, compared to those that are rooted in traditional isolation or those that masquerade as Professional Learning Communities (PLCs).

"Schools rise and fall based on the quality of the teamwork that occurs within their walls. Well-functioning leadership and teaching teams are essential to the continuous improvement of teaching and learning. That is particularly true when schools have clearly articulated, stretching aspirations for the learning of all their students. Effective teams strengthen leadership, improve teaching and learning, nurture relationships, increase job satisfaction, and provide a means for mentoring and supporting new teachers and administrators" (Sparks, 2013 p. 28).

This chapter will explore a vision of a collaborative school, obstacles to collaboration, the rationale for collaborative structures, the prerequisites and building blocks for collaboration, necessary conditions, collaborative learning–focused activities, and collaborative roles.

PORTRAIT OF A COLLABORATIVE SCHOOL: A PROFESSIONAL LEARNING COMMUNITY

Imagine a school where teachers work on teams to design curriculum, plan instruction, develop authentic assessment tasks based on specific standards, analyze data and plan instructional interventions, problem solve, counsel students, support each other, and teach. Teachers and other school leaders collaborate to design and participate in professional growth activities. As part of this effort, they peer coach with one another. Their focus is learning about learning. When one walks into the faculty room, the dialogue is about teaching and learning. There is a parent-teacher-student organization that meets regularly. Their work focuses on collaboration to support learning. When one visits classrooms, often cooperative learning is observed. At the classroom level, the students experience the same type of collaboration and respect that adults model at the building level. Teachers, the principal, and assistant principal work with students on the student council. Support staff, including bus drivers, cafeteria workers, custodial staff, instructional technology aides, office personnel, and playground supervisors, frequently meet to receive training and to discuss how they can facilitate and enhance the learning process.

Administrators and instructional staff meet frequently and share decision making to promote better and lasting decisions about the quality of the workplace and learning. There is open communication at all levels. Trust exists. People are committed to values, beliefs, and activities that focus on learning.

This school or collaborative center for learning extends its activities to include partnerships with parents and the community as well as local businesses. There is two-way dialogue about what skills students need to be successful in both school and life. Students develop important life skills as a result of service projects they do in the community. Community members attend school activities, and school community members take part in local civic activities. Business leaders and school staff attend shared professional development activities. There are learning fairs where all who contribute to learning are recognized and celebrated for their efforts.

AN IMAGE OF REALITY: OBSTACLES TO COLLABORATION

The preceding scenario is far from reality in many schools. "Collaboration, it turns out, is easier to value than it is to implement . . . the challenges to collaboration include a tradition of autonomy in classrooms, time and scheduling constraints, lack of supportive leadership, and pressure for individual accountability" (Armstrong, 2011, p. 1). The history of the teaching profession is rooted in norms of isolation, stemming from the original "school"—an isolated one-room schoolhouse. Thus professional isolation is a condition familiar to many teachers. In many of today's schools, this one-room schoolhouse structure is repeated every few yards down the corridor. In fact, Maeroff (1993) concluded that teachers go about their jobs as if each classroom were a separate building. Although classroom endeavors are largely communal—one teacher interacting with several students simultaneously—professional interactions within schools often tend to be one on one. A principal meets with a teacher in a supervisory visit or communicates about a particular student. A teacher inquires of another about a particular curricular issue. Teaching, in the main, tends to be a solitary, private act with regard to adult interaction. Whole-faculty gatherings for professional interaction offer one potential forum for articulation and communication about learning. Yet, in many cases, there are collective bargaining agreements that limit faculty meetings to one a month or, in some schools, one a semester!

Sometimes perceived as an intrusion on planning time—or, as a result of past experiences, not worthwhile—time for professional collaboration among colleagues is limited within many workplaces. In many schools, the schedule would need to be altered to create common planning time for professional colleagues to address Common Core or articulate and integrate curriculum and plan meaningful learning experiences.

Many recognition traditions tend to be individualistic as well, such as "Teacher of the Year" or "Staff Member of the Month." Success is defined as making it alone. As a result of these conditions and traditions in some schools, teachers seldom have the opportunity to experience the benefits of collaborative work and, as a consequence, lack the values and beliefs necessary to sustain collaboration. It seems ironic that the very individuals who are being asked to foster cooperative learning experiences for the students in their classrooms are sometimes not encouraged to engage in similar experiences with their professional colleagues. This lack of personal experience, in some instances, limits one's awareness of the subtleties that influence collaboration as well as the feelings and opportunities it brings. Some school staffs, however, have committed to challenge traditional isolation and have created cultures of learning-focused colleagues. They operate as PLCs.

THE CASE FOR COLLABORATION

Schools serve students best when staff members engage in collaborative work, the National Education Association and American Federation of

Teachers have endorsed the notion that educators should work collaboratively. "The National Commission on Teaching and America's Future (NCTAF) also call on educators to work as members of a professional learning community" (DuFour, 2011, p. 59).

The NCTAF's president wrote

> Quality teaching is not an individual accomplishment, it is the result of a collaborative culture that empowers teachers to team up to improve student learning beyond what any of them can achieve alone. . . . The idea that a single teacher, working alone, can know and do everything to meet the diverse learning needs of 30 students every day throughout the school year has rarely worked, and it certainly won't meet the needs of learners in years to come. (Carroll, 2009, p. 13)

In a study conducted by Odden and Archibald (2009) of schools and districts that doubled student achievement, the authors note, "It should be no surprise that one result of the multiplicity of activities was a collaborative, professional school culture . . . what is commonly called a 'professional learning community'" (p. 78). Hargreaves and Fullan assert that collaboration is key to improving schools for students and their teachers. In their book, *Professional Capital: Transforming Teaching in Every School* (2012), the authors address the critical roles that human and social capital play in sustained school improvement. Human capital addresses the qualities of individuals such as a teacher's knowledge and skills. Social capital is the ability of groups to work collectively and effectively toward school improvement. It includes the relationships among professional colleagues that increase the collective capacity of staff to serve students, school, or system.

Jan O'Neill and Ann Conzemius (2002), in "Four Keys to a Smooth Flight," report that "schools showing continuous improvement in student results are those whose cultures are permeated by: shared focus; reflective practices; collaboration and partnerships; and an ever increasing leadership capacity" (p. 15) characterized by "individuals who focus on student learning, reflect on student assessments, and learn as a collaborative team" (p. 17). Ann Lewis, quoted in an article by Mike Schmoker (2004), notes that schools that function as PLCs are four times more likely to be improving academically than those which operate in isolation.

In addition to the research, teachers report that their work is becoming increasingly more complex. Many report that students today have different needs and problems. A large number of teachers speak of increasing classroom demands and a discontented public. These difficult times point to the need for colleagues to join together in addressing them to ease the individual burden they pose. In the *MetLife Survey of the American Teacher*, teachers reported much greater job satisfaction when they had opportunities for regular collaboration (MetLife, 2012).

Research and experience tell us that collaboration makes a difference. Roland Barth, former director of the Principal's Center at Harvard University, once shared with a convocation of principals, "Four years of public school teaching—and 10 years as a principal—convince me that the nature of relationships among adults who inhabit a school has more to do with a school's quality and character, the accomplishments of its pupils, and the professionalism of its teachers than any other factor."

Judith Warren Little (1982), in a keynote address to mentor teachers in Napa, California, observed that in collaborative settings, such as the teachers' room, when the dialogue focused on teaching and learning, the school typically was improving. This was not the case when the teachers' talk focused on griping about students, administration, or one another.

Similarly, the late Susan Rosenholtz (1989) studied 78 schools and characterized them as "stuck," "in-between," or "moving." The moving schools were found to be learning enriched. Their environments were characterized by shared purpose and direction, teacher collaboration, teacher on-the-job learning, and teacher certainty (efficacy). In these settings, there was evidence of teacher commitment and student learning. Rosenholtz noted,

> In the choreography of collaborative schools, norms of self-reliance appeared to be selfish infractions against the school community. With teaching defined as inherently difficult, many minds tended to work better than a few. Here requests for and offers of advice and assistance seemed like moral imperatives and colleagues seldom acted without foresight and deliberate calculation. Teacher leaders . . . reached out to others with encouragement, technical knowledge to solve classroom problems, and enthusiasm for learning new things. (p. 208)

In the learning-enriched settings, Rosenholtz (1989) found that principals played a critical role in contributing to "an abundant spirit of continuous improvement" where no one ever stopped learning. They did this through "frequent and useful evaluations which seemed also a powerful mechanism for delivery on the promise of school improvement as they also served as guides for future work." In addition to evaluation, these principals often orchestrated collaborative relations between more and less successful teachers. Teachers came to realize that these relationships helped contribute to classroom success. Having experienced the power of these alliances with other professionals, teachers desired to continue such relationships. Collaborative principals were found who "uniquely rewove schools that had come altogether unraveled" (Rosenholtz, 1989, p. 208). In contrast, principals who seemed

> unsure of their technical knowledge and concerned with their own self-esteem, did teachers and students an enormous disservice. In protecting their turf, even the smallest attempts by teachers to solve school or classroom problems were met by distance, intimidation, or defeat. Most often, it was here teachers learned the unassailable lesson that they must shoulder classroom burdens by themselves. . . . [N]o teacher could impose upon another. (p. 207)

In an article titled "How Our Schools Could Be," Deborah Meier (1995) emphasized

> When schools see themselves as membership communities, not service organizations, parents and teachers discuss ideas, argue about purposes and exercise judgment, because taking responsibility for making important decisions is at the heart of what it means to be well educated. Students can't learn unless the adults who must show them the way practice what they preach. (pp. 369–370)

Indeed, William Cunningham and Donn Gresso (1993) in *Cultural Leadership* state that "collegiality is the most important element in the success of and commitment to school improvement." Robert Eaker and Janel Keating (2008) note

> Never before has there been such widespread agreement among researchers and practitioners regarding the most promising approach (Professional Learning Communities) to significantly improve schools. . . . [However] the concept will have little impact on schools unless professional learning community practices become embedded into day to day culture. . . . [C]ollaboratively developed shared values and commitments can be a powerful tool for shaping school culture. (p. 15)

Three cultural shifts are critical for PLCs to be sustained, Eaker and Keating (2008) explain. First,

> a shift in fundamental purpose from teaching to learning. This shift is seismic. . . . Second, a shift in the work of teachers. . . . [T]eachers organize into high performing, collaborative teams. . . . [T]hird, a shift in focus. Their focus shifts from inputs to outcomes and from intentions to results. (p. 15)

Thus, proponents of the research on collaboration and those experienced in it report "together, we are better than alone." Yet achieving the goal of collaboration is a distant target in many schools. Therefore, the movement toward it must be gradual. Gradual change allows for the provision of experiences so that individuals have the opportunity to participate in collective activities that will build the necessary values, beliefs, commitments, and desire for continued collaboration.

MOVING TOWARD COLLABORATION

Because the collaborative experience is an uncommon one in many schools, the initial activities designed to foster the development of values and desires for collaborative work and, eventually, the creation of norms for collaborative practice need to be introduced, facilitated, and structured by someone or some group outside or within the organization. Expect resistance. Staff members do not always perceive the need for this type of experience. Collaboration may be a foreign activity. People may not see a purpose for collaboration and view it as an invasion of privacy. Furthermore, adults have a lot to lose—especially their professional image and self-esteem. It is important that a staff's initial experiences with collaboration do not require them to put their professional selves on the line. Rather, the experiences should be designed to be "low risk," that is, activities that do not require participants to expose professional knowledge, skills, or talent. Examples of this might be reading and analyzing articles from professional journals, suggesting implications for practice, discussing challenges of Common Core State Standards, or watching videos of lessons posted on the Teaching Channel and discussing their applicability to one's practice.

As individuals become more comfortable with one another, they will be more willing to expose their professional selves. As they benefit from this type of collegial activity, they may come to value and seek additional opportunities for collaboration with colleagues. As individual values and beliefs within organizations begin to change, the organizations change. And as individual values that celebrate collective action develop, new traditions and collaborative practices will emerge. An example of this comes from Central Park East Secondary School in New York City:

Another priority for us was creating a setting in which all members of the community were expected to engage in the discussion of ideas and in "the having of their wonderful ideas," as Eleanor Duckworth (from Harvard University) has put it. "One of our most prominently stated, up-front aims was the cultivation of what we came to call 'Habits of Mind'—habits that apply to all academic and nonacademic subject matter and to all thoughtful human activities." The five we came up with are not exhaustive, but they suggest the kinds of questions that we believed a well-educated person raises about his or her world.

- How do we know what we think we know? What's our evidence? How credible is it?
- Whose viewpoint are we hearing, reading, seeing? What other viewpoints might there be if we changed our position—our perspective?
- How is one thing connected to another? Is there a pattern here?
- How else might it have been? What if? Supposing that?
- What difference does it make? Who cares?

In order to carry out our basic mission of teaching students to use their minds well and preparing them to live productive, socially useful and personally satisfying lives, we approach curriculum with these habits as a backdrop and specific "essential questions" at the core. (Meier, 1995, p. 371)

Judith Warren Little offers a cautionary note about

> when people are brought together to do work that is defined by others . . . data analysis, looking at evidence, mapping out standards, aligning curriculum and assessment. All of that may be really valuable work. The question is who owns it? So the leadership task becomes both organizing the school . . . to support that kind of ambitious work and creating conditions where people really endorse and claim it as central parts of what it means to be professional. If working as a community doesn't carry value added over what teachers are able to accomplish independently, then it won't be worth the transactional costs, the investment of time and the competition with what teachers feel that they have to do individually. (quoted in Crow, 2008, p. 54)

NECESSARY CONDITIONS FOR A COLLABORATIVE SCHOOL

In a collaborative school, all staff members engage in the study of learning and those practices that facilitate the learning process. The school becomes a PLC with a focus on continuous improvement. Although no specific recipe exists to make this a reality, Rebecca and Rick DuFour described some key ingredients at the 2002 Association for Supervision and Curriculum Development conference. These included "shared vision, mission, values, goals, collaborative teams, collective inquiry, action orientation, commitment to continuous improvement, and results orientation."

Tracy Crow (2013) reflects, "If time to collaborate were the only resource necessary to create high-performing teams, then countless schools would be achieving at the higher levels that effective collaboration facilitates. But time for collaboration isn't enough." Being able to know what work to focus on and the skills necessary to do the work are key. DuFour (2011) describes the right work: "Educators in a PLC work collectively to develop a guaranteed and viable curriculum to ensure that students have access to the same essential knowledge and skills regardless of the teacher to whom they are assigned. The team gathers ongoing information regarding the learning of their students through a comprehensive assessment process that includes common formative assessments developed by the [PLC] team. The team then jointly analyzes the evidence of student learning from the assessments and uses the information to improve the professional practice of the individual members and the collective effectiveness of the team" (p. 61). Students receive the support they need, as a consequence of this process, to achieve at high levels.

The process skills necessary to do collaborative work include creating an understanding that groups go through a variety of developmental stages as they evolve into a team, developing agreements about how collaborative work will take place, learning communication skills for listening and talking together, honoring team members perspectives, making decisions about how decisions will be made and how conflicts will be resolved, determining shared goals and a vision for collective work, and building trust among professional colleagues (adapted from Crow, 2013).

Yet, in some schools, individuals might not feel safe to demonstrate these behaviors. In schools where cultures of isolation exist, the path to collaboration requires that staff members change the way they think and relate to one another. One principal commented, "You want people to feel 'Hey, I'm part of this,' but it's hard to do when what is modeled is 'dog eat dog.'"

"Teachers are more likely to cooperate when barriers to common action are removed and they feel their problems are shared" (Bird & Little, 1984). When this is the case, teachers, inspired by a common purpose, may be able to bring about change at both the classroom and school levels.

Critical to the development of a collaborative school is the notion that collaboration cannot be forced. Therefore, groups of colleagues who desire joint work should be supported with resources to pursue it. Others, who have not yet developed values for collaboration, may be exposed to opportunities for collective action. Wells Junior High School, in Wells, Maine, developed a norm asserting the following: "Everyone has the right to participate. No one must. If you choose not to, however, you must go along with decisions of the collective group. If you choose to disagree verbally, we will take time with you to work out the disagreement."

The focus of collaborative work must be its ultimate impact on students. To that end, colleagues must engage in work that ultimately leads to a heightened awareness of the conditions necessary for learning to occur. In a collaborative workplace focused on learning, all staff assumes collective responsibility for the professional welfare and growth of both students and colleagues. For this to occur, however, requires—for many schools—a fundamental change in the school's culture. In a collaborative culture, the core values, which are reflected in the practices, reward structures, rules, sanctions, and traditions of the school, must be characterized by a spirit of curiosity about teaching and learning and a belief in joint work. When such a culture exists, staff members join together to share the responsibility of curriculum, instruction and assessment, developing and executing plans to address the specific needs of at-risk students, problem solving classroom frustrations, developing students' reflective and analytical skills, developing social and emotional intelligence, and creating meaningful academic tasks. They also celebrate one another's accomplishments and share the learning implicit in these feats. This recognition serves as an intrinsic motivator, creates synergy, and perpetuates the belief that "together we are better than alone." Cooperative goal structures are, as a consequence, reinforced and advanced.

Each school differs in how it evolves to have a culture of collaboration. Leadership; the history of professional development; experiences of the staff; and existing norms, values, and beliefs will influence the development of a collaborative workplace. However, there are some specific activities that tend to take place in a developmental way. Collaboration tends to emerge as staff members move from relationships characterized by congeniality, to cooperation, and then to collegiality (Figure 11.1). How much time is spent in each of these stages will be a function of the existing characteristics of an individual school.

The collegiality that exists when staff members collaborate is not created overnight. In fact, the building blocks for collegiality go beyond work and take considerable time. Thus, when a school principal visits a teacher or other staff member who has experienced a family crisis or is recovering from a serious operation or accident, he or she often finds that sharing the moment of crisis is invaluable in building trust. At times, several activities—some congenial, some cooperative, some collegial—might take place simultaneously.

A teacher and a principal, reflecting on how their staff grew to become a collaborative school noted, "We had come to know each other as human beings . . . sharing about our families, interests, and sports. This was essential to build the trust so you can bare your soul with your colleagues and say, 'Here's the problem.' To be intellectually honest requires a foundation of trust." They described a continuum:

As a staff moves from left to right on the continuum, trust increases among colleagues. This continuum is significant in that it reminds one that if a basic respect for one another as human beings does not exist, people will experience a more difficult time collaborating.

Hargreaves and Dawe (1989) provide a useful typology for considering the impact of school culture on the development of a collaborative workplace. They suggest that there are four types of cultures:

- *Fragmented individualism*—the traditional form of teacher isolation
- *Balkanization*—subgroups and cliques operating as separate subentities
- *Contrived collegiality*—leading to a proliferation of unwanted contacts among teachers that consume already scarce time with little to show for it
- *True collaborative cultures*—"deep personal enduring cultures central to teachers' daily work" (p. 14)

Thinking about these cultures, one could assume that if the nature of relationships among adults in a school is characterized by individualism or balkanization, it is very probable that individuals will not take much of a risk when revealing their professional selves in working with others.

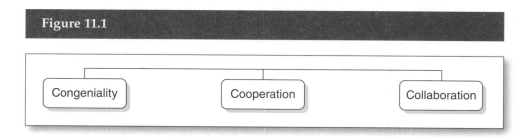

Figure 11.1

Congeniality   Cooperation   Collaboration

Therefore, when planning activities to foster the development of a collaborative workplace, low-risk activities in which individuals' professional knowledge is not at stake would be more likely to engage staff members than high-risk activities in which individuals might be asked to display their knowledge publicly. Cultures in which contrived collegiality exists might be transformed by inviting staff members to come together and share activities that have personal meaning for each of them.

Although congenial activities build rapport and community, it is critical to move swiftly into collegial work. However, congenial activities may continue to be interspersed. The following portrays a range of activities and examples as well as illustrates the difference between congenial tasks and collegial tasks.

Congenial activities. These are designed to create a sense of comfort with one another as human beings. The experiences typically are not professionally focused. Examples might include potluck lunches, volleyball games, swap meets to exchange educational resources, or Friday afternoon gatherings.

Collegial, professionally focused experiences. These develop interest, respect, and cooperation among and between individuals as professional colleagues. The focus of collegial interactions tends to be curriculum, instructional practice, assessment, and data analysis. Ultimately, the results of these activities must be an enhanced capacity to serve students and a staff commitment to help every student succeed. These are represented by a broad range of activities.

Low-risk activities do not require participants to expose their professional knowledge and skills. Rather, these activities are designed to raise awareness of the value of multiple perspectives and a realization of the resources that may exist beyond one's classroom door in neighboring classrooms. These tend to create a desire for collaborative work. Examples might include a cooperative learning activity in which a small group of teachers read different journal articles on CCSS or integrating reading across the curriculum and then meet to discuss them.

Medium-risk activities require professionals to expose some of their professional knowledge and skills. These activities generally occur outside of one's classroom and may include such tasks as professional sharing of successful practices, problem solving, or developing common assessments. These tend to build a desire for more knowledge about content areas or teaching practices. Examples might include workshops about teaching reading, writing, or thinking skills across content areas, working with English language learners, using technology in the curriculum, learning about research on the brain, or practicing specific instructional strategies associated with fostering student achievement.

High-risk activities require professionals to expose their professional knowledge and skills. These might include the rigorous examination of teaching, curricular, or assessment practices and their consequences. Training to prepare staff members for this type of collegial work might include sessions on conferencing skills, classroom observations, and data collection. Examples of high-risk activities might include peer coaching, mentoring, conversations about student work, lesson study, instructional walk-throughs, and learning walks.

Because there is an intrinsic similarity between the goals of the activities discussed in the previous list and the goals of supervision—the development of knowledge and practices regarding staff and student learning—in some schools that have actualized true collaborative cultures, these activities have become a way of addressing the professional growth goals of individual teachers identified during the initial supervisory conference (this concept is discussed at length in Chapter 10).

Differentiating professional growth experiences for staff increases staff members' understanding of the value of providing differentiated learning experiences for students. Collectively, this fuels the school's capacity to serve students.

Once a foundation of trust, comfort, and risk taking is created, the opportunities for peers to support one another through collaborative exchanges are limitless. As joint work among colleagues continues, norms of collaboration evolve. Working together becomes "the way we do business around here," as one staff member put it. Eventually, governance structures may reflect collaboration as well. For instance, one school designed a structure called the Principal's Advisory Committee (PAC). The PAC was made up of three teachers elected by the staff and the principal. Together they met and planned faculty meetings. The PAC members rotated responsibility for conducting the meetings as well. The teachers on the PAC provided a bridge for communication with faculty members at large. In the process of serving on the PAC, they received training in meeting management, problem solving, decision making, conflict resolution, effective professional development, and communication skills. Hence, in addition to serving their colleagues, they developed critical leadership skills.

TEACHER LEADERSHIP AND THE COLLABORATIVE SCHOOL

The number of tasks facing principals and assistant principals in 21st century schools are far too complex and numerous for those administrators to undertake alone. Further, teachers offer an important perspective of the work to be done to improve learning and schools because of the daily work they do in classrooms. They are knowledgeable about the learning needs of students, equity issues, social justice, the status of implementation of current (and past) initiatives, curriculum, instruction and assessment, scheduling needs, resources, the integration of technology, relationships among professional colleagues, needs for professional development, and more. Interestingly, research on "what contributes to a smart group shows that the best group diversity is not based on intelligence, racial, ethnic or cultural diversity, but on differences in backgrounds and life experiences (Page, 2007)" (von Frank, 2013, p. 5). Valerie von Frank adds, "When group members have different sets of mental tools, the group decision making process is less likely to get mired and more likely to result in different ways of looking at the problem" (von Frank, p. 5). The collective intelligence amassed by such groups "determines the group's ability to engage in complex cognitive work that results in improved outcomes" note Garmston and von Frank (2012). Individual intelligence is augmented by the collective perspectives of group members who represent different backgrounds and role types.

Teacher leadership capitalizes on the unique knowledge base that teachers possess and makes the leadership team smarter—enhancing the team's ability to tackle a wide array of tasks related to staff and student learning and school improvement. Providing "Leadership support is itself leadership" (Knapp, Copland, Honig, Plecki, & Portin, 2010, p. 28).

Another dimension of leadership support is the role that teacher leadership development plays. In order to maximize the effectiveness of teacher leadership, the role, responsibilities, and expectations must be clearly defined, goals should be collaboratively developed, norms need to be created, and decision-making parameters specified. In addition, in order to function maximally, teacher leadership teams benefit from professional learning about communications skills, conflict resolution, effective meetings, using data tools, consensus building, decision making models, and problem solving. These learning experiences provide the foundation underpinnings for team members to collaborate effectively as a teacher leadership team and do the work of the team.

Cindy Harrison and Joellen Killion (2007) describe a wide range of roles teacher leaders play that impact school and student success:

- *Resource Provider*—"sharing instructional resources"
- *Instructional Specialist*—helping "colleagues implement effective teaching strategies"
- *Curriculum Specialist*—using "the curriculum in planning instruction and assessment"
- *Classroom Supporter*—working "inside classrooms to help teachers implement new ideas, often by demonstrating a lesson, co-teaching, or observing and giving feedback"
- *Learning Facilitator*—"facilitating professional learning opportunities among staff"
- *Mentor*—"serving as a mentor for novice teachers"
- *School Leader*—"serving on committees . . . acting as a grade level or department chair . . . representing the school on community or district task forces"
- *Data Coach*—leading "conversations that engage their peers in analyzing and using information to strengthen instruction"
- *Catalyst for Change*—as visionaries, posing "questions to generate analysis of student learning"
- *Learner*—modeling "continual improvement, demonstrat[ing] lifelong learning, and us[ing] what they learn to help all students achieve" (pp. 74–76)

Expanding the leadership role to include teacher leaders can enhance efforts to build community and contribute rich resources to the repertoire of skills staff members have available to them to help every student succeed.

THE PRINCIPAL AND COLLABORATION

As noted earlier, a key factor in the development of a collaborative school is the principal's role. The principal and assistant principal must truly believe in and value professional collaboration for this type of work to be sustained over time. This must be reflected not only in what is said but also in the actions of the principal. For instance, if opportunities for professional collaboration are provided, do they occur during prime time, or are they placed at the end of a meeting's agenda? Does the principal collaborate as well? Is there a budget item to support this type of endeavor? For many principals who have not experienced collaborative efforts heretofore, such activities may be uncomfortable. Some principals, for example, have indicated a discomfort with shared governance because they felt, from the district's perspective, the principal still has accountability for decisions. In these cases, many principals solve the problem by requesting staff input but reserving the right to make the final decision. So that the staff did not feel "sold out" by this, one principal in Maine first facilitated a session in which the faculty brainstormed all the decisions to be made, which were recorded on butcher paper. The principal and the staff then labeled who would have primary responsibility for input for each decision.

SOME FINAL THOUGHTS ON COLLABORATION

Creating a collaborative culture has been described as "the single most important factor" (Newmann & Wehlage, 1995) for successful school improvement initiatives. Regardless of how a collaborative organization develops, schools that are able to reach such a state report a sense of synergy, creativity, and a capacity for innovation and learning uncommon to those that function in isolation. Moreover, in true collaborative cultures, joint work among teachers has developed as a daily norm for operating. It is reflected in work habits; meetings; and ongoing, planned, job-embedded professional growth experiences. In these cultures, staff members are willing to put their professional knowledge and practices on the line to be scrutinized by their colleagues. They view one another as sources for learning.

Time is a precious resource in schools. Therefore it is essential that collaborative time in schools is focused on capacity building to ensure high levels of quality student learning. There should be strong links between core beliefs, vision and mission, data analysis, goal setting, and site-level collaborative work. Planning in this way enables the realization of excellence.

REFLECTIONS

This space provides for you a place to write in ideas that have been generated by this chapter, things you want to try, or adaptations of ideas presented herein.

1. What do you believe are the obstacles and opportunities afforded by PLCs?

2. Thinking about the goal of enhancing student learning, what additional collaborative activities would you add to those offered in this chapter?

3. Thinking about the staff of which you are a part, how would you characterize their capacity to engage in risk-taking behavior (low, medium, or high risk)? What activities might you share?

4. What types of teacher leadership currently exist in your school? What new roles might you incorporate? What professional learning opportunities would enhance teacher leadership?

5. What insights or new questions do you have as a result of reflecting on the ideas presented in this chapter?

12

Fueling the Learning Organization Through Professional Development

It takes a whole village to educate one child.

—African proverb

WHY PROFESSIONAL DEVELOPMENT?

Educating a child begins with a village of elders who themselves model and find their lives enriched by the quest for lifelong learning. Students learn as a result of what they see modeled within the school. Building-based professional development, by design, provides opportunities for members of the school community to grow professionally in ways that will ultimately benefit both teacher and student. In the process, the entire system improves because of its increased capacity to influence productivity. Echoing this notion, Margaret Arbuckle, addressing a group of principals, stated, "Schools that support the continuous learning and development of students also support the continuous development of the educators. Schools must be places of learning for both students and educators. You can't have one without the other. Building a culture of professional learning in schools is a necessary condition for sustained learning and particularly critical if we are to link professional development with reformed concepts of teaching, learning, and schooling." And principals don't have to do it all. Leadership Teams can coordinate what and how professional colleagues learn.

PROFESSIONAL DEVELOPMENT DEFINED

"Professional development means a comprehensive, sustained and intensive approach for improving teachers' and principals' effectiveness in raising student achievement" (Learning Forward, 2013).

Professional development should result in improved student performance. It should be aligned with national, such as the Common Core State Standards (CCSS), or state academic achievement standards as well as school improvement goals. It should be ongoing and conducted by leadership teams, teachers, coaches, assistant principals, or principals. It can also include online courses, webinars, workshops, institutes, conferences, or university coursework. It should be designed and implemented to address data regarding teacher and student performance. Professional development should be supported by job-embedded learning opportunities such as coaching or lesson study. It should be evidence based and focused on improving the practice of teaching and staff, culminating in student learning. It should build the collective capacity of school community members to address school improvement goals as well as individual professional growth goals.

STANDARDS FOR PROFESSIONAL LEARNING

Learning Forward, with contributions of 40 professional associations and education organizations, developed standards for professional learning "that lead to effective teaching practices, supportive leadership, and improved student results. . . . Widespread attention to the standards increases equity of access to a high-quality education for every student" (Learning Forward, 2013). Using these standards to plan, implement, facilitate, and assess professional learning enhances the quality of learning experiences and increases the probability that the educator's heightened performance will positively impact student learning. Principals, assistant principals, teacher leaders, and other learning community members will benefit from examining the seven Standards of Professional Learning (Learning Forward) as they plan professional learning.

CREATING A CONTEXT WHERE PROFESSIONAL LEARNING THRIVES: SOME GUIDELINES

Creating an atmosphere for successful professional development involves focusing on the following guidelines:

- *Provide opportunities to create a sense of purpose for professional development.* This purpose should reflect the school's vision, organizational members' professional growth goals, data regarding student needs, school improvement goals, and current initiatives. For example, the staff can share professional growth goals and discuss student performance in relation to desired levels of achievement. Then, relevant professional development activities can be identified to enhance teachers' capacities to address student performance data so every student thrives.

- *Encourage and promote collaboration and mutual respect among all in the school community.* This can be a critical source of support and will contribute to the implementation and institutionalization of professional development practices. Keeping all individuals informed, inviting people to participate in follow-up activities after training, and recognizing and celebrating collaborative efforts are essential events. A common thread in professional learning sessions should be opportunities for staff members to interact in ways that create an appreciation for the different perspectives and unique talents of others.

- *Focus on continuous improvement in quality.* When training is developed that matches both staff and student growth needs, individual and organizational performance is enhanced. Time should be taken to discuss and analyze needs according to responsibilities associated with roles. Those engaged in analyzing data as a part of Professional Learning Community (PLC) work, for example, should have opportunities to practice with tools for disaggregating data and developing interventions as their role responsibilities for this function require the development of this expertise (see *The Data Toolkit: Ten Tools for Supporting School Improvement,* Hess & Robbins, 2011, for additional resources).

- *Conduct readiness-building activities and plan collaboratively prior to training and implementation.* Include maintenance activities to ensure institutionalization of professional development. Wood, Thompson, and Russell (1981) suggest five stages for a professional development program: readiness, planning, training, implementation, and maintenance.

- *When training is designed, attention should be paid to five key components* (Joyce & Showers, 1981): presentation of material, demonstration of skills, practice, feedback, and coaching in the appropriate use of the new skill. There should be a focus on providing frequent opportunities for staff members to revisit professional development content, share successes, problem solve, and refine skills. This ensures opportunities for staff members to adapt new behaviors and learnings to their own situations. It ensures that training can be designed to address teacher concerns (mentioned in Chapter 7) that initially focus on how the professional development will affect them personally; then, how they will manage a new program's implementation; and later, it may develop into how the programs will affect students (Hall & Loucks, 1978). In other words, there is a predictable series of stages that an individual goes through as they become increasingly familiar with and comfortable using a particular new skill associated with curriculum, instructional, assessment, or social justice initiative.

• *Design training for a variety of skill levels.* Training may be delivered to provide awareness, knowledge, skill development or application opportunities, or to foster internalization of concepts. Choose the appropriate focus given staff needs. In many contexts, training has been differentiated to address a wide array of teachers' skills and background experiences. Training should be spaced over time to promote the integration of new ideas, approaches, and behaviors into the classroom or workplace.

• *Design training that addresses learner needs and context variables.* Just as teachers plan learning experiences with specific students in mind, when professional development is designed, the plan should reflect the unique characteristics of the participants for whom the training is intended. In addition, both the setting in which the training will occur and the contexts in which participants will be applying the new skills, knowledge, and processes should be considered. Reflecting on the importance of learner needs and context variables, the late Susan Loucks-Horsley, in an interview with Dennis Sparks (1999), executive director emeritus of the National Staff Development Council, now Learning Forward, noted, "We recognize that young people learn in different ways, but often don't acknowledge that this applies to teachers as well when we plan learning experiences for them" (p. 56). Loucks-Horsley, describing contextual learning strategies for teachers, emphasized the following:

> Selecting strategies is really the process of designing staff development. It is a dynamic process similar to one teachers go through in designing lessons for their students. Staff development leaders have to ask themselves which strategies make sense to use at that particular time with that particular set of teachers for a particular set of outcomes. Context variables are important in making these decisions. What are the district or school standards and goals for student learning? What do teachers already know and what do they need to know? What current policies and practices influence student learning? What is the school culture? What is the nature of the student population? Teachers' levels of content understandings are also very important, especially at the elementary level where teachers may not have a deep understanding of content, as is often the case with science and mathematics. A lot of different aspects of the context come into play when selecting the right combination of strategies. (p. 56)

When training plans consider learner needs and contexts, the professional development that follows is more closely aligned with learner needs and context variables, leading to a greater degree of implementation.

- *Embrace the digital revolution.* As mentioned in Chapters 10, 14, 16, and 17, the digital revolution has transformed professional learning. On-demand learning provides virtual differentiated access to a range of professional development options. These include online learning, webinars, social networking, and the potential of massive, open, online, courses (MOOC).

Training activities need to reflect and model those attributes of good teaching that we want to promote in classrooms: outcomes focused, active learning, a brain-compatible approach, higher order thinking skills, time for reflection, and tasks that reflect multiple intelligences. The goal of professional development should always focus on enhancing educator skillfulness in ways that culminate in student learning. To illustrate:

1. Active learning opportunities can include cooperative learning tasks, small-group work, role-playing, simulation, direct instruction, reciprocal teaching, video analysis, discussion, e-learning, and case studies. Emphasis should be on teaching that engages the whole class. For example, questioning strategies should be modeled to increase participants' awareness of the power of questions to engage the entire class and give all students the opportunity to respond to a variety of thinking and skill levels. These would include the skills of convergent and divergent thinking and the use of wait time to enhance the quality of student responses.

2. The brain-compatible approach recognizes the need for active involvement of the learner with the learning task and with fellow participants. It highlights the need for participants to rehearse new learnings. It underscores the importance of not teaching too much too fast and linking new learning to previous experiences when applicable. Finally, it acknowledges the need to develop schemata or frameworks into which new information or knowledge fits.

3. Time for reflection allows the mind time for rehearsal and analysis. Reflection fosters the development of new neural connections. Insights can be gleaned as a result of providing time for thinking. Reflections may be recorded in logs or journals. They may be shared or remain confidential.

4. Multiple intelligences theory (Gardner, 2006) suggests there are at least nine *ways of knowing.* These include verbal-linguistic, logical-mathematical, visual-spatial, bodily-kinesthetic, musical, interpersonal, naturalist, intrapersonal, and existential. Designing professional development tasks with these in mind lends credence to the importance of highlighting the multiple ways we perceive and respond to the world.

- *Effective professional development programs use what is known about adult learning.* Adults are more likely to be motivated when there is a relationship between professional development and their on-the-job responsibilities. Adults come to any learning experience with a rich background that begs to be tapped. Also, adult learning is ego involved. Learning a new skill may promote a positive or negative view of self. There is sometimes a fear of external judgments that we adults are less than adequate, which produces anxiety during new learning situations. Adult learners need to see the results of their efforts and have accurate feedback about progress toward their goals.

• *Professional development programs should involve choice.* Respecting staff members as professionals and treating them accordingly means providing each individual with the right to set meaningful professional development goals and allowing them the freedom to choose how they will meet those goals. These goals should be related to building a staff member's capacity to serve students in areas identified by assessment data and other qualitative data. Expect that not all staff members will embrace wholeheartedly the notion of professional development. Often, however, when key individuals seek such experiences, peer examples and peer pressure are more powerful influences than mandates. Influence, pressure, and support will play important roles in generating participation among those staff members who do not jump on board immediately. Providing a variety of learning experiences that address common goals from which professional staff can choose is a way of modeling differentiation. For example some staff members prefer online courses. Others may enjoy participating in a book study. Still others would prefer a traditional professional development session.

When training is a "required opportunity" associated with implementing an initiative or using new materials or technology, provide the staff with choices regarding when training might be scheduled, the format, or the time frame. When professional development is designed for new staff members or beginning teachers, it is helpful to consult staff members who joined the previous year. They can lend valuable suggestions regarding their first-year needs that will contribute to planning responsive professional development.

• *Involve staff in planning professional development.* One way to increase participation or buy-in is to create a forum where teachers, teacher leaders, support staff, administration, and classified staff can talk about the tasks associated with their roles and define areas that professional learning would enhance. In addition, desired student outcomes could be examined in relation to current levels of performance. Topics and approaches are then identified that would provide all staff members with the knowledge, skills, and strategies to support students in reaching their potential.

• *Provide opportunities for the staff to learn about classical pedagogical knowledge and current practice.* It is important to provide staff members with information about current trends and developments in education, such as CCSS, powerful teaching strategies, new approaches to writing, technology resources, interdisciplinary curriculum approaches, critical thinking skills, and common assessment. Equipped with knowledge, understanding, application opportunities, and the chance to analyze and evaluate how these developments affect or fit with one's work, the practitioner then has the background to distinguish between fleeting fads and sound practice when confronted with professional development choices.

- *When professional development occurs away from the school site, encourage school teams to attend.* This provides a building-based system of support when colleagues return from professional development and begin to implement new practices.

- *Demonstrate administrative support for professional development.* Strategies include attending professional learning opportunities on- or off-site, including online learning, with the staff, using the techniques or approaches, and allocating time for planning and implementing new learnings. Discussion time should be allocated to provide opportunities to problem solve and share examples of practice. As the principal conducts Leading and Learning by Wandering Around visits, taking time to write a note regarding a teacher's implementation of a strategy learned in professional development is a great way to celebrate learning. It also fosters the development of schoolwide norms of practice.

- *Use professional development as a public relations tool.* With limited time, energy, and financial resources, using professional development as a public relations tool while it is being used to develop the individual and the organization provides the chance to get the most out of the investment. In some settings, the public relations venture might be an awareness session for parents about a new instructional, curricular, or assessment trend such as CCSS, technology applications, differentiated instruction, emotional intelligence, or student portfolios. For instance, one middle school adopted "Rachel's Challenge" to address problems with bullying and held a special session for students and their parents to promote an understanding of the program and its cherished outcomes. Providing information in this way also takes the mystery out of what the school is doing. In other schools, the public relations effort might be an invitation to businesses or key individuals from the community to attend training along with faculty members.

- *Avoid jargon.* One way to diminish the possibility that professional development will become alienating is to eliminate the use of jargon and acronyms as substitutes for phrases or structures. A principal recently commented, "It's like alphabet soup around here... Why can't they just use English?" Using language that a person on the street can understand helps make professional development activities user friendly.

- *Build local school capacity.* Once a staff has received training in a specific area and applied it in classrooms, one way to continue the development of individuals, while creating a local resource, is to provide opportunities for staff members to participate in training for trainers. This fosters the development of presentation skills, creates opportunities for teacher leadership, and helps a school build site-level support. Ultimately, this enhances the prospects that professional development activities will become institutionalized. It also affords the school on-site trainers who can provide professional development to newcomers to the building. The entire staff benefits from having a "common language" and experiences.

• *Assess the context in which professional development is to occur.* The questions that follow can serve as guidelines for program development.

> • Does the venture have relevance for the staff? Is it related to student needs? Required initiatives?
> • How much is already going on?
> • With what will the intended professional development activity compete?
> • What will be the financial and emotional cost associated with the effort?
> • How many cohorts of people will it affect (students, teachers, administrators, parents, substitutes)?
> • How complex will the implementation process be? What existing skills may come to bear on this?
> • Has the staff been involved in the decision to consider the professional development activity?
> • In what ways will follow-up support be provided?

To illustrate how context variables should influence professional learning experiences, an assistant principal recognized the difficulty staff members were experiencing with relating an initiative from the previous year to this year's initiative. She decided to "marry" the two. At a staff meeting she played the wedding march and then conducted a marriage ceremony to marry the two initiatives. Staff members enjoyed a wedding reception immediately following the ceremony. While there was a lot of laughter during this event, the assistant principal received several e-mails after "the wedding" expressing appreciation for clarifying the relationship between the two initiatives.

LEADERSHIP TEAMS AND PROFESSIONAL LEARNING

Teacher leaders, along with the principal and assistant principal, play an active role in designing professional learning at the school. In most cases, their work is driven by the goals in the school improvement plan and involves staff members in working together to identify needs and developing strategies to address those needs through a variety of structures: meetings, learning walks, peer coaching, data talks, and other job-embedded learning strategies. To illustrate, at one high school, the leadership team and principal researched teaching strategies for reading informational text. They presented the strategies to faculty members and asked them to try one or two in their classrooms and report on their experiences at the next professional learning session with an emphasis on student results. As well as learning from their own classroom experiences, teachers amassed additional strategies from their colleagues as application results were shared. Learning walks conducted after this session by teacher leadership team members provided affirmation that this professional learning experience directly impacted teachers' practices and resulted in student learning.

OPTIMIZING THE INDIVIDUAL'S PROFESSIONAL LEARNING EXPERIENCE

The following suggestions can enhance the value of participants' learning experiences:

- *Choose trainers who do their homework to learn about participants with whom they will be working and federal, state, and local mandates affecting the training and the trainees.* This information can then be used during a session to increase its relevance for participants.

- *Ask participants to share their expectations about what they hope to get out of the session prior to the session.* Eliciting expectations enhances the consultant's ability to tailor examples, comments, and activities to participant needs. In this way, as adults, participants feel they have control, or at least influence, over what happens during a session.

- *Focus on ways to build meaning into a session.* Stories or video clips, followed by time for discussion of personal experiences and time to reflect, contribute to meaning. When a session has personal meaning for participants, they are more likely to buy into activities and use them in their own context.

- *Relate the session content to formal and informal data about students.* Emphasizing how the professional learning experience will build staff capacity to address student needs is a critical strategy for creating commitment and implementation.

- *Use participants' names.* This makes individuals feel as if the consultant cares enough to personalize their experiences. Moreover, it indicates that the consultant has taken a personal interest in each individual from the first moment of contact. It models that the relationship is important and communication is key.

- *Provide participants with handouts or make handouts available for download that are copies of PowerPoint, Prezi, or Keynote presentations, and identify websites where they can access any videos or supplemental resources used in the session.* This allows participants to focus on what is being said, rather than on copying what is on the screen. Because the mind can only pay conscious attention to one thing at a time, this enhances the participants' ability to remember key aspects of the presentation. Research suggests that 68 percent of the population learns best visually. Providing visual support also models effective practice and increases the possibility that teachers will provide this for students.

- *Deliver training content in a user-friendly way.* Participants welcome overviews, agendas, and outcomes for a session. Instruction should reflect a healthy balance of research and practice. Frequent opportunities for movement should be provided, such as the "TalkWalk" (discussed in more detail in Chapter 13). There should be a variety of tasks that emphasize different cognitive demands and grouping structures. Refreshments are always appreciated!

- *Search for and use humor.* Cartoons, jokes, and sometimes seizing the moment add a special touch of warmth to a session. Consultants should be able to laugh at themselves. Humor often relaxes people. When the brain is in a more relaxed state, it is able to retain more.

- *Arrange furniture to reflect desired participant interactions.* For example, consider positioning tables to facilitate participant discussion and table-group tasks as well as access to the presenter's direct instruction and screen, if one is used. Create opportunities for participants to interact with other table group colleagues during activities throughout the training.

- *Establish norms regarding risk taking, participation, and accountability.* Consultants should model risk taking and accountability, for example, by asking participants at the end of a session to review the expectations they generated, reflect on the session's content, and offer feedback. In this way, the person who conducts the workshop models a commitment to continual growth. The participants should be invited to set goals for themselves, take risks, participate, and assess their learnings. These data are used for program evaluation and future program planning. The adult participants recognize, in this way, that input can influence a program. This contributes to a growing sense of efficacy. Modeling accountability in training also reinforces the importance of teachers focusing on the results that their instruction produces in the classroom.

Central Office Support for Professional Learning

Elsie Rodriguez, Assistant Superintendent for Curriculum and Instruction, Monroe-Woodbury Central School District, Central Valley, NY

Ideally, there is central office support for professional learning at individual schools. Assistant Superintendent Rodriguez explained her district's action plan to implement CCSS, "Our number one priority in implementing CCSS was to work as a team and involve key players: superintendent, business official, HR, building principals, teachers, parents, and board of education." The team identified the following tasks to accomplish their goal:

- Get up-to-date information (Log into EngageNY, the state website, on a weekly basis to review changes made to the ELA and Math modules; access curriculum updates).
- Educate staff.
- Collaborate with our local BOCES (Educational Service Center) and the building administrative team to develop a rollout for the modules.
- Ensure that all teachers receive districtwide in-service K–5.
- Provide teachers with time to review materials as a grade-level team.
- Make a plan, develop a timeline of events, implement plan.
- Teachers work with building principals and decide what grade-level resources are needed; allocate monies accordingly.
- Meet and review the "kick off" with building administrators.
- Conduct professional development (administrators/teachers).
- Implement Curriculum Nights to discuss with parents the changes in curriculum, as well as grade-level expectations and materials.
- Align report cards K–5 to CCSS (two-year process) and provide parents with their child's progress in relation to the new standards.
- Look at building schedules; try to get maximum learning time.
- Design local common assessments and software to analyze data.
- Implement Schoolnet software that houses benchmark data and student progress. Develop online assessments in preparation for the implementation of PARCC.
- Design a web page for parents to become more familiar with CCSS.

FINAL THOUGHTS ON PROFESSIONAL LEARNING

Principals play the key role in creating a context or culture in which adult learning flourishes (Champion, 2002). Principals who use the information in this chapter will increase the probability that professional learning will address both individual and organizational needs, will model effective practice, and will provide a variety of learning activities for the adults in the building who serve students. Student success will result. Professional learning must be ongoing and provide for continuous improvement. Implicit in this orientation is the need to constantly assess how well the professional development addresses the goals for which it was ultimately intended: student and staff growth as well as increased learning-focused collaboration among staff. As Roland Barth (personal communication, 2007) once said to a group of principals, "I've yet to see a school where the learning curves of students are upward and the learning curves of adults are downward. Learning goes hand in hand, or not at all."

REFLECTIONS

This space provides for you a place to write in ideas that have been generated by this chapter, things you want to try, or adaptations of ideas presented herein.

1. Visit the Learning Forward website and explore the standards for professional learning. How might they influence your practice?

2. Which of the guidelines for creating an atmosphere for positive professional learning are most meaningful to you?

3. What professional learning opportunities might teacher leaders guide?

4. Reflect on a professional development activity with which you have been involved. Evaluate it using your learnings from this chapter.

5. What insights or new questions do you have as a result of reflecting on the ideas presented in this chapter?

13

Faculty Meetings
A Tool for Capacity Building

Faculty meetings build our capacity to serve every student.

—A principal's voice

Faculty meetings create a forum for professional dialogue and learning that builds educator effectiveness and increases every staff member's capacity to promote student learning. The processes and experiences that staff members engage in during faculty meetings should model effective instructional practices and build relational trust among professional colleagues to develop, over time, a learning focused collaborative culture. Faculty meetings should be planned, much as lessons, with a particular end in mind. For example, they might address schoolwide goals, federal, state, or local initiatives, student performance data, professional growth goals of staff, sharing successful practices, site-level problems, promising practices, the school mission, current trends, or school culture. The lesson design for meetings should emphasize active participation, cooperative tasks, and higher order thinking skills. When teachers or the leadership team join the principal and share collective responsibility for planning the agenda, implementing and following up meetings, there is greater staff ownership and involvement.

At Parkside Middle School in Manassas, VA, Dr. Mary Jane Boynton, the principal, works with the leadership team to plan nine monthly learning focused faculty meetings. Five of the meetings are designed and facilitated by leadership team members. Four are conducted by the principal with leadership team support and address a districtwide mandate that focuses on building staff members' repertoires of strategies to work with English language learners. Mary Jane promised the faculty that because she valued their time and expertise, and because her number one priority was to create the support necessary to assure that every student thrives, no faculty meeting agenda would address administrivia. To model that meetings are reserved for learning opportunities, all notices that can be communicated by e-mail are included in a "Weekly Focus" newsletter, to which any faculty member can contribute. This preserves precious meeting time for learning. Every meeting ends with the question, "What have we learned, decided, or done today to make the life of each Parkside Student better?"

FACULTY MEETINGS AS LEARNING OPPORTUNITIES—GETTING STARTED

One of the first steps to building an inviting context for learning focused faculty meetings is giving staff members an opportunity to reflect upon:

> "What are those core values that underlie my fierce resolve to do whatever it takes to advance the organization's purpose and to ensure that every individual within the [school] thrives?" (Alvy & Robbins, 2010, p. 15)

Sharing core values and beliefs is an essential building block for collaborative work because staff members need to understand one another's perspectives as they engage in joint work. These understandings illuminate points of view in conversations about problems and practice. The following strategy can also be used to raise awareness of faculty members' values, beliefs, and actions.

Lantern Activity

Invite faculty members to "think of a person in your life who has acted as a lantern—a role model who has lit the way. Also consider the passion(s) in your life that fuel the fervor with which you embrace your role. Form groups of three. Two group members remain silent and listen as the third describes his or her "lantern" for two uninterrupted minutes. Repeat the process so that each member of the trio has the opportunity to share lanterns and passions (adapted from Maria Erb, Elon University as shared by Caley Mikesell, Elon University). This activity foreshadows the values that drive an individual's behavior and helps to explain what motivates a person and influences thinking about practice. K–12 principals who have used this strategy report that faculty members open up to their colleagues during the dialogue. This process helps to create the foundational underpinnings for collegial work. Later, if conflicts occur, this activity helps to clarify why individuals can interpret and react to the same situation differently.

Norms

Creating a context for learning also involves building norms so that faculty members can feel that it is safe to experiment, take risks, make mistakes, get feedback from colleagues, and experience being vulnerable in the learning process. These norms govern working relationships among professional colleagues and convey "this environment is a safe place for learning."

Doughnut Hole Norms

A strategy to establish shared norms that gives every faculty member a voice in the process works like this:

- Ask faculty members to sit in groups of 5 or 6 around a piece of chart paper on which a huge doughnut is drawn with a large open center.
- Divide the doughnut into as many sections as there are group members.
- Ask group members to reflect upon (1) how they want faculty meetings to function and (2) how they wish to be treated by colleagues during these meetings.
- Invite them to write their response to these questions on their individual section of the doughnut. Let them know that they will have two minutes to do this, and that no talking may occur during this part of the process.
- After two minutes have elapsed, ask group members to share, within their group of 5 or 6, what they have written. As sharing occurs, when several members have written similar responses, that response is written in the doughnut hole. For instance, if 4 out of 6 people have written "respect," then the group decides on how to phrase their desire for respect—"We agree to treat one another with respect"— and that is written in the doughnut hole. The process continues until each group member has shared his or her list. Then, table groups meet and merge their norms until one master list is developed that everyone signs. If the faculty is large, the process can occur within departments and then departments can come to consensus.

This process provides great consensus building practice and creates the opportunity for group members who are less vocal to get their thoughts on paper. In addition, the doughnut hole norms process can be used in the classroom to create classroom rules.

THE SCHOOL MISSION AND FACULTY MEETINGS

The principal and teacher leaders should view meetings as opportunities to emphasize the school mission. Certainly, in the beginning of the year and with new faculty, this is especially important. By coming back to the mission periodically, the message is communicated that the mission is not just an idea that looks good in the handbook or on the school website. Examples of classroom activities that are taking place to support the mission further reinforce the interrelationship between daily classroom activities, schoolwide goals, and the mission statement. Reviewing the mission statement and the corresponding goals periodically provides the staff with opportunities to tailor the guiding principles and documents of the school to current needs.

The following activity represents a mission-building strategy. It can also be used to refine a mission statement. Individual staff members are asked to reflect on the following:

- Describe the place you would like to go to work each day.
- Describe the place you would like to send your children to school.

Staff members are then asked to fuse these visions into one. Following this, individuals are asked to share at table groups and to develop a composite vision. Table groups then share these composites and ultimately create one that represents the collective vision. When this is recorded, it can become the basis of a school mission. Many schools have included parents and students in the mission-building process. Some schools have developed shorter slogans to remind everyone of the essence of the mission. Logos to encapsulate the mission or slogan have also been created.

INCREASING TEACHERS' ROLES IN FACULTY MEETINGS

As we work to foster greater teacher decision making in schools, faculty meetings become an important arena for teacher leadership and teacher involvement. As mentioned earlier, teachers can collaborate in setting the agendas, coplanning the meetings, and presenting or facilitating (with or without the principal or assistant principal). In many schools, the staff selects members to serve on a faculty advisory committee (FAC). The FAC works with the principal to develop the agenda and to plan, implement, and evaluate meeting effectiveness. The meeting agenda should be made public in advance by e-mailing a memo. This meeting memo can invite faculty members to submit additional agenda items in a designated space on the memo. Feedback, is then incorporated into the final agenda for the meeting. Meeting minutes can be recorded on butcher paper by faculty members so that staff members can provide immediate feedback on the accuracy of the record of meeting proceedings. The recorder and facilitator roles can rotate on an ongoing basis. This level of involvement increases staff ownership and commitment to the school's activities. Phones or iPads are used to take pictures of the notes and are e-mailed to all participants.

Teachers and support staff may also play a major role in determining the focus of presentations during a given meeting. For example, the jigsaw activity mentioned in Chapter 3 could be used to share articles on integrating technology, working with English language learners, or an innovative teaching strategy such as project based learning. At one school, several teachers shared classroom sets of iPads as an integral part of lessons. These teachers agreed to present mini lessons to share how they were using the iPads. Displays of student work and how the teachers implemented some of their ideas made for an engaging and successful meeting, helped build appreciation for teacher colleagues, and made teachers aware of resources just beyond the doors of their classrooms.

Time should be allocated for teachers to discuss specific teaching or assessment strategies, fine-tune questioning skills, or diagnose problematic areas of math, for example. Often, teachers can select DVD or video presentations, teaching and learning websites, guest speakers, or written materials that can be part of the faculty meeting. At some schools, teachers host monthly faculty meetings in their classrooms. This increases awareness of what is going on in individual classrooms across the school. Still other schools use faculty meetings to study and analyze data or to articulate the curriculum.

SUCCESSFUL FACULTY MEETINGS: STORIES OF PRACTICE

Dennis Sparks observes in *Leading for Results*, "Some of the most important forms of professional learning occur in daily interactions among teachers in which they assist one another in improving lessons, deepening understanding of the content they teach, analyzing student work, examining various types of data on student performance and solving the myriad of problems they face each day" (Sparks, 2007, p. 29).

In one Southern California high school, the principal asked faculty members to select three of their students who were the most at risk for dropping out. She challenged the teachers to meet with and tutor them as well as dedicate time for meaningful dialogue. This intervention went on through the entire school year. Teachers shared progress updates at every faculty meeting. The principal conducted video interviews of students. At the beginning of the year, before the intervention, the students' stories communicated a sense of alienation and hopelessness. At the end of the year, the students' stories were uplifting—and communicated hope, inspiration, and gratitude for the teachers who had invested in them. At the last faculty meeting of the year, the principal surprised the faculty and played the before and after videos of selected students. Teachers watched silently, wiping tears away as they sat spellbound, mesmerized by the students' testimonials. At the end of the meeting, the principal said, "On a daily basis, your dedication and commitment to students like these ultimately change life paths. I sincerely thank you for the difference—individually and collectively—that you've made. You are, in a very real sense legacy makers!"

This meeting was transformational. It was a segue to a new version of faculty meetings that focused all 120 staff members, working in small groups, sometimes across departments, sometimes within, on student performance data. Faculty members carefully analyzed student work or assessment data in relation to performance goals or Common Core State Standards (CCSS) and prescribed learning interventions. When these professionals recognized they needed additional professional learning to support their work, the teacher leadership team researched their requests and arranged for face to face or online professional development. A student survey was designed by teacher leaders in response to a request from faculty. Survey results were aggregated and provided data that indicated students perceived that teachers were going the extra mile and demonstrating compassion on their behalf. Data also indicated that reading informative, explanatory texts to convey complex ideas were two areas in which students needed additional help. The learning focused orientation of faculty meetings with related student feedback served to create trust among faculty colleagues, staff cohesiveness, and morale, as well as develop teacher skillfulness that enhanced student learning.

A school district in Connecticut adopted a teacher evaluation system based on Charlotte Danielson's *Enhancing Professional Practice* (2007). The principal at one school in the district wanted the evaluation experience to be meaningful to staff members. He wanted them to understand that the new evaluation system was based on a clear set of standards that define effective teaching and respects its complexity. To introduce the *Framework for Teaching* (Danielson, 2013), "which defines a comprehensive set of responsibilities connected to student learning," the principal asked staff members to bring to the faculty meeting a list of factors that characterize effective teaching—the kind that results in student learning. Teachers were then asked to work in groups of six to eight and share their lists, comparing and contrasting the contributions of group members as they did this. Finally, each group was asked to categorize the data that was generated from their collective lists. Categories were posted and staff members engaged in a "wisdom walk," which involved walking around the room and examining the charts of their colleagues in relation to the one their group had generated. When the faculty completed the walk and returned to their tables, they found a handout that explained the Four Domains of the Danielson Framework (Planning and Preparation, Classroom Environment, Instruction, and Professional Responsibilities). The principal facilitated an examination of the four domains. He invited the staff to notice the similarities between the domains and the categories staff members had generated. Staff members expressed appreciation that there were so many similarities. The "exit ticket" for the faculty meeting that teachers were asked to complete read, "Please jot down a few thoughts about what you would like walk-throughs to focus on this year in relation to our work today." The exit ticket data was summarized, distributed to every faculty member, and will drive walk-throughs conducted by the administration.

This faculty meeting provided the foundation for future meetings and professional development work. When Pam Robbins led a professional development session on "Instructional Strategies for the Modified Block Schedule," the principal actively participated and, as instructional strategies were being explained and practiced, staff members also had the opportunity to relate the strategies to the Four Domains of the Danielson Framework. In this way, staff members became knowledgeable about how strategies to address the new scheduling initiative related to the teacher evaluation initiative—building their capacity to promote student learning.

"Faculty meetings should mean something" Peter DeWitt, principal, declared in an *Education Week* blog (2013). As a consequence of this declaration, he met with the school's Principal Advisory Committee (PAC). Collectively, they decided that every faculty meeting would have a meaningful "Faculty Focus." At the first faculty meeting of the year, the faculty shared their collective thoughts about "What we want students to look like when they leave us." The intent was to develop a collective vision of the work to be done. The October meeting focused on evidence-based observations. Teachers explored a definition and model, and then watched a video to discuss the evidence of learning they saw. In November and December meetings, the Faculty Focus was on providing effective feedback—feedback teachers provide to students, students provide to teachers, and what school leaders provide to teachers. DeWitt reflected, "A Faculty Focus will bring our collective thoughts together and hopefully help us (teachers, students, and administrators) become even better in our practices."

In a large Georgia High School, the administrative team decided that the staff was too large for meaningful faculty meeting dialogue. They decided to conduct "all day faculty meetings!" Here's how they were structured. A faculty meeting was conducted by the principal, two assistant principals, or dean in every one of the four daily instructional blocks that made up the school's schedule. Teachers attended the faculty meeting during the block that they did not have student responsibilities. In this way, smaller, cross-departmental faculty members were able to meet and engage in thoughtful learning focused meetings. This faculty meeting approach also forged stronger relationships among professional colleagues across departments and created a common schoolwide focus on teaching and learning.

FACULTY MEETING STRATEGIES THAT WORK!

The following examples represent a compilation of strategies that could be used during faculty, team, or department meetings, professional development days, or job-embedded learning opportunities. The broad goal of their use is to provide experiences to develop values for collaboration that will lead to joint work among professionals and ultimately enhance the resources the collective staff possess to ensure every student thrives.

Listening posts. In listening posts, staff members are asked to generate professional topics about which they would like to chat. For example, some may wish to talk about common assessments, whereas others might want to converse about CCSS, differentiated instruction, or grading, to name a few. Each topic is assigned to a specific area or "post" in the room by the facilitator. Staff members gather by the topic area of their choice and have a discussion for 15 to 30 minutes. At the end of this time, the individuals who have discussed each topic develop a 1- to 2-minute summary of their discussions and report back to the larger group. In this way, the entire group benefits from hearing about the separate topic area discussions. In fact, seeds of interest across topic areas are often planted as a consequence of such sharing.

Carousel brainstorming. As trust begins to develop and values for collaborative work are created, staff members become more comfortable sharing professional knowledge. Carousel brainstorming promotes this type of sharing within a relatively safe context. In carousel brainstorming, four to six sheets of butcher paper are posted around the room. Topics are assigned and written on each sheet. For example, if a faculty is implementing CCSS, sheets might be labeled: Reading: Literature; Reading: Informal Text; Reading: Foundational Skills, Writing, Speaking and Listening, Language. Staff members are then divided into groups and position themselves in front of one of the sheets. They brainstorm for three minutes, writing their brainstormed ideas about instructional strategies to address anchor standards on the sheets. They then rotate to the next sheet, taking with them the colored marker that has been assigned to their group. The process continues until each group has brainstormed at every chart. At this point, the group members walk around the entire room, reading the completed charts. Frequently, iPads or phones are used to take pictures of the charts and distributed to faculty members.

Consulting colleagues. As staff members feel increasingly comfortable and trust one another, they are willing to let their rough edges show, resulting in greater adeptness in joint problem solving. Consulting colleagues provides a structure for the problem-solving process. Peers form groups of three and designate one person as A, another as B, and the third as C. During Round 1, which lasts five minutes, A shares a problem while B and C listen. During the next five minutes, B and C ask clarifying questions about the problem. Finally, during the last five minutes, B and C offer solution ideas to A, who writes them down. The process is repeated so that B and C have a chance to discuss their problems as well.

Pinwheel activity. Another problem-solving strategy that engages larger numbers of faculty is the pinwheel activity. Groups of six are formed and stand in a pinwheel configuration. That is, three people stand in the center, each facing a person in an outer circle. The three individuals in the center each pose a professional problem or dilemma they are experiencing to the person facing them. The people they face generate possible ideas about how to address the specific problem posed. After they brainstorm solution ideas for three minutes, the people on the outside rotate. In this way, the individuals in the center are able to gain additional ideas about how to address their problems or challenges. The process continues until each person in the center has three different sets of ideas from the three outside "consultants." Then the pinwheel is turned inside out, and the outside people who had brainstormed solution ideas previously have a chance to share their problems and garner ideas from professional colleagues. This process makes the staff aware that other people share similar problems or challenges and that a tremendous amount of expertise exists among faculty members that begs to be tapped.

Success stories. Generally, a note to faculty is sent out in advance so that teachers and support staff can plan what they want to share:

> What works? Often we read about research studies that draw broad conclusions regarding how we should teach. These studies are very helpful. However, they frequently miss the day-to-day successes that teachers experience in our particular school. Please share with your colleagues a success story from your class that you have experienced recently. Why were you satisfied with this experience? Can the experience apply beyond the context of a particular student or class? If the success story involves instructional resources or student work, please bring these items to the meeting.

Using Humor

Humor is a great tool for faculty meetings. Goleman, Boyatzis, and McKee (2002) note, "Research on humor at work reveals a well-timed joke or playful laughter can stimulate creativity, open lines of communication, enhance a sense of connection and trust, and, of course, make work more fun. . . . Small wonder that playfulness holds a prominent place in the tool kit of emotionally intelligent leaders" (p. 14). In one school, a teacher approached a principal on the morning of a faculty meeting and mentioned that she would probably have to leave during the meeting for emergency root canal work. She was sorry that she would miss part of the meeting. To open the faculty meeting that day, the principal mentioned that one of the teachers had to decide which was worse, the faculty meeting or having to get a root canal. The teacher was such a masochist, the principal said, that she chose to accept a little of both! That opening got the meeting off to a good start. When necessary, such remarks also can come in handy at the end of a meeting. Often, an anecdote about a student can fit the occasion and emphasize an important theme. One teacher shared such a story by telling about a second-grade student who, while completing a math paper, counted on her fingers, recorded the answer, and then blew a kiss for every problem. When questioned about this technique, the student explained that her first-grade teacher told her, "When you get to second grade and do math, you can just kiss your fingers good-bye!" The story added humor to the meeting and reminded everyone about the importance of meaning in our actions.

Supporting Vertical Articulation and Interdisciplinary Curriculum and Instructional Practices

Faculty meetings are great opportunities for teachers in elementary, middle, or high schools to meet across grade levels and within departments. Traditionally, the social studies, science, and world language departments meet separately following a faculty meeting or on a different day. However, the principal can allocate time to facilitate departments meeting across disciplines to explore the possibilities for interdisciplinary curriculum work and to promote the sharing of effective teaching practices across disciplines and grade levels. Interestingly, when we discuss the interdisciplinary curriculum, we usually overlook the interdisciplinary instructional practices that should be considered. For example, if only one teacher is using cooperative learning, performance assessment, or reflective writing in a classroom, students may not see the practice as valuable throughout their other classes. The faculty meeting provides a special forum to foster the development of interdisciplinary planning for curriculum, instruction, and assessment. Approaches to differentiating learning experiences for students may also be shared. Interdisciplinary department meetings also give the staff opportunities to pursue consistent strategies and activities to meet the school mission. Some teachers have had students submit one product for two different classes, emphasizing the importance of integrating disciplines.

In the elementary school, faculty meetings offer wonderful opportunities to break up into small groups across grade levels or departments. For example, teachers across grade levels can meet to share successful instructional strategies they have used with English language learners. In another school, groups of second- and third-grade teachers met together to reflect on the following questions: What are you finding out about the students we sent to you last year? What are their strengths and weaknesses? State test results can also be reviewed in this way. What are the students' strengths and weaknesses based on the test results? How can we work together across grade levels and disciplines to meet our school or district goals to help all students succeed? In one high school, all departments and grade levels examine how they can promote writing across the curriculum.

The following faculty meeting guides have been used to pursue some of the goals mentioned previously while promoting articulation across grade levels.

Discussion Guide: Vertical Articulation of the Curriculum

Grade Levels _____ (two or more)
The following questions are intended to stimulate discussion across grade levels. Please add to these as you see fit.

1. When your students leave your grade, what do you expect them to know? To do (key concepts, content, and skills)?

2. What would you like the incoming students to know? To do (key concepts, content, and skills)?

3. What are the congruencies and discrepancies in your view regarding the expectations?

4. What are your conclusions?

5. What next steps do you plan to take?

At certain times during the year, staff members have found it helpful to meet to discuss standardized test results. The following guide has been used as a conversation starter.

Analyzing State Achievement Tests Results

Grade Level _____ Subject Area _____

1. What response patterns emerged as important for your grade level/subject area?

   Strengths:

   Weaknesses:

2. How can the results be helpful for the remainder of this year?

3. Do you have any recommendations for the previous grade level or the next grade level?

4. What are some of the major similarities and differences between the objectives of the state tests, CCSS, and our school curriculum? Differences between state tests and how assessment occurs in classrooms?

5. What are some of the major goals of the CCSS and our curriculum that cannot be assessed through state tests? How should we assess these goals?

6. What are your conclusions?

7. Examining data from subgroups, what inferences can we make about student learning? What do we need to keep doing, stop doing, and start doing?

8. What next steps should we take?

With software programs available to disaggregate data, many principals and teachers have found this information useful in schoolwide conversations about student learning and student needs.

The Standing Faculty Meeting for Short, Informative Sessions

Often when the staff has been promised a short faculty meeting on an immediate or emergency issue, the meeting tends to drag on. If you ask the staff to stand during the last five minutes of the meeting, you are symbolically illustrating that you are serious about holding a brief meeting. The staff member who wants to hold up the group with his or her own agenda will be very reluctant to do so when colleagues are standing and ready to go. Or, staff members can be asked to stand near the end of a regular meeting and are promised the meeting will end in five minutes. This promise must be kept! Furthermore, the staff will enjoy the opportunity to stretch!

TalkWalk for Energy, Exercise, and Dialogue

Teachers often come to meetings exhausted after a hard day's work. Imagine their surprise at an invitation to take a walk with one or two colleagues for 10–15 minutes! The TalkWalk (Caro & Robbins, 1991) engages the staff in professional dialogue while providing exercise, energy, a change of environment, and the opportunity to share expertise. Staff members tend to return from the walk in a more relaxed, reflective mood. They then articulate key points from their TalkWalk dialogue. (This promotes accountability.)

Video-Stimulated Discussions for Fun, Reflection, and Dialogue

Many staffs have begun a practice of bringing in a popular video from a website like Teacher Tube, Teaching Channel, YouTube (TedTalks website), or Edutopia and playing a portion of it to stimulate discussion. Examples range from *Freedom Writers*, to stimulate a dialogue about working with at-risk students and ELA Standards, to viewing Ted Talks that address teaching math standards. Staff members rotate responsibility for bringing in videos. A variation of this approach is to use stories (literature for either adults or children) as a springboard for conversation.

Swap Meets for Clean Rooms and Effective Use of Resources

To build a positive climate and to facilitate sharing, some faculty meetings periodically include a swap meet. Swap meets provide the opportunity for teachers to exchange instructional, curricular, or assessment resources. To illustrate, for the swap meet, teachers bring items they no longer use to exchange for items that other teachers bring. Sometimes these meets are preceded by classified ads in which teachers identify needs for resources in a "want ad" format. Requests range from coupons to books, plastic jars to magazines, and ideas—either written or recorded—to Internet resources.

A Template for Faculty Meetings

The following figure (13.1) can be used as a template to plan and structure faculty, team, or department meetings. It is based on effective instructional practice.

Figure 13.1 Using Meetings as Transformational Tools

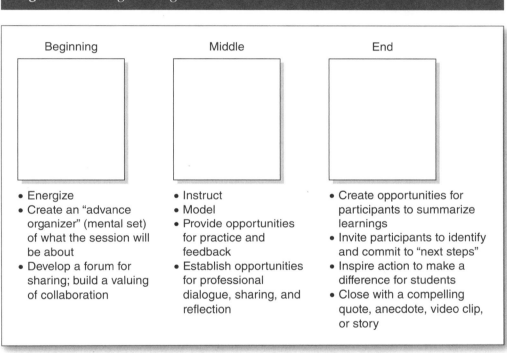

Beginning	Middle	End
• Energize • Create an "advance organizer" (mental set) of what the session will be about • Develop a forum for sharing; build a valuing of collaboration	• Instruct • Model • Provide opportunities for practice and feedback • Establish opportunities for professional dialogue, sharing, and reflection	• Create opportunities for participants to summarize learnings • Invite participants to identify and commit to "next steps" • Inspire action to make a difference for students • Close with a compelling quote, anecdote, video clip, or story

A FINAL THOUGHT

It is important to reiterate that the faculty meeting is an opportunity for professional growth and the celebration of teaching as professionals gather together to share and learn. We often hear that teaching is the second most private act. The faculty meeting is the perfect forum for teachers to interact, build community, and break down the traditional barriers that serve as obstacles to discussing what goes on in our classrooms. Faculty meetings also provide the context to model those teaching behaviors that educators wish to see implemented in the classroom with students. Further, it is a powerful stage for building culture and schoolwide norms of practice. Most importantly, it represents a forum for enhancing instructional practice in ways that culminate in staff and student learning.

REFLECTIONS

This space provides for you a place to write in ideas that have been generated by this chapter, things you want to try, or adaptations of ideas presented herein.

1. Describe what typically goes on in a faculty meeting at the school in which you work.

2. Which idea from this chapter might you implement during the next faculty meeting?

3. What are some ways teacher leaders might take a greater role in faculty, team, or department meetings?

4. What is an initiative your school is currently implementing? How might faculty meeting activities support this?

5. What insights or new questions do you have as a result of reflecting on the ideas presented in this chapter?

14

Asking the Right Questions About Curriculum, Instruction, and Assessment

Getting to Know the C.I.A.

Are we preparing students to be college and career ready or how to successfully take a test? Can we do both?

—A principal's voice

WE LIVE IN INTERESTING TIMES

As things now are, the high school teacher finds in the pupils fresh from the grammar schools no foundation of elementary mathematical conceptions outside of arithmetic; no acquaintance with algebraic language; and no accurate knowledge of geometric forms . . . The college teacher of history finds in like manner that his subject has never taken any serious hold on the minds of pupils fresh from the secondary schools.

—Report From "The Committee of Ten" in 1892
(Educators tasked with redesigning secondary school curriculum)

We have been here before, in fact lots of times. The challenge that our schools can do better is a theme that has been around since the growth of U.S. public schools in the 1840s. Why? Because we are never satisfied with how much we know and how that knowledge can be transferred and applied to college and the workplace. This challenge is actually a healthy characteristic because it implies that we want to do better—the status quo is not good enough. But the challenge also begs a question: What have educators learned from this historical challenge about how to improve curriculum, instruction, and assessment to ensure that our students succeed in the 21st century?

Educators know this next decade will be critical. Administrators and teachers feel the pressure to address the Common Core State Standards (CCSS) and the assessments that accompany the standards. No Child Left Behind (NCLB) and Race to the Top (RTTT) make accountability a very public exercise. It is not pleasant to be labeled "in need of improvement" (the NCLB euphemism for a failing school) or to lose out on a competitive RTTT grant. Ironically, districts and schools are expected to implement the democratic ideals of local control and yet embrace federal and state expectations related to curriculum and high-stakes testing. Not surprisingly, most teachers are uncomfortable with "teaching to the test" if the test does not meet curriculum expectations and the unique needs of the students in their classes. In fact, although the overwhelming majority of administrators and teachers welcome the CCSS, the enthusiasm for standards has been partially clouded by testing issues that are fairly or unfairly linked to standards.

ASKING THE RIGHT QUESTIONS

Principals and assistant principals, because of their daily interaction with students, teachers, and parents, may be in the best position to reflect on how the curriculum is affecting the total school community. From this vantage point, principals must consider and facilitate discussion concerning the following questions and issues as curriculum, instructional, and assessment decisions are made. By promoting these questions and encouraging dialogue among the staff, principals can do a great deal to facilitate teacher thinking about curriculum, their students, and ways of teaching.

How Should Curriculum Be Defined?

There is no one definition of curriculum that is universally accepted. For example, curriculum can mean a sequenced plan to educate students or a broad field of study (e.g., examining various curriculum models). However, defining curriculum is a very difficult and important task. The definition says much about the scope of school experiences that one believes has a direct impact on student learning. For example, a **narrow definition** of a curriculum plan usually focuses on specific and discrete subjects, with a scope and sequence addressing content and skills that are tied to class outcomes and expected evidence. A **broader definition** also includes specific subject area content and skills but in addition supports activities that address college and career readiness with outcomes and evidence expectations that sometimes are not easily tested. Additionally, a broader definition implies that almost all of the actions of a classroom teacher and activities within a school may have far-reaching social, emotional, and cultural implications for students beyond academics. Although a narrow subject specific definition of curriculum is easier to grapple with, especially when considering the testing implications, reality tells us that a broader definition is more likely to prepare students for college and career readiness. Hence our preference for a broader definition.

What Are Some Important Shifts Related to Curriculum, Instruction, Assessment, and Learning That Influence the Practices of Principals and Others in Supervisory Positions?

To gain a clear understanding of the shifts, it is important to consider five conceptual themes that illuminate logical categories of division among these shifts.

First, there is the conceptual theme of supervision and evaluation being distinctly different from one another in focus, but nonetheless interrelated. Supervision is, by its nature, a growth-oriented process, not a punishing one. Its intent is to foster teacher growth and deeper conceptual understanding of the interplay between instruction, curriculum, and assessment practices that promote student learning. Evaluation, in contrast, is a process (usually district or state mandated) focused on examining areas of teacher competence. The following are shifts related to this theme:

• The clinical supervision process, traditionally focused primarily on observing summative teacher behaviors, is now refocusing around quality, meaningful, and engaging student work during class and teacher selected (preferably) instructional components from district instructional frameworks. Consequently, formative preobservation and postobservation conferences are targeting data and teacher-driven initiatives related to: student work samples, teacher strategy preferences, CCSS expectations, differentiated instruction, data-driven decisions related to student learning, student voice, and traditional and alternative assessments.

• Differentiated supervision is customized for novice, proficient, exemplary, and at-risk teachers (needing intensive assistance).

The second conceptual theme of shifts is that of supervisory practices focused on learning. Some of these practices focus on student learning, some on staff learning. The following are shifts related to this theme:

• There is a shift toward observing quality, meaningful, and engaging student work that is sustained and based on the CCSS. We must ask: What are the students learning, not just, are we teaching. Previously, supervisors concentrated primarily on the teacher delivery system.

• Quality, meaningful, and engaging work must be personalized and offered to each student, with feedback (student voice) and success *for each student in the school as a goal.*

• Decisions related to social justice, student diversity, and exceptionality are being addressed through instructional, curricula, and assessment differentiation—that is culturally responsive to economic, racial, ethnic, gender, sexual minority, and pre-existing achievement opportunity issues.

• The digital transformation is empowering both educators and students. Supervisors are supporting teachers retooling 21st century classrooms using digital devices, blended learning, digital content, social learning networks, and self-directed student learning strategies based on full access to information. Making the transformation thoughtfully includes ensuring that high-poverty schools and students without privilege are not left behind (e.g., the Digital Divide) and that student success and effective teaching govern all technology decisions.

• Continuous teacher growth, in contrast to mastery, is a more suitable approach for addressing the complexities of teaching, learning, curriculum, and assessment for lifetime learners. Moreover, complexity and accountability "demand" that effective teachers become lifelong learners. Individual growth and collaborative synergistic growth are both critical objectives for continual learning.

• Individual principals or assistant principals are serving as culture-building instructional leaders by shaping faculty meetings as learning opportunities, increasing their classroom visibility to celebrate student and teacher work and success, using technology and Web-based systems to facilitate data analysis and sharing, involving parents, and fostering trust in nonhierarchical Professional Learning Communities (PLCs).

The third theme of shifts embraces supervisory actions in response to school-site data. Here the goal is to examine promising assessment practices that are contextually relevant. An example might be a supervisor identifying specific teachers who, according to school-site data, have narrowed or closed the achievement gap. Supervisory visits would focus on promising practices that are particularly influential when embedded in the local context. Through peer interventions and PLCs, supervisors would help facilitate the lateral influence of successful teachers. The following are shifts related to this theme:

• Data-informed assessment decisions, especially decisions related to *closing the achievement and opportunity gaps,* are influencing professional development, supervision and evaluation, *proactive early intervention* programs to assist students (e.g., Response to Intervention), and detracking policies to maximize *high achievement opportunities* for all students.

• Summative tests (including state and national tests) and innovative formative assessments are addressing rich content and 21st century expectations related to authentic tasks and the world of work, global citizenship responsibilities, media literacy and technology, student voice, problem solving, and critical and self-regulated thinking to enhance independent learning.

The fourth shift theme addresses professional development as an extension of the supervisory process and, at the same time, an embedded part of it. The explicit goal is to build the capacity of staff members to address a wide spectrum of student needs and foster student learning. Capacity building is accomplished in a variety of forums and led by both administrators and teacher leaders. The following are shifts related to this theme:

• Educators are addressing the "best and promising practices" research on teacher quality, instruction (e.g., current frameworks) and evaluation; student learning, CCSS, assessment, and leadership behaviors.

• School leaders, recognizing the *holistic relationship* of instructional, curricular, assessment and professional development work, are intentionally, coherently, and systematically aligning decisions among these four areas. The goal is to promote student learning and teacher capacity.

• Teacher leaders are initiating, directing, and celebrating collaborative work in PLCs related to individual and group professional development, coaching, and mentoring; CCSS planning, data sharing and analysis, peer-coaching teams, book study groups, critical friends groups, lesson study, curricular and instructional breakfasts, and action research. These practices have inspired teachers to shift from isolated to collaborative work leveraging collective wisdom.

• Supervisors are supporting teacher leaders engaged in collaborative professional development, embedded in individual and group reflection related to student work, reflection-in-action (e.g., Schön, 1983), self-evaluation, and professional goal setting. Supervisors recognize that capacity building and the sharing and distribution of leadership responsibilities are essential cultural goals to address the core challenges of teaching and student learning.

• Teachers collaborating online through social media and digital educational sources (e.g., Personal Learning Networks, Twitter, TeacherTube, ASCD EDge) are encouraged by supervisors to seek and share best practice strategies, helpful apps, rich digital content, and approaches to current challenges (e.g., CCSS, teacher evaluation).

The fifth theme is simple, rare, and powerful: feedback on feedback. The intent of practices that relate to this shift engage the supervisor in asking staff members for feedback about strategies employed during conferences and observations. The supervisor might ask a teacher in a postobservation setting, "What strategies did I employ that facilitated your thinking and learning? What other approaches or techniques might

I have used? Is there anything I did that impeded your learning?" These questions and related actions build trust, emphasize a focus on learning about learning, and portray supervisory actions that focus on the core work of schools: teaching and learning. The following are shifts related to this theme:

- Recognizing that personal professional growth is imperative in today's complex world, supervisors are embracing George's (2007) notion that "to be an effective leader, *you must take responsibility for your own development*" (p. xxxiii).

- Hattie's (2009) insight on visible learning, "that feedback was most powerful when it is from the *student to the teacher*" (p. 173), encourages both supervisors and teachers to honor and use student feedback as an opportunity to fine-tune, and possibly transform, professional practice.

- Expert supervisors and teachers must not be overlooked as recipients of feedback. As Jim Collins (2005) has stated, "Greatness is an inherently dynamic process, not an endpoint. The moment you think of yourself as great, your slide toward mediocrity will have already begun" (p. 9).

The Common Core State Standards: What Enduring Lessons Are Principals Learning From a Real-Time Exercise in Reform and Leadership?

It's difficult to draw conclusions about the success of a major initiative when in the middle of the venture. But that is where we are with the CCSS. However, being "in the middle" also has an upside: you are living with process in the here and now and, at times, *process is more important than product*. There are lessons to be learned as we reflect-in-action (Schön, 1983). These lessons can help us make sound decisions related to change five years, or twenty-five years, into the future. Indeed, there are four enduring lessons concerning the implementation of the CCSS that can be drawn today: (1) stand up for important values, (2) empowerment creates trust and ownership, (3) build consensus, and (4) the tortoise really did beat the hare.

Stand Up for Important Values. Let's start with common sense. Robert Rothman (2012b) draws an analogy between President Lincoln's 19th century decision to build a transcontinental railroad (using a standard gauge track width), with the 21st century support of educators for the CCSS. Before Lincoln's proposal, the rail gauges varied by state, "so each region of the country built its own rail line" (Rothman, 2012b, p. 1). This resulted in passengers often having to change trains whenever reaching a different state border. Today we live in a highly mobile society and students are disadvantaged if they move to a state in which the new grade level or subject area curriculum is significantly different from their previous experience. Also, the NCLB Act may have put K–12 education on the front burner but, "the act made variations in state standards conspicuous" (Rothman, 2012b, p. 3). So the enthusiasm for greater conformity in standards and tests not only seems logical but also fair to students on the move. In fact the NCLB experience begs the question: Did we have to first go through NCLB to reach a consensus for national standards?

The issue of social justice must also be addressed. Every student is entitled to a high quality, 21st century education, which is a major goal of the CCSS movement. The Declaration of Independence states that as citizens we have certain "unalienable rights," they are "life, liberty and the pursuit of happiness." These rights cannot be achieved unless all of our state and local school leaders—administrators and teachers—are committed to providing a superior education for all students whether they are privileged or not. As Rotherham and Willingham (2009) note,

> Many U.S. students are taught these [21st century] skills—those who are fortunate enough to attend highly effective schools or at least encounter great teachers—but it's a matter of chance rather than the deliberate design of our school system. . . . If we are to have a more equitable and effective public school system, skills that have been the province of the few must become universal. (p. 16)

The alternative to first-rate schools and dull classrooms is devastating; approximately 75 percent of U.S. prison inmates are high school dropouts, illiterate, or both. "The young men who go to prison rather than college face a lifetime of closed doors, discrimination, and ostracism" (Alexander, 2012, p. 190).

Empowerment Creates Trust and Ownership. When the standards were rolled out in 2010 many educators and community stakeholders believed that a rigid curriculum would be mandated by fervent CCSS advocates. Nothing could be further from the truth. Consider these four guidelines from English Language Arts Literacy Design Standards (National Governors Association, 2010; http://www.corestandards.org/ELA-Literacy),

1. The Standards define what all students are expected to know and be able to do, not how teachers should teach . . .

2. While the Standards focus on what is most essential, they do not describe all that can or should be taught. . . . The aim of the Standards is to articulate the fundamentals . . .

3. The Standards do not define the nature of advanced work for students who meet the Standards prior to the end of high school . . .

4. The Standards set grade-specific standards but do not define the intervention methods or materials necessary to support students who are well below or well above grade-level expectations . . .

Clearly a lot is in the hands of teachers and school leaders. No one is being told how to teach. Standards "focus on outcomes, not curriculum or instruction. The implication is clear—educators must translate the Standards into an engaging and effective curriculum" (McTighe & Wiggins, 2012, p. 3).

Thus, teachers have ownership of instruction and curriculum. As curriculum is developed, principals and assistant principals should encourage teacher leaders to play a role getting involved in state and district work to shape decisions.

Build Consensus. EngageNY is a wonderful website (www.engageny .org) created by the New York State Department of Education dedicated to assisting administrators and teachers as they usher in the standards. The "Professional Development Kit for Principals" includes a video with Louis Cuglietto, Principal of J. F. K. Magnet School in the Port Chester-Rye S. D. After attending a common core workshop during the summer of 2012, he felt it was time to move ahead with state curriculum aligned to standards but thought it best to make it voluntary at first with the teaching staff. By giving folks a choice he built consensus. To start, over 60 percent of his faculty decided to use the new curriculum pacing guides and modules. Cuglietto stressed four words as consensus built: teamwork, leadership, ownership, and trust.

Discussing their experiences with introducing the CCSS in Maryland Judy Jenkins and R. Scott Pfeifer (2012) recommend that principals facilitate K–12 vertical articulation teams so that the college and career ready goals are seamless. They stress also the importance of creating "collaborative work groups" to work on transition topics and timelines to address assessments coming from the Smarter Balanced Assessment Consortium and the Partnership for Assessment of Readiness for College and Careers. Maryland also implemented a "gap analysis that compared its state curriculum with the CCSS" (p. 32). As a result of the gap analysis, text complexity and close reading emerged as topics that needed to be addressed as curriculum is rewritten. This certainly is not a surprise. Both topics are often mentioned as part of a national shift taking place, along with the use of evidence (not just opinion) to support one's position, and engaging in more nonfictional writing. Finally, by taking the lead and supporting transition teams, principals and assistant principals become curriculum leaders, not because of an expertise in each content area but because the teams build consensus, an indispensable ingredient to the success of the CCSS.

The Tortoise Really Did Beat the Hare. On August 7, 2013, the New York State third- through eighth-grade reading and math exam scores were reported. Across the state "31 percent of students passed the exams in reading and math. Last year, 55 percent passed in reading, and 65 percent in math" (Hernandez, 2013). Although the curriculum and teaching of the CCSS is still a work in progress in New York, and most teachers are making significant strides with the curriculum developed from the standards (i.e., EngageNY), no one suggests that the students were ready for the tests. In Rochester, New York, 5 percent of students passed in reading and math. A week after the tests results were reported, Randi Weingarten, President of the American Federation of Teachers and a supporter of the CCSS, stated, "I am worried that the Common Core is in jeopardy because of this . . . The shock value that has happened has been so traumatic in New York that you have a lot of people all throughout the state saying, 'Why are you experimenting on my kids?'" (Richie, 2013). Did New York state do the right thing by administering the tests? The voices in support of "moving ahead" with the assessment as a first step toward more rigor and those who believe it was a mistake to administer the exams are equally vocal and sincere in their passion about doing what is best for the students. It is a tough call, but this is what we think of the decision. For economically comfortable families and those with privilege whose children are attending schools that normally score well it might be easier to absorb the scores as a one-time experience. Worst-case scenario the families might have to pay for extra tutoring down the road to make sure college works out for their children. But for families in poverty, without privilege, telling those families that it's okay their child performed poorly, well, we just don't think that works. An eighth grader whose family is struggling economically and who failed the test may decide to drop out of school in another year. The student might say, "Why bother? I'll just look for a job to help out at home." We are not suggesting that children without privilege should be sheltered from exams; but is it fair to give an exam to students who are already at-risk of dropping out? Not everyone is resilient.

Another pressure point related to the CCSS implementation relates to the billions of dollars companies are poised to make as a result of the reform effort. The caution flags are out there warning school districts that they don't have to be the first education community (the hare!) to purchase resources. Assessment expert James Popham (2013) warns, "Not surprisingly, commercial publishers are inundating U.S. educators with instructional material ostensibly directed at promoting student mastery of the standards. But let's be honest we really won't know the true nature of the common core's success until the two assessment consortia . . . complete their test-building by the spring of 2015" (p. 29). Michael Q. McShane (2013) of the American Enterprise Institute asks, "What do we do about the tens of thousands of resources that are being published branded as 'common core aligned' even before assessments come online? What kind of quality control mechanisms are available for teachers and school leaders to make sure that what they are using is appropriate" (p. 3). During the spring of 2013, the Next Generation Science Standards (NGSS) were completed. Stephen L. Pruitt, who is a vice president at Achieve, a company that helped to manage the development of all three sets of standards, advises those in charge of implementing the new standards to go slow, building capacity and an infrastructure. Peter McLaren, the president of the Counsel of State Science Supervisors, echoes Popham and McShane by cautioning science supervisors to avoid vendors who enthusiastically state, "'This is NGSS-ready,' stay far away from them, or laugh at them" (Robelen, 2013, p. 13). Finally, James Pellegrino, co-chair of the National Research Council, soberly suggests, "Our greatest danger may be a rush to turn the NGSS into sets of assessment tasks for use on high stakes state accountability tests" (Robelen, p. 13). Keep your eyes on the tortoise.

Preparing Students for a 21st Century Democracy: How Can We Use Authentic Work and Feedback to Sustain Success?

It is important to consider student work and related outcomes, assessments, and feedback strategies that go beyond traditional school-related tasks and expectations. Each proposed outcome should answer satisfactorily the question: Will this learning help students when they are not in school, as citizens and in the workplace? For example, if we accept Drucker's (1992) view that to work successfully in an organization one must have "the ability to present ideas orally and in writing; the ability to work with people; [and] the ability to shape and direct one's own work, contribution and career" (p. 5), then we must teach the appropriate content and skills to foster these competencies.

Thus a 21st century approach to teaching and learning, led by educators determined to see student success in a diverse society, should include: rigorous content, multicultural experiences, cooperative learning activities, independent and challenging complex text and close reading activities; oral and written higher-order thinking, creative, and self-directed experiences; and interdisciplinary activities. This range of experiences is essential, not because they are fashionable but because they provide essential content and skills that can be transferred to the workplace. Moreover, when deciding on key student learnings, it is essential that one asks: What are the specific instructional techniques and activities (e.g., fostering conceptual understanding in mathematics, cooperative learning, drafting several versions of a report, debating) that best teach specific curricular expectations and foster transfer and applications of these learnings in the workplace? To illustrate further, in elementary, middle, and high school community service programs and in middle and high school courses, workplace experiences become essential links to support and highlight the connections between K–12 schools and career experiences.

To develop relevant curriculum expectations, a structured approach that covers essential questions is very helpful. As noted in Chapter 1, the classic Tyler Rationale still provides us with four essential questions that should be addressed by individuals and committees when developing curriculum. These questions are: "(a) What educational purposes should the school seek to attain? (b) What educational experiences can be provided that are likely to attain these purposes? (c) How can these educational experiences be effectively organized? (d) How can we determine whether these purposes are being attained?" (Tyler, 1949, p. 1). Add to this model what we now know from research on the human brain and developments in teaching methodology, and we have key elements to engage in a meaningful dialogue on curriculum, instruction, assessment, and learning within a school setting. An approach close to Tyler's, but subtly different, is expressed by Wiggins and McTighe (1998) as they effectively tackle curriculum "backward" with a design strategy that initially may appear counterintuitive:

This backward approach to curriculum design also departs from another common practice: thinking about assessment as something we do at the end, once teaching is completed. Rather than creating assessments near the conclusion of a unit of study (or relying on the tests provided by textbook publishers, which may not completely or appropriately assess our standards), backward design calls for us to operationalize our goals or standards in terms of assessment evidence as we *begin* to plan a unit or course. It reminds us to begin with the question, What would we accept as evidence that students have attained the desired understandings and proficiencies—before proceeding to plan teaching and learning experiences? (p. 8)

In addition to recognizing the type of learning needed to succeed in the future, and how curriculum and assessments should be aligned, schools need to ask: Are the assessments democratic? Are the assessments addressing the needs of all students? Are we using feedback to improve teaching and learning? Assessment expert Rick Stiggins (2005) laments that, traditionally, educators competitively ranked students and seemed gratified with that broad distribution of tests scores that labeled a large segment of the student population as failures. These students either dropped out of school or failed to develop needed basic skills because ongoing feedback and skill development were not part of the assessment equation. According to Stiggins,

> The driving emotional force cannot merely be competition for an artificial scarcity of success. . . . The student must believe that, "I will succeed at learning if I keep trying." Students must have continuous access to believe evidence of credible academic success, leading to the new role for assessment in school improvement: We use it to help students see and understand the achievement targets from the beginning of the learning, and we use it to help them watch themselves grow and succeed. (pp. 73–74)

Stiggins (2005) calls this process *assessment FOR learning* in which students have the opportunity to work on and improve performance in a supportive environment. He contrasts this with *assessment OF learning,* the traditional summative process, that lets students know if learning occurred following the instruction. According to Stiggins, "Assessments OF learning ask if students are meeting standards . . . [and] assessments FOR learning ask if our students are making progress toward meeting those standards. One is for accountability, while the other is intended to support learning" (p. 75). Bransford, Brown, and Cocking (2000), using the more popular term *formative assessment,* note that this type of assessment is "ongoing," "make[s] student thinking visible," and "help[s] both teacher and students monitor progress" (p. 24).

Chris Tovani (2012), motivated by the powerful visible learning notion expressed by Bransford et al. and Hattie (2009), reflects that, "When students have the chance to tell me what they need, they empower me to revise and rethink my instruction. Such two-way feedback puts students—instead of just the curriculum—in the driver's seat" (p. 51). One cannot overstate this aspect of formative assessment and feedback as an instructional strategy. Popham (2008) emphasizes, "Assessment-elicited evidence of students' status is used by teachers to adjust their ongoing instructional procedures or by students to adjust their current learning tactics" (p. 17). When both teachers and students value feedback, it becomes an indispensible instructional strategy to build trust and personalize learning. The bond between student and teacher becomes almost symbiotic—they need each other to achieve outstanding work. Teachers, as reflective practitioners, modify their strategies, often on the spot, as a response to the level of student understanding and students, through feedback, deliberatively gain confidence in their ability to gauge and make choices about the direction of their work. As a 21st century skill, students using that feedback to make independent decisions about their learning become "self-regulated learners . . . and masters of their own destiny" (Brookhart, 2008, p. 113). Finally, as is often the case, this brings us back to Madeline Hunter and a phrase that has influenced millions of educators: checking for understanding. Mike Schmoker in his book *Focus* (2011b) passionately argues that we are spending way too much time and money on a "parade of popular initiatives and trainings" (p. 61) while overlooking the compelling research on student achievement and the power of checking for understanding (i.e., feedback). The mandate is clear, school principals as supervisors, and quite frankly just as colleagues, need to share with teachers how their practice will benefit by using feedback as an everyday part of their repertoire to make learning visible.

How Can Data-Driven (and Data-Informed) Curricular, Instructional, and Assessment Decisions Help Educators Foster Student Achievement?

Effective principals look at data and analyze trends, gaps and insights. And yet they know that their role goes beyond the actuarial; instead they must be aspirational.

(National Association of Elementary School Principals [NAESP], 2008, p. 2)

Background

In the past, when student test scores on national norm-referenced tests were shared with faculty or parents, few changes were made based on the testing results. The tests may have given us some insight into how a particular child, school, or district was performing, but there was little concern about teacher or student accountability. With NCLB the situation changed. Today with the CCSS, state tests, and two major testing consortiums developing assessments aligned with the standards, the goal is to use the test results as student and teacher accountability measures. In addition, unlike in the past, districts expect to receive the test results within a few days so interventions can be made to help students that same school year. At least that is the plan.

The Purpose of Data-Driven Decision Making

Quite simply, data-driven decision making takes an analytical and hard look at the question: How are the students doing? This question is grounded in school, district, state, and national expectations for student achievement (i.e., standards) that hold administrators and teachers accountable in each school. Both quantitative and qualitative trends and patterns of student progress should be monitored and interpreted based on worthy outcomes. As Manobianco (2002) notes, "Interpreting data in isolation is useless without linking the data to what we want students to know and be able to do as well as looking at our instructional strategies" (p. 17). In addition, effective data-driven decision making implies that teachers will use multiple sources of data to fine-tune their teaching in order to meet various student needs. Scherer (2001) refers to this important assessment responsibility as the examination of "multiple data waves" (p. 15). Importantly, on this point, Nidus and Sadder (2011) remind us that data are more than test scores,

> It encompasses all the talk and work of teachers and students. Data may come from homework assignments, writing samples, portfolios, exit slips, journals, or any information that provides the opportunity to discuss student work in the context of the lesson and instruction. (p. 33)

Supporting a Culture That Engages in Data-Driven Decision Making

It is not easy to create a school culture that embraces the examination of test results that may very well indicate instructional weaknesses on the teacher, school, or district level. Yet it is one of the most important trends occurring in schools today. Schools that embrace data-driven decision making are often led by principals who are "effective school leaders [and] are hunters, gatherers and consumers of education" (NAESP, 2001). Research on effective school principals sponsored by The Wallace Foundation (2013) strongly supports this approach by concluding that one of their five key principalship practices is, "Managing people, data and processes to foster school improvement" (p. 4).

Effectively led schools, often with thriving PLCs and teacher leaders, are willingly examining curricular, instructional, and assessment practices that account for strengths, weaknesses, and puzzling student scores without blaming or pointing fingers because of testing outcomes. Instead, teachers comfortably ask: How can we use the data to target difficulties and improve teaching and learning? This reflects a climate in which accountability is balanced with honest analysis in a nonthreatening manner. Lachat, Williams, and Smith (2006) suggest using a team approach to examining data: "A data team expands the control of data beyond a handful of administrators and allows a group of staff members to develop and model data analysis skills" (p. 19). Lachat et al. also suggest that schools should develop essential questions relevant to the specific site to organize the data and use a data coach to facilitate the process until the school team has a greater understanding of how to maximize the use of data. Asking questions can also help schools get beyond the numbers. Is there a story, a narrative, that emerges from the data (The Wallace Foundation, 2013)? For example, with a difficult economy have more homeless students become part of our school community? Are the low test scores, frequent absences, and increase in free or reduced-price lunch applicants a part of a pattern that we should have picked up already? It is important that schools are deliberate about the steps of collecting, organizing, and analyzing data because thoughtful action should be the culminating activity (Parsley, Dean, & Miller, 2006). The team approach is endorsed also by DuFour and Mattos (2013), "The most vital support a principal can give these collaborative teams is helping them use evidence of student learning to improve their teaching" (p. 38).

Leaders can set a positive tone in schools by promoting a dialogue about assessment. To illustrate, principals can encourage data analysis during faculty meetings, pre- and postobservation conferences, classroom teaching, grade-level meetings, and other professional development activities. One middle school assistant principal stated, "The most exciting activity that we encountered as a faculty concerned data-driven decision making related to sharing writing samples across the curriculum during a faculty meeting. During the meeting we established rubrics aligned with state standards as we scored student work together. This activity made all of us aware of the writing expectations that students should be held accountable for within each discipline." Also, faculty meetings can provide forums for inviting representatives from other schools, with demographic profiles similar to your own school, to share information about progress and concerns with their curricular standards and assessment measures. Principals can help with purposeful scheduling to provide time for teachers to diagnose data in teams to more effectively plan teaching and learning.

Recently, a retired teacher shared the following observation: "When I was teaching I did not worry about standardized tests because the tests were not given until the following year. Today, with standards and the increased testing and accountability, teachers cannot ignore how the progress in their class might affect testing the following year." Consequently, opportunities must be provided that allow teachers to compare notes with grade-level or department colleagues to review standards and benchmarks and discuss effective instructional strategies. During these meetings teachers can remind one another to concentrate on essential curriculum elements, pinpoint areas that need greater emphasis, identify strengths, and explore grade-level or subject area trends (e.g., "How are our students doing with their non-fiction writing? Are they using evidence or just sharing their opinions on topics? With our emphasis on STEM objectives, are the students writing about connections between their math and science classes? Are student technology projects showing creativity and design rigor?").

This horizontal articulation must be complemented by vertical articulation with grade-level or subject-area colleagues above and below a particular grade to reduce curriculum repetition and share successful teaching strategies. These horizontal and vertical grade-level meetings provide opportunities for PLC and critical friends activities to occur, linking CCSS, state, and consortium assessments with actual classroom performance.

Pre- and postobservation conferences and class observations should also be used to promote data-driven decision making. During preobservation conferences, principals need to ask teachers about targeting standards, benchmarks, and assessment data with student work in particular classes.

Data-driven decision making also uses feedback generated from student, parent, or community surveys. For example, data revealing how present high school students or recent graduates are succeeding in college or with their careers can help schools with curricular and instructional decisions. One high school that has significantly improved its graduation rate is aggressively seeking data to discover why this has not yet translated into success at the college level.

A portfolio, as a record of student growth over time, is especially promising as a rich source of student data. When a teacher, parent, or community member can look at a specific student's work, generated during a year or over several years, one can see progress right before one's eyes. Hard-copy evidence of student work as artifacts of progress is very powerful. Hearing and/or seeing a brief audio or video recording, generated over several months, of a first grader learning to read is equally powerful. The popularity of student-led conferences showcasing student work attests to the power of these sources of data. Paperless electronic portfolios are also very popular and enable students to display a variety of work samples in a digital format that can include artifacts that range from a math exam, to video of a field trip, to an interactive dialogue with British students debating the causes of the revolutionary war.

Diane Ravitch (2010) in her thoughtful book *The Death and Life of the Great American School System* supports the use of a variety of data sources to make decisions about student progress. However, she strongly believes that our schools should be very cautious about data,

> Data are only as good as the measures used to create the numbers. . . . If the data reflect mainly the amount of time invested in test-preparation activities, then the data are worthless. If the data are based on dumbed-down state tests, then the data are meaningless. (p. 228)

Ravitch also shares a powerful idea from Deborah Meier, the well-known public school activist and early supporter of the small schools movement.

Meier believes that "our schools should be 'data-informed,' not 'data-driven.'" Essentially, Meier is saying, "Hold the horses, and let's not jump to conclusions. Maybe the data isn't telling us everything we need to know. In fact, maybe the data isn't telling us anything." Meier's insight reminds us of the quote attributed to Albert Einstein, "Not everything that can be counted counts, and not everything that counts can be counted."

Disaggregating Data

Data-driven (or data-informed) decision making seeks "to look deeper into the surface data" to help schools identify why some students are doing better than others (NAESP, 2001, p. 64). With the Web-based school management data systems available to districts, disaggregating information is much less difficult today than even 10 years ago. Principals can lead this effort, along with guidance counselors, teachers, department or grade-level leaders, PLC groups, school psychologists, and central office assessment specialists.

Multiple demographic variables can be examined by disaggregating data. Examples of demographic variables include gender, attendance patterns, ethnicity, race, student mobility, teacher mobility, teacher tenure, free or reduced-price lunch eligibility, tardiness, behavioral referrals, and second-language learners. It is critical to engage in a dialogue when disaggregating data to examine trends or patterns that emerge as variables are considered.

One cannot exaggerate the importance of analyzing data demographically. For example, a majority of students in a particular school may have achieved outstanding results on the state's math assessment test. However, disaggregated data may reveal that 75 percent of the students in the school who are eligible for free or reduced-price lunch scored below the minimum expectation on the test. Clearly the school needs to target this population to help these students improve their test scores.

Finally, a cautionary note. Disaggregating data helps principals, teachers, and parents examine whether schools are succeeding with their various populations. However, whenever we separate groups and highlight differences, there is a risk that data might be misinterpreted or misused—leading to stereotypical remarks and possibly racist or prejudicial generalizations. Unfortunately, the history of standardized testing, going back to the 1920s and the original intelligence testing movement, is filled with prejudicial use and abuse of data results that led to limiting school and career opportunities for both indigenous and immigrant American populations (*Education Week,* 2000). School leaders must guard against this abuse of data. This sentiment is supported by the American Educational Research Association's position statement on high-stakes testing. That statement includes two key recommendations: "The intended and unintended effects of the testing program must be continuously evaluated and disclosed" and "the negative side-effects of a high-stakes assessment program must be fully disclosed to policy makers" (Amrein-Beardsley, 2008, pp. 72–73).

What Is the Best Way to Determine Whether Students Have Grasped the Key Curriculum Goals?

This question presents one of the most difficult and controversial issues in education: finding the best way to judge what students know and are able to do. Unless educators and other stakeholders are satisfied with the ways of assessing students, curriculum accountability will always be questioned. Standardized tests give us some insight into how students in each school "rate" when compared to each other and to students in other schools. State assessments, based on curricula standards, serve as a crucial and very public source of information for comparison and accountability purposes. This is especially true when high-stakes tests are used to make decisions for promotion and graduation. It remains to be seen how educators, students, the consortium states, and the public receive the Smarter Balance and Partnership for Assessment of Readiness for College and Careers assessments. However, we need to go further if each teacher's expertise about his or her class is to count—and if we are to identify the diverse strengths and needs of each student. The nature of assessments may need to vary in each class. Thus a major part of a school's discussion on curriculum must be related to the learning tasks and expected outcomes at each grade level that indicate whether students have grasped the essentials of the curriculum. Clearly, assessment is not separate from curriculum and instruction.

Probably one of the richest activities for a teaching staff is to develop an authentic performance task that aligns with the CCSS, the local curriculum, and expected outcomes. To illustrate, let us assume that an 11th-grade American history class has just studied the governmental system of checks and balances. Instead of giving a traditional essay exam to assess their knowledge of the system, why not try a simulation activity in which groups of students represent the three branches of government (executive, legislative, judicial) and debate over which branch or branches should be responsible for handling scenarios presented by the teacher? Before beginning the activity, a teacher should have a strong sense of which concepts (outcomes) are critical for understanding. The activity should be structured so students have an opportunity to display and reinforce their understanding of the concepts (e.g., When does a police action by our military become a war? What role does each branch of government play if America is fighting a war?). This will give students an opportunity to really wrestle with issues, debate, think on their feet, and see the different interpretations that are possible. This type of performance task addresses the following concern: developing student tasks that provide evidence as to whether the students are college and career ready. Such a task also presents opportunities for students to practice critical thinking, decision making, public speaking, and listening skills in addition to demonstrating knowledge about the branches of government.

The positive response of so many teachers to alternative assessment strategies probably indicates a realization that the search for ways to authenticate learning has brought greater meaning to both teachers and students. Principals would be wise to encourage these explorations if teachers are taking ownership of the various strategies to pursue meaningful curriculum goals. Portfolio assessment, for example, has enabled teachers to see significant growth over time and has encouraged students to take greater ownership and reflect more on their work (Tierney, Carter, & Desai, 1991).

Curriculum and the Future: What Do We Need to Do to Keep Our Eyes On the Prize?

Toward the end of the American Civil War as the winds started to blow favorably for the North many citizens wanted to give President Lincoln credit for the progress. In character, Lincoln, in a letter to his friend Albert Hodges, stated, "I claim not to have controlled events, but confess plainly that events have controlled me." That is kind of how we feel about the future direction of U.S. curriculum. It is easy to say, "Hey, you need to control your own destiny." But, just like in Lincoln's time, there are many factors and players. For example, what will be the status of the CCSS in five years? What about the Smarter Balance and the Partnership for Assessment of Readiness for College and Careers (PARCC)? How those initiatives fare will, to a great extent, determine what happens next. As we noted earlier in this chapter, the flaws of NCLB provided the opening for national standards and broad assessment consortiums. There was just too much variety under NCLB concerning state standards and variance related to the quality of state assessments. The CCSS, NCLB, and RTTT are just some of the factors that will "control events." Some others include the nation's economy, politics, the infrastructure condition of the nation's schools, energy issues, foreign competition, business needs, immigration, progress concerning the achievement and opportunity gaps, technological developments, pop culture, how families manage, the teacher and administrative pipelines, the quality of schools of education, societal mobility, graduation rates, and unpredictable events. Although it is impossible to weigh how these factors will influence the future of U.S. schools, these are prominent curriculum issues that we need to keep an eye on for the future. And, if we are quick enough, maybe we can even influence outcomes before anyone notices!

(1) *Will we commit to writing curriculum (scope and sequence) aligned to the CCSS and will we provide the professional development that teachers need to implement the new standards?* Writing CCSS and awarding two consortia funding to develop assessments for the standards will not be enough. The work that states and districts are engaged in today, developing curriculum and organizing professional development opportunities for their teachers on teaching with the standards, will be the real test. Can we keep up that effort? Much of the teacher training is online; we will see how that goes. And, will we take the time to develop rich curriculum?

Schmoker's (2012) concern is real; commenting on the "current blitz" around CCSS workshops, he maintains, "These workshops are seldom designed to help schools complete a coherent, literacy-rich curriculum now, not years from now. Make no mistake: When we postpone the implementation of curriculum, we forfeit the benefits of the most powerful lever for improvement" (p. 68).

(2) *Are we committed to ensuring that students without privilege have the same access to superior curriculum, teachers, and resources as privileged students?* Linda Darling-Hammond in her influential book, *The Flat World and Education* (2010), addresses this question by referring to the **Opportunity Gap**, "the accumulated differences in access to key educational resources—expert teachers, personalized attention, high-quality curriculum opportunities, good educational materials, and plentiful information resources—that support learning at home and at school" (p. 29).

(3) *What will be the status of subjects that are not part of the high stakes testing related to the CCSS?* We have been here before. Can we thrive as a society if we do not address the social studies, the arts, foreign languages, health, and physical education (our assumption is that the STEM expectations will be addressed as part of the Next Generation Science Standard, which is part of the plan)? We are not suggesting that all of these subjects should be tested—but that does not mean they should receive second-class status within the curriculum and within the culture of our schools. Teachers and principals need to be creative in how they keep these subjects on the front burner. Greece may be having financial difficulties, but the nation will live forever because of the Parthenon, a perfect example of the Arts and the STEM disciplines in harmony. Yong Zhao's (2009) position is compelling, "I am convinced that no one subject or skill, regardless of its perceived importance, should be elevated to a level that excludes other subjects or skills in the school curriculum" (p. 155).

(4) *Can we commit to both rich content and 21st century skills?* Content may not sound as romantic as 21st century skills, but students will certainly need to be strong in both areas to succeed with the standards. To be college and career ready, the standards are asking for teachers to emphasize the importance of evidence. For example, consider this Grade 5 Literacy Standard (CCSS.ELA-Literacy.RL.5.1): "Quote accurately from a text when explaining what the text says explicitly and when drawing inferences from the text." Clearly creativity alone (a vital 21st century skill) will not enable a student to meet this Literacy Standard. But here is where we can fall in a trap. We should not "fall" for the notion that it is an either/or choice: content OR 21st century skills. As noted in Chapter 1, Collins and Porras's (2004) notion of the "The Genius of And" is an approach educators should take whenever facing false choices (e.g., phonics vs. whole language; fiction vs. nonfiction; teacher-centered vs. student-centered). Let's hope that as we move forward, content and 21st century skills are perceived as complementary elements of learning.

(5) *Do we have the courage to practice less is more?* Long before the CCSS movement, the late Ted Sizer encouraged educators to go deep instead of wide, "Let us do a few things exceedingly well, rather than many things superficially."

(6) *Where is the digital transformation taking us?* In the 1920s, a revolutionary invention was poised to change schools forever, and for the better: the radio. An innovative idea at that time was to teach penmanship over the radio! Today the opportunities are infinite. We are enthusiastic about the 21st century classroom because of possibilities related to digital devices, social and educational networks, digital content (e.g., eliminating traditional textbooks), blended learning with teachers as guides, on-demand professional development, Personal Learning Networks (PLN) for online teacher collaboration, Massive Open Online Courses (MOOC), digital interactive teaching strategies, apps that generate immediate classroom feedback, and greater empowerment for students and teachers because of instant access to information. However, the Opportunity Gap is a troubling technology concern that must be addressed (i.e., the Digital Divide) since high-poverty schools are less likely to have access to school devices, extensive bandwidth, 1 on 1 computing, and Bring Your Own Device (BYOD) options. Again, courage is critical, school leaders and teachers need to constantly ask: Will a proposed technology option improve teaching and learning and will students without privilege have equal access?

(7) *Can we say "No" to the next big thing?* Today we are facing a perfect storm. New teacher evaluation systems, the CCSS, and the PARCC and Smarter Balance assessments are all arriving in a relatively short time period. Consider this: student test scores will be used to judge the competency of a teacher, yet we don't know at this point what those tests will look like or whether they will be effective.

(8) *Will "teaching to the test" become the dominant factor as we move forward with the CCSS?* This fear has already been expressed as a concern when the Next Generation Science Standards were introduced this spring (Robelen, 2013). The leaders of that movement are encouraging science educators to just concentrate on the standards. Educational historian Diane Ravitch's concern must be taken into consideration as we move forward, "The things that have made a difference for our country are freedom and the encouragement of creativity, imagination, and innovation—things that are not encouraged by our obsession with standardized testing" (Dodge, 2011/2012, p. 55).

(9) *Will our concern with curriculum content diminish the importance of personalization and making connections with students?* The pressure will be on the next few years to succeed with the CCSS and the Smarter Balance and PARCC assessments. But if we become obsessed, it will get in the way of relationships. Teaching and learning is just as much about enthusiasm for a class, because the teacher sparks student curiosity, as it is about rich content.

Again, let's not get caught up in an either/or dilemma as we move forward with the CCSS. Relationships are important—they open the door to learning.

Let's revisit these factors in five years, and in ten years, to discuss how we are doing on these nine issues!

CONTINUING THE CURRICULUM DISCUSSION

Today, a principal's most important responsibilities regarding curriculum may be in providing the forum or setting to facilitate teacher curriculum discussions about the CCSS and displaying empathy for the frustrations and concerns teachers have as they move forward with the new standards and assessments. Principals also have to stay on top of the changes, be assertive about ensuring that the state or district scope and sequence documents align with the standards, and promote professional development for faculty. Too often in the past we have asked teachers to make changes without providing the training or resources to do so. Finally, "We should be aiming to help children become caring adults, builders of communities, sharers of learning, lovers of the printed word, citizens of the world, and nurturers of nature" (Teeter, 1995, p. 360).

REFLECTIONS

This space provides for you a place to write in ideas that have been generated by this chapter, things you want to try, or adaptations of ideas presented herein.

1. Do you agree or disagree with the definition of curriculum provided in this chapter? Discuss your ideas with a colleague.

2. Are the shifts related to curriculum, instruction, and assessment relevant to your setting? What would you add to the list?

3. What are the most important curriculum issues that currently need to be addressed in your school? Why are these issues important? How can you begin energizing the staff to address these issues?

4. Speculate on some societal trends that could affect the curriculum. Are schools addressing the curricular areas necessary to cope with these trends?

(Continued)

(Continued)

5. Should the curriculum reflect current societal trends or ideal societal possibilities?

6. How might staff interest in curriculum review, development, or implementation be enhanced?

7. What are the strengths of the CCSS? What are your greatest concerns?

8. What insights or new questions do you have as a result of reflecting on the ideas presented in this chapter?

PART V

Starting Effectively and Staying the Course

15

First Days of School

A time for renewal.

—A principal's voice

The first days of every school year are always both exciting and nervous times for students, parents, new principals, seasoned administrators, and teachers. Regardless of how many years one has spent in the profession, the new year is always a time of renewal and uncertainty. This is a time of renewal because it is a chance to try a fresh approach with new and returning students and teachers. It is a time of uncertainty because, whether one is a newcomer or a veteran, there are always questions: Will I succeed this year? What will be the new challenges? Which state and federal mandates need to receive particular attention this year? This will be particularly challenging during the next few years with the Common Core State Standards (CCSS), new teacher evaluation systems, regional assessment consortia aligned with the standards, and the economic difficulties school districts are facing. Often, principals try to speculate about what the challenges and issues will be for a new year. The best approach to take may simply be, "I don't know what challenges or issues will come our way, but I'll try to be ready!"

The beginning of the year also has special significance because the brain remembers beginnings and endings. The first impression that a principal makes with the staff will be a lasting impression. Additionally, in the beginning of the year our senses are heightened, and the opportunity exists to face new and old challenges with a fresh perspective. On the other hand, too much change in the beginning of the year can be unnerving—especially if the changes come as a surprise to the staff. A blend of tradition and change may be the best approach.

LOGISTICAL CONCERNS

Distributing a schedule of beginning-of-the-year activities to teachers with a "Welcome Back" letter a couple of weeks before school begins is a good way to let teachers know that all is moving along smoothly and to remind them of the School Improvement Plan goals. The letter can help encourage the staff to begin thinking about the new year and plan activities and actions that need to be taken care of before initial school meetings begin. In a year-round school, this will be necessary for each track. The letter also models valuing preparedness.

During the first days of the new school year, the principal needs to be very concerned about logistics, yet ensure that human needs and curricular, instructional, and assessment goals are not overlooked. The following "Beginning of the Year Checklist" addresses many of these concerns:

- Thoroughly examine the Web-based school management software system to make sure all critical administrative, teacher, student, and parent portals are up to date. It may be helpful to meet with the district or school Technology Integration Specialist to walk you through the system, since there will likely be upgrades or new functionalities that should be reviewed. For the beginning of the year, it is particularly crucial that student demographic and registration systems are operating efficiently. Other crucial systems to check on the administrative and teacher portals include: the master schedule, teacher assignments, class lists, attendance, student transportation, discipline, grade book, seating chart, lunch data, updated curriculum scope, and sequence and pacing charts.
- Review district and school mission, curriculum goals, and school and grade-level testing data—alone, and then with key personnel. Although all of the documents and data are online, consider what needs to be hard copied or posted in the school.
- Consider which district, state, and federal mandates will need special attention this year.
- Review Individuals with Disabilities Education Act regulations, and consider whether any particular compliance issues will need special attention. Discuss these issues with district and school special education experts.
- Carefully review previous beginning-of-the-year memos and newsletters to staff, students, parents, and the community.
- Examine faculty assignments and last-minute hiring issues.
- Review master schedule, enrollment trends, and class lists with counselors and administrators.

- Review timelines for projected supervisory and evaluation visits and block schedules with appropriate administrators and staff.
- Review the budgetary expectations for the year—alone and with the district budget manager.
- Meet with assistant principals, department chairs, and grade-level leaders concerning goals for the year and beginning-of-the-year logistical issues.
- Review with secretaries the beginning-of-the-year tickler file (see Chapter 16).
- Review orientation for new students with counselors and appropriate staff.
- Review orientation for new teachers with key veteran faculty or coaches.
- Meet with special services team, including counselors and teachers.
- Remind secretaries of their role as ambassadors for the school.
- Walk through the school with the head custodian to make sure rooms have sufficient furniture for students and staff and that outlets, lights, windows, ceilings, walls, halls, and playgrounds are all meeting cleanliness and safety standards.
- Ensure that restrooms have necessary supplies and are absolutely clean.
- Review security, health and safety plans and procedures, and critical phone numbers for fire, ambulance, police, and poison control.
- Make sure procedures are in place for preventing intruders.
- Develop the year's calendar (likely with the district office) for fire, lockdown, intruder, and active shooter drills. Depending on the region, weather-related drills need to be scheduled.
- Meet with transportation director (e.g., review traffic patterns, bus lanes, signage) and food service personnel.
- Review the year's activities with athletic/activities director.
- Review disciplinary procedures, especially new mandates, with assistant principals.
- Working with the Technology Integration Specialists, make sure digital hardware, projectors, and software are ready to go to minimize first-day glitches (which will happen!).
- Invite student government representatives to lunch.
- Make sure substitute teacher policies are in place.
- Carefully organize beginning-of-the-year faculty meetings, combining professional development and logistical concerns. Seek input from faculty and other administrators. Consider reviewing the School Improvement Plan during the faculty meeting.
- Meet with Parent Teacher Association representatives. Ask for volunteers to help the first week with orientation, soliciting parents from various communities, with translators.
- Make sure orientation signs for "first days" of school are completed. Include a banner in the front of the school with a slogan that students are familiar with, such as "Good Things Are Happening"

(ABC News, 2002). If appropriate, post the first day signs in various languages to meet student and parent needs.

- Block your schedule to be especially visible during the first few days of school.
- Walk through the school on your own, "visioning" a typical day.

One principal thought he was ready on the first day, except for one problem: the automated school bells had not been calibrated for the year. The custodian had forgotten about the bells, and the principal did not know how to set them. The principal quickly learned. What a way to start! Although operating the school bells should never be confused with educational leadership, the ability to calibrate bells in this case contributed to things running smoothly.

Before classes begin, teachers want to make sure they have resources and time to work in their classrooms. Scheduling a workshop in lieu of providing time to set up classrooms could be a "kiss of death" to the feeling tone in the school. There should be a balance between how time is organized and used prior to classes and a sensitivity to teacher and classroom needs. Regarding instructional resources, each teacher should receive, without asking, essential technology resources and traditional classroom supplies (pencils still come in handy!). The Web-based school management system should have a teacher portal that includes items such as student demographic information and programs for attendance, lunch data, grade book, seating charts, transportation, and discipline; also an activities calendar and school policies and procedures manuals should be available. The instructional management system should include curriculum guides, scope and sequence and/or pacing guides, templates for monthly or unit planning and lesson planning, testing programs, and student assessment data. Depending on the system, the district or state may align the CCSS with district curriculum for availability on the website. Whether the district goes with digital textbooks or traditional textbooks will also affect teacher resources. Classroom resources should include:

Pens, pencils, erasers	Paper, tape, tissues, and a stapler
Flash drives	Garbage cans
Whiteboard markers	Eraser fluid for whiteboards
Chart paper	Markers for chart paper
Smart Board supplies	Bulletin board material

Having these Web-based and traditional items in classrooms when teachers arrive tells them that you care. If you have not used this procedure, develop a beginning-of-the-year technology and supply list with three or four veteran teachers and a secretary. Also check with the library media center personnel and technology area personnel to make sure they have necessary resources and are ready for the first day of school. Teachers welcome lists of new library, technology, and media acquisitions.

Another logistical concern should be school maintenance. The principal should review the summer maintenance requests with the custodian and walk through the school several days before the year begins to make sure that the repairs have been completed and that the school is well lit, clean, and safe. In elementary schools, the playground areas should be carefully checked for hazards. In middle and high schools, checking locker conditions and common gathering areas is a must.

To remain on top of logistical concerns from year to year, keep a beginning-of-the-year digital or hardcopy folder as part of your "tickler file" (see Chapter 16). Although the monthly tickler file will include important activities covered during each month, the beginning-of-the-year file is especially important to help you begin successfully. Remember to update the file a few days after the school year starts. Soliciting staff input can be helpful in enhancing beginning-of-the-year activities. The file is especially valuable to a principal who will be taking over a new school. Typical items that may be in the file include letters to parents, the previous year's teaching schedules, the master schedule, programs from various school productions, minutes or agendas of faculty meetings, and reflections on how to improve Back to School Night. Keep everything online, make sure the items are backed up, and make hard copies to review any items that will be distributed to parents, teachers, students, or the community.

BEGINNING-OF-THE-YEAR FACULTY MEETINGS SET A TONE

Faculty meetings are extremely important in the beginning of the year as colleagues, old and new, gather together, work collaboratively, and, it is hoped, grow professionally. These meetings present special opportunities for principals to strengthen staff cohesion and morale. Your first obligation during the meetings should be to remind staff members that you are there to serve them. We cannot overstate the importance of these meetings as culture-building opportunities. Research strongly supports the notion that when school leadership creates a positive tone teachers want to remain in that school (Grissom, 2011). Moreover, teachers take pride when working with colleagues who care about students and believe they can make a difference, "In fact, studies show that one of the greatest incentives in teachers' choices of schools is the opportunity to work with other skillful and committed colleagues, and to be in environments where they can be efficacious" (Darling-Hammond, 2010, p. 208).

Consider a specific theme to set the tone for the year. For instance, if the theme is "The School as a Community of Learners," activities need to be structured to reflect that. One such activity is to remind teachers of the wealth of knowledge that exists among the staff. During a faculty meeting, teachers might be asked to add up their collective years of teaching at a table group and share. The table group members with the greatest number of years might be awarded a prize. Such activities remind one of the rich resources that exist just beyond one's classroom door. By seeking advice from colleagues, staff members are able to tap the wisdom of practice that exists in a school. Without doing so, one runs the risk of repeating an initial year of teaching several years in a row. At Cheney High School in Cheney, Washington, the administration and faculty instituted a student motivational program based on the "212°" degree theme (the extra degree boils water!) and video that stresses the importance of taking personal responsibility and making the extra effort. With videos, displays in the school, and teacher buy-in the program was successfully implemented. Throughout the year, students and faculty were recognized for making the extra effort. With the CCSS emphasis on writing, a "Think Write" theme could be implemented across the curriculum with any elementary, middle, or high school. The theme could include emphasizing both higher level thinking skills (Think) and meaningful writing (Write). David Conley, after conducting extensive research on college readiness, stated,

> If we could institute only one change to make students more college ready, it should be to increase the amount and quality of writing students are expected to produce. Develop student writing skills systematically in all classes and across a range of writing genres, especially expository, descriptive, and persuasive writing. To increase the amount of writing that high school students do, assign many short, three- to five-page papers that require careful reasoning supported by research and citations. Expect students to edit and revise these papers rather than submit them only once.
>
> (2007, p. 26)

Again, with the CCSS movement, writing has become a critical point of focus for schools, and adopting this theme could make a big difference in helping students become college and career ready.

Professional development should always be a significant part of faculty meetings. The beginning of the year is the perfect time to make this point. A principal should consider activities that help teachers think about the year and possibly create a vision of the kind of year they can have with their students and colleagues. Before beginning this visioning activity, review the school's philosophy and mission with the staff. Ask whether they believe it needs revisiting or revising. Here is a variation on a "reverse visioning" activity from *If It Ain't Broke . . . Break It!* (Kriegel, 1991) that has been used successfully in the beginning of the year:

Reverse Visioning—A Variation

1. You are 85 years old . . .

2. What did you do with your life?

3. What were the significant milestones at 30, 40, . . . 80?

4. What qualities did you exhibit?

5. How do other people describe your life?

6. Do you have any regrets? If so, what are they?

7. What would you have done differently?

8. As you are sitting in your rocking chair, a former student comes to visit you on your 85th birthday. The student states that he or she remembers you very well. Ideally, what would you hope that the student would say about you?

9. Pair up with a new teacher or someone who is not on your grade level or specialist area and discuss your ideas.

After the exercise, teachers were asked to write on a small poster what they wanted the students to say about them. Teachers used tablets or markers and poster paper to complete the activity.

These faculty meetings should be used also as a link with previous years. Review the school's traditions, successes, and what characterizes the culture of the school. This is not a time to review every topic in the faculty handbook. Certainly, new or very significant school changes should be mentioned, but teachers should read the handbook on their own. This is the time, however, to remind staff members of the noble purpose of their profession and their years of dedication to students. Remember, what you pay attention to communicates what you value.

If yearly goals are developed, then a review of last year's recommendations and the refinement of that document need to begin (see Chapter 8). These goals are important for teachers and students. The common goals can send a signal to students while they are in a class that the teachers are working together. For example, if fostering critical thinking is a school goal, emphasizing the goal in each discipline can be especially powerful in high schools as students move from class to class and realize that teachers are encouraging the same behaviors. This lets students know that teachers are communicating and working together.

Team-building activities should also be part of a school's opening. For example, the following activity helped the staff in one school become better acquainted and proved to be a pleasant icebreaker:

1. Teachers were divided into groups of four.

2. Each group member listed four statements about him- or herself— one statement was false.

3. Each person then read his or her list, and the other group members guessed which statement was false.

4. After all guessed, each person revealed which of the statements was false.

5. Points were awarded for accurate guessing and for "stumping" the group.

One school engaged in an activity in which teachers, paraprofessionals, and administrators brainstormed about the "One Big Thing" they wanted to accomplish with their students during the new school year. After deciding on the "One Big Thing," everyone had to write out their decision in six words, not more, or less. It was a fun exercise. Everyone was asked to post their six words in a place that they would frequently pass by. Another staff had a back-to-school breakfast. Following the meal, a scavenger hunt was scheduled so staff members could find additional resources. The winning team received gift certificates to a local teaching supply store.

DEPARTMENTAL AND GRADE-LEVEL MEETINGS

These meetings should be prescheduled because the time for small groups to get together to plan the year is critical. Grade-level and departmental meetings should be held for reviewing and refining curricular, instructional, and assessment goals and estimating timelines for completing work. This should include a review of the successes as well as hurdles of the previous year. The emphasis should not be to cover everything but to discuss key outcomes that should be stressed for the year. Also, this time should be used to review some of the major activities that are held during the year (e.g., Thanksgiving program, Spirit Weeks, Martin Luther King commemoration, state testing dates, Earth Day activities) to adjust time accordingly. Ensuring that all members of the grade-level and department teams have sufficient supplies should also be a goal of these meetings. During this time, seasoned teachers should discuss the instructional resources available and share their materials with new teachers.

Reviewing the vertical articulation of the curriculum and aligning the curriculum with the CCSS and assessment expectations should be an objective of these meetings. For example, sequential grades (e.g., Grades 3 and 4) can meet to review the expectations for the present and following year. Too often, we forget to consider the next year and micromanage the curriculum for the next day. To facilitate a more far-reaching view of the curriculum, the third-grade teachers, for example, should ask the fourth-grade teachers: What do you expect fourth graders to be able to do when the year begins? This helps the staff project for the next year, not the next day, and can have important implications for how one teaches. In middle and high schools, departmental members should be asking similar articulation and alignment questions of one another to project for the future. Ideally, the teachers in exit grades in each school should talk about their expectations to all of the teachers in grades below them as well as to those receiving teachers in the grades above them. Discussing interdisciplinary curriculum and instructional strategies should, in addition, be considered at this time. Often Professional Learning Communities schedule dates several months at a time for various departments to meet and discuss possibilities for a parallel curriculum (e.g., teaching related topics at similar times), developing common assessments, or actual interdisciplinary teaching (e.g., teaching common themes and concepts, developing interdisciplinary essential questions, working on projects and activities together, team teaching, celebrating successes, and monitoring student progress). In elementary settings, grade-level meetings can also be devoted to these possibilities.

ORIENTING TEACHERS WHO ARE NEW TO THE SCHOOL

Separate orientation sessions for new teachers and teachers who are new to the school should be set up. Usually one or two days before veteran school staff members return is sufficient time to hold the meetings. Whether a teacher is new to the profession or simply new to the school, this is an anxious time. A veteran teacher who may have been very successful in previous schools can find this time especially taxing because he or she will be experiencing some of the same frustrations as the total newcomer: Exactly how does that copier work? What are the rules for duplicating material? What is the schedule? Where are resources housed? Is it a Mac or PC school? What kind of Web-based student management software system is the school using? Will I develop strong professional relationships?

As with the general faculty meetings, the principal should view this time as an opportunity to set an example with the new staff by not only responding to their immediate needs but also emphasizing the school mission and the possibilities that exist for students when teachers are committed, have energy and enthusiasm, and care about children. The principal should talk about the school culture and celebrate teaching. Also, the principal can use this time to stress that the school is a learning community and that the principal, too, is learning along with the teachers.

• Devote very little time during the meetings to the faculty handbook—emphasize only those procedures that are new or essential. Send the message that you know the teachers are professionals and can read the manual on their own. Welcome questions about the handbook for the next meeting. Because they will be anxious about curriculum material, make sure the material is available on the first meeting day with curriculum guides, teacher editions, and supplementary resources.

• A tour of the school and available instructional resources (both basic and enrichment) should be a priority.

- Suggest resources to create a positive class climate. Encourage teachers to review basic school and classroom routines with their classes during the first few days of school. (This should help save time and reduce possible student problems as the year progresses.) For the beginning teacher, stress the importance of structuring the classroom early in the year.

- Provide a variety of models for room arrangement.

- Offer time for teachers to check out resource materials.

Asking new and veteran teachers about the needs and questions they considered during their first year of service can be useful in determining elements for an orientation session. The following guidelines for assisting new teachers were developed by a combined group of new and veteran teachers in the school supervision graduate class at Eastern Washington University:

- Develop a new teacher packet with school philosophy and mission, schedules, staff data, routines, crisis plan, holiday policy, copier directions, hardware availability, Web-based school management system instructions, and community information.
- Purposefully use a mentor/coaching program through the district and school, and initially assist with curriculum, instruction, assessment, time management, the teacher portal program of the school management system, and social issues.
- Assign equitable course loads and grade-level responsibilities.
- Share strategies for working with parents.
- Schedule luncheons with the principal every few weeks during the first year. During one session explain district and school jargon related to educational and informal issues.
- Visit classrooms, observing veteran colleagues, possibly with help of coaches or other teacher leaders.
- Minimize extracurricular commitments during the first year.
- Provide funding for professional development workshops related to the school's curriculum, instructional, and assessment initiatives.
- Allocate sufficient instructional resources and office supplies (e.g., curriculum guides, teacher editions, manipulates).
- Plan social events.
- Encourage team planning with department, grade-level, and/or special service faculty.
- Schedule a welcoming coffee with parent and community representatives.

Many school districts have new teacher induction programs that systematically help newcomers during their first and second years. If your district does not have a formal program, instituting a buddy or coaching system for new teachers is a wonderful way to ease their transition into the school. Research suggests that induction programs can have a positive impact on the newcomers and minimize the number of new teachers who quit during their early years usually because they feel isolated and unsupported. Encouraging the veteran staff to show newcomers around and take them out to dinner or breakfast, at the school's expense, can go a long way in helping newcomers feel like part of the group. By simply answering the various questions that newcomers have—and are reluctant to ask the principal—the buddies can give teachers a sense of security and help them get off to a successful start.

TEACHER TIME IN THE CLASSROOM

Besides receiving their instructional supplies, teachers want to spend time in their classrooms. Teachers should have ample opportunity to do so. If you have several days scheduled of pre-school-year meetings with teachers or an annual retreat (this varies from district to district), try to make a symbolic statement by having one day, or the greater part of a day, without any meetings to show staff members that you respect their need to get into the classroom. Certainly, classroom time should be built into every day before school. Moreover, many teachers will want to work in their classrooms the weekend before school opens. Make it easy for them. If building security is a problem, facilitate the process to keep classrooms open so teachers know you are serving them; the bureaucracy should not become an obstacle during this critical period. Besides, you will be at school the weekend before classes begin!

WELCOMING STUDENTS AND PARENTS

If possible, hold an open house for new students and their parents either late in the spring before the new school year or during the week before school opens. For middle schools, alternative schools, and high schools, ask selected veteran students attending the school to come to the open house to give the newcomers a tour of the school. Many middle, alternative, and high schools have peer support groups supervised by counselors, activities directors, teachers, or administrators to organize social activities and/or academic strategy sessions for new students. Many programs extend throughout the school year, especially to help high school freshmen make the transition. An open house is a good time to introduce assistant principals, teachers, counselors, secretaries, support staff, paraprofessionals, and custodians to the students and parents. This should be a light function, a social gathering, with refreshments. It should be scheduled for about an hour. The gathering can include ice cream for students. A few students from the upper elementary school, middle school, or high school, depending on the setting, can serve as guides.

Ask the parent association to assist on the first day, orienting new parents, serving coffee, and so on. Encourage the association to have a welcome table for parents. Try to have parent volunteers, including several parents who can serve as translators, to assist new families for whom English is a second language. Consider posting direction signs in languages that represent the major school demographic groups.

BE VISIBLE ON THE FIRST DAYS OF SCHOOL

Finally, on the first day of school, plan on being visible to teachers, students, and parents throughout the day. One principal wears a funny hat on the first day so people will gravitate toward him with any logistical questions. Again, the time needs to be built into your schedule well in advance. Circulate on the campus, in the hallways, and in the cafeteria. Also try to visit as many classes as possible during the first couple of days to personally welcome students and wish them a successful year. Some elementary school principals have classes visit their office to emphasize school rules, review activities, answer questions, and generally get acquainted.

Often, assemblies are held to go over school goals and rules. During the assembly, emphasize the school's commitment and personal concern for all students and the importance of community. Introduce the new teachers and classified staff, and honor veteran staff. Remind students that academic success and caring about each other are mutually important school goals that both faculty and classified staff are committed to achieving with students. If there is a theme for the year, the first assembly is the time to roll out the idea. If possible, consider holding the assemblies on the second day so teachers and students can start smoothly and begin their classroom routines.

Most importantly, by being out there (e.g., in the cafeteria and corridor, on the field, by the buses) on the first days of school, the principal reaffirms that important events in the school happen in the classroom and on the campus, not in the administrative offices. In doing this, the principal can proactively troubleshoot logistical problems to see that the school year gets off to a smooth start.

REFLECTIONS

This space provides for you a place to write in ideas that have been generated by this chapter, things you want to try, or adaptations of ideas presented herein.

1. Make a list of 5–10 priorities that a principal should act on before the school year begins.

2. Develop a two-day orientation schedule for faculty.

3. Create an agenda for the first faculty meeting. Consider collaborating with staff members to plan it.

4. Share one or two fun activities that could be included during the faculty orientation period.

5. What were two or three particularly difficult situations for you as a first-year teacher? How could the effect of those situations been minimized?

6. What insights or new questions do you have as a result of reflecting on the ideas presented in this chapter?

16

Tips
Ideas That Work and
Align With the School's Mission

Let's not reinvent the wheel.

—A veteran teacher, now a principal

We are often advised to work smarter, not harder. This chapter will help you follow this advice. We have several practical ideas that can help enhance your performance and tackle new problems. Also, there are many suggestions that we have made throughout the book that are really tricks of the trade, so we are bringing some of these ideas together in this chapter for you as a quick read. In addition to the tricks of the trade, we include suggestions that can firm up the core values important to your school. Each idea has gone through a kind of litmus test. That is, the idea is included because it has been used successfully.

ORGANIZING YOUR TIME

Using a Tickler File

Probably one of the most practical organizing tools a principal can use is a "tickler file" that includes all of the important events, critical activities, memos, e-mails, and time deadlines (e.g., end of semester or quarter, testing, grading periods, open house, parent conferences) for each month; you "tickle" the file monthly. Thus, when November is about a month away, the principal and secretary meet, review a list prepared by the secretary of items in the November file, and examine each previous November memo or important activity description. It is helpful to have separate "beginning of the year" and "end of the year" files, a "graduation" file, a "state testing procedures" file, in addition to the August/September and May/June files. A useful addition to the file is a monthly section that includes your reflections on the events so errors are not repeated, successes are noted, and ideas for next year can be immediately added to the file. A tickler file is invaluable to a principal new to a school.

Blocking Your Personal Schedule

We know that if principals are not careful about monitoring their time—and often interruptions are unavoidable—they will have little control over their schedule. A very helpful tip is to block in time well in advance if you want to be in certain places and engage in particular activities; even personal family events or exercise! We are not only talking about scheduled assemblies or formal observations. Principals should also block in morning walk-throughs to classrooms and short periods to greet or say good-bye to students during the day if these activities are important. Principals must ask themselves, "What message(s) do I need to send to the staff, students, and parents through my behavior? What are my priorities? Am I spending time on these priorities?" As Kent Peterson said, "What you pay attention to communicates what you value." It is especially vital that the school secretaries know the principal's priorities because secretaries can have tremendous influence on the schedule. Finally, principals often feel conflicted because they want to be available, but know that the question "Do you have a minute?" often means a half hour. One principal responded this way: "I have a minute if you can walk and talk with me on my way to my next appointment." This allows the principal to be responsive and to save precious time.

ADDITIONAL HELPFUL IDEAS TO STAY ON TASK

Reflection Log

Keep a log of your reflections. This provides an avenue for a "professional time-out" and increases your capacity to be reflective and analytical. The art and practice of reflection allows one to view a situation from a different perspective because time has elapsed between the occurrence of an event and when one creates the time to think about it. Often fresh insights emerge. Or, one resolves to handle future, similar situations in a different way.

The Digital Morning Daily

An excellent way to communicate daily morning announcements is to use the "Digital Morning Daily" for all teachers to quickly read. It works equally well in elementary, middle, or high schools. The principal prepares the morning announcements the previous afternoon and schedules the announcements for distribution via e-mail the following morning at 7:00 a.m. Most of the announcements will relate to items that could not have been anticipated with the master calendar (e.g., "Because the debate team won the regional competition they will be leaving at 2:30 this afternoon. Wish them good luck!"). The daily should also be used to build spirit with announcements of faculty achievements, inspirational phrases, and humorous comments. Post hard copies in prominent places such as the faculty lounge or reception area for staff that like to socialize or say "hi" to folks before going to their classrooms. If funding is available an iPad or other tablet device can be dedicated to carry the "Digital Morning Daily" in the prominent places just noted. Here is an example of morning announcements.

1. Introducing the standards-based report cards this quarter was quite an accomplishment. But you did it! The comments were thoughtful, objective, and informative. Your hard work is much appreciated. I've already received some great feedback from parents.

2. Assembly at 10:10 instead of 10:15 because we are recognizing five students for their environmental work.

3. Building Leadership Team meeting at 12:05.

4. Math Department meeting during 8th period.

5. Reminder: Student Council representatives will be visiting seventh-grade classes during homeroom to generate interest in the charity drive.

6. Today is Mr. Abram's birthday; we can't give his exact birth year because records were not kept in those days!

The Digital Morning Daily keeps everyone informed, enhances the idea of community, and, when humor is added, can create a friendly and positive tone to begin the day. The daily has another benefit: It serves as a permanent record of important daily events. It really works!

Tips From a Superintendent: What Makes a Successful 21st Century Principal?

By Dr. Deb Clemens

(Superintendent, Cheney Public Schools, Cheney, WA)

Like most superintendents, Dr. Clemens is leading her district through the Common Core State Standards (CCSS) reforms, a new teacher and principalship evaluation system, assessments aligned with the standards, and the usual challenges that all superintendents face. Her reflections on what superintendents seek in today's

(Continued)

(Continued)

building leaders insightfully capture the essence of the 21st century principalship. She identifies 10 critical qualities:

1. Focusing on the Mission and Vision

I think successful principals clearly understand the mission and vision and understand how their schools fit into a bigger picture, into a system. You have to understand the power of being on the same page, to minimize the personal workload and get further by working with the district team.

2. Effectively Communicating Purpose and the "Why" to Teachers and Parents

Principals need to stand in front of teachers and parents and say what the purpose of our school is and why. They need to talk about why the mission and purpose is important and take care of the action plan that helps them achieve the why. The communication piece is so important, not just for articulating the mission and vision but also for timing and choosing the right media resource. When do you communicate? How do you communicate? When do you send handouts? When do you send emails? When should you use the school's audio system? When do you send it by email or print it? Principals need to recognize the importance of timing with all messages.

3. Serving as Instructional Leaders

The instructional leadership piece is crucial. Over the last 15 years, the conversation around instructional leadership has increased. Now principals and teachers are engaged in conversations about standards, curriculum, teaching, assessment, and particular units of study. Those conversations are now a much bigger part of a principal's role. It is critical to stay current, but difficult. The new standards are really just another piece since we have been working the past few years in the district aligning standards, curriculum, teaching, and assessment. With standards principals look for those things that are present in classrooms. For example, what opportunities do students have that indicate they are mastering the common core (e.g., compare and contrast)? Principals are understanding this so they can help teachers adjust their classroom practice, it is not just a checklist of standards.

Concerning the CCSS, principals need to develop strong teacher leaders within each elementary level and at the secondary level within departments. The teachers know the standards and curriculum. It is really hard for a principal to know the standards really well. Principals are not spending everyday on standards with kids and aligning lessons like teachers are doing. But principals still need to own it and engage in those conversations with teachers and spend time attending the same professional development workshops as the teachers. That is true with any initiative. You need to be right there with your teachers, so you have a good understanding. Principals need to build the capacity of their teacher leaders and have that mutual respect. If schools have instructional coaches principals need to build shared responsibility. Principals have to be a part of it and lead it; but a principal cannot be an expert in every part of it. Our principals know how important it is to be with their teachers when they are getting professional development.

Our principals are learning and spending a lot of time on the new teacher evaluation instruments. They are saying that they are having the best conversations they've had with their teachers. They feel it is the right work to spend time on. Principal and teacher evaluation instruments have some similar elements. They both have student growth sections that we need to spend time on. At the elementary level teachers are looking at assessments to see student growth, using multiple measures. Principals are also looking to show multiple measures of growth with their teachers.

One thing that is important for the long range is having principals serve on some district committees. It is hard to leave the building, maybe to work on math standards, but dedicating your time to that work helps principals stay connected to the long-range work, which can be over seven years.

4. Setting Priorities in Action, and Managing Time Effectively

Principals have to set priorities. They should not get lost in every single initiative. Principals have School Improvement Plans. They have to decide what is going to happen to make sure they hit the main points well. What are the priorities? For example, we have six building collaboration meetings in each school during the year. Principals have to decide what their priorities will be with the staff at each meeting. Our principals use emails for nuts and bolts stuff so collaboration meeting time is not wasted. You have to decide what you will prioritize with staff. If pre- and postassessment information is going to be big, then principals need to schedule that early on with the building collaboration meetings. You need to intentionally schedule your building collaboration meetings, conferences, and staff meetings. Consider, what are the important topics that we must make sure we address?

Principals need to be good time managers. They need to be organized and manage their time to make sure goals for that month, day, trimester, or year get achieved. Principals need to address the most important priorities of their work, and be proactive. If your goal is to be visible in the classroom then you must schedule it. 'Got a minutes' are always there and you have to schedule classroom time or else the 'got a minutes' will take up all of your time, if you let it. You need to prioritize how you use time so you get in the classroom. A principal really needs to be sure of the calendar time and get the cyclical nature of the year down to move the staff, students, and parents forward. The electronic calendar is really a good thing, but you have to schedule your key priorities.

5. Building Relationships

Our successful principals have the relationship thing down with teachers, and students and parents too. You have to make hundreds of decisions in five minutes, and getting 99% of those decisions right depends on relationships.

6. Sharing and Learning as Collaborative Leaders

Our principals participate in walk-throughs together, and go to each other's schools. Their willingness to share is important. You want your school to be the best, but you want to share. Principals also share and learn from what is happening with different grade bands. They learn from seeing what practice needs to be worked on for students by observing the different grade bands and learning

(Continued)

(Continued)

from what they can see teachers doing. This is not just in elementary schools. Principals share and support similarities in instructional practices across the spectrum of grade levels and schools from elementary to high school.

7. Exercising Visibility

What I appreciate is how visible our principals are with their staff and the community. They are there for important events, science night, greeting parents, the co-curricular piece in high school, you need to be present at events to support teachers, coaches, and parents. Visibility is really critical.

8. Leading Autonomously but Getting Support From the Superintendent

Principals have a lot of autonomy, but to be successful you need to understand the district, the mission, and the benefits to being part of a team, and catch the wave of the support structure. The superintendent or assistant superintendent has to let the principals make the decisions, remain autonomous. But sometimes things go sideways. A parent might get involved and want to see the superintendent. You have to listen to the parent and not just jump in. Recognize that the principals have good background knowledge and understand the greater context. Superintendents need to support principals when they make decisions. Things go sideways, that happens to everyone. When this happens, you have to help principals recover.

9. Welcoming Feedback: Principals Need to Have Good Feedback Loops

Principals receive feedback on school events. For example, instead of doing the Open House in October principals moved it to the night before school started. The reason our principals changed from October is because of parent feedback. Kids got their schedules, knew where their desks were, and had lockers before school started.

10. Creatively Managing Limited Resources

We are working with limited resources. Because we have limited resources our principals have taken on the responsibility for leading professional development in our schools. Our principals are fine teachers, and they model effective teaching during meetings and in classrooms.

THE SCHOOL BUDGET: COMMONSENSE EFFICIENCY TIPS BASED ON THE MISSION

Let's be blunt: No one makes tough choices in flush time.

—Frederick Hess (2011, p. 60)

Economists project that these lean financial times will last several more years. This will have a major effect on school resources, both human and material. The following tips are intended to help school leaders make commonsense choices that can significantly impact budgetary decisions:

1. *Prioritize and Think Strategically.* It is tough to decide what needs to be eliminated or trimmed, but doing so without first deciding on what is most important lacks vision. Ask yourself, based on our mission, what are our five top priorities that positively affect student learning? Educational Resource Strategies (ERS), working with schools throughout the United States, maintains that the most resource efficient schools "start with a clear vision and instructional model, and they align all their resources around it" (Calvo & Miles, 2011/2012, p. 19). ERS indicates that resourceful schools focus on quality teaching, individual student attention, and efficient use of time. The ERS website is an excellent source, with scenarios and other resources for making sound budgetary decisions (http://holdem.erstools.org).

2. *Personalization Counts More Than Class Size.* Class size has always been a popular cause for educators. Concentrating on personalization, however, appears to be a sounder strategic approach, "Reducing class size by one or two or three students doesn't make much difference, on average, and can be very expensive. . . . Rather than focusing on how many students are in a class, think about ways to individualize students' learning experiences and increase the amount of personal attention they get" (City, 2013, p. 12).

3. *Be a Skeptical Consumer of Products and Services.* Cherokee County School District in Georgia and Henry County Schools in Virginia are discriminating consumers. In Henry County, teachers experiment with new apps for about a year before purchasing products, while Cherokee County recently piloted "five types of math software . . . while examining findings about the software from other districts" (Flanigan, 2013, p. S10). Thoughtfully vetting products, programs, and technology options will help districts avoid fads and literally save millions of dollars.

4. *So What Does a Discriminating Consumer Ask?* After speaking with experts, *Education Week* recommended raising several issues when companies indicate that their educational products are supported by research: (a) Can we observe where the study occurred and speak with the local educators? (b) Does our community context match the community where the study was conducted? (c) Is the company willing to speak with various constituencies in our district about their product and study, and can they do it with clarity? (d) If significant achievement is claimed, what is it based on? Was there a comparison group with similar characteristics? (e) Was the study conducted based on the standards of the American Educational Research Association or a similar professional organization? (f) Was the research conducted by an independent third party (Flanigan, 2013, p. S13)?

5. *Promoting Online Learning and Advanced Placement Courses.* Small schools that do not have enough students to hold an Advanced Placement course will often find the class online. The cost is about $500 to $700 for each course. Even high schools with enrollments of 2,000 to 3,000 should consider online offerings for students when only a few seek to enroll. Blended learning online options can also save schools dollars. Creating a foundation for online possibilities (e.g., "Meeting the Needs of Each Student"), or applying for grants with in-house grant writers or volunteer

grant writers from businesses or service clubs, could prove to be creative options (Marrs-Morford & Marshall, 2012; Odden, 2012). Consider these websites to get started: Foundation Center: http://foundationcenter.org; Grant Alerts: www.grantsalert.com; Lowe's: www.toolboxforeducation .com; or Wal-Mart: http://foundation.walmart.com

6. *If You Can't Make a Commitment, It Ain't Gonna Happen.* District and school leaders have to take a hard look at long-term commitments. Billions have been wasted on initiatives that, for various reasons, lost momentum. Again, consider the school mission—is the initiative or innovation going to survive when its greatest advocates move on or the legislature trims funding? Is the support for the initiative strong enough so that each component will be addressed? For example, is the initiative doomed to fail if faculty do not receive professional development training? At the end of the day, the success or failure of any initiative depends not on how much money is thrown at the project—it depends on the people, our beliefs, our hearts, our hopes, and our vow that *this* is the right decision for our students.

PROVIDING EXPERIENCES TO CELEBRATE THE SCHOOL'S CULTURE

The following activities, events, projects, strategies, and professional development recommendations have all been successfully implemented. A few of the ideas may be right for your school or, we hope, may spark an idea that will strengthen the values essential to your school.

See Them Teach Before They Leave

When teachers are permanently leaving a school, especially the retiring veterans, ask the departing teachers if it would be okay for other teachers to watch them teach during the final month of the school year. Use the slogan "See them teach before they leave" (e.g., in the Digital Morning Daily) for a couple of days to encourage teacher visits. The principal should offer to cover some of the classes while staff members visit their departing colleagues. This type of project could become a catalyst for increasing classroom visits among teachers during the school year. At one school that observed this tradition, the departing teacher was presented with a plaque with the doorknob from her classroom mounted on it. Under the knob were the words, "Thank you for opening your door and sharing well-kept secrets. You saved the library of knowledge from burning."

Principal for a Day

A contest can be held in which individual students send the principal letters stating why they should be chosen from among their classmates to "take over for a day." The principal would become the student when the exchange takes place. To get several students involved, the position can change each hour or class period. Principals have also exchanged jobs with business leaders for a day as a community project.

Phoning the Good News

How often do principals call parents to communicate good news? Unfortunately, the reflex goes like this: Billy has messed up again; is it time to call his parents? It is rarely: Johnny was very helpful with that new student; should I call his parents? Principals need to call home and send letters home when good news takes place. Principals use smartphones while Leading and Learning by Wandering Around and call parents about positive student behaviors with the student present. In some schools, students call from the principal's office to give the good news themselves. Phones can even be used to send instant photos home when a student receives an award or wishes to "show off" a great test score. This has served to favorably influence parental attitudes toward the school.

The Principal as Reader and Teacher

Students, especially in elementary schools, enjoy having the principal visit class to read a story or a poem. The holiday season is a perfect time for this type of activity. The school librarian can be very helpful in selecting a variety of stories for each grade level to be read by the principal. About 15–20 minutes of time in each class works. Two or three classes a day for several weeks will do the trick. One principal who is a combat veteran teaches when secondary students are studying the Gulf War or combat operations following 9/11. It is very important for students to see the principal in a role other than the traditional one—the disciplinarian or person "in the office."

The Principal's Three-Dimensional Scrapbook

School principals receive notes, pictures, artwork, poems, photographs, and so on from students throughout the year. Posting these items as a principal's bulletin board scrapbook is a rewarding exercise. Students are drawn to this interesting three-dimensional scrapbook as it "grows out" on a bulletin board near the principal's office. It becomes a folk history of the principal's school year.

Building Traditions to Celebrate Important Values

October 24, United Nations Day, is an excellent opportunity for any school to unify around themes such as respecting all humanity, global unity, strength in diversity, exploring other cultures, or the work of the United Nations. A school should celebrate and commemorate the importance of respecting one another regardless of race, ethnicity, religion, gender, or sexual orientation. Having the faculty working together on an activity such as United Nations Day reminds everyone of one of the most important reasons for schools: learning to get along with one another. There are, of course, other special days that can equally serve this type of theme, such as Earth Day, Martin Luther King Jr. Day, Presidents' Day, and 9/11 commemorations. These days also give a school opportunities to celebrate a theme that should go to the heart of schooling. A variety of activities stressing particular themes should occur throughout the day, or possibly week, of the special occasion. Student projects, films, and outside speakers should all be involved in the activities. School principals should do whatever they can to support faculty committees organizing these special events. Faculty, students, and parents all take an interest in the important values that are brought forth on these days and, one hopes, throughout the school year.

Student Tutors and Peer Counseling

High school students enjoy tutoring younger students, and elementary school students welcome help offered by older students. A relationship between a high school and middle or elementary school to develop a student-tutoring program is an extremely worthwhile activity. It is especially helpful for elementary school students who need special attention and for high school students who can use a boost with their self-confidence. For all involved, this process builds important social and emotional skills. Often, these programs can be set up following the regular school day. Many secondary schools offer course credit for this type of work. In one high school, seniors in the French Club tutor first graders one day a week.

Peer counseling is also a very worthwhile activity for middle and high schools when organized by school guidance counselors who can provide meaningful orientation sessions and monitor the peer counseling during the year. The peer counselors work with fellow classmates who may need someone to talk with because of a personal difficulty or just someone who can help them get into gear regarding their studies. Peer counselors have even worked with upper elementary school students, especially in conflict resolution on the playground. School principals should view these student-to-student programs as important opportunities to assist students in their social and emotional growth.

School Recognition Assemblies

These assemblies should be scheduled every six to eight weeks to recognize students for positive accomplishments. Teachers submit student names for recognition by the principal for a variety of accomplishments: attendance, citizenship, improved academic performance, service, persistence, and so on. The assembly gives the principal an opportunity to emphasize important themes (academic, behavioral, social, emotional, or physical), wish happy birthday to students and staff, and welcome newcomers or say good-bye to students leaving the school. A student musical interlude or class play may be a part of the assembly program. A high school variation is to hold a Recognition Assembly in late spring to celebrate student successes, especially for freshmen, sophomores, and juniors. This is apart from the traditional athletic and activities award nights. Seniors often have their own event or receive awards at graduation.

Tips on Opening a New School

By Dr. Becky Berg

*(Dr. Berg is Superintendent of Marysville
School District, Marysville, WA, and a former planning principal.)*

The following tips are offered for school leaders who have been designated as "Planning Principals" charged with opening a new school. The tips are offered in two parts: Bricks and Mortar pertains to building the actual building, and Creating a High-Performance School Culture pertains to planning a start-up school that has not yet existed.

Bricks and Mortar

As with all aspects of leadership, process is important. How you go about the process of planning a school is a reflection of your values and vision.

Use participatory teams that include a mix of global thinkers and detail people. The detail people are those who know that the ideal storage space in a closet is a "Xerox box plus four inches"—so that the size of boxes found commonly in schools can fit neatly in the spaces created (true story!).

Visit other sites and staffs who have gone through the process recently. Learn from their victories, challenges, and defeats.

There are various stages commonly known to the construction industry but are a little more mysterious to educators. They are educational specifications, schematic design, design development, construction document development, construction, and final punch lists. The educational specifications are the key to the entire process. What the architect hears from the team as the priorities and the vision will be reflected in the design and referenced as a rudder to guide decision making. Be very deliberate and careful in this process.

The construction documents development is the other vital step. These documents are extremely detailed plans that all the trades use in the construction of the school. As soon as they are ready, sit down with the architect, your facilities manager, or someone in the field to go over them with a fine-toothed comb because they become essentially unchangeable. The interpretation of the educational specifications by the design professionals is sometimes very different than how the users (educators) would want them interpreted. This is the time to clarify your ideas so changes can be made. There really is no realistic and affordable way to go back after the construction documents are firm.

Planning for a school building with an indefinite life span, compared with planning for technology that is out of date the moment it is purchased, provides for an interesting contrast. Remember all of the users of technology in the planning of the building. Consider computer projectors, document cameras, laptop or desktop computers, and sound amplification systems as a start for classrooms and meeting spaces. Many of these need power sources and cabling, so again ensure that they may be used however the room is configured and for any number of users. Remember also that in this world of BYOD (bring your own device), parents and community members will increasingly want wireless access when

(Continued)

(Continued)

they visit your school. Some schools even have afterschool parking lot users of their Internet, which is a way of enhancing your community beyond the walls of the schoolhouse. Again, "maximum flexibility" is the mantra.

Building a new school will test your mettle. Know when to be firm on things that will significantly impact the use of the facility for the education of students and when to give on more subtle issues. Keep your integrity, and build relationships. When the building is completed and the process is done—the relationships remain. Give credit to the many members of your district staff who were participants in the process in addition to the design team.

Celebrate with the voters and community. It is their school. Ensure that you have a groundbreaking ceremony, a dedication ceremony, and an open house. The district began way before your arrival and will continue on past your departure. Honor all of the participants. Build connections.

Some keys to an educationally efficient facility:

- *Storage, storage, storage:* If materials are individually managed and in classrooms rather than communal storage rooms, no one has to go clean out the storage room periodically. Anyone who has worked in schools knows that cleaning out the storage room of old fish tanks and art projects is a thankless task that is continuously repeated across the country. Individual storage is much easier to manage.
- *Maximum flexibility:* Try to ensure that rooms are similar in size and detail. You never know if that kindergarten classroom will end up serving sixth graders in future years. Remember: Kindergarten-aged students use regular-sized toilets and sinks at home, with accommodations. They can do it!
- *Furniture:* Try out the furniture options in classrooms with students. They will quickly and clearly let you know about quality and usability.
- *Lighting:* Natural light is a bonus in the learning environment, but remember potential afternoon glare on screens and whiteboards.
- *Displays:* Consider how to best display student work in hallways and common areas. Some well-placed wall strip mouldings can help set off displays and make them look more intentional. Remember to coordinate with your local fire department in order to determine how much wall space may be covered with student work and design the spaces around that agreement.
- *Traffic flow and supervision needs:* Dark corners and congested areas result in potential safety and disciplinary concerns.

Creating a High-Performance School Culture

Begin with a planning grid that includes significant activities dealing with the construction and with the development of a positive school culture. The construction process can easily overtake time spent on planning to shape a positive culture if you are not extremely intentional about attending to both.

Understand the non-negotiables from your district and state. Keep district leaders informed all along the way.

Be thoughtful about your vision from the outset. Although it will certainly be influenced by the team that you build, teachers and other staff want a picture of what they are signing on to before they decide whether to join your staff. Your vision, leadership, and who you are as a person are perhaps under the most scrutiny of your career at this stage—so be sure you communicate about these aspects every chance you get.

Work with your human resources department and your educational association to agree on hiring practices that will result in creating a "best-fit" staff rather than staffing solely on seniority. For instance, one high school principal, advertising for teaching positions in a new school, created a brochure that highlighted the vision and core values they were looking for in candidates. After the list of core values was a simple, but powerful line: "Those who do not embrace these student-focused values need not apply."

Remember to involve parents from the beginning, not only on the building of the facility but in the creation of the culture. They are full partners in creating the vision and mission of the school.

Create your parent organization a year in advance, and meet periodically. Under your leadership, they can create by-laws, establish 501(c)3 tax status, and elect officers. You can then hand over the reins of the group to the officers and participate as you normally would. With careful planning, this group can be your biggest asset in quickly establishing celebrations and traditions with the student body and the parent community.

Carefully design a participatory decision-making process and norms for working together. If you go slowly at this stage, you can eventually go quickly through the plethora of decisions that need to be made, while developing trust and relationships along the way. This process, pertaining to adults, may be applied to building trust and relationships among the student body as well.

After you have the foundational work completed, work on the way you will do business for the future. As a team, read the research and the works of leaders in the field, partner with higher educational institutions in your area, set specific and measurable goals, conduct job-embedded professional development based on those goals, conduct Action Research, ensure that you design vertical and horizontal teams, and model curiosity.

This is a once-in-a-career opportunity, so use it to inspire all of the participants to be their best. This may be some of the most generative work you will ever do—dream big.

Remember the words of Robert Jarvik: "Leaders are visionaries with a poorly developed sense of fear and no concept of the odds against them. They make the impossible happen."

Tips on Using Technology to Enhance a Principal's Performance

Brent Howard and Scott Friedman

(Brent Howard is the Professional Development and Innovation Support Specialist, Central Valley S.D., Central Valley, WA. Scott Friedman is the Nine Mile Falls Elementary School Principal, Nine Mile Falls, WA)

(Continued)

(Continued)

The Principal's Role: Modeling the Use of Technology

Today's principals must be prepared to use and lead others as technology users on a daily basis. When used thoughtfully, technology is a gateway to increased professional efficiency, connections, and opportunities to learn with others from around the globe. Most importantly, it is a means to prepare students with the 21st century skills to compete in a high tech world. As a principal, you do not have to be a technology expert to lead your staff, and you don't have to do it alone. By asking for help from Instructional Technology (IT) staff or from tech-savvy colleagues (and students!) you are modeling just the kind of behavior that others need to embrace.

Our first tip is to consider these reflective questions, a self-assessment, as a starting point to develop a plan for yourself, and with the help of a team, a technology integration plan for your school:

- Do you have a clear vision for technology use in your school?
- Do you consistently model the ethical use of technology?
- Do you take actions that support the use of technology?
- Do you take advantage of professional development opportunities about technology?
- Can you describe what digital citizenship would look like in your school?
- Do you advocate for technology use in support of student learning?
- Do you discuss the role of technology in teaching and learning with your school and/or district IT staff?
- Do you communicate with your community regarding the use of technology in teaching and learning?
- Do you share technology ideas and thoughts with other administrators in your district?
- Do you regularly use technology to connect and network with other school leaders around the world?
- Have you identified the tech-savvy teachers in your building?

Overview of ISTE/Nets-A. In 2009, the International Society for Technology Education (ISTE) published their latest technology standards for administrators. The standards were developed to help school leaders focus their professional learning around skills and abilities necessary to support digital age learning and technology implementation. The standards are divided into five sections: Visionary Leadership, Digital Age Learning/Culture, Excellence in Professional Practice, Systemic Improvement, and Digital Citizenship. These standards serve as a foundation to enhance your leadership and vision around technology integration in your school (http://www.iste .org/standards/nets-for-administrators).

Visionary Leadership. Principals should help create an instructional vision for the school with the support of others. Developing the school vision involves establishing a context for technology, restructuring learning through technology, empowering teachers, and helping students become more technology literate (Brockmeier, Sermon, & Hope, 2005). Principals must be highly skilled at consensus building and articulate a shared message that promotes technology integration to maximize instructional practices for students and teachers. This shared vision must be ongoing. Principals must engage themselves in continuous learning and actively advocate for a thoughtful technology plan.

Tips to Support Visionary Leadership:

- Examine the ISTE standards for both teachers and students. As you are reading the standards, always think about their practical application.
- Become familiar with future trends in technology. Subscribe to a technology journal and read the latest *Horizon Report* (5th edition) to keep abreast of emerging technologies and K–12 education (http://www.nmc.org/publications/2013-horizon-report-k12).
- Explore research on the transformation of schools through technology. For example, ISTE publishes Project Red's *Revolutionizing Education Through Technology*. The project shares research on the transformation of schools through technology (http://www.projectred.org/images/books/ISTE_Book.pdf).
- Subscribe to podcasts that describe how to use technology in schools. A list of podcasts can be found at: (http://gettingsmart.com/2013/02/50-educational-podcasts-you-should-check-out/ **and** http://www.stevehargadon.com/p/interviews.html).
- Model the use of technology. Become an active user of social media. We recommend networking through sites such as Twitter and Google Plus.
- Participate in an online learning experience with other educators.

Digital Age Learning/Culture. Helping to shape the school culture is one of the most important responsibilities of a principal. Today that culture includes Digital Age learning. Principals can support digital learning by endorsing risk-taking and the adoption of technology among staff.

Tips to Support Digital Age Learning:

- Be transparent about your own technology journey and share your own highs and lows. Showing your vulnerabilities and willingness to take risks will help build trust.
- Model technology use during staff meetings, community events, Parent Teacher Association meetings, and daily activities. It is imperative that the technology enriches the learning and is not perceived as a gimmick.
- Include technology tip, links to great Web pages, and articles that support classrooms and technology during daily or weekly staff updates.
- Start a volunteer book study group. A good technology related topic would be the learner-centered classroom. Clayton Christensen's *Disrupting Class* discusses how computers could be used to individualize learning focusing on a student's talents.
- Retrieve survey data, gather questionnaire information, provide feedback for teachers on walk-throughs, and helpful evaluation information, using tools such as Google Forms. The following sites will provide helpful information to get started: (https://support.google.com/drive/answer/87809?hl=en **and** http://www.youtube.com/watch?v=IzgaUOW6GIs).
- Provide opportunities for students to showcase technology-generated work at staff meetings and community events.

(Continued)

(Continued)

- Celebrate successes and embrace risk-taking and "failure" during the school's technology journey.
- Communicate with staff and the community through social media such as Facebook, Twitter, Google Plus, and Instagram, and create podcasts with Audioboo.

Excellence in Professional Practice. Staff needs to engage in deliberate, ongoing, and engaging professional learning opportunities to become comfortable with technology. Principals should allocate time and resources to ensure this learning occurs and actively participate with staff. Leading a school from the Industrial Age to the Digital Age is not easy and takes a team effort.

Tips to Support Professional Practice:

- Establish a "Tech in 10" agenda item at all staff meetings. During this 10 minutes, share information about beneficial technology tools or resources. Always ask staff to share their ideas too.
- Use Web-based student management systems. Many programs use mobile applications for student schedules, attendance, grades, discipline, and other items. Use technology to support an online calendar for school events, and public aspects of your schedule. Use technology tools that make management tasks easier so staff sees the benefits of going digital.
- Provide staff incentives, maybe in a fun way, for pursing professional development options (e.g., "Take a class in podcasting and win a microphone for your classroom!").
- Start a districtwide learning community around a topic or book of interest that uses a learning module system (e.g., Moodle, Edmodo, Blackboard).
- Host virtual guest lecturers during meetings or staff development sessions with tools such as Skype or Google Hangouts.
- Seek out virtual learning experiences for staff that demonstrate the positive impact of classroom technology; Edutopia is a great place to start.

Systemic Improvement. Effective principals are focused on systemic improvement of the organization and buildings as technology leaders and managers. The principal should thoughtfully share resources, engage in long-range planning, and ensure that technology purchases align with district and building goals based on data-driven decisions for collecting and analyzing student achievement.

Tips to Support Systemic Improvement:

- Create a school technology committee to establish long-range plans focused on: technology integration, purchasing digital resources, professional development, and budgetary realities.
- Earmark school funds for faculty professional development.
- Pilot innovative technologies as demonstrated on this site: (http://wiki.canby.k12.or.us/groups/innovation).
- Partner with community leaders and agencies and exchange expertise on 21st century learners.

- Network with district, regional, state, and the federal education departments. Share ideas and pursue grant opportunities.
- Insist that all new technology purchases include staff development training for teachers.

Digital Citizenship. Never before have students experienced so much immediate access and exposure to information and communication sources. This access increases the need for principals and staff to understand the social, ethical, and legal aspects of our evolving digital culture. Of particular importance is the equitable access issue for all students. It is imperative for principals and staff to model and demonstrate appropriate social and ethical behavior related to technology with students, and parents.

Tips to Support Digital Citizenship:

- Help staff, students, and parents see the connection between character education and digital citizenship.
- Adopt and implement with appropriate colleagues an acceptable use policy for today's learners. Also, a comprehensive Internet safety education plan for staff, students, and parents. Examine Common Sense Media Resources: (http://www.commonsensemedia.org/educators/curriculum).
- Develop, with the appropriate curriculum committee, a grade-level scope and sequence for the teaching of digital citizenship skills aligned with district goals. Excellent resources include: (http://www.commonsensemedia.org/educators/scope-and-sequence **and** http://k12digitalcitizenship.wikispaces.com).
- Share strategies for finding and using media licensed under a Creative Commons License: (http://creativecommons.org/). One strategy would be using Flickr: The Commons at http://www.flickr.com/commons.
- Support a social media presence for your school and use it to share the great work that is happening. For example, encourage classes to create webpages and provide the professional development assistance (e.g., mentors, savvy faculty) and resources to demonstrate your support.
- Ensure that your students and teachers have equitable access to appropriate digital tools and resources.

What Else Can I Do?

First, share student-learning experiences. Work with your superintendent to schedule a yearly or biyearly school board presentation to celebrate how technology is used in your school. Focus on learning outcomes (not the tech tools) and the increased engagement that the use of technology provides. Continually highlight how technology aided your students in meeting proficiency goals for the year. Second, address the challenge of enriching technology in your school under tough budget constraints. It is important that technology is seen as an ongoing funding priority and not a one-time expenditure. Your technology plan should be used as a road map *based on student needs* to determine the yearly expenditures for district and building budgets. Be transparent—share budgetary issues with your staff. Third, in today's digital age the principal needs

(Continued)

(Continued)

to establish positive ongoing relationships with IT staff in and out of their building. The principal and IT district technology director should always keep the lines of communication open so issues between teachers (e.g., "I need this blocked website opened!) and IT building technicians can be worked out in the best interest of students. These open communication lines will help IT staff better understand classroom instruction desires and needs while helping the principal better understand the demands of network management.

Final Thoughts

As administrators we must look to embrace the shifts that are already happening in education around the use of technology. It is critical that we become active participants in this process. Our active participation begins with a dialogue about what is best for students and how does the technology improve learning (Couros, 2013). We need to seek out information, learn, and connect with others. Lead and embrace the digital journey!

USING TIPS IN YOUR SETTING

The ideas in this chapter are all tried-and-true strategies used by principals and other school personnel to improve their effectiveness or positively influence the culture of the school. Although only some of the ideas may work in your school, all of the ideas are intended to identify themes or strategies that might lead principals and their professional colleagues to come up with successful activities for their schools. Perhaps one of the most powerful ways to continue this tradition is by organizing support groups of principals (no larger than 10 members) to meet regularly, problem solve, and share successful practices.

NOTE

1. More tips: We encourage our readers to send their tips for us to use in subsequent editions of this book. Send tips to Pam Robbins, 210 North New Street, Staunton, VA 24401 (e-mail: probbins@shentel.net), or Harvey Alvy, 808 Summit Drive, Cheney, WA 99004 (e-mail: halvy@ewu.edu).

REFLECTIONS

This space provides for you a place to write in ideas that have been generated by this chapter, things you want to try, or adaptations of ideas presented herein.

1. What are some tips that you can offer to your colleagues?

2. What kind of events, activities, or strategies might be added to those mentioned in the chapter to positively affect the values of a school?

3. What advice would you offer to school leaders concerning budget management during these difficult economic times?

4. What insights or new questions do you have as a result of reflecting on the ideas presented in this chapter?

PART VI

Embracing Your Constituencies

17

Working With Parents and Partnering With the Greater Community

Working with parents is a two-way street. We expect parents to respond to our calendar, but we also have a responsibility to reach out.

—A principal's voice

EFFECTIVELY COMMUNICATING WITH PARENTS

A strong parent-school partnership is an invaluable resource. Jean Johnson, of Public Agenda, speculates that "Unless teachers, parents, students and community members become allies and partners in the mission of improving schools, the United States will likely stumble in its efforts to build a world-class education system" (2013, p. 19). This chapter examines facets of this partnership with parents and the greater community and offers several tools to enhance these relationships. It is clearly the responsibility of all school personnel and especially principals to communicate effectively with parents. Thus schools need to take the initiative in this area, engaging in two-way communication and seeking to initiate partnerships with various organizations and businesses. The Race to the Top (RTTT) federal grant competition strongly endorses this approach with public and private partnerships as one of the grant approval criteria. In the past, school leaders and teachers were reactive with parents or viewed the relationship as a back-burner priority. This should not be the case. As one assistant principal noted, "Principals must be PR persons today. You have to welcome parents and be much more accommodating to a very demanding public. Parents need to be courted." What is troubling however is that some low-income parents of color and their communities feel unwelcome and powerless in schools because of a history of discrimination and the unwillingness of some schools to reach out beyond traditional avenues (Khalifa, 2012; Ishimaru, 2012). Additionally, it is important that LGBT parents feel as welcome in the school as everyone else (Cianciotto & Cahill, 2012).

Principals, assistant principals, and faculty members need to be proactive when communicating with parents regarding all school issues, from a new program to an individual child's progress report. For example, unsatisfactory grades on a report card should not come as a surprise to parents. Parents should be notified if their child is having difficulty, and school intervention should be occurring well before the report card is distributed. School principals need to build this idea into the system and communicate ways this can be done. Moreover, the benefit of partnering with families goes beyond improving communication: "Studies confirm that when families are involved, more students earn higher grades in English and math, improve their reading and writing skills, complete more course credit, set higher aspirations, have better attendance, come to class more prepared to learn, and have fewer behavior problems" (Epstein, 2007, p. 18).

When schools have good news to report, parents should hear about it. There is no better public relations strategy than reporting good news. For example, an elementary school principal may hold recognition assemblies about every six to eight weeks to positively reinforce students for a variety of accomplishments. These may include a current student helping a new classmate in school, a first-rate math test score, having a painting sent to a museum, intervening appropriately when a classmate was bullied, or improved behavior. Following up the assembly with e-mails or handwritten notes to parents that compliment students and explain how the students were recognized sends a clear message concerning what is important in that school. Recognition assemblies, in this way, not only serve as public relations tools but communicate cultural values to parents as well. Another effective strategy to report news to parents is through the student-led conference. These conferences, appropriate from kindergarten to the 12th grade, can be arranged as special events or as part of scheduled parent-teacher conference days. Student-led conferences give parents opportunities to observe and hear their children report and reflect on their progress. Whether teachers help students prepare working or showcase portfolios or specific samples of student work, students, by engaging in a dialogue with their parents and by showcasing their work, have an opportunity to demonstrate what they have learned. These conferences are a powerful tool, transcending, by far, the minimal effect provided by traditional report cards.

When considering how parents view schools, it is interesting to note that, as an institution, a school is one of the few professional organizations with which all feel some familiarity. We all attended school. The mysteries of medicine, for example, may cause parents to hesitate about questioning a particular diagnosis of their child. This is not the case when schools are concerned. Most parents, especially parents of privilege, are likely to be much more assertive about questioning the school system. Their own experiences in school, good and bad, have left many parents with firm ideas on how to approach schools and how schools should operate. For some parents, school was a very unpleasant experience, and the school principal may remind them of memories better forgotten. Khalifa (2012) in his research on the concerns of many urban, Black, and Latino families states that "traditional school principals in urban areas expect parents to come into the school and for the partnerships to exist within the paradigm of school-driven goals (e.g., how can parents partner with schools to raise test scores?)" (pp. 460–461). Thus a smile, handshake, warm welcome, and sincere questions about how a child is doing or what can we do better as a school can be important icebreakers for those who feel less comfortable in schools.

The role that parents play in schools varies greatly and depends on factors such as whether the school is public, private, elementary, middle, or high; the nature of the parent community; the administrative approach with parents; current issues; teacher comfort with parental involvement; parent comfort with teachers; and the degree of parent input formally built into the system for educational and political reasons. Thus parents may play roles ranging from the more traditional role of attending school only on Back to School Night and during parent conferences, to volunteering several days a week as a class tutor, to serving on school boards and making general policy decisions, to becoming a member of a School Improvement Team involved in setting important yearly goals. Schools have the responsibility of informing parents about the various roles they can play.

Again, principals should be proactive with parents and not assume that they are an adversarial group. The overwhelming majority of parents will support the school as long as the school is communicating with them and has kept them aware of important issues. When there are interest groups that have a personal agenda that may interfere with the best interests of the students, it is very helpful to have a majority of parents familiar with the issues. When conflicts occur, a principal should look at the conflict or problem as a challenge and an opportunity to work out a solution. When working out solutions, principals must take the higher ground, not viewing the conflict as a personal battle. This, of course, is easier said than done.

When parents raise questions regarding general school issues or changes they would like to see, the school philosophy or mission statement should play a major part in helping the principals and teachers remain focused regarding the direction of the school. This is why it is advisable to involve parents in mission building to create understanding and ownership. One must consider the key question: Is the proposed change consistent with the school mission?

Additionally, it is important for the principal to actively listen to all ideas and factions. This does not mean that the principal is not aligned with a particular point of view—one should have strong feelings on significant issues—but the appearance of an inflexible position quickly tells parents that you are uninterested and not listening. It is important also for principals to meet routinely with the president or head of the parent association. Particular parents, however, should not be seen as the principal's favorite or the decision makers for other parents.

BUILDING BRIDGES WITH THE PARENT COMMUNITY

To build up parent interest in a school, an open house before school officially opens or early in the year can be held for parents (and students) to meet the administration and teachers. This kind of positive interaction can help build the bridges that will come in handy when communication on important issues is necessary.

Holding monthly parent coffees is an excellent proactive forum to discuss school issues. Although you cannot eliminate griping by some parents at these meetings, the forum can be used to present important school issues with the administration taking the initiative. The following format has been used successfully to carry out monthly coffees: (a) general announcements updating parents on school events and student successes, (b) a presentation to parents on a topic in which they have expressed interest (e.g., the CCSS, a sample of the hands-on science curriculum, trends in education, an update on the new school crisis management plan), (c) occasionally breaking up into small groups to talk about the presentation issues, and (d) open comments and announcements by parents. Holding these meetings in the morning or evening with a one-hour time limit lets the community know that the sessions will be both meaningful and doable given a parent's busy schedule. Furthermore, it emphasizes the value placed on two-way communication in a clear, concise way.

This format works because many parents attend coffees if they think a topic of substance is on the agenda. By setting a positive tone with planned presentations of interest to parents, the meetings proceed in a supportive climate. The climate of these morning or evening coffees can be an essential element in maintaining positive family-school relations throughout the year. The discussion of hot button topics can be helpful to eliminate rumors and clarify important issues.

Although it is more convenient for school personnel and many parents to hold the coffee gathering on-site, principals should consider parents' homes and community centers as other venues for coffees. For some constituencies, a community center may seem less threatening and an indication that the school is reaching out to the community. This may be particularly true in some low-income settings.

Parent reading groups sponsored by the school are another effective way to build bridges with the parent community. A school principal, assistant principal, counselor, librarian, or teacher can help sponsor the reading group. A joint letter from the principal and parents association should state the purpose of the group, how to obtain selected books, and when and where meetings will be held. Often the parents provide coffee and cake. *Letting Go: A Parent's Guide to Understanding the College Years* by Coburn and Treeger (2003) was a popular choice in one school.

Another strategy for building bridges with the parent community is to make teacher and administrative home visits to school families (Henke, 2011). A successful home visit program in the Maplewood Richmond Heights School District (just outside of St. Louis, Missouri) was initiated in 2005 with the help of the Kalish Foundation. The foundation sponsors training sessions to help teachers develop their listening skills and learn about support services to share with parents. High school principal Kevin Grawer shared a story about a pleasant visit with a Spanish speaking family. As Mr. Grawer was getting ready to leave,

> the mother pointed to a large pile of letters and newsletters from the district, all stacked neatly on her table. He was impressed with all the communication that the school had sent out—until she explained that . . . she couldn't read it. "I went back to school," Kevin said, "and used the Google Docs translator program and sent her everything. Now all of my letters to Hispanic families go out in Spanish." (p. 41)

The traditional Back to School or Open House Night and parent conference days provide unique opportunities for schools to show what they are all about. Creative variations during these traditional activities can have very positive long-range results in the parent community. For example, teachers should be encouraged to show parents videos of students working and student-teacher interaction in their classes. Parents appreciate the effort made by teachers who prepare videos, and they love to see their children in action. As noted earlier, student-led conferences are very effective. The use of student portfolios displaying the work and progress of each student significantly affects parents. One parent, after viewing her child's portfolio, remarked, "I wasn't aware that my child was capable of that work." Furthermore, the walls of a school should be lined with student work every day, especially on these special days. Student work should be the heart of these events. Open School Night, if organized to start with presentations by the administration and the parent association, provides a special opportunity for principals to reassert the vision of the school, publicly thank teachers and parents, and recognize the important role that they play in the lives of children. The following suggestions from a school principal to faculty members are helpful tips for successful Back to School Nights and Individual Parent Conferences.

Back to School Night Guidelines for Teachers

- Welcome parents and guardians at the classroom door. Consider including some music playing and/or videos of the students in action as parents enter and at the conclusion of the session.
- Clearly display, or verbally note, the room number, your name, and class (sometimes parents are lost and in the wrong room!).
- Review curriculum expectations of the class, sharing samples of books and instructional resources to clarify points.
- Review major class activity, assessment, and homework expectations, possibly showing samples of exemplary work.
- Let parents know that you are accessible to their children.
- Let parents know how you can be reached and that they are welcome to get in touch with you. Exchange appropriate phone numbers and e-mail addresses.
- Tell parents that if their child is experiencing difficulty, they will be notified (e.g., progress reports, e-mails), and that positive news will also be reported.
- If time permits, consider having parents write a short note to their child to be read privately by their child the following day.
- Try to have parent or student translators available if necessary.
- If possible, provide child care for young children while parents are with teachers.
- Finish with positive comments.

The following suggestions for teachers apply to individual parent-teacher conferences, usually held a couple of months after the school year begins.

Guidelines for Individual Conferences With Parents and Guardians

- Pleasantly greet parents and thank the parents for taking the time to meet with you. Instead of sitting behind the desk consider a more relaxing setting in the room for the conference.
- Some parents know their children are doing poorly and are quite uneasy about the conference. It is especially important to comfort these parents and let them know that "we are in this together." Remember the meeting is about more than grades. It's about building relationships.
- Be specific about strengths and weaknesses, and include samples of student work to emphasize a point. Again, consider student-led conferences as an option for the evening.

- Ask parents for helpful information about their child that might be of assistance to you. For example, "Do you believe your child learns better by seeing, hearing, or through a hands-on approach?" Also, inquire as to whether a student has access to a computer or the Internet at home.
- Discuss specific strategies for their child to achieve success in your class.
- Ask parents for help, and review activities that they can do at home with their child to strengthen the home-school partnership.
- Avoid educational jargon when talking about the curriculum, instructional strategies, assessment, or concerns about a child.
- Before closing, ask parents if there is anything else that they would like to know, or share, about their child.
- Keep the meetings on time so waiting parents do not have to wait longer than expected.
- Telling a story about each child, possibly with some artifact, is a recommendation from parent Nancy Flanagan (2012). She shared a wonderful story about a parent conference involving her own child:

One of the most heart-warming observations I heard as a parent was when my son's 8th grade English teacher showed us some sketches of cars Alex drew in his journal during free-writing. "Aren't these cool?" he said. "Someday that boy's going to work in the automotive industry." What that told us: He's paying attention to Alex. He knows Alex, and values Alex's interests. (p. 2)

- Try to finish on a positive note. Thank parents for coming, remind parents that you enjoy working with their child, and let them know that you are accessible and how you can be contacted. Exchange contact information.

(Principals or assistant principals should make sure that refreshments are available during conferences in central locations, or in each classroom.)

A school might consider a Saturday morning parent workshop or academy sponsored by the administration and teachers for parents to provide information on important topics. Topics might be faculty or parent generated and include helping children with homework, the role of technology in education, tips on writing, or suggestions to instill greater responsibility at home. In settings where parents' own experiences with school were so negative that they feared school, the school has extended an outreach program. In Hawaii, for instance, school personnel took blankets to the local park and set up learning stations for parents.

Joyce Epstein (2007) is probably the most respected researcher and advocate for school, home, and community partnerships in the United States. Her well-known school partnership framework rests on six pillars: parenting, communicating, volunteering, learning at home, decision making, and collaborating with the community. Epstein's theory of partnership embraces the notion that schools, home, and communities are "overlapping spheres of influence" that greatly "benefits children's learning and development" when collaboration is effective (Epstein, Galindo, & Sheldon, 2011, p. 466). Further, her 2011 study, involving school programs and partnerships with district and school leaders, found that leadership was more important than demographics (e.g., free and reduced-price lunch), dispelling the idea that a challenging local environment is too high a hurdle to build a supportive school community culture. In short, "Principals' active support for family and community involvement remained a significant predictor of the quality of school-based partnership programs" (p. 485). The *PTA National Standards for Family-School Partnerships: Implementation Guide* includes six standards based on Epstein's work (and excellent activities). The guide is an invaluable resource for school leaders and involved parents and is available at: PTA.org/partnerships.

ADDITIONAL WAYS TO BRING PARENTS AND COMMUNITY MEMBERS INTO SCHOOL

Involving parents in school-related activities can build bridges with parents and help the school in areas in which resources may be scarce. To illustrate, parents can serve as volunteers to help with tutoring, with field trips, in the cafeteria, in the office, or in the media center. It is critical to conduct background checks prior to using parents in schools. Volunteer tutoring is especially helpful. Using retired community members for tutoring can be a wonderful experience for both students and retirees. It is important, though, that when tutoring takes place, volunteers are aware of the importance of confidentiality and working hand in hand with the classroom teacher. In one school, parents and community members joined together to create assistive technology devices, such as communication boards, to support special education students.

A parent or community resource file can be set up by each school to note parents and community members who have a particular expertise or hobby that they can share with the school. Having adults from the community visit classrooms to tell about their careers or hobbies brings the real world to the classroom and lets students know that there is a clear link between what they are doing and what is taking place in the world of work. Furthermore, it fosters great public relations. Students, parents, community members, and school all benefit from the experience.

Also, booster clubs have been an important traditional way for parents to become involved in schools. Frequently, these clubs help with sports activities and marching band, but these organizations can also help purchase technology for a school, raise funds to improve playground equipment, and repaint the walls of a school. The variety of possibilities is limited only by one's imagination.

Many parents do not reach out to a school because they do not know how they might help. Some schools facilitate the outreach effort by sending home a list of suggestions. Suggestions range from supporting the school on campus to assisting students by sponsoring a homework group. Working parents may appreciate that even by saving labels from cans—something they can do with limited time—they can help. A school starting a new science program asked parents for jars, lids, and bottles to build up the science resource room supplies.

In summary, effective communication with parents is a primary responsibility of each school. Why? Because it is very difficult to succeed with children if relations with parents are unsatisfactory. We need to create a partnership. So often, a school looks to what parents can do for the school. We must also examine what the school can do for parents and the community. In the end, the school principal is in the most effective position to lead the way in taking the initiative with teachers, parents, and the larger community.

BROADENING SCHOOL SUPPORT AND PARTNERSHIPS

Developing relationships with parents is essential. Schools, however, need to reach out and create partnerships with the broader community as well. Thus Johnson notes, "That's why the crucial next step in improving k-12 education is unleashing the human factor—transforming these pivotal groups into allies and partners, rather than passive audiences or constituencies to be managed" (2013, p. 17). This provides opportunities to counter the traditional skepticism about the effectiveness of schools in communities. Partnerships address the need to get public support for schools and enable schools to maximize existing and potential human and financial resources. In pursuit of building broader support, schools need to communicate with a wider circle of people. One principal suggested, "Schools need to meet folks on their turf." The outreach effort may extend to the beauty parlor, barbershop, senior citizens center, supermarket, plant nursery, local business association, chamber of commerce, churches, mosques, and synagogues. Muhammad Khalifa (2012) in his study of building partnerships with urban school leaders through trust, credibility, and rapport states,

> I would argue that visiting a church, fighting for the rights of marginalized and abused children in the community, leading a rally against racism in schools, or going to homes on personal visits all contribute to students success in school and therefore *are* leadership behaviors. Through such activities, urban principals earn an asset essential to successful school leadership—the community's trust. (p. 461)

Partnerships also include bringing younger and older students to retirement communities for seniors or nursing homes to sing for the adults, provide companionship for walks, and play board games. In return, the senior citizens can serve as tutors, mentors, or surrogate grandparents. For these retired senior citizens, as noted earlier, the experience can be rewarding and meaningful. For students, these experiences build important values about reaching out and serving others. Also, senior citizens or disabled veterans served by community organizations can be invited to schools for special programs at the holiday season or even special programs just for them. When appropriate, professional development opportunities in a school can include participants from the business community who can benefit from the experience (e.g., learning about education-related apps).

Today, approximately 70 percent of school districts are involved in some type of business partnership, a 35 percent increase since 1990 (Sloan, 2008). At the Kaneohe Elementary School, Kaneohe, Hawaii, sailors from the naval base are helping students with tutoring and PE, and are building benches and helping to beautify the school grounds. The Carpenters Union built a $70,000 storage facility and charged only $6,000 (cost of material) for the whole project! Principal Mitchell Otani stated, "In a day of tight budgets, schools can't do it alone anymore. . . . It makes good sense to enlist all the resources of the community and parents" (National Association of Elementary School Principals, 2008, p. 10). Thomas Jefferson High School for Science in Alexandria, Virginia, is a STEM-focused school with labs similar to what one would expect on a college campus. However, when students need assistance beyond the school's capabilities one of its partners is the National Institute of Health in Bethesda, Maryland. The appreciative school principal, Evan Glazer, reflected that, "Whenever there's connectivity to an outside organization or a real problem that we experience, it creates greater meaning for the students" (Ash, 2013, p. S26).

COMMUNITY-BASED ORGANIZATIONS

In urban and rural areas, community-based organizations (CBOs) may provide the greatest direct support to schools other than the help of parents. This is especially true in areas with large numbers of disadvantaged youngsters. Often, the organizations provide support that cannot be offered at home. CBOs provide direct or indirect assistance to schools, individual students, parents, and teachers. The organizations usually work in collaboration with a school to enhance educational opportunities and provide the kind of individual or family aid that can make the difference between dropping out of school and making it. CBOs provide support to help with such questions as these: Where do I go for a job? Where can I get adequate day care? Where can I find food or shelter? How can I get health care?

Both public and private agencies are involved in community-based support efforts. Community agencies are reaching into schools, and schools are learning how to reach out to the community. This is reflected in the growth of full-service schools and community-school partnerships.

Jane Quinn, who today serves the Children's Aid Society of New York as Vice President and Director of the National Center for Community Schools, emphasized in 2002 that as a result of these partnerships, "The principals in these schools no longer have to double as educational leaders and social workers because our agency provides social services (as well as medical, dental, and mental-health services; before and after-school enrichment; summer programs; and parental involvement opportunities)" (Quinn, p. 40). Quinn emphasizes that joint planning will be a key to successful partnerships in the future. A prime example of the first-rate service provided by the Children's Aid Society is the partnership it maintains with Fannie Lou Hamer Freedom High School in The Bronx, New York. The school was founded as one of the original small high schools. The principal, Nancy Mann, knew that the social service infrastructure in the neighborhood would be insufficient, so in 2005 she contacted the Children's Aid Society. The Society responded by offering numerous services, including medical, dental and mental health, support to families, and enrichment activities out of school. If families are facing eviction, the society works on providing emergency relief services. More than 70 percent of Fannie Lou Hamer graduates go on to college. Principal Mann states, "Through our Children's Aid partnership, the teachers are less likely to feel helpless and hopeless . . . . They know the students are being taken care of so we can get back to academics. This is crucial" (Jacobson, Hodges, & Blank, 2011, p. 20).

Harkavy and Blank (2002) of the Coalition of Community Schools maintain that successful community schools foster "after-school enrichment opportunities, programs in such areas as violence prevention, service learning, family literacy, mentoring, mental health, and others, and services that go beyond a narrow focus on core academics" (p. 52). Community-based support efforts may include the following:

- Health clinics, including dental facilities
- Hospitals
- Neighborhood associations
- Religious organizations
- Homeless shelters
- Women's centers
- Gay, Lesbian and Straight Education Network
- Community colleges and universities
- Youth centers
- Art organizations
- Museums
- Young Men & Young Women Christian Associations (YMCA & YWCA)
- Boys and Girls Clubs of America
- Girl Scouts and Boy Scouts
- Merchant associations
- Sports associations
- Drug and alcohol rehabilitation centers
- Zoological parks

- Teachers' unions
- Parks and recreation departments
- U.S. Forest Service and National Park Service
- U.S. Postal Service
- U.S. Armed Forces
- Police, fire, and emergency service personnel
- Newspapers, television networks, radio stations, online news services

Often, major city school districts or local, state, and federal agencies will list the CBOs in a particular area that provide resources to schools. For example, the New York City Department of Education maintains an Office of Public and Community Affairs that partners with hundreds of organizations. The community affairs website builds enthusiasm for partnerships with very informative links that demonstrate the variety of partnership work from academic to social service (schools.nyc.gov/community/city/publicaffairs/).

SEEKING SCHOOL SUPPORT THROUGH EDUCATIONAL GRANTS

In addition to CBOs, another source of assistance for individual schools can be public or private grants. Millions of dollars in grants are available to schools from public and private sources for worthy and innovative school programs. These grants may be from federal, state, or community agencies; from private industries or foundations; or from different educational associations. Often, a grant is targeted for a specific community or general region in which an industry operates. The hope is that the grant will eventually "pay off" for the community or possibly the corporation. One source of information about grants is the weekly report *Education Grants* Alert (www.grantsalert.com). A typical issue will list grants from federal agencies (e.g., Department of Labor, Department of Commerce, Department of Health and Human Services) and many industrial or private industries and foundations (e.g., Scott Paper, Bill and Melinda Gates Foundation, Danforth Foundation, Annenberg Foundation). Grants can range from a few hundred dollars to millions of dollars and may be available for early childhood learning; academic achievement; technology opportunities, STEM projects, innovative educational reforms; environmental issues; consensus building; substance abuse education; teen pregnancy prevention and assistance; afterschool and summer activities for inner-city youths; professional teacher reform; Native American education; and math, science, and technology projects. The five top educational grant contributors for K–12 in 2010 (most recent available information) were the Bill and Melinda Gates Foundation—208.5 million, Walton Family Foundation—109.5 million, W. K. Kellogg Foundation—58 million, Michael and Susan Dell Foundation—54.8 million, and the Silicon Valley Community Foundation—35.2 million (Ash, 2012, p. 10).

REACHING OUT AND WORKING WITH THE MEDIA

Newspapers, television, and the radio are always competing for an audience. The competition is even more intense today because millions of Americans only use smartphones, tablets, and laptops with online news—shunning conventional media. And the education market is up for grabs. For example, *Education Week,* with excellent print and online services, has to compete with online "newcomers" like *Huffington Post,* which has a daily education section.

Conventional wisdom and marketing research indicate that the news is often dominated by negative stories: "If it bleeds, it leads." Of course, if good news sold, then good news is what would be presented most often. How can schools overcome this conventional logic concerning news stories? Well, they cannot overcome it completely, but interestingly, some schools have succeeded incredibly well in getting their story across. For example, one school district in Washington state conducted a news audit and found out that during a 180-day school year, 105 articles were printed about the district in local papers—only 3 articles were negative! How did this occur? What can a school district do to minimize the negative news and get the true message out about school success? Larger districts do this by hiring a public information specialist (that "PR" person!) responsible for collating and distributing news about the schools for dissemination to various media. Smaller school systems must rely on superintendents, principals, and classroom teachers to work with the media. Regardless of whether you are a principal in a big city system or in a small town, the following guidelines can help you reach out to spread the message of success:

1. *Focus on the school vision and mission.* Every television appearance, radio interview, newspaper article, and online opportunity that you are involved in should focus on teaching and learning and the health and welfare of the students. Always consider the school mission and your responsibility to students, teachers, and the community. A trick of the trade is to quietly ask oneself before an interview: How can I focus (or redirect the interview) on teaching and learning during this media opportunity? Remember, each time you speak it is an opportunity to step forward, be an advocate, and state what is best about the school. Even when a tragic incident occurs, drawing media to the school, the direction of the interview from the school's standpoint should be toward the health and welfare of the students and getting back to teaching and learning.

2. *Build a reputation based on honesty and trust.* Successful public information officers will tell you that it is vital to build an honest and trusting relationship with the media. This is especially true when there is bad news to report—and the bad news should be reported just as we report the good. The community is entitled to know what takes place in the tax-supported public schools. Sadly, there are times when an administrator, teacher, or

classified worker engages in inappropriate or criminal behavior. Trying to hide a major incident will backfire on the school district. After receiving legal advice, schools must be up front about incidents that may hurt the image of the school. However, if a trusting relationship between a reporter and a school district has been nurtured, even the most difficult situations can be ameliorated at times. For example, in one school district an embarrassing incident concerning a staff member was going to be reported in the local newspaper. Because of the trusting relationship between a reporter and a school administrator, the school was told when an article about the incident would be in the paper and whether the incident was going to be in the widely circulated main section of the newspaper or in the "zone" (local) section. This forewarning helped the school prepare for the fallout. Trust is also maintained with a little common sense. For example, it is considered poor form to ask to see a story in advance. As a courtesy, send a brief "thank you" note when a positive story is published.

3. *Recognize that each story needs an angle.* Consider that the average 30-minute television news show may select from hundreds of stories for the evening broadcast. Maybe 10 stories will be selected as "news," with only about 20 minutes of actual broadcasting time. Why should the station show a story about a school? What makes your story news? It is only news if the media says so! So the story needs to be unique or have an angle. For example, the ecology club in one school created a trail with Braille signs for visually impaired hikers. A newspaper and a local television station picked up the story. The story was inspirational and sent a strong signal to the community about the school's devotion to service and its ecological mission.

Interestingly, because of NCLB, RTTT, standards, high-stakes testing, and accountability issues, school test results are big news. Public interest on national, state, and local levels means that test scores often are listed in newspapers as columns of statistics with a school's score, compared to others in the district or state. When school leaders are asked to comment on these data, it is important to keep a perspective. Thus, if interviewed about a school's test results, one might consider avoiding the appearance of being overly thrilled or overly disappointed depending on a school's scores. (Don't set yourself up for the surprise of next year's scores!) Further, let reporters know that high-stakes testing is only one of many ways to assess students and that some students simply do not test well.

4. *Seize opportunities to showcase students.* In small and midsize cities, newspapers and television networks will often showcase stories about students receiving awards or special recognition. This is especially true when a major state or national honor is achieved. In small towns, local newspapers will publish honor roll information, and zone editions of some major papers will publish local school information

about awards, the work of clubs, special class activities, and big school events. A key to all of these opportunities is that they are about local kids, with local names that stakeholders will know. If a newspaper lists the names of 300 high school students who made the honor roll or a photo of the citywide chorus made up of four middle school groups, there is a good chance that all of the parents or guardians of the children mentioned would buy papers.

5. *Serve as an educational resource.* Although most reporters are college educated, it is unlikely that they are familiar with all of the issues facing schools. A commandment of working with nonschool personnel is avoiding jargon. To illustrate, using the phrase "differentiated instruction" or acronyms "CCSS" or "PARCC" with reporters is unhelpful. Additionally, you may be asked about issues related to testing, data-driven assessment, students with special needs, NCLB, RTTT, and so on. Reporters may not have a comprehensive understanding of an issue and will want to check with a trusted educator they know. Help out!

6. *Be accessible and visible.* As with other principalship roles, accessibility is critical. When the media call, try to get back to them as soon as possible. Obviously, if there is a serious issue, it may be necessary to check with the superintendent, and in larger districts with the public information specialist, before returning a call or accepting an interview. When positive or negative issues arise, the community expects the principal to be there.

7. *Approach news proactively—good or bad.* Districts should keep a steady stream of school news flowing to the media, and they will check out the school websites and social networking resources. As noted previously, there will be negative stories that need to be shared. Keep the media informed consistently about district and school events. Moreover, schools must advocate for students at every opportunity and get the message out. The best way to do this is by raising the consciousness of all staff about the importance of sharing school successes beyond the classroom walls and by developing a system in which interesting stories are routinely sent to the principal and the district's public information specialist.

8. *Respect deadlines.* Because newspapers, television, and radio are different media, they handle deadlines differently. Check with newspaper reporters and editors and radio and television producers to find out about local deadlines. For example, ask: What kind of advance notice is necessary for a human interest story? If you request video or a photographer, will that change the deadline? Television producers often meet about 10 a.m. with the anchors and reporters to decide on the evening stories. Anyone who has been in a television studio before an evening news show or in a newspaper's newsroom knows that the deadline pressure is extraordinary; schools do not need to complicate the situation. For a crisis or emergency situation, the media most often will work with you if a deadline is tricky.

9. *Get to know the key media players.* Part of building a professional relationship with the media is simply getting to know the key players. For example, find out if there are particular newspaper, television, and radio reporters who cover the education beat. Identify the influential editors and producers. Keep this information easily accessible for future use. Meet these important contacts for lunch, invite them on a tour of your school, and prepare a press kit for them with essential and lively information about your school. It is essential that all media are treated equally when returning phone calls and meeting deadlines.

10. *Develop partnerships with the media.* Members of the media should be actively courted for school-community partnerships. Career Days, journalism classes, media technology production classes, and social studies, English, and science classes all present opportunities to actively involve the media. Students enjoy visiting newspaper offices and radio and television studios. School-to-work courses and media internships are excellent credit-earning possibilities for high school students. Also, the media should be routinely invited to unique class events, showcase assemblies, science and math exhibitions, fund-raisers, and other major academic and nonacademic programs and sporting events.

11. *Prepare for interviews.* A public information officer once advised us: "Don't say dumb things, and don't do dumb stuff!" Here's some good advice: First, decide on the critical points of your message, and state the message by sticking to the facts during the interview. Second, remember that short 10- to 20-second sound bites are what the public remembers. Thus, brevity! Third, because the brain remembers beginnings and endings best, state your point firmly at the beginning and repeat it at the end of the interview. Fourth, when television interviews are recorded, the dead time will likely be edited, so patiently collect your thoughts before answering. Fifth, if a reporter gets argumentative, stay calm and above the fray. Sixth, at the end of the interview, express your thanks for the opportunity to talk about the school.

12. *Recognize that there are no "off-the-record" comments.* Reporters are trained to supply the public with news. When school leaders try to confidentially share a little "off-the-record" news with reporters, sometimes hoping to avoid an unfortunate consequence, the school leaders force the reporter into an ethical dilemma. Thus, principals should only make comments that are on the record. In fact, even during a newspaper interview, it is a good idea to record the interview so both sides can recognize that the whole story is on the record.

13. *Contact non-English-language newspapers, television, radio stations, and online news services.* A very powerful message is sent to all of the school communities when an effort is made to contact non-English-language news sources about school events. Through the non-English-language media, the school can notify the non-English-speaking community that translators are needed or will be available especially for events like Back to School Night.

It may also be possible to initiate a liaison relationship to share information between the English media and non-English-language media.

14. *Respect the legal and moral privacy of your students.* We noticed a front-page newspaper photo of a student in a school lunchroom being admonished by a police officer for poor attendance. The story's purpose was to highlight budget cuts that would curtail the services that city police could offer to schools. However, the photo was disturbing because anyone who read the paper would know about the child's attendance issues—and yes, the child's name was written below the photo. The budgetary cuts, purportedly the purpose of the article, could easily have been stressed with a positive photo of students and the police officer. The child's rights (e.g., privacy of attendance records) under the 1974 Family Educational Rights and Privacy Act (Public Law 93–380) may very well have been violated.

15. (*And now you have your "own" media option*): *Maximizing Internet possibilities with websites and social media showcasing the school.* "New tools have paved the way for principals to communicate with all stakeholder groups with the push of a button" (Smith, 2013, p. 2). Yes, instant access is a powerful tool, but leaders must be thoughtful about how to use that power. For example, sending several messages to other media services and the parent community each day via Facebook or Twitter will quickly become ordinary; leaders should remain selective about information. Websites and social media news from the school do provide an advantage: you control the information. Thus, a principal's recorded message to parents and the community welcoming in the new school year, or sharing of exciting information concerning student awards at a STEM event (with student explanations and artifacts) are wonderful opportunities to show off the school. Also, many districts and schools have sophisticated television studios that if used effectively by staff or students also provide an opportunity to control the message. Finally, it is important that the parent portal is up to date as many parents will look to the school website before checking traditional news sources.

A REFLECTION ON PARTNERING WITH PARENTS AND THE COMMUNITY

Today, the needs of many students extend far beyond the resources schools have traditionally offered. Thus, teachers and administrators cannot accomplish their mission alone. School leaders must creatively reach out to the community to bring in resources that can positively impact students. Resources can range from programs that enrich academic and extracurricular activities to essential survival services for students in need. Collectively, through relationships with parents and partnerships with the broader community and public and private agencies, schools can provide the services to enhance student life in and out of school.

REFLECTIONS

This space provides for you a place to write in ideas that have been generated by this chapter, things you want to try, or adaptations of ideas presented herein.

1. Download the *PTA National Standards for Family-School Partnerships: Implementation Guide.* Review activities that promote parent-school involvement. Which activities would be particularly relevant for your school?

2. Thinking about the school in which you work, in what ways are parents involved?

3. What strategies would you introduce to increase parent involvement, especially with parents who are more reluctant to get involved?

4. What kinds of school-community partnerships are established in your school and district?

5. Based on ideas from this chapter, how can the partnership arrangement be enriched?

6. What community-based organizations play an important role in your school? What organizations would you like to see play a larger role in your school? How can this be achieved?

7. How is your district/school successfully using the Internet to get its message out?

8. What insights or new questions do you have as a result of reflecting on ideas presented in this chapter?

18

Making a Difference for Students

The Heart of the School

When our "school goes home" at night, can we say, "On this day, each student was affirmed"?

—A principal's voice

It is not the building or instructional resources that make a school; it is the students, teachers, parents, and community. A school is made up of people. When the doors close, we only have a building, an empty shell without a soul. The soul of the school is the students.

In this chapter, we will try something a bit unusual. It is often through anecdotes about students that we get our greatest insights regarding their needs and how they think. Humorous anecdotes are especially interesting and often poignant. The stories of children, often comical, remind us of our special connection to students and the joys of innocence. Thus a portion of the chapter will be spent on anecdotes about students from elementary school through high school. However, we will begin the chapter by examining the challenge of excellence and equality, social justice, and school leadership. Following the humorous anecdotes we will share a poignant story from World War II and then review important components of the

Individuals with Disabilities Education Act, Response to Intervention (RTI), and how principals affirm that each student is valued. Next, the chapter offers key considerations related to effective school discipline options, bullying, cyberbullying, and support for lesbian, gay, bisexual, and transgender (LGBT) students. Strategies to increase our high school graduation rate and related student homelessness issues will next be addressed. The chapter will conclude with reflections on resiliency, September 11, 2001, and the tragedy at Sandy Hook Elementary School on December 14, 2012.

THE CHALLENGE OF EXCELLENCE AND EQUALITY, SOCIAL JUSTICE, AND SCHOOL LEADERSHIP

Reaching for both excellence and equality is a tall order, but a noble one. As we move further away from ability grouping and traditional high school tracking, provide the least restrictive environment for children with disabilities, and successfully meet the needs of students from diverse backgrounds, our democratic ideals can become a classroom reality. Many nations track students early for high schools, colleges, and careers. In this context, the "late bloomer" would not have a chance to reach his or her potential.

Today, this quest for excellence and equality has become an important moral issue for school principals and educators under the phrase *social justice*. In fact, Standard 5 of the *Educational Leadership Policy Standards: ISLLC* (2008), related to integrity, fairness, and ethical leadership, includes social justice as a critical principalship function: "Promote social justice and ensure that individual student needs inform all aspects of schooling." McKenzie et al. (2008) define three social justice goals to help school leaders make decisions for students with moral purpose. The goals include the following:

- Rais[ing] the academic achievement of all students in their school, that is, test scores do matter. . . . Thus, although we advocate for a variety of measures of student learning and are well aware of the problems associated with standardized achievement tests, we contend that they still have a place in the social justice discourse.
- Requir[ing] that educational leaders for social justice prepare their students to live as critical citizens in society. . . . Thus, it is not enough for leaders to focus on student achievement only to produce students who can read, write, and compute at high academic levels but who do not use their academic skills to challenge injustices in society and thus become no more than uncritical operators in the production economy.
- Require[ing] leaders to structure their schools to ensure that students learn in heterogeneous, inclusive classrooms. Thus, the third prong of our definition of social justice links social justice to inclusive schooling. (p. 116)

The current interest in social justice comes at an important time for schools and school leaders. Leaders often feel torn between meeting mandates and addressing individual needs. For example, leaders worry that high-stakes testing may be forcing some students to drop out of school. We often see issues as either/or propositions. Yet as the preceding social justice goals demonstrate, excellence and equality are both worthy aims. Furman (2012) takes this a step further, imploring social justice leaders to stand for the marginalized and underserved and defining "leadership for social justice [as] identifying and undoing . . . oppressive and unjust practices and replacing them with more equitable, culturally appropriate ones" (p. 194).

"THOSE KIDS" AND THEIR STORIES

Let us talk about kids for a few minutes. First of all, to consider kids, it is important to get into their shoes. A good way is to try to recall your own school experience. What do you remember about school? Do you recall a specific class? An incident in the hallway? Were you bullied? What special events do you remember? Which teacher had the greatest effect on you? Why? As a school principal, are you promoting the kinds of experiences for students in school that reflect your own positive memories of school?

As ideas flash through your mind, consider what you remember about your school principals. We all remember our interactions as students with principals. How many of us, when growing up, never saw the principal except on the stage during school assemblies or in his or her office because of a disciplinary infraction? One of the authors recalls playing with drumsticks on the school stairs as an eighth grader. All of a sudden, two legs appeared on the stairs. They belonged to the principal. Fortunately, the principal's reprimand was in a soft tone—he had obviously decided that this was not a major infraction. More than 30 years later, the feeling of that incident remains!

A principal recalls many memories of students. At high school graduation, pride flows when the student speeches surpass those of celebrities and politicians who are asked to address the senior class. The humor of simulated U.S. presidential debates by students in middle or high school always brings a smile to the principal's face. In one example, the principal recalled the vehicles with their tops down bringing the "candidates" to the debate accompanied by "secret service" personnel with secure earphones (from their iPods). The goal of both excellence and equality emerges when a teacher, assessing students for entrance to calculus class, mentions to the principal that a student new to the school who did not have the grades and did poorly on the assessment test asked some great questions during the test. The teacher indicates the student should be given a shot at taking calculus. The student eventually received a B in the course. The teacher's intuition paid off! Another memory is crystallized when recalling the high school student whose captivating violin solo led to a standing ovation during a school assembly. The student's reputation among the faculty as indolent and unmotivated needed to be revisited after the memorable performance.

The elementary school stories often tend to be comical, yet valuable. During the morning of the first day of school, one principal walked into every classroom to greet students. He mentioned to the second-grade students how lucky they were to have Ms. Smith as their teacher and that this would be a special year for them with this special teacher. A little girl smiled and raised her hand. The principal confidently called on her. She said, "You said the same thing last year."

In the beginning of the year, one child new to the school saw the principal a few days after school began as he was walking downtown. The child looked at the principal with an odd expression on his face and then smiled and said, "Do you know who you are? You're the principal!" A first grader walked up to his teacher a few days before the school year ended and said, "You know, in the beginning of the year I didn't like you. But now I like you better than I like my dog!"

In kindergarten class, a teacher told students that 10 bears were going on a picnic. They had only eight cups. Would that be enough cups? All the students, except one child, said no. When the single child was called on to explain his answer, he said that eight would be enough because "they could share." In another kindergarten class, a teacher asked the students to draw a picture of a birthday party. One child approached the teacher with a picture of a house, flowers, trees, and a picket fence. After looking at the picture, the teacher immediately thought to herself, "This child is a product of poverty and has never experienced a birthday party. I was foolish to assign this project." Still the teacher asked the child, "Where is the birthday party?" The student, after hearing the teacher's question, fashioned a facial expression that could only mean one thing: The teacher must be an idiot! The student proudly pointed to his picture and announced, "The birthday party is out back!"

While saying good-bye to students by the school buses one day, another principal asked Nicholas, a second grader, "Did you learn a lot in school today?" He said, "No." (The principal was immediately disappointed.) Then Nicholas added, "You don't learn a lot in one day. You learn a lot in a whole year."

A library teacher shared a story in which she was explaining to the children that previously it was legal to separate Blacks and Whites in some parts of the United States. She asked the children to state the word that indicates a separation between races. The children could not come up with the word. So she gave them a clue and said that the word starts with the letter *s*. A student raised her hand and said that the *s* word for separating the races is the word *stupid!*

THE RIGHT TO BE A CHILD AND TO MAKE MISTAKES

Janucz Korczak is one of the best-known European educators from the first half of the 20th century. He was a Polish doctor, teacher, and great advocate of children's rights. Tragically, he was killed with his students in Nazi concentration camps. Korczak was so famous the Nazis offered to let him escape the camps, but he chose to remain with his students, knowing that they would be arrested and later murdered. This story is told of him:

> In 1919 Korczak was giving a series of lectures at the Institute of Special Pedagogy in Warsaw. His first lecture was titled "The Heart of the Child." He asked the assembled group to accompany him with a child he was holding by the hand to the X-ray room of the children's hospital. The child was placed behind a fluoroscope and the lights in the room were dimmed. Everyone assembled could see only one light. It was the light of the child's heartbeat. Korczak then stated: "Look, and remember in the future, sometime, when you are tired or angry, when children become unbearable and distract you from your thoughts . . . remember what a child's heart looks like." (quoted in Brendtro & Hinders, 1990, p. 239)

Korczak also wrote a Bill of Rights for Children, which included the admonition that "children have a right to make mistakes." This is a key point to keep in mind when encouraging students to take risks as they answer questions or respond in class. In the end, if school does not provide an environment where it is safe to make mistakes and learn from them, where might this occur?

We must help children overcome their concern about failing in front of classmates or their teachers. If failure can be viewed as a source of learning, rather than a defeat, it takes on a positive air. This cannot be accomplished without caring. We have to nurture students so they are not afraid of trying to experiment, even though they may not succeed. Trial and error are part of learning. The risk for society is that a fear of failure may inhibit a child's desire to take on new challenges or creative enterprises. Many important intellectual leaps have come about as the result of risk-taking, intuitive, and creative behaviors.

MAXIMIZING OPPORTUNITIES FOR STUDENTS WITH DISABILITIES

Introduction

Special education programs have mushroomed since the original Individuals with Disabilities Education Act (IDEA; Public Law 94–142) legislation in 1975, which mandated Individualized Education Programs (IEPs), free and appropriate education for students with disabilities in the Least Restrictive Environment (LRE), and due process rights. Citing the U.S. Department of Education 2011 statistics, Heward (2013) states that approximately 6 million children and youth receive special education services. Males outnumber females two to one in special education and the number of autism students jumped tenfold in a decade. Approximately

95 percent of special education students spend at least part of their day in a general education classroom (Morrison, 2009), while 25 percent of special education students are in self-contained classes and 3 percent are in special schools or facilities (Ornstein & Levine, 2003).

The 2004 Individuals with Disabilities Education Improvement Act (IDEIA) Legislation: Continuing the Academic Emphasis of the 1997 Law

Federal law mandates that all students, regardless of their degree of disability, must receive a free and appropriate public education. The 1997 IDEA legislation, stipulating that special education is a service, sent a clear message that special education students should not be isolated. A key feature of the 1997 law, reinforced in the 2004 law, was the mandate that IEPs must relate more clearly to the general curriculum. The 2004 legislation took this notion a step further, aligning IDEIA legislation with NCLB accountability requirements. Umphrey (2006) notes, "When the requirements of IDEIA 2004 and NCLB are combined, students whose academic performance could at one time blend into the background and go unnoticed are now readily visible on a school's accountability landscape. IDEIA 2004 raises the bar for a good reason—to support all students as they pursue an education and prepare for life" (p. 6).

Although many in the education community have complained about the 2004 requirement that students with disabilities be included in the district and state assessments, some teachers welcome the change. One veteran California special education teacher stated, "Finally my kids get the same books as the general education students because now our test scores count, just like everyone else. Previously, we received old or outdated resources."

The 2004 law also provides for more flexibility on the part of the school related to disciplinary issues. The legislation "does not require that schools hold an IEP meeting or a manifestation determination review (MDR) before suspending a student for 10 days" (Arnberger & Shoop, 2006). The legislation also permits schools to place students in an alternative educational setting for up to 45 school days (increased from 45 calendar days in the 1997 legislation) for weapons, drug charges or inflicting "serious injury upon someone at school or a school function" (Heward, 2013, p. 24).

Individualized Education Plans and Program Compliance

The Individualized Education Plan (IEP) is at the heart of the movement to serve students with disabilities. IEPs must be developed before permanent placement is decided upon. The goal is to place a student in the least restrictive environment with appropriate accommodations and resources. *It is critical that principals recognize that the IEP is a contract and any decisions made to provide a particular service or meet an expectation becomes part of the contract.* To reinforce this point, a lawyer representing a school district on special education issues counsels principals with this simple advice: "If it is on the IEP, the school must comply. If the IEP states that a paraprofessional will serve a child in a general education classroom, then that paraprofessional must be in place. Compliance is nonnegotiable, otherwise lawsuits will occur." Also, legislation requires that the IEP team consist of parent(s), school social workers, regular and special education teachers, school psychologists, an administrator, the student (if appropriate), "and other individuals who have knowledge or special expertise about the child who can help plan for the student's unique needs" (Miller, 2007). Armenta and Beckers (2006) note that although the legislation does not specifically require that the school principal attend the IEP meeting, "some state statutes may require it. Other state laws simply mandate that a principal's designee attend. If that is the case in your state, care should be exercised in selecting that designee" (p. 23).

Section 504 of the Rehabilitation Act of 1973

"Section 504 prevents discrimination against students with any disabilities in all programs and activities receiving federal financial assistance. Examples of Section 504 handicapped conditions not covered by the 13 categories specified in the IDEA legislation include disabilities such as HIV, asthma, allergies, attention deficit disorders, behavioral difficulties, and temporary medical problems" (Alvy & Robbins, 1998, p. 125). Other common disabilities covered by Section 504 include alcohol or drug abuse (but not illegal drugs), hepatitis, and environmental disabilities. Student accidents that require home schooling for a temporary period are also covered under Section 504.

Although Section 504 assistance does not provide the extra funding or extra services that the IDEA legislation requires, it does offer a broad range of services to level the playing field for students who are experiencing difficulty in school. Although an IEP is not mandated for a Section 504 child, a specific plan to help the child is required. Furthermore, parents must be notified regarding identification of needs, evaluation, placement, and significant changes made in the child's program. Again, if our mission is to meet the needs of all students in the school, Section 504 special needs students also must receive the attention of school principals to ensure that proper services are provided.

The Principal's Role: Affirming Students With Disabilities

Principals can set an ethical tone for a school by embracing the spirit and law of the IDEA legislation and Section 504. For example, although a principal's designee can attend an IEP meeting, attendance by the principal sends a strong message of support for students with special needs. Principals can also address the needs of special education faculty, and the parents, by providing time for staff to meet and plan lessons for special education students. Arranging teacher schedules to accommodate parent meetings can be very helpful. In addition, principals can facilitate relevant professional development for special education, regular, and paraprofessional staff. Using faculty meetings for professional development is a worthwhile option.

Recognizing the accomplishments of special education students, displaying their work, and paying attention to the students in one-on-one situations will send a strong and positive signal to students, staff, parents, and the community. Principals can help "cut through the red tape" to ensure that proper assistive technology devices are available and that regular instructional resources are modified. Spending time with parents of special needs students, and giving them an opportunity to share their hopes, can help build trust and confidence in the school's program.

Social Justice, Equity, and Students With Disabilities

Ornstein and Levine (2003) note that "Data on special-education placement show that students from some racial minority groups are much more likely to be designated for mental retardation programs than are non-Hispanic white students" (p. 390). This news is disturbing. Fair testing, with extensive documentation and a variety of culturally sensitive assessment tools, is necessary. States, therefore, are required to gather data to ensure that school districts are not identifying and placing minority students and limited-English-proficiency students disproportionately in special education classes. School principals must examine disaggregated data to ensure that race and ethnicity are not student placement factors. Greater cultural sensitivity from the staff and support for multicultural curriculum practices are also recommended to mitigate this injustice (Heward, 2013).

Further, principals must ensure that students with special needs do not feel isolated from the general population. When portable classrooms, resource rooms, or study skills classrooms with special needs students are located away from general education classes, the "spirit of educating these students in the least restrictive environment" is compromised (Armenta & Beckers, 2006). At the end of the day, principals must ask: Have I done everything possible to address the needs of students with special needs?

RESPONSE TO INTERVENTION

The 2004 IDEIA authorized RTI as a proactive intervention strategy for all students to "catch" learning difficulties early on and, through a three-tier process of increased assistance, minimize the possibility of a minor problem becoming a major one. RTI really comes down to good teaching practices. Buffum, Mattos, and Weber (2010) reflect that when students are having difficulty we usually assess the students to learn about "their problem." RTI turns this thinking around and raises the question: What kind of targeted interventions should I be using to help the student? Another key point is that many teachers think that RTI is supposed to lead a student to special education because it was part of IDEIA 2004. Really the purpose is just the opposite; every student deserves a teacher who responds early on: "RTI's underlying premise is that schools should not wait until students fall far enough behind to qualify for special education to provide them with the help they need. Instead schools should provide targeted and systematic interventions to *all* students as soon as they demonstrate the need" (Buffum et al., p. 10). Finally, the support of principals is essential for the success of RTI programs—a study of middle schools that successfully instituted RTI programs revealed that the faculty in these schools believed that the key to program success was the active participation of the principal, leadership made the difference (Mellard, Prewett, & Deshler, 2012).

SCHOOL DISCIPLINE: THE PRINCIPAL'S ROLE, THE DISCIPLINE GAP, AND PROMISING OPTIONS

Handling disruptive behavior is certainly one of the most difficult and potentially controversial aspects of a principal or assistant principal's job. Of course, helping students with behavioral issues is one of the most important aspects of our job. Teaching and learning cannot occur if classrooms are unsafe. Yet, the very best disciplinary guidelines may reduce, but will not prevent, disruptive behavior. Educators have to set limits and show a caring attitude when disciplinary problems occur. Students need to see that principals and teachers separate inappropriate behavior from how they feel about the students. Major responsibilities for principals, then, include helping teachers develop effective classroom management plans and consistent schoolwide plans as well as working directly with the more difficult disciplinary problems. Often, middle and high schools assign an assistant principal to be responsible for discipline. However, principals need to let these administrative colleagues know that the principal should be kept informed and consulted when difficult situations occur. Ultimately, the principal is responsible for disciplinary decisions taken by the assistant principal.

Before discussing discipline management plans, it is important to define *effective classroom management*: Effective classroom management is the conscious use of proactive strategies and procedures to help students behave in a way that provides maximum learning opportunities for each student in the class. Through such a management system, students are encouraged to develop skills for self-discipline. Based on this definition, attention should be devoted to behavior management at both an individual and a schoolwide level. Thus there should be an overall school procedure for handling disruptive behavior and specific recommendations to teachers on how to resolve problems with individual students. Both situations, however, must always be viewed as "embedded in a social system; it [a disciplinary problem] is never an isolated event" (Ross, 1981, p. 211).

This is a critical point because principals and teachers must act on the assumption that every student is a witness to the decision. In this setting, fairness and a justifiable rationale are essential. Ross (1981) also stresses the importance of clear rules but adds that showing praise—catching the child being good—and ignoring undesirable behavior when possible have proven to be effective management techniques.

The strategy of catching the child being good raises the important issue of intrinsic versus extrinsic motivation. If, while catching the child being good, the teacher uses too many extrinsic rewards, students may become dependent on external reinforcement and teacher behaviors that diminish the value of being good simply because it is the right thing to do. Too often in school we resort to instant extrinsic rewards and reinforcement (e.g., stickers, exaggerated praise) to promote desired behaviors. As Kohn (1996) reminds us, "The promise of a reward is sometimes not just ineffective but counterproductive, that is, worse than doing nothing at all" (p. 33). We need to adopt long-term strategies to foster intrinsic behaviors that encourage the joy of learning or the personal satisfaction of reading a book or helping a classmate who is having difficulty with a math problem.

The Discipline Gap

Before discussing specific disciplinary approaches, *the discipline gap*, which includes troubling similarities to the achievement gap, needs to be addressed.

> In school districts throughout the United States, Black, Latino, and American Indian students are . . . subject to a differential and disproportionate rate of school disciplinary sanctions, ranging from office disciplinary referrals to corporal punishment, suspension, and expulsion. (Gregory, Skiba, & Noguera, 2010, p. 59)

The researchers stress that this issue was first raised back in 1975 when the Children's Defense Fund shared data indicating that *Black students were suspended disproportionally two to three time over other groups nationally.* Not surprisingly, there is a connection between suspensions, expulsions, and achievement. When you are not in school your grades go down. Further, connectedness to school and building relationships with teachers have often been cited as factors that keep students in school—when students are suspended or expelled they are unconnected and not building school relationships. Gregory, Cornell, and Fan (2011), in their study of ninth graders and suspensions, refer to the disparity as the "racial discipline gap," noting, "Correlational and longitudinal research has shown that suspended students are more likely to be truant, miss instructional time, and drop out of high school" (p. 906). Shah (2013), reporting on recent data from Florida linking graduation rates and suspension, reveals that when Florida ninth graders completed their freshman year without a suspension, they graduated at a 75 percent rate; if suspended once that year their graduation rate dropped to 52 percent, two suspensions drop the rate to 38 percent. In this data review "Black students, special education students, and low-income students were disproportionately affected by the disciplinary measure" (Shah, p. 6).

So what can schools and their leaders do? Although Gregory et al. (2011) did not come up with specific strategies to reduce the Black/White discipline gap, they did provide strong evidence on how to reduce suspensions in general. A healthy school climate is critical: schools that exhibited *both* structure (i.e., behavioral rules and academic demands) and support (i.e., caring and concern) reduced suspensions for both Black and White students. They did speculate that historical inequities cannot be overlooked in relation to the suspension gap, "a lack of closeness and trust between teachers and students . . . may be especially deleterious for groups who have been historically stigmatized" (p. 925). School leaders cannot ignore these statistics, conclusions, and the importance of school climate and trusting relationships. As we take a look at three disciplinary approaches it is important to ask: Can these approaches be used to correct historical injustices?

Schoolwide Positive Behavioral Supports and Social Emotional Learning

In a very comprehensive review, Osher, Bear, Sprague, and Doyle (2010) describe the two dominant disciplinary approaches of the past decade: Schoolwide Positive Behavioral Supports and Social Emotional Learning (SEL). It is critical for school leaders to understand the rationale for these approaches and evidence of success since most schools are likely using one or the other, or a blending of the two. Like any other aspect of the principalship, one's success rests on understanding the "why" behind one's action (e.g., Why are schools supporting the CCSS?). So by reviewing these approaches principals can decide: is this the best path forward for how we discipline our students?

Schoolwide Positive Behavioral Supports (SWPBS) is also linked to PBS or PBIS (with "Intervention" in there), and is similar to RTI because it uses a three-tiered approach in which all students begin on the primary tier. If they do not "respond to intervention," then they move on the continuum to another tier. According to Osher et al. (2010), SWPBS and SEL differ in some fundamental ways that all educators will recognize. SWPBS is more teacher centered and aims to manage student behavior while SEL is more student centered and aims to foster self-discipline. Both systems however use elements of an "ecological approach" in which the setting, the environment, is considered critical. Also, suspensions, expulsions, and separating students from their peers are not options that appeal to the proponents of either approach. SWPBS rests on the notion that when educators teach, model, and catch the students being good based on the teacher expectations, then "academic effort . . . safe behavior, [and] the proportion of students with mild and serious behavior problems will be reduced and the schools' overall climate will improve" (Osher et al., p. 50). Prevention is the cornerstone of SWPBS and includes modeling prosocial skills (and posting behavioral expectations in classrooms) and using data-driven decision making to decide whether students are responding appropriately. All students begin on the first, "universal" tier, about 5–10 percent based on observations of at-risk behavior move to the "secondary" tier, and 1–5 percent of students who need individual interventions move to the "tertiary" tier (PBIS.org, 2013). Research that supports SWPBS include studies that indicate reductions in antisocial behavior, 50 percent fewer disciplinary referrals, and fewer students sent to the principal's office (Osher et al., p. 51). Finally, it is important to note that SWPBS as a schoolwide approach is perceived by teachers as an intervention that improves school safety and one in which they can play a major role in helping students make good decisions through modeling.

SEL focuses on building students' understanding of "self-awareness, self-management, social awareness, relationship skills, and responsible decision making" (Osher et al., 2010, p. 51). Building strong relationships with teachers and classmates is critical, with cooperative learning, class meetings, and service learning as important elements of the approach. An excellent example of the SEL approach is described by Maurice Elias (2002), called the "Keep Calm Force." Elementary school students who display appropriate behavior are selected for the Keep Calm Force and help maintain good behavior on the playground wearing their Keep Calm Force T-shirts. When they observe dissension or fighting, the students walk over to the conflict and point to their T-shirts. Among the Keep Calm Force students are former "troublemakers." Also, students who no longer qualify for the Keep Calm Force (possibly because of bullying behavior) are reminded that they are Keep Calm Force alumni—good behavior is part of their history! Research studies supporting SEL indicate that the approach minimizes bullying, antisocial behaviors, and aggression (Osher et al., p. 52).

In some ways comparing SWPBS and SEL takes us back to the John Locke ("The environment is a problem, we need to teach positive modeling!") vs. Jean-Jacques Rousseau ("The environment is beautiful, let the children exercise self-discipline!") views of the world. Again, we can learn from the "Genius of the And" (Collins & Porras, 2002). There is a lot to like about both approaches. As a principal, assistant principal, or teacher, we would be comfortable with a system that teaches very specific behavioral strategies, using data to monitor success, and having students learn self-discipline to make it on their own. Restorative Justice includes elements of both systems.

Restorative Justice

The popularity of Restorative Justice, to some extent, is a result of frustration with severe disciplinary consequences and zero tolerance policies. This is particularly an issue in urban areas and with disadvantaged youth, in which suspensions and expulsions lead to extensive periods out of school, and the logical consequences: missing class time, lower grades, disengagement from teachers and classmates, and a greater likelihood of dropping out of school. *Implementing Restorative Justice: A Guide for Schools* (Ashley & Burke, n.d.) published by the State of Illinois, is an excellent source to gain an understanding of the fundamentals and approach implementation strategies. To begin, Restorative Justice is not a quick fix, it is about changing the culture of the school and community, with acceptance of both consequences and the need to develop ("restore") relationships beyond a particular disciplinary issue. The method is used worldwide and is grounded in the practices of indigenous cultures. For example, Restorative Justice uses: (1) the circle—to bring people together to talk about issues, conflicts, and foster collaboration, (2) mediation and conferencing—to resolve disputes, using peer mediators, (3) peer juries—in some cases to provide guidance with low-level cases of misconduct (Ashley & Burke, n.d., pp. 14–15).

Today Restorative Justice is being used in 21 Oakland schools, and in other cities such as Denver, Chicago, and Portland, Oregon (Brown, P., 2013). In these schools, teachers and administrators are working with students "to come up with meaningful reparations for their wrongdoing while challenging them to develop empathy for one another through 'talking circles' let by [their school coordinator]" (Brown, P., 2013, p. 1). One student attending Ralph Bunche High School in Oakland, Damon Smith, discussed how he was suspended 15 times before getting involved in the Restorative Justice program at the school. He is now an A student. Talking about the suspensions, Damon said,

> You start to think it's cool [to get suspended] . . . You think you're going to come back to school and catch up, but unless you're a genius you won't. It made me want to mess up even more. [On restorative justice] I didn't know how to express emotions with my mouth. I knew how to hit people. I feel I can go to someone now. (Brown, P., 2013, p. 2)

Ashley and Burke state that the Illinois Restorative Justice program has three main goals: "accountability, community safety, [and] competency development" (n.d., p. 6). To explain how the three goals are integrated they use an example of how truants, without Restorative Justice, can miss how their behavior impacts a community. The truant may think that he is doing no harm to others, but in reality there are at least three victims. The truant is missing work and will fall behind, the teacher will have to spend extra time with the student to help him catch up, and classmates will lose that time with the teacher. All of these issues would be discussed in a restorative circle in which the truant has to face how his behavior affects others.

BROAD DISCIPLINARY GUIDELINES

After reviewing the general aspects of SWPBS, SEL, and Restorative Justice, principals and assistant principals must still answer the question: What broad disciplinary guidelines should be in place that emphasize both safety and respect? Guidelines must be clear about expectations and provide information that students need to be successful in school. Specific school rules must, of course, align with federal, state, district, and local school board policies. School law and the legal system often are in flux, yet general guidelines concerning the extent of the school's responsibility with regard to discipline and student rights must be followed by school principals. Taking a school law class and following legal updates in principalship journals is a must. For example, school principals must be familiar with laws related to due process, random drug testing, search and seizure, truancy, disruptive students in special education, zero tolerance, censorship, and bullying prevention related to violence, intimidation, sexual harassment, and cyberbullying. Access to a lawyer with school law training is an imperative for today's school leaders.

When developing disciplinary guidelines for a school, consider the following:

1. State the guidelines positively and with clarity. A list of don'ts sets a negative tone and shows a lack of confidence in, and respect for, students.

2. Except when absolutely necessary (see Guideline 3), avoid guidelines that are too specific; consider general principles that include specific offenses.

3. Guidelines that should be absolutely specific include the right to undisturbed teaching and learning and total intolerance for weapons, physical violence, and drugs; hurtful, sexual, sexist, homophobic, or racist language; bullying behavior; academic dishonesty; and vandalism.

4. If you are not sure that a particular guideline (e.g., students are not permitted to smoke within three blocks of the school) is the responsibility of the school, consider leaving the guideline out.

5. Safety must be the prime consideration when developing guidelines; a school must first be safe.

6. Try to involve students in the development of guidelines; their commitment will increase—however, remember that student responsibilities go along with student rights.

7. All guidelines should have a rational basis. "It has always been a rule" is not good enough especially in a culture that promotes mediation and peer discussions.

8. School rules should align with the school mission.

9. School rules must reflect district, state, and federal legal statutes.

REDUCING BULLYING BEHAVIOR

"Bullying presents one of the greatest health risks to children, youth, and young adults in U. S. society" (American Educational Research Association

[AERA], 2013, p. 1). Unfortunately AERA maintains in its 2013 report *Prevention of Bullying in Schools, Colleges, and Universities* that because children and youth are in schools already, these environments have become the "epicenter" for bullying activities, with about 28 percent of students bullied. Citing Dan Olweus, the AERA report defines bullying as "unwanted, intentional, aggressive behavior that involves a real or perceived power imbalance that is often repeated over time" (p. 5). Bullying should be stopped, and not just because it may lead to a worst-case nightmare of a school shooting. Bullying is unacceptable because it is wrong to verbally or physically intimidate or harass others. And obviously, students cannot learn successfully when fear is a part of their lives. Bullied students "experience higher rates of anxiety, depression and physical health problems . . . are less engaged in school . . . [experiencing declines in] grades and test scores" (AERA, pp. 9–10). In today's high stakes environment in which accountability, testing, and high school graduation rates are prominent issues, we must take a hard look at data that indicate, "In schools where bullying and teasing are prevalent, the student body is less involved in school activities, perform lower on standardized students, and has a lower graduation rate" (AERA, p. 10). Citing federal sources Lerman (2010) reports that approximately 160,000 students stay home from school on the average day because of fears of being bullied. Goleman (1995) notes that bullies often lack empathy, are unable to interpret social cues, and misread neutral expressions as hostile actions against them. Elias (2002) indicates that if bullies are going to change their behavior, they must learn to internalize and practice appropriate skills. Also, those who exhibit bullying behavior often "experience a greater degree of depression than is found among adults who did not bully others at school," and they are more likely to receive future criminal convictions (Harris, Petrie, & Willoughby, 2002, p. 6).

School principals must communicate to the school community that bullying is unacceptable—it is violent behavior. Sadly, the victims of bullies do not feel that school officials care, and bullied students are unlikely to tell about their victimization for fear of reprisals. Interestingly, school officials are more likely to intervene in bullying incidents when race, religion, and disability are involved than when the "harassment [is] related to sexual orientation, gender presentation, and body size" (AERA, 2013, p. 26). To support bullied students, states and school districts have established antibullying, harassment, and intimidation policies. Washington state mandated as part of its legislative bill a section that provides immunity to school employees, students, or volunteers who willingly report incidents of harassment, intimidation, and bullying. Furthermore, staff workshops and other professional development programs that stress positive character traits and values are part of the antibullying policy as mandated by the state legislation (Substitute House Bill 1444, State of Washington, 2002).

Based on the recommendations of AERA (2013), Goodwin (2011), Harris et al. (2002), Lerman (2010), and (Yetter, 2012), our own experiences, and the suggestions of other educators, the following recommendations are suggested to reduce bullying behavior in schools:

- If possible, organize large schools into smaller "units, families, or houses" to reduce the feeling of alienation some students may experience in larger settings.
- Initiate personalization programs that connect an adult with every student in the school, and that connect students with peers. Mentoring programs and peer intervention programs should both be instituted so that every student has someone to talk with and receive effective intervention strategies from when difficulties occur.
- Recognize that bullying is a systemic school and community issue, the *whole community needs to be involved* in prevention strategies.
- Use community resources (e.g., mental health agencies) to help students prone to bullying, especially those students from families unable to provide positive support.
- Survey students concerning their perceptions about the school climate and bullying, and share results with staff, parents, and community members.
- Ensure that students who are victims of violence recognize that the administration, counselors, classroom teachers, and community resources are firmly in their corner and are there to support them.
- Use student leadership organizations or other appropriate avenues to get the message out that a dialogue concerning antibullying prevention and intervention strategies is a major school priority.
- Recognize that overt acts of bullying (e.g., violence) are not the only concern; verbal harassment and intimidation must also be addressed.
- Supervise "hot spot" areas where bullying behavior may occur, and *talk with students in these areas to build relationships.* These venues include hallways, lockers, cafeterias, restrooms, playgrounds, buses, areas immediately surrounding the school, and even classrooms. Provide extra supervision in areas that are especially problematic. Also consider that support staff (e.g., bus monitors, cafeteria workers, janitorial workers, security personnel) can play a major preventative role in "hot spots."
- Consider anonymous bullying reporting possibilities for students like hotlines, voice mail, and text-messaging alerts.
- Initiate professional development programs that emphasize character and values, and work with the faculty to model and support a positive school climate and a culture that promotes antibullying behaviors.
- Keep students informed concerning the school's antibullying policy and consequences relating to suspension and expulsion for students who defy the policy.
- Initiate programs to assist students who bully others by providing social, emotional, personal, and academic skill support to cope appropriately in a school environment.

CYBERBULLYING AND SOCIAL RESPONSIBILITY

The Center for Safe and Responsible Internet Use has defined cyberbullying as "being cruel to others by sending or posting harmful material using the Internet or a cell phone" (Willard, 2005). Cyberbullying includes online verbal attacks with hostile or vulgar language; sending or posting hurtful messages, rumors, or photos; intimidating through cyberstalking; disclosing private information; and blocking someone from online access (Parker-Roerden, Rudewick, & Gorton, 2007). A report on cyberbullying noted that 81 percent of administrators were confident that they were preparing students sufficiently concerning online safety; teachers were less optimistic—only 51 percent expressed confidence about student preparation (Yetter, 2012). Cyberbullying is particularly pernicious because the bully (who perpetrates the Internet, text messaging, or other electronic bullying act) can easily remain anonymous while engaging in harmful behavior toward an innocent target. Often the bully sends a copy of the hurtful message to bystanders, similar to the act of the schoolyard bully who punishes another in front of a crowd. Bystanders, who may initially be innocent recipients of the "message," have three basic choices: (1) they can forward the hurtful message to others and become bullies themselves, (2) they can remain as bystanders, or (3) they can intervene to end the bullying behavior.

How a bystander responds to cyberbullying can determine whether the hateful behavior continues. Experts have different opinions about the role of bystanders, some believing that they should "have the courage to intervene" (Long, 2008). Weissbourd and Jones (2012) maintain that it is a bit more tricky, "relying on isolated bystanders to become upstanders does little to change the social norms that fuel the cruelty. . . . No widespread system of prevention can depend on the capacity of individual children for heroism and self-sacrifice" (p. 27). Behaving with courage is not easy, especially for teenagers surrounded by peers who are participating in cyberbullying or other forms of harassment. Additionally, school leaders must make sure that student disciplinary policies define cyberbullying and the consequences for inappropriate behaviors. Because cyberbullying can begin off school grounds, students may rationalize that it is not a school issue. Administrators need to let students know that cyberbullying is a form of harassment, bullying, and intimidating behavior. Parents must be informed about the anticyberbullying policy and provided with guidelines to help them understand the issue and what they might be facing at home. Also, faculty professional development should be included as part of a school's anticyberbullying strategy, just as professional development has been offered in response to other forms of inappropriate behaviors. Finally, Weissbourd and Jones (2012) and Goodwin (2011) believe that a more holistic approach that taps into the values of the school culture and community has the best chance of mitigating the offensive bullying and cyberbullying behaviors.

SUPPORTING LESBIAN, GAY, BISEXUAL, AND TRANSGENDER YOUTH

In the most recent report sponsored by the Gay, Lesbian and Straight Education Network (GLSEN) on the school climate for LGBT youth, 84.9 percent of the LGBT youth heard "gay" used negatively, 71 percent heard other homophobic remarks, 56.9 heard homophobic remarks from teachers, 63.5 percent felt unsafe because of sexual orientation, and 38.3 percent were physically harassed (GLSEN, 2012; www.glsen.org). The picture is clear and disturbing. Bullying and harassment of LGBT students is a major issue for our schools, and thus a social justice issue for principals, assistant principals, and teachers. As with other bullying situations, LGBT youth attend school less, receive poorer grades, and feel unconnected to their schools when they are targeted. Moreover, "suicide among sexual minority youth is a major public health concern" (Robinson & Espelage, 2011, p. 316). Young (2011) reports that "in a school of 1,000 students, up to 100 will be gay, lesbian, or bisexual, 10 will be transgender; and one will be intersex (biologically neither male nor female)" (p. 35).

Although the GLSEN report is sobering, with over 80 percent of LGBT youth experiencing harassment, it was also optimistic, stating the positive interventions in schools are beginning to make a difference. LGBT youth are heartened when a teacher stands up to bullying, and schools with Gay-Straight Alliance Clubs are safer places where fewer homophobic remarks are made and where teachers intervene when inappropriate behavior occurs. It is also critical to stress that even with the high percentages of bullying and societal pressures, the majority of LGBT youth, "are *not* at risk. . . . and develop as healthy teenagers" (Robinson & Espelage, 2011, pp. 325–326). Jason Cianciotto and Sean Cahill (2012) in their book *LGBT Youth in America's Schools* cited the *Respect for All* program sponsored by the New York City Department of Education as an exemplary professional development model for teachers and staff. Program goals include:

1. Building the capacity of school personnel to actively promote a community of inclusion in each school so that all students feel both safe and respected.

2. Increase the likelihood that school personnel will intervene when witnessing anti-LGBTQ language, harassment, and/or bullying.

3. Build the capacity of school personnel to serve as a resource and support for students who may be lesbian, gay, bisexual, transgender, or questioning.

4. Build the capacity of school personnel to serve as a resource for other school personnel regarding issues faced by lesbian, gay, bisexual, transgender, and questioning students.

5. Decrease hurtful, offensive, or exclusionary language and/or practice (Cianciotto & Cahill, p. 97).

If you would like information on the program, contact: RespectForAll@ schools.nyc.gov.

Robinson and Espelage (2011) make a significant point toward the end of their research study—a lot has happened on the social front related to the LGBT community. Don't Ask Don't Tell has been repealed, President Obama recorded a video supporting the "It Gets Better" project after multiple gay teen suicides, and pop culture has many pro-LGBT artists like Lady Gaga with her huge hit, "Born This Way." We would add that the number of states that have legalized same-sex marriage is an additional indicator that times are changing. But the bullying, harassment, and intimidation continue. School leaders should seize this issue just as other civil rights issues were seized in the past and take a stand to demonstrate that our schools exemplify what is best about our democracy—we welcome diversity because through diversity we have become a great nation.

GRADUATING AMERICA'S YOUTH: MAKING PROGRESS ON A LONG ROAD

Graduating from high school is a first step to opportunity. For students and society, failure to graduate has far reaching implications. While about 75 percent of U.S. high school students graduate, 1 million students fail to do so each year. That is about 5,500 each school day! Colin Powell called the drop out crisis a "catastrophe" ("Feds Take on Dropout Crisis," 2008). When the high school dropout data are disaggregated, the statistics show significant disparity. After four years of high school, 81 percent of Asians, 80 percent of Whites, 68 percent of Latinos, 62 percent of African Americans, and 51 percent of Native Americans graduate. The positive news is that during the last decade, the national graduation rate has gone up 8 percent, the Latino rate 16 percent, and the Black student rate 13 percent. On the sobering side, the Native American rate has increased only 3 percent in a decade, and has actually dropped since 2008 (Swanson & Lloyd, 2013).

Academic Press, Social Support, and Community Efforts

Promising practices to increase graduation rates are being implemented throughout North America. An approach supported by the Chicago Annenberg Challenge (Lee, Smith, Perry, & Smylie, 1999) recommends a two-pronged strategy employing both *Academic Press* and *Social Support* to make a difference in the lives of students. Although the study concentrated on sixth and eighth graders, fieldwork involved observing high schools that were using both social support and academic press strategies. Social support is defined as "the personal relationship that students have with people who may help them do well in school" (Lee et al., 1999, p. 9), while "academic press . . . focuses on the extent to which school members, including teachers and students experience a normative emphasis on academic success and conformity to specific standards" (Lee et al., 1999, p. 10). The power of this approach rests on rejecting the notion that schools must choose between providing emotional and social support *or* press for academic achievement. This strategy is similar to the *structure and support* approach noted in the section on the Discipline Gap. The results of this Annenberg study indicated that when academic press and social support were instituted, achievement scores were highest. Interestingly, the approach to supporting students in historically Black colleges and universities is provided as a working example. These institutions of higher education succeed due to "strong academic programs and strong systems of social support to help students succeed academically" (Lee et al., 1999, p. 6).

Based on the research study, strategies to enhance social support include supplemental one-on-one tutoring, creating smaller learning communities, personalized learning, schools within schools, parent education programs, and building relationships with mentors and older community members. Academic press strategies include higher expectations for students, teacher professional development related to higher-order thinking and challenging student work, and formative assessments to impact instruction (Lee et al., 1999, pp. 21–22). Finally, the researchers report, "For students who may receive little support from home, peers, and community, it becomes even more important that principals, and teachers create school and classroom environments that provide personal support for learning" (Lee et al., 1999, p. 25).

As noted in Chapter 17, community organizations like the Children's Aid Society work with schools to offer social, emotional, and health-related services. One of the nation's top-rated agencies devoted to working with potential dropouts is Communities in Schools (CIS). The Virginia-based organization, presently serving 1.2 million potential dropouts, coordinates local services with schools committed to its program. Each school has a CIS site-coordinator who works on prevention and intervention, "On a typical day [the coordinator offers] intensive case management, academic help, mentoring, clean clothes, or just a kind word to a kid whose day got off to a rocky start" (Boss, 2013, p. 2). CIS uses evidence-based data to increase the program's local impact on students—each student's situation is going to be different. Finally, the organization is committed to providing wraparound services that, although available in the community, are often disconnected.

Breaking Ranks II

The academic and social support recommendations of the Chicago Annenberg Research Project parallel the three "Core Areas" of the National Association of Secondary School Principals (NASSP, 2004) in its publication *Breaking Ranks II*. Adding a leadership dimension, the NASSP calls for

(1) collaborative leadership, in PLCs, that strategically use data; (2) personalizing the school environment into smaller, caring units; and (3) implementing curriculum, instruction, and assessment practices that are personalized based on high expectations and student needs (pp. 17–18).

Educators with the Chicago Annenberg Research Project and NASSP clearly believe that to reduce the number of high school dropouts, school leaders and teachers need to make personal connections with students that focus on academic rigor and success. Additionally, creating community is a major element stressed by both groups, with community having an in-school dimension focused on building connectedness and trust, and a reach out dimension that engages community resources to meet the needs of all students.

Homeless Students: In Need of Intense Support

When we discuss at-risk students in need of social support and structure, there is no group more at risk concerning graduation than homeless students: less than 25 percent of homeless students complete high school (Murphy & Tobin, 2011). According to the National Association for the Education of Homeless Children and Youth (NAEHCY), during the 2010–2011 school year, almost 1.1 million homeless youth enrolled in schools. For homeless youth, school is the only place "where they see the same faces, sit in the same seat, and can put their hearts and minds into pursuits that ease their daily troubles" (NAEHCY, 2013, p. 1). The McKinney-Vento Homeless Assistance Act, first authorized during the Reagan Administration and reauthorized in 2001, requires each school district to have a "homeless liaison" to advocate for these students. In some smaller districts the principal or assistant principal may take on that role. Aspects of the McKinney-Vento law that are sometimes overlooked include (1) a student's right to enroll immediately if he/she is homeless even if residential documentation is unavailable, (2) recognizing that a student who is living with other individuals is still considered homeless if the "new" residency is a result of an economic, housing, or other severe circumstance, (3) the right to attend one's school of origin (before the homeless circumstance) with school transportation rights (Dill, 2010). Principals and teachers need to be acutely aware of possible bullying of homeless children because of clothing, hygienic, social, and academic issues that may disadvantage the students. Dill suggests that teachers need to use their "caring detective radar" to spot changes in a child's life that may indicate homeless. Teachers should contact the homeless liaison who can implement support strategies that include school supplies, clothing, scholarships, and coordination with residential homeless serving agencies. Finally, the NAEHCY website has numerous links that can help principals, assistant principals, and teachers take the lead on this issue, with excellent sources of assistance, including information on postsecondary scholarships (http://www.naehcy.org).

Principal Lori Wyborney:
Making a Difference at Rogers High School

Principal Wyborney has served as the leader of Rogers High School in Spokane, Washington, for the past five years. During that period, the on-time graduation rate has risen from 55 percent to 87 percent. She was kind enough to spend time with us to discuss how the teachers, students, parents, community, and administration have worked together to make a difference. Her remarks fell into four categories: (1) keep an eye on the mission and vision; (2) reflections, big ideas and strategies; (3) teacher leadership; and (4) student pride and the community.

1. Keep an Eye on the Mission and Vision

The only thing I am not flexible about is the mission. You need to have a center, a true north. Then the flexibility is easier. You know your values and what you can be flexible about. I purposely don't write everything down concerning the mission because sometimes ideas get lost on paper. Here's my story. I'm passionate about equity. I had a student, Hector. He was brilliant, 13 yrs. old. I had all the opportunities possible because of what my parents were able to provide for me. Hector did not have the same opportunities because of background issues. I had to ask myself, "Why did I get this?" "Why doesn't Hector get to go to college?" "Why doesn't he get the same opportunities that I was lucky enough to get?" All kids have to have an adult advocate. School has to provide Hector with opportunities. These are questions that we constantly raise at faculty meetings.

2. Reflections, Big Ideas and Strategies

Passions motivate people. There is no secret to what we do. All we try to do is teach kids to learn a lot so they can go on to be great. We never feel like we have arrived. The nature of the job is that change is always taking place; things are always changing.

We look at our data. Our African-American kids, our Native American kids who were underperforming are succeeding. We have all access for all kids in our AP courses. Our African-American and Native American kids are graduating on time and going to college.

I have no problem with accountability. High-performing schools like Rogers can almost always wipe out the gaps that some kids have when they come to school. When you say all kids have to reach a certain standard, you can eliminate the gap. When you say a kid does not have to reach a standard, then you are hurting that kid. Seventy percent of our kids enroll in college, but only 21 percent persist through the second year. We are working on this. Our students all take four years of math, about 80 percent take four years of science. They are taking harder academic programs.

Interventions—that is the difference between us and another high school: our kids have to get it here, if they don't get it at home. We try a lot of different interventions until we find out what works. Our interventions relate to our use of Academic Mentors who work with a demographic group; a group of kids from a specific culture. They notice kids, know the culture, and have made a difference.

Previously faculty meetings were about disseminating information. What I now realize, and one of my most effective moves, was realizing that now it has to be about passion, the mission. We need to inspire, use videos, data, and examples. It is not just words. What do the changes mean to us as people? At every Tuesday meeting I bring up and stress these ideas: All kids have a right to graduate on time. The transcripts of all kids should show that they are career and college ready. All kids must meet standards in reading, writing, math, and science.

3. Teacher Leadership

We have to own our student learning, be accountable. Teacher leadership drives what goes on at our school. Teacher voice. They decide on the interventions. I expect the teachers to make so many of the decisions in this school. I've worked hard to give voice to a lot of teachers, and a voice directly to me. I welcome when people say, "Lori, you did this wrong." Teachers who are upset need to be heard, face-to-face. I say to them, "Tell me why you don't like this idea. Tell me how to fix it." For example we are working on moving intervention time, from first to third period. They have a direct voice to me on how they feel about this.

Principals have to let teachers know that they respect their work; they respect teachers. Whether it is what they are teaching, or an idea for making change in the school. It should not come from the top. It has to come from the teacher ranks. (Lori mentions Susan Szachowicz, the award-winning principal of Brockton High School in Massachusetts.) Doc Szach said, "I always tell everyone, if you want to change a school, empower a team." She is totally right!

The staff welcomes acknowledgements, recognition and accolades. We need to recognize them more, let them know we appreciate their work. To me, what goes on in a school that works will remain, the teachers will make sure of that.

4. Student Pride and the Community

Kids will do what we expect them to do. It is about expectations. They will rise to the expectations. The kids are loving that we expect more.

Rogers is a neighborhood high school. A community school. So the pride in the school has always been there. In the past the pride was about being fighters. That is not how it is in our school anymore. Now it is about academics, not fighting. Having a new building has helped build more pride.

I have to work on how the kids and their parents view the school. Now they take pride in the school and academics. We don't know about the potential of our kids until we see them grow. Sometimes parents don't know about the opportunities. At school we have to provide opportunities and let parents know about opportunities and interventions.

Leaders as Builders of Dreams

A school principal from a high school with a large population of at-risk youth took an unusual but powerful approach to address the dropout problem. As you read this principal's story, consider how a vision can be realized when school leaders, faculty, and students are committed to the idea:

"Sometimes, leaders are 'keepers of the dream' when it comes to students' aspirations. But sometimes, the leader encounters students who are dreamless. They are beaten down and have a sense of hopelessness. In this case, the leader must help construct dreams for, and with, students. Last year, I took on the role of 'builder of the dream.' I shared this idea with teachers and asked them to collaborate as 'builders of the dream.' During the first week of school, we called in every senior. We shared our collaborative vision of graduation day. We asked the seniors to put themselves in the picture, specifically the lineup to receive a diploma. Then we said, 'To make this vision closer to reality, put on a cap and graduation robe. And we'll take your picture.' Students seemed surprised, but pleased. We photographed every one of them in a cap and gown, approaching a podium where they would be handed a diploma. That picture served as a magnet for many of the kids—it pulled them through the year, despite tough times. As a staff, we are convinced many more graduated because of this approach. We'll plan to do this again every year."

STUDENT AND TEACHER RESILIENCY

As the tragic events of September 11, 2001, were unfolding, we learned a great deal about heroes. "On September 11th, more than 8,000 children—from day care to high school seniors, from fully mobile to multiple-handicapped—were safely evacuated from the vicinity of Ground Zero in lower Manhattan. Not a single child was harmed or lost in all of the chaos. The principals, teachers, staff, and parents were heroes in every sense of the word" (Lehmuller & Switzer, 2002, p. 54). Paul Houston (2002), executive director of the American Association of School Administrators, reflected,

> Perhaps the most powerful lesson for me was to find that all I had learned about heroes was wrong. Most of us were raised to think of heroes as those extraordinary people in history books who do extraordinary things. What we learned on September 11th was that we are genetically programmed to act heroically. Heroes are ordinary people who do extraordinary things and they are all around us. It is in each of us to act heroically when called upon. What a wonderful lesson for our children. (p. 46)

School principals all around the country were tested concerning their leadership skills on September 11, 2001, and the following days. On September 11, teachers, students, and parents wondered if their schools would be closed or if lockdown procedures would be implemented. Following September 11, teachers looked to principals to determine whether they should stick to their routine or teach about death, grief and anxiety, tolerance, current events, the tenets of American democracy, or the geography of Afghanistan.

Let's recall that a consistent theme in all of the nation's schools was a desire to express appreciation to New York and Washington firefighters, police officers, and emergency service workers and to the heroic civilian and military men and women who were attacked at the World Trade Center and the Pentagon. Students in elementary and secondary classrooms created banners, drew pictures, collected money, and wrote thousands of letters to express their feelings. Like thousands of other classrooms across the nation, Shannon Collinge's class of second graders in Spokane, Washington, received the following thank you from the Uniformed Firefighters Association of New York:

> Thank you for the drawings and letters from the children in your class. Please convey to them our gratitude for the concern and compassion they have shown us in this difficult time.
>
> We have received an outpouring of kindness from the children of America in such letters as those you sent and we have taken the letters and drawings to fire stations all over the city so that they can be displayed where firefighters can see them. We also placed as many pictures as would fit in the front window of our building so that other New Yorkers could see them as they pass by.
>
> Again, please let the children know how much their kindness means to us.
>
> Sincerely,
> Uniformed Firefighters Association
> Widows' and Children's Fund

Sandy Hook Elementary School

On February 15, 2013, President Obama awarded the Presidential Citizens Medal, the nation's second highest civilian honor, to the six educators martyred at Sandy Hook Elementary School, with 20 innocent children. Reflecting on the legacy of the six educators the president said, "It defines our way of life. It captures our belief in something bigger than ourselves—our willingness to accept certain obligations to one another and to embrace the idea that we're all in this together" (Lederman, 2013). Dawn Hochsprung was the school principal. Like the other educators on that tragic day, her courage symbolized the first obligation of each educator: protect the children. If Dawn Hochsprung had continued to live as principal of Sandy Hook Elementary School, protecting the children would have meant ensuring that they learned to read and write, problem solve, collaborate, think for themselves, explore their creativity, and understand the world. Each day educators protect and serve children by making sure they gain the knowledge and skills necessary to break through barriers, to become great, to find their destiny. By continuing that work we can do justice to the memory of the principal, teachers, and children of Sandy Hook Elementary School.

FINAL THOUGHTS ON "THOSE KIDS"

Caine and Caine (1991) remind us that creating a positive climate in school can directly affect how students think and function. They stress that under threat, the brain actually "downshifts" and does not perform at its maximum capacity. Thus communicating often with students, setting a supportive tone in class, and sending positive nonverbal signals are as critical as the rules. Finally, learning what responsibility is all about is a lifelong challenge. If schools can foster responsibility through positive guidelines and valuable activities, then the possibility of developing the tools for lifelong learning can become a reality.

REFLECTIONS

This space provides a place for you to write down ideas that have been generated by this chapter, things you want to try, or adaptations of ideas presented here.

1. What do you remember about your school principals?

2. What aspects of social justice resonate with you?

3. What humorous anecdotes can you recall about students in your school that tell a larger story?

4. What are some of the effective strategies used in your school to assist students with disabilities? Which strategies need to be improved?

5. What broad disciplinary guidelines would you add to, or delete from, the chapter list?

6. Review the recommendations in this chapter described to reduce bullying and cyberbullying behavior. What else would you suggest to mitigate these problem?

7. How can principals shape the school climate to support LGBT students?

8. Why has the high school dropout rate become a major issue? What solutions do you think could be offered to reduce the crisis?

9. What insights or new questions do you have as a result of reflecting on the ideas presented in this chapter?

PART VII

The Principal's Professional and Personal Worlds

19

The Newcomer to the Principalship

There were some days, you know. It's like when you're a kid and you're about to go up [to bat], and there are three teammates on base, and it was the bottom of the ninth. Your stomach has this feeling like, hey, I've got to do it! There were some days I had that feeling all day long in my stomach.

—Comment from a first-year principal

First-time principals experience five interrelated threads of influence (Alvy & Robbins, 2008) that help explain why the job is so complex. The unique experiences of all newcomers affirm their individual signatures. Review each factor below, and consider your personal situation.

Newcomer experiences—negotiating the many "firsts" one encounters during any fresh experience such as moving to a new community, meeting new people, driving a new car, or navigating a new laptop.

Challenges all principals face—experiencing the daily work of any principal, new or seasoned.

Personal and professional baggage—considering all the experiences one brings to the job, including family background, education, values, teaching experiences, previous supervisory relationships, one's unique career ladder, social and communication skills, attitude, and talents.

> *Local and immediate context of the school culture*—reflecting on the special nature of each school, district, and community—the teachers, students, and parents—that newcomers encounter.

> *The chemical mix*—reflecting on the unique "mark" that emerges for each individual when the above four factors are synthesized.

By reflecting on these factors, new principals gain important insights about the challenges of the job, previous experiences that influence present behaviors, and one's performance. Most important, these factors should provide newcomers with a sense of relief, reminding them that they are not alone. But the relief does not diminish the daily challenges that new principals face; on-the-job training is not an option. *From day one, you have full principalship responsibilities.* Schools obviously cannot afford to suspend operations while new principals are learning the ropes. Thus it is crucial to identify the problems that are especially challenging for new principals and offer practical suggestions to assist new and prospective principals. Experienced principals, who find themselves "new again" in a different setting, will find the ideas discussed in this chapter useful, as will superintendents and veteran principals serving as mentors for new principals.

PROBLEMS THAT CHALLENGE NEW PRINCIPALS

The literature on the principalship indicates there are several areas of difficulty that seem to frequently surface with new principals (Alvy, 1983; Alvy & Robbins, 1998; Alvy & Robbins, 2010b). In the following paragraphs, these difficulties are described, not to scare off prospective principals or newcomers but to reduce their anxiety, knowing that other very talented individuals are experiencing the same challenges. This chapter will then move forward with suggestions to acquaint prospective as well as new principals with important socialization concepts and offer some practical suggestions to get started on the job.

The limitations of preservice training. When moving into the principal's role, newcomers usually find that the preservice training could not possibly duplicate all of the challenges that one immediately faces. For example, there are many unique situations in each school, regarding staff relations, curriculum and instructional demands, student needs, and the physical plant, so that on-the-job trial and error is simply a necessity. For some, it has been helpful to experience the realistic and practical training provided through a vice principalship, administrative internship, or administrative assistantship. Preservice courses generally do not address how to use the latest Web-based student information software, design a temporary schedule to implement the statewide testing, or prepare for a lockdown. Yet these frequently are the responsibilities of a principal. Universities and principals' centers are working to improve their ability to provide more realistic experiences (e.g., case study analysis, simulations, in-baskets, internships with support networks). Increasingly, school districts and universities are pursuing mentoring programs to help newcomers face the job challenges.

It's lonely at the top. New principals are not only on unfamiliar ground but will find that, by virtue of their positions at the top of the management hierarchy in their schools, they do not have professional peers with the same responsibilities in their immediate environments. Quite simply, there may be no one else around who can relate to the problems being faced. Elementary principals may find themselves even lonelier because many elementary schools have only one building administrator. Role models and on-site assistance may be desired but not possible. "I felt like I was alone. I couldn't go across roles and confide with somebody" (a principal's voice). Because the superintendency and high school principalship in many areas are still dominated by males, the loneliness of the principalship may be heightened for women in some contexts.

Ironically, although the principal may be lonely with regard to having a professional peer on the same organizational level, a principal is anything but alone during the school day. The principal is constantly interacting with teachers, students, secretaries, parents, security personnel, student teachers, and community partners. Thus, for someone who enjoys human interaction, the principalship can be very rewarding. Yet opportunities to sit down at the lunch table with other principals may occur only at districtwide meetings or at annual regional, state, or national association meetings.

Developing a personal mission and vision. At the same time that new principals are learning about the district mission, the culture of the school, and priorities that were previously established, the newcomers must revisit their own beliefs in order to complement district goals. It is one thing to develop a mission statement as part of a graduate course; it is quite another when you are part of a district and school team.

Time management—finding time to visit classes and juggling the various roles. It is an understatement to say new principals quickly learn that there are frequent and various demands on their time. For many newcomers, time management becomes their most significant problem. Unfortunately, the first casualty of a new principalship may be the instructional responsibility of taking the time to visit classes (Alvy, 1983). If one's early actions are a predictor of future actions, it may be difficult for newcomers to reverse patterns that develop early in their principalship. Managing one's time, then, becomes a challenge to be addressed from the first day on the job.

New principals may also feel resentment about the amount of time required of them. Why do I have to return to school in the evening? Should I turn off my smartphone during dinner? Should I check my e-mail before going to bed? What happened to my summer holiday? "I've been surprised at the amount of time, and weekends, that this particular superintendent has asked me to give. . . . It surprises me, and that's the one thing about the job that bothers me" (a principal's voice).

A related time and responsibility management issue is juggling the various roles one has to play. Principals can pretty much forget their job description. In addition to serving as instructional leaders, principals must be child advocates, budget managers, personnel mediators, cheerleaders during "down" days, community healers, curriculum planners, public relations experts, basketball timers, culture shapers, actors in school plays . . . and what else?

Managing when resources are scarce. Tough economic times are here to stay. Without the experience of seasoned principals who know how the informal network operates (How did he get new lighting fixtures for the performing arts auditorium?) newcomers have to prioritize, gain allies, and creatively manage resources. The key question becomes: What is essential? It is helpful to consider the advice of Apple's lead design engineer, Jonathan Ive, "You have to deeply understand the essence of a product in order to be able to get rid of the parts that are not essential" (Isaacson, 2011, p. 343).

Staff relations and introducing change. There is always some nervousness when a principal is new to a school—especially when a first-timer takes over responsibilities. The nervousness, of course, is mutual. Newcomers usually find that staff resistance to change is one of the major obstacles they face. The resistance may be even more pronounced with the more seasoned teachers, who may comment, "We tried this two principals ago." Implementing change may be especially hard for the principal who is hired in-house. Relationships with longtime friends may have to change. In this context, the teacher evaluation process can be a particularly difficult hurdle to overcome.

Honoring the various constituencies. Teachers, students, superintendents, unions, school boards, parent associations, specific parent interest groups, businesses, and community agencies often have conflicting interests. Just trying to find out what these individuals and groups desire is a considerable task for the new principal. Principals may be tempted to state simply, "My responsibility is to follow the directives of the superintendent, and school board in the best interest of the students." But reality tells us that interest groups will not be satisfied with this bureaucratic response. Group conflict and the consequences are a given. Staff and parents will be very interested to see how the newcomer reacts when conflicts emerge. Having more knowledge and facts is not enough; people look for respect. Facts and technical competency may get you hired but without interpersonal skills your administrative career will be short-lived (Zenger & Folkman, 2002).

Unrealistic expectations—making immediate instructional changes. When hired for the principalship, one usually can take pride in knowing that he or she was selected for the job over some pretty stiff competition. Also, with all of the literature on the principal as instructional leader, often the newcomer hopes to make a quick and significant curriculum change or implement an instructional innovation. However, these ideas usually will need time to be nurtured as staff members adjust to the newcomer and the newcomer learns about the culture of the school. Thus, implementing immediate curricular, instructional, or assessment changes will probably have to wait until the principal has the opportunity to assess the cultural context and build trust with staff. For a change to be institutionalized, one should know the organization well—the mission, teachers, parents, students, and resources. One veteran principal advises newcomers to be patient with the staff: "Trust took almost five years to build. But we created a world together."

Meeting individual student needs. Principals and teachers want to address the needs of each student. However, many new principals see the school population as a whole—instead of considering individual students. After all, principals see all the students at an assembly, in the hallways, by the buses, in the cafeteria, or during a fire drill. This is quite a change, especially if the principal recently served as a teacher. It is a challenge and a dilemma. One must take responsibility for the whole institution but still consider the personal needs of each individual. The same dilemma can be applied to faculty, classified staff, and the parent community.

It's difficult to become an instant sage. A new principal in his mid-30s had a veteran teacher, who was close to retirement, enter the office one afternoon after school to ask the principal for advice about what to do in retirement. The newcomer was struck by this image of the older, white-haired teacher coming to this newcomer for advice. If anything, it was the new principal who should be going to the veteran teacher for advice. However, as the weeks progressed, many others raised critical issues and questions. The newcomer slowly realized that because of his position many people just expect the principal to know. If only they knew the truth! The short-term solution was to show respect through active listening.

A PROFILE OF THE NEW PRINCIPAL

The following brief characterization summarizes the previous remarks concerning the school life of a new principal.

After a few days on the job, the newcomer realizes that the preservice training program insufficiently prepared her for the job. The new principal is having trouble with experienced staff who are resisting state-mandated teacher evaluation and curriculum changes and two former teaching colleagues from a previous school who refuse to take the beginner seriously. The principal is not sure how to respond to a few teachers who seem very frustrated concerning students who are experiencing academic difficulties. The principal is struck by the notion that too many students are not succeeding. She too is frustrated and thinks, "This job has more responsibilities than I had anticipated. However, I am eager to accept the challenges."

As the year progresses, the new principal is somewhat disheartened because numerous daily interruptions, job details, and personal ambivalence concerning the evaluation process stand in the way of spending more time as an instructional leader. She wants to visit classrooms, observe student work, and assist teachers. Yet the beginner is still unsure—and a little fearful—about delegating responsibilities to free herself to engage in more instructional leadership. The new principal also is learning about the norms and customs of significant others in the school, district, and community and how they effectively operate outside of the official line and staff expectations. Finally, toward the end of the year the newcomer is becoming more confident in her work and open to asking veteran district administrators about important end-of-year responsibilities. She reflects while shaking her head, "Why didn't I ask for assistance in August and September? I certainly will seek assistance next year!"

HELPING PROSPECTIVE AND NEW PRINCIPALS MAKE THE GRADE

Identifying the problems of new principals is, of course, a first step in helping newcomers make the grade. Now let's examine socialization strategies necessary for the principalship and close by offering practical suggestions to succeed during those critical first years.

Socialization for the Principalship

Developing a positive mind-set is critical to success in a new position. As you reflect on the ideas that follow, consider how these suggestions can enhance your performance.

The leader as learner—a habit of mind. The leader-as-learner mind-set is essential to a new principal's success. Why? Because the concept is based on the premise that the leader who is willing to learn has an excellent chance to succeed. Thus, when new principals ask questions and solicit ideas about how the school works, they are not revealing a weakness or ignorance but a strength, the desire to learn. Let others know that their ideas are important and that without their information you could not succeed. This is a refreshing attitude to see in a leader and sets a wonderful personal example. Most professional colleagues will appreciate the newcomer who wants to know how things really work. The key, though, is to keep this characteristic throughout your career.

Reflecting on your professional background. Sarason (1982) reminds us that as teachers we often remember the supervision and evaluation process with some disdain. With regard to teaching experiences, prospective principals need to consider their feelings about classroom isolation; how they felt when supervisors entered their classrooms; relationships with teachers and supervisors, students and parents; and the professional climate in their schools. For example, what kind of supervisory role models has one worked with? In addition to teaching experiences, new principals need to evaluate the type of university training received and how previous administrative positions may affect their performance. For instance, if one has served for several years as an athletic director, will he or she be able to make budgetary decisions fairly when the athletic budget may need slicing to provide more funds for a major group of non-English speakers entering the school district?

Developing a broad view. When teaching or taking responsibility for a particular program, one does not have to consider the broad scope of responsibilities and decisions that a principal experiences. To illustrate, imagine a cone-shaped funnel. The teacher can look toward the narrowing end of the funnel while the principal must look at the funnel becoming wider with increased responsibilities.

> There is a tendency, and I went through it myself, for teachers to feel that administrators forget that they were teachers once, too. I don't think that's the case. I think that once you start operating from a different frame in the system, your outlook changes from single program to total program. (A principal's voice)

Thus, for the principal, it is critical to look at the big picture. What is the mission of the school? What are the important goals of the school? Are we addressing inequities? Are we meeting the needs of all students with disabilities? Is our school providing a caring environment for students, teachers, parents, and the community? When one sees the big picture, then it becomes easier to discern which battles are worth fighting. For example, is it really important that a particular bulletin board was not changed on the due date? Shouldn't the real question be: How effective is that teacher with students? A principal must "Step back, look at the whole program, and then step in again" (a principal's voice).

Exercising patience and flexibility—yet holding on to your convictions. Leaders often have to deal with impatient individuals who want to see things change—immediately. Yet, "being decisive often means having the courage not to make decisions until a problem has been thoroughly examined" (Richie, 2013, p. 21). A principal must remain patient when that irate parent shows up or a teacher is upset because the server is down or the school air conditioning system is broken. Listening patiently is very important. However, when false information is presented, it is important to politely correct the errors. For example, an angry parent might say, "That teacher just doesn't care for my child." The principal's response: "I'm sorry you feel that way, Mr. Smith, but if the teacher did not care about your child, or any other child in this school, he would not be working here. We just don't operate that way."

Remaining flexible and actively listening is critical during discussions if one is going to remain open to various points of view. Yet when all is said and done, it is very important to state your convictions. People need to know where the principal stands on issues.

> But the one thing about change is that you're supposed to do it over a long period of time, and I've got to learn that. However, if something has to be done to change academic achievement of kids or their mental health, I'm not willing to wait one, two, or three years. I simply will not settle for that. (a principal's voice)

Coping with the loneliness and time factors. As stated previously, two problems that many newcomers face are loneliness and the difficulty of managing time effectively. Interestingly, these two factors are connected since there are extensive periods after school, in the evenings, or on the weekends when principals are alone at the office or working at home. However, because the principal's job can be so fragmented, it may be that productive work only occurs during these "lonely" times when true reflections take place.

PRACTICAL SUGGESTIONS FOR NEWCOMERS

The buck stops here . . . for everything. Harry Truman was right. Thus, it is important that the new principal accepts responsibility for whatever takes place in the school. Indeed, 89 percent of principals feel they should be held accountable for everything related to students in school (MetLife, 2013, p. 5). Regarding the school operation, it is especially important to take responsibility for items that may appear to be routine but are very significant for teachers in the beginning of the year. For example, the principal needs to make sure that there are enough desks in each room, drinking fountains are working, all light fixtures are operational, and toilets are flushing. It is important that one does not misinterpret "the buck stops here" to mean the principal cannot delegate and trust others. Competent people welcome and need responsibilities.

Seek out people and communicate—especially with the experienced staff and the secretary. If the three rules of real estate investing are location, location, location, then the three rules of the principalship are communication, communication, communication. In the principalship, you are investing in people. New principals should track down experienced staff (especially the school secretary) and gain their opinions about what works and what does not. They know the history of the school. Through your summer letter and first faculty meeting, let folks know that you look forward to visiting with them and learning from them.

One principal spent time before school began in August with a longtime veteran and asked, "What, in your opinion, separates this school from others?" The veteran stated, "Our teachers are always accessible to students." The new principal used that information as a positive theme with students, teachers, and parents whenever he wanted to describe the school culture.

As the year progresses, continue to take the initiative regarding relationships with faculty, students, and parents. As you develop relationships, try as much as possible to meet on their turf. The principal's office is daunting for many, and until others see you as approachable, it may not be the best place to meet. Teachers appreciate the principal who says, "Let's meet in your room."

Be visible and support the school vision and mission. Visibility is crucial. The teachers and secretary need to know that you believe the most important events in the school take place in classrooms, not the principal's office. Thus, principals need to Lead and Learn by Wandering Around (LLBWA). Research indicates that finding time to visit classrooms is especially difficult for new principals. By visiting the classrooms, library, cafeteria, labs, gymnasium, art studios, and music rooms, the principal is sending a strong message to the staff and students that what they are doing is important. Also, consider the school mission, vision, and School Improvement Plan during your school walks. Honor the school's history. When opportunities emerge, compliment individuals for behaving in ways that support these school goals. For instance, one principal regularly celebrates teachers who consistently share good news and seek feedback from parents and the larger community. These efforts address the school improvement goal of enhancing two-way communication between the school and the community.

Keep in mind that LLBWA may very well be a new approach for faculty. Make sure you let them know during the beginning-of-the-year faculty meetings that you believe the important events of a school take place in classrooms, so you intend to be visible, use walk-throughs, support the school mission and vision, and celebrate teaching and learning. Some of the staff may be skeptical about your motives at first, but most will soon appreciate the effort. As a consequence, classroom visits later in the year for teacher observations will be less stressful.

Control your schedule. This book provides several suggestions regarding time management strategies. However, a few points should be emphasized for newcomers. Although it is very difficult, try to take control of a significant part of your schedule. Block out time for events that demonstrate your commitment to the educational goals of the school. If the effort is not made, "events" will quickly fill up your schedule. During the year, constantly think about the school priorities and consider whether your schedule reflects them. There will certainly be days and even weeks when you will not be able to meet your objectives, but keep coming back to them. The teachers and your secretary should know your basic strategy concerning time use. The secretary needs to know that teachers should never feel shut out when they want to see the principal. If the principal is unavailable at a particular time, then the secretary should take the initiative and set up an appointment for the next available time. LLBWA also allows for numerous miniconferences during the day.

Additionally, it is crucial to learn to say no and to take a backseat on some committees and community requests for your time. For example, if the Cub Scouts ask you to speak at their annual awards ceremony, you should probably say yes, but that does not mean you should also say yes to the request that you join them on the overnight campout in April.

Make sure that you leave time for your own lunch and for leisure activities. Otherwise, your productivity and spirit will suffer, and resentment may surface if the job becomes all consuming.

Model the desire to grow professionally. In the long run, this may be the area in which you make your most significant contribution in serving students and teachers. Begin modeling a desire to grow professionally as a principal. Share evidence-based research, make suggestions based on sound data, distribute professional articles and recommend journals and Web sites to the staff. Let staff know about professional growth opportunities. Share with them your professional growth objectives during your first year. For example, as a new principal, one should try to get involved with a mentor, either in the district, through a local university, or possibly through a state principals' association. Consider joining a Professional Learning Network for principals, or join or create a blog for school leaders. Subscribe to professional journals, and try to attend state and national association meetings. Share your learning experiences with the staff. When you have time, continue to read about leadership. It can be very therapeutic—and you will find out that you are not alone!

FINAL THOUGHTS ON THE NEWCOMER EXPERIENCE

Coping with the daily events and constituencies in a school can be very overwhelming for a new principal. Yet there is no greater feeling than to be part of a school community and to know that you made a difference. New principals during their first year can make a contribution to their school communities every bit as significant as that of the 10-year veteran.

Often, new principals are told they will experience a honeymoon period and be forgiven for early mistakes. However, it may be foolish to hope for such a present. It is more important for the newcomer to assume that many mistakes will be made, not only during the first year. If the principal is a learner, he or she will grow professionally through each mistake. If the teachers, students, and parents perceive that the newcomer is growing, trust will build. Everyone wants to be proud of the principal. Together, as a community of learners, the principal, teachers, and students can grow together.

REFLECTIONS

This space provides a place for you to write down ideas that have been generated by this chapter, things you want to try, or adaptations of ideas presented here.

1. What were some of the major challenges you faced (or are facing) during your first year as a principal?

2. What characteristics would be suitable for a principal mentor? On what areas of study would you like to focus, given the opportunity to work with a mentor?

3. Do you agree with the characterization of the principalship as a lonely position?

4. To add to the advice offered in this chapter, what suggestions do you have for aspiring or new principals?

5. What insights or new questions do you have as a result of reflecting on the ideas presented in this chapter?

20

Taking Care
of Yourself

I used to think it was selfish to engage in activities like scheduling time for sports, movies, and reading. Now I realize if I don't do those things, my ability to nurture others is compromised.

—A principal's voice

Principals must take care of themselves in order to care for others. Setting an example as a leader does not end with the leadership, instructional, and management roles of a principal. How a workplace "feels" plays a profound role in influencing creativity, commitment, and productivity. The leader's behavior is observed by organizational members and serves as an emotional barometer and guide. One's job performance is impacted by one's home life and vice versa. In all professions, if the leader comes to work unhappy or stressed out, it takes a tremendous amount of energy and psychological manipulation to reverse one's disposition in order to function effectively for others and oneself. If a leader wants the staff to perform optimally, the leader must model both a zest for professional learning and enthusiasm for leadership that influences learning. Just as important, however, is modeling taking time to relax, reflect, and renew. If the school leader and staff are not refreshed when the year begins, then the school year is off to an ominous start.

What Is Burnout?

According to Miller and Smith (1993), "If in the beginning your job seems perfect, the solution to all your problems, you have high hopes and expectations, and would rather work than do anything else, be wary. You're a candidate for the most insidious and tragic kind of job stress—burnout, a state of physical, emotional, and mental exhaustion caused by unrealistically high aspirations and illusory or impossible goals" (p. 107). Other possible causes of burnout may include a loss of meaning for the work and frustration resulting from top-down mandates that do not align with what is best for students. Lack of rapport, common beliefs, or communication with assistant principals can also contribute to job stress. A toxic school culture, and the daunting task of transforming the culture, can be still another contributing cause of burnout. Finally, many principals cite the long hours and time away from family and friends as another burnout factor.

ACHIEVING SUCCESS OVER STRESS

"Making a concerted effort to build your resilience is a major stress-prevention technique" (Singer, 2013, p. 24). Leaders play many roles besides those formally assigned—counselor, psychologist, nurse, mediator, scheduler, facilities director—to mention only a few. Balancing these duties that are assigned or befall you with challenges and responsibilities at home can leave one feeling overwhelmed. The following seven strategies, cited by Jack Singer (2013), can "inoculate you against . . . stressors":

1. **Take charge of your internal dialogue or self-talk.**

"Research has shown that thinking patterns have a dramatic effect on moods, attitudes, and emotions" (Singer, 2013, p. 24). Stress results when one encounters disturbing events and then talks to oneself about those happenings in a negative way. William James, an American philosopher and psychologist, once said, "The greatest weapon against stress is our ability to choose one thought over another" (Singer, p. 24). Stress mastery involves choosing positive self-talk instead of negative.

2. **Develop the 3 C's of stress resistance: Commitment, Control, and Challenge.**

Singer (2013, p. 25) suggests that in addition to taking control of one's thoughts, it is important to revisit the **commitment** one made to become a leader—to serve students, staff, and the larger community. By focusing on the vision you possess for your role, you can rise above daily stressors. Let those over which you have no control fade away. The second "C" has to do with **control**. There are many stressors over which you have no control. So focus on that which you can control or influence, through participation on a committee, for instance. The third "C" is **challenge**. Essentially, challenges can either be viewed as obstacles or opportunities. Embrace them as opportunities, make lists on your e-tablet, phone, or pad of paper. Check them off as you address each one. For problems that you have yet to overcome, create a step-by-step strategy to address these over time.

3. Breathe!

When one breathes through the diaphragm, a full volume of breath is afforded—critical to stellar performances. In contrast, when one is stressed, shallow rapid breathing often occurs.

4. Let the endorphins flow!!

Endorphins "are referred to as natural opiates because of their effect on reducing stress and anxiety and creating euphoric feelings" (Singer, 2013, p. 26). Endorphins also positively impact wellness because they enhance the immune system. Physical activity such as sustained fast-paced walking, jogging, swimming, or tennis produces endorphins, as does laughing! Research also suggests that endorphins are produced as a consequence of enjoyable activities—yoga, massage, or a walk on the beach.

5. Take time to participate in random acts of kindness.

A sense of well-being, positive moods, and feelings of satisfaction are generated by doing for others—especially when such deeds are unexpected. These feelings serve to counter feelings of stress. Random deeds of kindness can include such acts as donating food, volunteering in the community, writing notes, or surprising all staff with treats.

6. Indulge in positive reflections.

Often at night, lying in bed, our minds are occupied with all that went wrong or could have gone better during the day. These negative thoughts rob us of sleep and increase the stress factor. Instead, try writing positive reflections in a notebook or electronic journal.

7. Choose to spend time with positive people.

Negative people bring doom and gloom to those around them. Choosing, whenever possible, to enjoy the company of positive people engenders feelings of optimism, hope, possibility, encouragement, and wonderful opportunities for a bright future state. Invite feedback from these people, read books, or articles about these topics.

TAKING CONTROL OF TIME

Unless we proactively organize our schedules with a lunch hour, leisure time, exercise, and other activities that refresh us, they will not happen. Thus, as you plan your schedule, build in leisure time. Place it on your schedule just as you place a school meeting on the calendar. The idea, obviously, is not to place these activities during the school day at prime times but, rather, to allocate time for daily personal activities at the beginning or end of the day to recharge your batteries. For example, if you need to leave at 5:00 p.m., it should be noted on your appointment calendar so you do not miss that jog, basketball game, or tennis match. Set a reminder on your phone.

Interestingly, the professional development time that you might take to read a journal to stay current in the field is the first thing to go when unimportant but pressing items arise in the schedule. Yet if we are to grow and our staff are to grow, we need to recognize that reading a professional journal or taking time to participate in a webinar in our office is as important as any other aspect of the job. Professional growth time should be calendared. This can also be a time to inform our practice. One principal routinely writes quotations down on index cards from articles she reads. She uses these to open faculty meetings with an approach called "Quote of the Day." Individuals read a quotation they are handed and can swap quotations with others. Also, we need to allocate time to watch videos, reflect, write, and read about the principalship and follow other professional interests. These interests need to become part of our professional and personal schedules. Taking time out for yourself gives you an opportunity to reflect upon your own experiences and your interactions with staff. You can gain a greater understanding of the faculty by taking the time to ponder why a teacher acted in a particular way or made a comment that seemed inappropriate. This can help a principal respond appropriately when addressing the needs of faculty colleagues. Reflection often affords a principal a valuable new perspective, providing valuable insights not available when one is rushing from one task to the next.

TOWARDS REALIZING THE VISION: A PERSONAL MISSION STATEMENT

Taking time to develop a personal mission statement based on professional and personal goals can help transcend the day-to-day responsibilities and keep your long-term vision in mind (Covey, 1989). As you develop the mission statement, consider the following questions:

- When you retire from education, how do you want to be remembered?
- What do you want teachers, parents, and, most of all, students to say about you?
- What will you, and those with whom you work, say are the highlights of your life story?
- What will be your legacy as a principal?
- What kind of a friend are you?
- How productive are you outside of your professional work?
- What would you want written on your tombstone?

Such questions cause one to connect daily activities with a meaningful, long-range vision. After your mission statement is developed, post it in a place where you can glance at it. Reflect upon your actions and decisions. Do your actions and decisions align with the mission statement?

GAINING PERSPECTIVE BY SPENDING TIME WITH STUDENTS

A principal's "batteries can be recharged" by taking time to visit with a class or spending a few minutes with students on the playground, in the halls, or in a courtyard. Students appreciate spending time with the principal, and this helps spread the message that the principal is more than the office figure or school disciplinarian. Having students see you as a real person helps in the process of building relationships with all students. One principal rides the bus with students once a month. Another greets students at the door when they arrive every morning. Still another participates regularly in book club discussions with different classes. These acts not only build relationships but also inform the principal about the pulse of the school.

BODY AND MIND: HEALTHY AND ILL TOGETHER[1]

If you do not feel well, it is hard to help others. From a practical viewpoint, the better you feel, the better you will perform. Your personal level of health and well-being must be maintained if you are to perform effectively on or off the job. This concept of well-being is dependent on attention to four areas: physical, physiological, emotional, and psychological. Although these are four separate areas, their functions are interrelated. For example, when you are anxious or tired, you may indulge in too many sweets, which can adversely affect your blood sugar level and put your system out of balance. A quick examination of these four interrelated categories can help you assess your personal well-being and identify areas you wish to monitor or change.

Physical Awareness

We all value having energy. An essential way to gain greater energy is to exercise. Increased energy and endurance can sustain us with a greater degree of alertness throughout the day. Yet we often fail to take the necessary steps, before or after work, to fine-tune our bodies to perform at a higher physical level while on the job.

Systematic exercise can improve cardiovascular fitness. As mentioned earlier, sustained exercise releases endorphins in the body that can have a soothing, pleasurable effect on the mind and relieve stress. And, of course, from a physical standpoint, exercise, energy, and longevity are inextricably linked for most people. According to John Medina, affiliate professor of bioengineering at the University of Washington School of Medicine and author of *Brain Rules* (2009), "Aerobic exercise reduces the level of brain loss and keeps cognitive abilities sharp" (p. 12). Exercise increases blood to the brain, increasing the release of what has been called brain-derived neurotrophic factor (BDNF), often called "Miracle-Gro for the brain." This chemical stimulates "the development of new neurons in the hippocampus, the area involved in memory, learning and the ability to plan and make decisions" (Rosen, 2013, p. 12). It also repairs damaged cells and strengthens connections among brain cells.

Unfortunately, when schedules get full, exercise is often the first thing to go. Planning your own prescheduled exercise program or joining an exercise group or club that meets at a specific time may be a good start. The exercise program should be written on your schedule, and you should not be shy about saying that you need to leave work at a certain time to make your appointment. Because of the facilities often available in schools, you may be able to get your exercise on-site if you do not feel that you need a different environment in which to relax. Another possible solution is to try to commit to an exercise program or sports activity with a friend. This serves two purposes. First, the friend will expect you to show up! Second, having a friend to talk with can provide a sounding board for dilemmas and someone with whom to share private victories. Many principals in Clark County, Las Vegas, Nevada, wear pedometers to measure how much exercise they derive from daily activity. They set targets for the number of daily steps they will take. This action makes the principal more visible as well.

Physiological Awareness

The old adage "You are what you eat" holds some truth. Overindulgence in food or inappropriate foods can lead to adverse consequences for your body and mind. Excessive food intake at meals can lead to marked swings in blood sugar levels. This physiological occurrence can lead to unwanted alterations of brain function, adversely affect attention and creativity, and contribute to lethargy. Unfortunately, overindulgence or erratic eating habits are most common when we are under stress.

Even when one strives to maintain a balanced diet, often the rapid pace of the day makes a principal skip meals or choose inappropriate foods. Principals should prepare for this eventuality by planning ahead and having some healthy food that is quickly accessible and provides for both energy and brain power. Complex carbohydrates such as fruits and vegetables are a good source of nutrients. Low-fat foods are helpful. For example, there are many low-fat breakfast foods and snacks on the market (e.g., bagels, granola bars, low-fat crackers). Keep these items readily available in your desk or refrigerator. Too often, it is a temptation to grab a candy bar and indulge in the wrong snack when a busy schedule may lead to omitting a meal.

Emotional Awareness

As discussed in Chapter 4, the leader's emotions influence the emotions of constituents. In fact, it has been said that the heart gives out an electromagnetic signal that is perceivable within three feet! Keep in mind that emotionally intelligent leaders exceed their goals by at least 20 percent (Goleman, 1995).

Psychological Awareness

Psychological rest or peace of mind takes place when your behaviors match your values and beliefs. There is more to life than the job. If you have peace of mind, that feeling can positively affect the level of energy that you give to your job or personal life. Unfortunately, principals may often experience psychological discomfort by doing things that they do not enjoy (e.g., responding to hundreds of e-mails). You need to anticipate that this will happen and have a plan for it. Different people handle discomfort in different ways. Some take comfort in spending time with family or friends; others go for a walk, exercise, read a book, travel, or pursue a hobby such as art or music. Having an outlet is very important because it affords a fresh perspective and brings a richness to our lives, enabling us to be more well-rounded and aware of other ways of doing things.

Finally, it is very difficult to make an effective contribution to an organization if one is functioning below par because of physical, physiological, emotional, or psychological reasons. When principals invest in their physical, physiological, emotional, and psychological well-being, their professional colleagues, their work, and their families will all benefit!

Finding an Inner Balance

Highly effective leaders work to find an inner balance or harmony within themselves. Doing this builds the capacity to portray oneself as a caring leader. Zach Kelehear (2004) suggests some useful strategies for doing this:

- Reflect on what matters most in your life; strive to align your decisions and actions accordingly.
- Remember, "Attitude is everything."
- Make time to take care of your health.
- Ask yourself, at the end of the day, "Has the practice of my life today reflected what matters most to me? In what way have I made the life of at least one child better?"

In the fast-paced life of the principal, it is tempting, and sometimes necessary, to dash from task to task. Only when we pause to reflect do we find the inner resources we need to serve others and thrive as a leader.

NOTE

1. We would like to thank Dr. David Jay Caro, from San Mateo General Hospital (CA), for his assistance with this section of the chapter.

REFLECTIONS

This space provides a place for you to write down ideas that have been generated by this chapter, things you want to try, or adaptations of ideas presented here.

1. Have you learned how to say no in order to provide yourself with quality time away from the job? Think of three school situations, and practice how you would say no in each situation.

2. How do you feel about focusing on professional learning while in your office? How do you think the staff would react to seeing you read a journal during the day? Consider inviting staff members to participate in a webinar. Reflect upon your collective learnings.

3. How do you find inner balance?

4. What are you doing or might you do to reduce stress? Which of the seven strategies designed by Jack Singer might be most important for you?

5. Google "The Last Lecture by Professor Pausch." Read or listen to it. Reflect on how the messages embedded in the lecture might influence your life. Share your insights with a trusted colleague.

6. What insights or new questions do you have as a result of reflecting on the ideas presented in this chapter?

21

Keeping the Professional Candle Lit

You have to be on the balls of your feet all of the time in the principalship.

—Lori Wyborney, Principal

"Things change on us. . . . We always have to be ready for what is next," reflected Lori Wyborney, principal of Rogers High School, in an interview about dramatically increasing the graduation rate with the support of teachers, support staff, parents, and the community. We are reminded by these reflections that more than ever before, the principal (and other educators) must remain on the cutting edge of the profession. Interestingly, while one is preparing for the principalship, we frequently engage with professional books, newsletters, and online resources—all devoured as part of course work and the certification process. However, once in the position of principal, it is easy to become so busy that it is difficult to keep the professional candle lit. Professional journals stack up as do digital files of articles intended to be read. Committing time away from school for professional learning, when so many demands call, make the learning-serving balancing act a delicate one. Planning a strategic proactive approach is the only way to stay current in the field and equipped with the necessary resources to address current demands, new initiatives, and serve the learning organization so it flourishes.

INSTITUTIONALIZING PROFESSIONAL LEARNING

The key to becoming and remaining proactive when it comes to professional learning is to institutionalize specific activities devoted to professional growth. For example, memberships in professional organizations, online courses, podcasts, webinars, writing, reading, conferences, participation in Learning Community team meetings, and the creative use of time can all yield learning that builds one's capacity to serve. When the principal models being a learning leader, it sets an example for all staff members and communicates an expectation that professional learning is a valued, activity that builds the capacity to promote student learning. Further, when the principal is perceived by teachers and other staff members as knowledgeable and current, it instills a sense of confidence and increases the possibility that members of the school community will look to the principal for resource recommendations to support their work. Involvement in professional learning activities with faculty colleagues builds relationships, keeps one mentally stimulated, and reduces burnout! Infusing the learnings that result from professional growth activities into faculty, team, or department meetings helps to build staff members' capacities to help students succeed.

In today's world, there are so many activities to which one can become dedicated that it is important to choose what is best for you, as principal or assistant principal. Such decisions can be informed by the shared vision of the school, student and staff data, survey results, current initiatives, and one's interests. To be sure, working style, in terms of when you have time available, can influence the selection of activities as well. Probably one of the most important actions the principal can take is to become actively involved in one or two professional organizations. Active involvement means attending state and, if possible, national conferences of the organization and reading the journals sponsored by the organization. Many organizations offer e-learning courses and webinars on a variety of topics in addition to journals or conferences. Online learning opportunities are relatively easy to access and can be attended without leaving school.

The logical organizations for principals are the National Association of Elementary School Principals (NAESP) and the National Association of Secondary School Principals (NASSP); both of these organizations address the needs of middle school principals, as does the Association of Middle Level Education (AMLE). The Association for Supervision and Curriculum Development (ASCD) and Learning Forward (formerly the National Staff Development Council) are also valuable national organizations for principals. All five organizations and state affiliates hold annual conferences that keep practitioners on the cutting edge in the field. Each one publishes excellent journals and newsletters. Some publish professional books. For example, Learning Forward, whose vision is "ensuring that every educator engages in effective professional learning everyday so that every student achieves" (Learning Forward, 2013), publishes the following resources in an effort to "build the bridge between . . . high quality professional development . . . and practice": *JSD* (a bimonthly professional magazine focused on leadership and learning), *The Learning System* newsletter (for superintendents and central office staff), *The Leading Teacher* (for coaches, mentors, instructional specialists, lead teachers, and master teachers), *Team Tools* (for teams or entire faculties), *The Learning Principal* (focused on principal's work, strengthening leadership practices, and leading learning), *Tools for Learning Schools* (focused on a single component of school improvement and tools and resources to support professional learning), *Connect* (a monthly electronic newsletter with resources, news, and learning opportunities), *Professional Learning News* (an e-news brief), *PD Watch* (a blog), and *Implementing the Common Core* (a professional learning system to support the implementation of Common Core State Standards). In addition, Learning Forward provides its members with access to reports on research and studies related to professional learning.

In addition to subscribing to national principal association journals and Learning Forward publications, *Educational Leadership* (ASCD) and *Phi Delta Kappan* would be excellent additional choices. *Teacher* and *Instructor* would be good hands-on choices for elementary school principals. *Education Week* is a good source of information about current events in education, especially as related to national and state political agendas.

To keep the professional candle lit for teachers, each school should be getting journals in the various disciplines. Publications for elementary, middle, and high schools are produced by all the major organizations such as the National Council for Social Studies, the National Council of Teachers of English, and the National Council of Teachers of Mathematics. Each department should keep up to date. In elementary schools, *Teaching Children Mathematics* or *Reading Teacher,* for example, should be subscribed to and distributed to the staff or kept in a professional library. All organizations such as these maintain active websites that carry important information about available resources.

As principals are in key leadership positions, they have much in common with those leading noneducational organizations. Thus it can be very helpful to subscribe to a professional journal outside of the educational field. For example, *Harvard Business Review* has excellent articles on leadership that not only give ideas that principals can use but also let principals know what is taking place in the business world. This can be very helpful information when making curriculum decisions to prepare students to be college and career ready.

Beyond journals, the practitioner should maintain a professional library with modern classics in the educational field (to revisit) and current books of interest on leadership and educational issues. A good selection would include books on educational philosophy, curriculum, the life of principals and teachers, and leadership books from the business and education world. (It goes without saying that books other than those that are education related are certainly welcome.) Important educators of the last century are always interesting to study; this enables one to compare contemporary writers with classical ones (e.g., Dewey, Tyler, Hutchins, Cremin).

Listening to CDs, audio books, or podcasts when driving to and from work or jogging can also be professionally productive. If one prefers, there are a wealth of e-books and online publications, as well as DVDs with structured activities and support materials. A variety of apps are available to provide online access to educational resources. For example, NAESP, NASSP, AMLE, and ASCD have apps for their annual conferences; and ASCD has an app for its online magazine (EL). Online courses (from respected universities such as Harvard and Stanford), webinars, videos, tutorials, and lesson plans are available on iTunes University. "The George Lucas Educational Foundation is dedicated to improving the K-12 learning process by documenting, disseminating, and advocating innovative, replicable, and evidence-based strategies that prepare students to thrive in their future education, careers, and adult lives" (George Lucas Education Foundation, 2013; edutopia.org). To that end, the foundation has created Edutopia. where there are resources on a broad spectrum of topics for teachers, principals, and other school leaders. Additionally, www .teachingchannel.org offers a newsletter, blog, and quality videos documenting successful practices. Collectively, these resources address current initiatives such as implementing Common Core, teacher evaluation, new-teacher support, teacher leadership, best teaching practices, brain-based learning, assessment, student engagement, project-based learning, flipping the classroom, social and emotional learning, ending cyberbullying, working in a digital culture, and education trends. Principals and teacher leaders can play a key role in ensuring that schools provide these resources for all school professionals.

The national associations also sponsor leadership academies in the form of one- or two-day workshops throughout the school year and longer workshops during the summer. Many states have principals' centers, often affiliated with universities. The opportunity to network with colleagues through the associations, workshops, webinars, principals' centers, and universities should not be missed. In fact, the loneliness of the principal-ship as a day-to-day feature of the job almost makes the networking through the various organizations imperative.

The opportunity to meet with other principals is especially important for the newcomer who needs affirmation that he or she is on the right track. Developing a mentor relationship through an organization can be an asset for newcomers and veteran principals. Becoming a member of specific associations will ensure that time will be set aside to meet with colleagues and keep up on issues in the field. With social networking, many principals can join or create blogs related to the principalship and develop personal learning networks (PLN).

Visiting other schools can also be informative. Drucker (1992) refers to this as managing by wandering around—outside. Spending a day in another school with another principal can offer insights on how others do the job. The opportunity to visit a school outside of your district or in another state may be advantageous because one is likely to see activities and curriculum projects a bit differently from those in the home district. These experiences may even lead to strong professional friendships and resource sharing across district lines.

REFLECTION AS A TOOL

The importance of reflection has been stressed throughout this book. Keeping a traditional or electronic personal journal can certainly help one reflect about the principalship and any other aspect of one's life. Often, the experience of seeing one's ideas in writing helps affirm convictions and brings greater insight to a particular problem. As the journal grows, one can reflect upon past experiences—so **that** is how I handled this problem last time! Reflection is a great asset and can help one avoid making the same mistake. To illustrate, in July of 1993, golf great Jack Nicklaus played the Senior Open Golf Tournament. As he led the tournament until the 12th hole, he recalled playing on the same course and approaching the 12th hole more than 30 years ago. He reflected back to that earlier tournament. He vowed not to make the same mistake that he had made in 1960. He won the Senior Open by one stroke!

Writing can extend beyond the journal to professional articles authored alone or with colleagues. Writing with another principal, teacher, consultant, or university professor may be the best route for the practitioner because it becomes very easy to drop a project when you are working alone and busy with the day-to-day responsibilities of the principalship. It is very helpful to have someone driving you on. (An electronic file will hold your ideas until you are ready to return to them!) Involvement in Action Research projects with teachers in your school can also be very rewarding. Presenting the results of a research project as a workshop during a state or national conference can be an important extension of the effort.

Holding a mini conference in a school or on a university campus could be a great way to intellectually stimulate a staff. The faculty could get together to recommend speakers to the administration. Administrators and faculty members could present at the conference, possibly during a professional development or in-service day or afternoon. This highlights the importance of keeping learning as a valued centerpiece of the school.

A PRINCIPAL'S PORTFOLIO

Developing and updating a principal's portfolio is a valuable resource to keep a record of and reflect on one's growth during a particular school year and cumulatively, over one's career. In some districts or counties, new evaluation systems for the principal require portfolios organized by leadership standards. The portfolio could open with a personal vision and mission statement, professional goals, and schoolwide goals and objectives. The orientation of the portfolio should be to demonstrate growth within a particular area or areas. At times, principals may elect to identify themes for their portfolios: enhancing student work, building positive parent-community-school relationships, professional development, teacher supervision and evaluation, professional presentations, or reflections. In addition to its role in evaluation, the portfolio also can serve as a valuable resource when applying for new positions.

Artifacts may include photographs of the faculty, students, and classroom activities; important professional development ideas; journal entries; speeches; staff evaluations; newspaper articles about the school; successful grant applications; important memos; faculty meeting agendas; letters or notes from students, parents, community members, and faculty; a video of school activities and the activity calendar of the school year; notes for possible journal articles; student work; information on awards given to students or faculty; data on student performance; information on workshops or conferences attended; presentations made to the school community or at professional meetings; and organizations to which one belongs. Many principals use flip cameras or iPads to video the work they wish to be a part of their portfolios. The actual portfolio may be in a notebook or in electronic form.

OTHER GROWTH OPPORTUNITIES

A strategy for ensuring one is current is to examine National or State *Educational Leadership Standards* with which your role is aligned. One can reflect upon these and assess personal strengths and areas for professional growth. Another opportunity to assess personal strengths is to examine the work of Marzano, Waters, and McNulty (2005), who identified 21 leadership responsibilities associated with student achievement, the work of the late Kathleen Cotton who wrote *Principals and Student Achievement: What the Research Says* (2003), or The Wallace Foundation's publications or videos regarding school principals (2012, 2013). These highlight leadership behaviors that impact student performance.

Involvement in interest groups can also be rewarding. Some professional organizations such as ASCD, AERA, NAESP, and NASSP sponsor interest groups that address topics such as the Whole Child, English Language Learners, global education, the at-risk student, increasing graduation rates, closing the achievement gap, differentiated instruction, assessment, working with special needs students, brain research, or effective instructional practices. The group may meet at lunch or even during dinner at various homes during the year. In one school district, K–12 administrators and department heads got together for dinner and conversation prior to board meetings. They read and discussed selected books chapter by chapter. Book group activities were so rewarding that they continued throughout the year.

Working to develop an inviting professional resource area in the school can be a significant professional boost for administrators and teachers.

This should be an area to exchange professional articles, books, websites, online resources, and ideas. Principals should encourage teachers to pass on professional articles and other resources to colleagues and the principal to help him or her stay on top of particular issues and, probably more important, remain informed regarding what teachers think is important. Having an area in the school dedicated to professional learning just might make it easier for administrators and teachers to spend time there during a school day—actually building the time into their weekly schedules. The actual physical structure for professional reflection can symbolize the importance of remaining on the cutting edge.

Finally, remaining intellectually stimulated throughout one's career is a tall order. Yet doing so benefits the principal, staff, students, and the organization. For instance, underlining important quotations while reading a journal and sharing these at faculty meetings, followed with a discussion, can show that the leader is academically up to date and can provide valuable resources to staff members in a time-efficient way. We need to create our own opportunities for professional growth through institutionalizing interaction, reflections, and readings. It is through these encounters that we remain alert and ready to approach the next challenge. Focusing on our own professional development builds an incredible resource bank from which to draw. By nurturing our own growth, we are able to enhance our ability to serve and to help others grow.

REFLECTIONS

This space provides a place for you to write down ideas that have been generated by this chapter, things you want to try, or adaptations of ideas presented here.

1. Are you keeping your professional candle lit? Discuss this with a colleague.

2. Which two or three professional development activities discussed in this chapter can you use? Which do you use already? What others might you add?

3. What inspirational article or book have you read recently? What about an inspirational story? How might you share it?

4. What insights or new questions do you have as a result of reflecting on the ideas presented in this chapter?

22

Reflections on the Principalship

I have never had a more complex, demanding, energizing, meaningful role. The stress and heartache are outweighed by the tremendous difference we make in lives—and shaping our tomorrow.

—A principal's voice

A school is much more than a physical structure; it is a community made up of adults and children engaged in a journey that will lead to greater understanding, learning, and a force in society. To promote student learning, a principal serves teachers by empowering them to be the best they can be. As servant leaders, school principals discover that their professional vocation is, in many ways, a calling. When principals answer that calling and serve teachers, students, parents, and the community effectively, students have a greater opportunity to enhance their skills in a climate that promotes growth, understanding, and a love of learning. Principals, through their words and deeds, grow the citizens of tomorrow.

SERVING THE SCHOOL COMMUNITY

As a school leader, a principal's foremost asset may be his or her ability to lead by example. How principals conduct themselves on the job—what they pay attention to—says more about ethical practice and their leadership ability than any specific decision, regardless of how important. Nair (1997), commenting on the life of Gandhi, notes that "leadership is not a technique, but a way of life" (p. 92). Leading by example must be sincere; if a principal is uncomfortable with small children or teenagers, the non-verbal cues will quickly be observed by the students. Moreover, if the personal example lacks consistency, others will soon comment about the lack of sincerity on the part of the principal. Credibility is an attribute of highly effective leaders. It is an essential trait for anyone leading a learning organization. When reflecting on the principalship and considering examples of exemplary practice and sound theory, the authors believe that the following behaviors and characteristics, if modeled consistently, will support a principal in best serving a school.

Principals thrive on the ethical responsibility of promoting teacher learning so they can make a difference for students. Principals serve teachers by empowering them to be the best they can be. James MacGregor Burns (1978), in his classic study on transformational leadership, noted that "Transforming leadership ultimately becomes *moral* in that it raises the level of human conduct and ethical aspirations of both leader and led, and thus it has a transforming effect on both" (p. 20). George (2007) adds, "Authentic leadership is empowering others on their journey. This shift is the transformation from 'I' to 'We.' It is the most important process leaders go through in becoming authentic" (p. 44). Principals who enthusiastically accept the responsibility of helping others grow foster the aspirations of teachers by distributing leadership throughout the system. Promoting teacher growth also includes helping colleagues become autonomous decision makers who engage students successfully when the classroom door is closed. These teachers are confident in their decisions, partially because they are part of a school culture that thrives on collaboration, peer coaching, mentoring of new teachers, and teacher-generated and -led professional development opportunities so that, at the end of the day, they can impact student learning.

Principals respect and dignify others. The importance of positive human interaction has been a main feature of this book; therefore, it should not surprise the reader that leading by example must include respecting and dignifying each individual connected with the school. Students must see the principal as someone who believes in them and respects them for what they are and what they can become. Teachers must see in the principal someone who has great respect for the teachers' professional role and what they can bring to students. Dignifying the classroom teacher is of paramount importance and should be modeled often by the principal during public and private occasions. Parents should see the principal as someone who listens to them and displays concern and interest when they are with students and in the community.

Principals lead through learning. There is no setting in which the concept of leader as learner is more applicable. The learning leader role can be modeled in several ways. For example, when working with teachers in a supervisory role, principals must create an atmosphere that fosters mutual trust and growth. Trust is a requisite characteristic if one is to take chances in a professional relationship. Teachers must feel that they can trust the principal if risk taking is to occur during a class lesson. Furthermore, principals and teachers need to believe that they will both grow from the relationship if they are to talk honestly during conferences about their profession and discuss what they think they are doing right and ways they can improve.

Additionally, as a leader of learners, the principal needs to provide the structure and forum to ensure that a dialogue concerning curriculum, teaching, assessment, and student learning takes place throughout the school. The principal needs to participate in this dialogue as an equal member, sharing articles and websites, structuring faculty meetings to facilitate conversation, promoting professional development in and out of the school, analyzing and discussing data, creating areas in the school for professional discussion, promoting classroom visitations by colleagues, and recognizing those teachers who are growing professionally. The dialogue that develops can create lasting relationships and a synergy that demonstrates the strength, potential, and desire of the group to continually grow professionally and never be completely satisfied with the current state. As Collins (2005) reminds us in *Good to Great and the Social Sectors*, "Greatness is an inherently dynamic process, not an end point. The moment you think of yourself as great, your slide toward mediocrity will have already begun" (p. 9).

Principals promote and embrace the success of others. As ideas are generated, the school principal must give credit to teachers and others whose ideas and dedication improve the school and contribute to student success. Stephen Covey (1989) calls this strategy the abundance principle in which credit for successful actions is spread around as much as possible. Furthermore, principals need to hire the best personnel available, provide supervisory and professional development support, and show a willingness to give personnel the freedom to use their talents to maximize student learning and address the never-ending challenges that face schools.

Giving credit to others, inspiring colleagues to take on difficult tasks, and taking satisfaction when the accomplishments of associates bring them into the limelight is a necessary requirement for successful leadership. Thus Drucker (1992) emphasizes,

> Precisely because an effective leader knows that he, and no one else, is ultimately responsible, he is not afraid of strength in associates and subordinates. . . . [A]n effective leader wants strong associates; he encourages them, pushes them, indeed glories in them. Because he holds himself ultimately responsible for the mistakes of his associates and subordinates, he also sees the triumphs of his associates and subordinates as his triumphs, rather than as threats. . . . An effective leader knows, of course, that there is a risk; able people tend to be ambitious. But he realizes that it is a much smaller risk than to be served by mediocrity. (pp. 121–122)

Encouraging others to be strong associates and distributing leadership can be challenging. Principals often are concerned about accountability. Can one empower another as leader and trust that person to follow through? Principals often ponder, "How does distributed leadership and shared decision making fit with the reality that "the buck stops here?" Some make a distinction between a kind of shared decision making, in which the principal takes input but ultimately decides and takes responsibility, versus shared governance, in which decision makers exchange ideas and share accountability for decisions. We have learned that the factory worker may know more about how the company works than the executive on the top floor. Barth's insight regarding this dilemma may be helpful: "It's far more powerful to join with others to do what needs to be done" (quoted in Sparks, 1993, p. 20). School principals are joining with others to try to make schools work better. But principals know and accept that, in many cases, teachers, students, parents, and the community continue to expect the principal to take ultimate responsibility.

Effective principals recognize active listening as an essential communication skill. The image of the leader who truly listens in a setting that thrives on teamwork and developing ideas through mutual understanding is a powerful one. Effective school leaders are good listeners and reflective thinkers. Creative ideas and solutions are often born after listening, reflecting, and working in groups.

Authentic listening with patience and attention is critical if one is truly trying to support and foster growth in others. Showing concern for students, teachers, and parents means hearing them out. Listening shows support and may go a long way in meeting the needs of colleagues or others in the school community. Often, individuals do not come right out and say what is bothering them. In fact, Soder (2001) warns leaders "that many people will be likely to tell you what they think you want to hear, and the likelihood poses dangers for the leader" (p. 33). Active listening, then, means trying to find out the subtle messages—what is really being said? At that point, it is possible to begin meeting the needs of others. To illustrate, when conferencing with teachers, principals will find that as the trust relationship begins to grow, teaching colleagues will take small leaps of faith to explore how sincere the principal is about trust and working with them. Unless a principal is listening carefully to the teacher, the principal may very well and quite inadvertently miss the leap on the part of the teacher.

Principals address their own needs. The school principal should also remember that it is important to recognize one's own basic needs. That is, one's private life, responsibility to family, and need for leisure and recreation should not be sacrificed. A workaholic is not a better principal than someone who knows how to manage his or her time and who takes the time for family and friends. A principal's life outside of school must receive the time and energy necessary for success so a positive attitude on the job results. Principals have to understand themselves, their strengths, and weaknesses. George (2007) insightfully reminds leaders,

"First, you have to understand yourself because the hardest person you will ever have to lead is yourself. . . . Second, to be an effective leader, you must take responsibility for your own development" (p. xxxiii). Balance is essential.

Principals accept success and frustrations. As part of our basic humanity, it is important also to take in stride both the successes and frustrations of the job. One should not be too enthralled with the positive press—when it happens. On the other hand, do not get too upset with the negative reviews. Reflection is a characteristic needed in both situations. What happened? What can I learn from this experience? Find the humorous side when possible. Bringing in humor often helps relieve tension, reduce one's feelings of self-importance, and place an issue in different perspective. Looking at a situation from another perspective can be enlightening.

Effective principals take the high road. When the negative reviews appear or when individuals complain, one should behave in an ethical manner. Regardless of tactics used by others, the school leader should always represent the best in society. Character is very important when crises occur. In fact, character is the key in a crisis, and character is often judged not by what one says but by how one acts. Persons who whisper but act righteously are heard loud and clear. Stay above the fray and avoid the shouting match. As one principal said, "What you do speaks so loudly I can't hear what you say!"

Effective principals are intentional. They are motivated by a passion to do things right and do the right things. They align their actions and words with their beliefs. They are strategic in accomplishing the vision for the school. Their actions are purposeful, and guided by ethical behavior.

WHERE DO WE GO FROM HERE?

Of course, there are no formulas for successful leadership that can be universally applied. An individual who exhibits or models some of the preceding characteristics may still fail if he or she is unable to analyze situations appropriately. The challenge is to find out what works in a particular setting. In his seminal work, Newell (1978) stressed that "effective leadership is possible only through an analysis of the situational elements in a particular system" (p. 242). Each school is different; therefore, each leadership situation is different. In the end, the effective leader, collaborating and building relationships with teachers, parents, and students, must discover how to meet the needs of students in a specific setting. And the discovery will show that no secret formula exists; the setting will dictate the approach.

Because there are no secret formulas, frustration can be a constant companion in the principalship. Yet the frustration can lead to success if one always searches for solutions and has faith in one's ability to face challenges with the help of others. In facing the challenges, a vision of the good school is essential. So what is our vision of the good school? What will one see on entering the doors of the school?

THE GOOD SCHOOL

When entering the school, a visitor quickly perceives that students and teachers are enjoying their time there. Here is where they want to teach and learn. The visitor notices that most students are actively interested and engaged in learning. Teachers are enthusiastic about their work. Student interest is shown through obvious excitement while working at a hands-on activity or through a look of serenity when quietly reading a book.

Some classroom teachers may, at first, be difficult to spot—they are sitting with students or with groups of students and examining student work. In another room, a teacher is talking to the class, his gestures indicating excitement about a student comment. In fact, the visitor notices that most teachers are enjoying their work and are patiently listening to and helping students. In various classes, students display looks of concentration and puzzlement, mixed with expressions of satisfaction and frequent smiles. The school visitor observes that some students seem less interested than others, yet the teachers are giving them equal time and showing patience when necessary. No students appear to be overlooked.

The visitor observes that the library and Internet café are busy throughout the day. In both areas, there are students working individually, in groups, or with teachers. Several students are gathered around computers. One group is sending an e-mail to a scientific team in Antarctica while another group is analyzing a recent presidential speech. In other areas, such as the music, art, physics, or world language rooms, students are all actively engaged, talking about their work, singing, writing, reading, drawing, experimenting, and showing interest in what they are doing. In the cafeteria the visitor notices that various racial and ethnic groups, and younger and older students, are sitting together and interacting during lunch. Also, several students are helping new Russian immigrant students with their English. Two elderly individuals, likely retired, are engaged in serious conversations with two middle school students.

Dropping into various classrooms with the principal, the visitor and principal notice a variety of teaching techniques. Some teachers are using Smart Boards or iPad labs and speaking with students, others are using PowerPoint presentations and simulations to communicate the content of the lesson, some teachers are sitting with students, and a couple of teachers are walking around their rooms observing groups or watching students work individually. One teacher is facilitating a stock market game, another is reading silently with his class, and another is writing in her journal with the class. Interestingly, the principal and visitor observe a lot of lively, engaged, and smiling faces in the various classrooms. The principal notices that students are unafraid to give "incorrect" answers and, at times, respectfully challenge a teacher's answer.

Our visitor notices that the teachers' lounge is frequented by colleagues who enjoy one another's company and share in the joys and frustrations of their classroom experiences. While in the lounge, teachers share a light experience, the humor of a classroom event. One teacher asks a colleague to read a poem written by a student the previous class period. It is clear that this group of teachers works and plays together. They share professional articles, problem solve, and encourage one another to pursue professional development opportunities. They team teach, coplan, and peer coach.

On the playground, students are obviously enjoying themselves playing games or sitting and talking. In the middle and high schools, peer counselors are spending time with students who are new to the school or are having difficulties with peers and at home. In the elementary school, a couple of kindergarten students run up to the principal, proudly announcing that they picked up some litter from the sidewalk to keep the school clean. At the middle school, a teacher and students enthusiastically invite the principal to watch the Lego robots as they go through the obstacle course!

The school buildings and grounds are inviting. The entrance doors to the school are murals, painted in bright colors by students. The halls of the school are lined with student work. The high school includes a fine arts display that rotates the art, poetry, photographs, and ceramic work of various students. The restrooms and cafeteria are clean and graffiti free.

In general, the visitor perceives pride and a caring attitude regarding how adults feel about students and the school. The visitor's perception is based on the positive interaction observed between teachers and students, secretaries and teachers, maintenance personnel and the principal, and students and the cafeteria workers.

At the end of the day, the visitor notices that neither teachers nor administrators rush to leave the school. Many staff members remain in their classrooms either working quietly, helping individual students, or conferencing with parents. The principal is seen standing by the school buses saying good-bye to students and asking them how the school day went.

TAKE TIME TO SMELL THE ROSES

A vision of the good school can help principals hold on to their convictions concerning what schooling should be all about. The vision and one's convictions can steer the school through rough seas and keep the school on course—a course guided by the needs of the students, needs that can be satisfied when exposed to a challenging school experience in a climate nurtured by caring adults.

As you reflect on your role in accomplishing this, take time to celebrate your deeds, learn from mistakes, smell the roses daily, make connections with others, and maintain a positive outlook for the future. Your dedication and hard work will change lives.

REFLECTIONS

This space provides a place for you to write down ideas that have been generated by this chapter, things you want to try, or adaptations of ideas presented here.

1. In *True North,* George (2007) states, "True North is the internal compass that guides you successfully through life. It represents who you are as a human being at your deepest level. It is your orienting point—your fixed point in a spinning world—that helps you stay on track as a leader" (p. xxiii). Describe your True North. What guides you successfully through life?

2. Create two or three questions representing your own reflections on the principalship. Share these with a colleague.

3. What actions will you take as a result of these readings?

4. What topics do you want to explore in greater depth?

5. Describe your vision of the good school.

References and Additional Readings

REFERENCES

ABC News. (2002, June 17). *Good Morning America.* New York, NY: American Broadcasting Company.

Alexander, M. (2012). *The new Jim Crow.* New York, NY: The New Press.

Alvy, H. (1983). *The problems of new principals.* Unpublished doctoral dissertation, University of Montana, Missoula.

Alvy, H., & Robbins, P. (1998). *If I only knew: Success strategies for navigating the principalship.* Thousand Oaks, CA: Corwin.

Alvy, H., & Robbins, P. (2008, March). *Helping new principals succeed: Strategies to support courageous leadership.* Presentation at the Association for Supervision and Curriculum Development Annual Conference, New Orleans, LA.

Alvy, H., & Robbins, P. (2010). *Learning from Lincoln: Leadership practices for school success.* Alexandria, VA: ASCD.

Alvy, H., & Robbins, P. (2010, March). *Responding effectively in turbulent times: Critical issues for new principals.* Presentation at the Association for Supervision and Curriculum Development Annual Conference, San Antonio, TX.

American Educational Research Association. (2013). *Prevention of bullying in schools, colleges, and universities: Research report and recommendations.* Washington, DC: Author.

Amrein-Beardsley, A. (2008). Methodological concerns about the education value-added assessment system. *Educational Researcher, 37*(2), 65–75.

Angelou, M. (2013, March 17). *Second general session: Maya Angelou.* Speech given at the ASCD 68th Annual Conference and Exhibit Show, Chicago, IL.

Armenta, T., & Beckers, G. (2006). The IEP: How to meet its demands and avoid its pitfalls. *Principal Leadership, 6*(9), 22–26.

Armstrong, T. (1994). *Multiple intelligences in the classroom.* Alexandria, VA: ASCD.

Armstrong, A. (2011, Winter). 4 key strategies help educators overcome resistance to change. *Tools for Schools, 14*(2). Retrieved from http://learningforward.org/docs/tools-for-learning-schools/tools1-11.pdf.

Armstrong, A. (2011, Summer). Lesson study puts a collaborative lens on student learning. *Tools for Schools, 14*(4).

Armstrong, A. (2012, Summer). The art of feedback. *The Learning System, 7*(4), 1–5.

Armstrong, D. G., Henson, K. T., & Savage, T. V. (2009). *Teaching today: An introduction to education* (8th ed.). Upper Saddle River, NJ: Merrill/Prentice Hall.

Arnberger, K., & Shoop, R. (2006). A principal's guide to manifestation determination. *Principal Leadership, 6*(9), 16–21.

Ash, K. (2012, November 14). George Lucas' promise to invest in education prompts speculation. *Educational Week, 32*(12), 10.

Ash, K. (2013, May 22). STEM schools digital push. *Educational Week, 32*(32), S24–S26.

Ashley, J., & Burke, K. (n.d.). *Implementing restorative justice: A guide for schools.* Chicago, IL: Illinois Criminal Justice Information Authority.

Astor, R., Benbenishty, R., & Estrada, J. N. (2009, June). School violence and theoretically atypical schools: The principal's centrality in orchestrating safe schools. *American Educational Research Journal, 42*(2), 423–461.

Bagin, D., & Gallagher, D. (2001). *The school and community relations* (7th ed.). Boston, MA: Allyn & Bacon.

Bambrick-Santoyo, P. (2012, November). Beyond the scoreboard. *Educational Leadership, 70*(3), 29.

Bambrick-Santoyo, P. (2012, October). Take back your time. *Phi Delta Kappan, 94*(2), 70–71.

Barber, M., & Mourshed, M. (2009, July, 7). Shaping the future: How good education systems can become great in the decade ahead. *Report on the International Education Roundtable.* Singapore: McKinsley & Co.

Barnard, C. (1938). *The functions of the executive.* Cambridge, MA: Harvard University Press.

Barth, R. (1990). *Improving schools from within: Teachers, parents, and principals can make the difference.* San Francisco, CA: Jossey-Bass.

Barth, R. (2001a). Teacher leader. *Phi Delta Kappan, 82,* 443–449.

Barth, R. (2001b, February 28). Teachers at the helm. *Education Week,* 32–33, 48.

Bennis, W. (1991). *Why leaders can't lead.* San Francisco, CA: Jossey-Bass.

Bennis, W., & Nanus, B. (1985). *Leaders: The strategies for taking charge.* New York, NY: Harper & Row.

Berman, P., & McLaughlin, M. W. (1978). *Federal programs supporting educational change, Vol. VIII: Implementing and sustaining innovations.* Santa Monica, CA: RAND.

Bird, T., & Little, J. W. (1984, April). *Supervision and evaluation in the school context.* Paper presented at the annual meeting of the American Educational Research Association, New Orleans, LA.

Blanchard, K., & Johnson, S. (1983). *The one minute manager.* New York, NY: Berkley.

Boss, S. (2013, Summer). Keeping kids in school. *Stanford Social Innovation Review,* (3). Retrieved from www.ssireview.org/articles/entry/keeping_kids_in_school.

Bower, M. (1966). *Will to manage.* New York, NY: McGraw-Hill.

Boykin, A., & Noguera, P. (2011). *Creating the opportunity to learn.* Alexandria, VA: ASCD.

Bransford, J., Brown, A., & Cocking, R. (Eds.). (2000). *How people learn: Brain, mind, experience, and school.* Washington, DC: National Academy Press.

Brendtro, L., & Hinders, D. (1990). A saga of Janusz Korczak, the king of children. *Harvard Educational Review, 60,* 237–246.

Brockmeier, L. L., Sermon, J. M., & Hope, W. C. (2005). Principal's relationship with computer technology. *NASSP Bulletin, 89*(643), 45–63.

Brookhart, S. (2008). *How to give effective feedback to your students.* Alexandria, VA: ASCD.

Brown, E. (2013). *Leadership in the wilderness: Tyranny in the book of numbers.* New Medford, CT: Maggid Books.

Brown, P. (2013, April 3). Opening up, students transform a vicious circle. *New York Times.* Retrieved from http://www.nytimes.com/2013/04/04/education/restorative-justice-programs-take-root-in-schools.html.

Bryk, A. S., & Schneider, B. (2004). *Trust in schools: A core resource for improvement.* New York, NY: Russell Sage Foundation.

Buffum, A., Mattos, M., & Weber, C. (2010, October). The why behind RTI. *Educational Leadership, 68*(2), 10–16.

Burns, J. M. (1978). *Leadership.* New York, NY: Harper & Row.

Caine, R., & Caine, G. (1991). *Making connections: Teaching and the human brain.* Alexandria, VA: ASCD.

Calvo, N., & Miles, K. H. (2011/2012, December/January). Turning crisis into opportunity. *Educational Leadership, 69*(4), 19–23.

Carnegie Corporation. (2013). *StoryCorps.* Retrieved from http://www.greatteaching .carnegie.org.

Caro, D. J., & Robbins, P. (1991). Talkwalking: Thinking on your feet. *The Developer,* 3–4.

Carroll, T. (2009, October). The next generation of learning teams. *Phi Delta Kappan, 92*(2).

Carter-Scott. C. (1991). *The corporate negaholic.* New York, NY: Villard Books.

Chaltain, S. (2006, October 25). To make schools safe, make all children visible. *Education Week,* 48.

Champion, R. (2002). *Good principals use informal and formal approaches to staff development: White paper for principals.* Alexandria, VA: ASCD.

Chenoweth, K., & Theokas, C. (2013, April). How high-poverty schools are getting it done. *Educational Leadership, 70*(7), 56–59.

Cianciotto, J., & Cahill, S. (2012). *LGBT youth in America's schools.* Ann Arbor: The University of Michigan Press.

City, E. (2011, October). Learning from instructional rounds. *Educational Leadership, 69*(2), 37–41.

City, E. (2013, April). Leadership in challenging times. *Educational Leadership, 70*(7), 10–14.

Clifford, M., & Ross, S. (n.d.). *Rethinking principal evaluation.* Alexandria, VA: NAESP & NASSP.

Coburn, K. L., & Treeger, M. L. (2003). *Letting go: A parents' guide to understanding the college years* (4th ed.). New York, NY: HarperCollins.

Collins, J. (2005). *Good to great and the social sectors.* New York, NY: HarperCollins.

Collins, J., & Porras, J. (2002). *Built to last.* New York, NY: HarperBusiness Essentials.

Conley, D. (2007, April). The challenge of college readiness. *Educational Leadership, 64*(7), 23–29.

Costa, A., & Garmston, R. (1991, April). *Cognitive coaching action lab.* Workshop presented at the Association for Supervision and Curriculum Development Annual Conference, San Francisco, CA.

Costa, A., & Garmston, R. (1994). *Cognitive coaching: A foundation for renaissance schools.* Norwood, MA: Christopher-Gordon.

Cotton, K. (2003). *Principals and student achievement: What the research says.* Alexandria, VA: ASCD.

Council for Corporate and School Partnerships. (n.d.). *Guiding principles for business and school partnerships.* Retrieved from http://www.corpschoolpartners .org/principles.shtml.

Couros, G. (2013, March 2). *Guiding questions for your IT department.* Retrieved from http://georgecouros.ca/blog/archives/37024.

Covey, S. (1989). *The seven habits of highly effective people.* New York, NY: Simon & Schuster.

Crow, T. (2008, Summer). Declaration of interdependence: Educators need deep conversations about teaching and learning to spark real changes in practice (Q & A with Judith Warren Little). *Journal of Staff Development, 29*(3), 53–56.

Crow, T. (2013, April). Time together is time well spent only when educators know how to collaborate. *JSD The Learning Forward Journal, 34*(2).

Cunningham, W., & Gresso, D. (1993). *Cultural leadership: The culture of excellence in education.* Boston, MA: Allyn & Bacon.

Danielson Group. (2013). *The framework for teaching.* Retrieved from http:// danielsongroup.org/article.aspx?page=frameworkforteaching.

Danielson, C. (2007). *Enhancing professional practice: A framework for teaching* (2nd ed). Alexandria, VA: ASCD.

Danielson, C. (2010/2011, December/January). Evaluations that help teachers learn. *Educational Leadership, 68*(4), 35–39.

Danielson, C. (2012, November). Observing classroom practice. *Educational Leadership, 70*(3), 32–37.

Danielson, C., Axtell, D., Bevan, P., Cleland, B., McKay, C., Phillips, E., & Wright, K. (2009) *Implementing the Framework for Teaching in Enhancing Professional Practice: An ASCD Action Tool.* Alexandria, VA: ASCD.

Darling-Hammond, L. (2010). *The flat world and education.* New York, NY: Teachers College Press.

Darling-Hammond, L., Amrein-Beardsley, A., Haertel, E., & Rothstein, J. (2012, March). Evaluating teacher evaluation. *Phi Delta Kappan, 93*(6), 8–15.

Deal, T. (1985). Cultural change: Opportunity, silent killer, or metamorphosis. In R. H. Kilmann, M. J. Saxton, & R. Serpa (Eds.), *Gaining control of the corporate culture* (pp. 292–331). San Francisco, CA: Jossey-Bass.

Deal, T., & Kennedy, A. (1982). *Corporate culture.* Reading, MA: Addison-Wesley.

Deal, T. E., & Peterson, K. D. (1990). *The principal's role in shaping school culture.* Washington, DC: Office of Educational Research and Improvement, U.S. Department of Education.

Deal, T., & Peterson, K. (1993). Strategies for building school cultures: Principals as symbolic leaders. In M. Sashkin & H. J. Wahlberg (Eds.), *Educational leadership and school culture* (pp. 88–99). Berkley, CA: McCutchan.

Deal, T., & Peterson, K. (1994). *The leadership paradox.* San Francisco, CA: Jossey-Bass.

Deal, T. E., & Peterson, K. D. (1999). *Shaping school culture: The heart of leadership.* San Francisco, CA: Jossey-Bass.

Deal, T. E., & Peterson, K. D. (2009). *Shaping school culture: Pitfalls, paradoxes, & promises.* San Francisco, CA: Jossey-Bass.

deGoeij, K. (2013). *Making meaning of trust in the organizational setting of a school.* Doctoral dissertation submitted to the faculty of graduate studies and research. Edmonton, Alberta: University of Alberta.

Dean, D., & Webb, C. (2011, January). Recovering from information overload. *McKinsey Quarterly.* Retrieved from http://www.mckinsey.com/insights/organizationrecovering_from_information_overload.

Department of Education. (2013, April 16). Proposed priorities, requirements, definitions, and selection criteria-race to the top. *Federal Register, 78*(73), 22451–22467.

DeWitt, P. (2013, September 7). What will be your faculty focus? *Education Week.* Retrieved from http://blogs.edweek.org/edweek/finding_common_ground/2013/09/what_will_be_your_faculty_focus.html.

Dictionary.reference.com. (n.d.). *Ritual.* Retrieved from http://dictionary.reference.com/browse/ritual.

Dill, V. (2010, November). Students without homes. *Educational Leadership, 68*(3), 43–47.

Diplomas count 2008: School to college. Executive summary. (2008, June 5). *Education Week,* 3–4.

Dodge, A. (2011/2012, December/January). Changing the poisonous narrative: A conversation with Diane Ravitch. *Educational Leadership, 69*(4), 54–58.

Drucker, P. (1992). *Managing for the future: The 1990s and beyond.* New York, NY: Dutton.

DuFour, R. (2001). In the right context. *Journal of Staff Development, 22*(1), 14–17.

DuFour, R. (2004). What is a "professional learning community"? *Educational Leadership, 61*(8), 6–11.

DuFour, R. (2011, February). Work together but only if you want to. *Phi Delta Kappan, 92*(5).

DuFour, R., & Mattos, M. (2013, April). How do principals really improve schools? *Educational Leadership, 70*(7), 34–40.

DuFour, R., DuFour, R., & Eaker, R. (2008). *Revisiting professional learning communities at work.* Bloomington, IN: Solution Tree.

Dwyer, K., Osher, D., & Warger, C. (1998). *Early warning, timely response: A guide to safe schools.* Washington, DC: U.S. Department of Education. Retrieved from http://cecp.air.org/guide/guide.pdf.

Dyer, K. (2001). The power of 360-degree feedback. *Educational Leadership, 58*(5), 35–38.

Eaker, R., & Keating, J. (2008). A shift in school culture. *Journal of Staff Development, 29*(3), 14–17.

Education Update. (2013, August). A closer look at principal evaluation. *Education Update. 55*(8), 5.

Education Week. (2000). *Lessons of a century: A nation's schools come of age.* Bethesda, MD: Editorial Projects in Education.

Education Week. (2013, April 24). What to ask about research. *Education Week, 32*(29), S13.

Educational Leadership Policy Standards: ISLLC 2008. (2008). Washington, DC: Council of Chief State School Officers.

Elias, M. (2002, March). *Building character education and social-emotional programs: A school leadership manual.* Presentation at the Annual Conference of the Association for Supervision and Curriculum Development, San Antonio, TX.

Elmore, R. F. (2004) *School reform from the inside out: Policy, practice and performance.* Cambridge, MA: Harvard Education Press.

Environmental Protection Agency. (n.d.). *Fact sheet: Mold in schools.* Retrieved from http://www.epa.gov/iaq/schools.

Environmental Protection Agency. (2012a, September). *Indoor air quality for schools.* Retrieved from http://www.epa.gov/iaq/schools.

Environmental Protection Agency. (2012b, November). *Student health and academic performance.* Retrieved from http://www.epa.gov/iaq/schools.

Epstein, J. (2007). Connections count. *Principal Leadership, 8*(2), 16–21.

Epstein, J., Galindo, C., & Sheldon, S. (2011, August). Levels of leadership: Effects of district and school leaders on the quality of school programs of family and community involvement. *Educational Administration Quarterly, 47*(3), 462–495.

Evans, R. (1996). *The human side of change.* San Francisco, CA: Jossey-Bass.

Fairbanks, A. (2013, May 22). Changing the role of K–12 teachers. *Education Week, 32*(32), S4–S7.

Feds take on dropout crisis. (2008, April 2). *eSchool news.* Retrieved from http://www.eschoolnews.com/news/top-news/?i=53380.

Flanagan, N. (2012, October 5). Seven ideas for meaningful parent-teacher conference. *Education Week.* Retrieved from http://blogs.edweek.org/teachers/teacher_in_a_strange_land/2012/10/seven_ideas_for_meaningful_parent-teacher_conferences.html.

Flanigan, R. (2013, April 24). Vetting product research to determine what works. *Education Week, 32*(29), S10–S12.

Flannery, K. B., Guest, E., & Horner, R. (2010, September). Schoolwide positive behavior supports. *Principal Leadership, 11*(1), 38–43.

Friedman, T. (2005). *The world is flat.* New York, NY: Farrar, Straus, and Giroux.

Friedman, T. (2008, February). Tom Friedman on education in the 'flat world.' *The School Administrator, 65*(2), 1–7. Retrieved from http://www.aasa.org/schooladministratorarticle.aspx.

Fullan, M. (2007). *The new meaning of educational change* (4th ed.). New York, NY: Teachers College Press.

Fullan, M., & Miles, M. (1992). Getting reform right: What works and what doesn't. *Phi Delta Kappan, 73,* 745–752.

Fullan, M., & Stiegelbauer, S. (1991). *The new meaning of educational change.* New York, NY: Teachers College Press.

Furman, G. (2012, January). Social justice leadership as praxis: Developing capacities through preparation programs. *Educational Administration Quarterly, 48*(2), 191–229. Retrieved from http://eaq.sagepub.com/content/48/2/191.

Gardner, H. (2006). *Multiple intelligences: New horizons.* New York, NY: Basic Books.

Geertz, C. M. (1973). *The interpretation of cultures.* New York, NY: Basic Books.

George Lucas Education Foundation. (2013). *Edutopia.* Retrieved from http://www.edutopia.org.

George, B. (2007). *True north: Discover your authentic leadership.* San Francisco, CA: Jossey-Bass.

Georgia Association of Educators. (1998–2001). *Teacher tips: Avoiding burnout and staying healthy.* Retrieved from http://www.gae.org/teacher/te_burnout.html.

GLSEN. (2012). The 2011 national school climate survey. New York, NY: Author.

Glickman, C. D., Gordon, S. P., & Ross-Gordon, J. M. (2010). Supervision and instructional leadership (8th ed.). Boston, MA: Allyn & Bacon.

Goleman, D. (1995). *Emotional intelligence.* New York, NY: Bantam.

Goleman, D., Boyatzis, R., & McKee, A. (2002). *Primal leadership: Learning to lead with emotional intelligence.* Boston, MA: Harvard Business School Press.

Goodwin, B. (2011, September). Bullying is common—and subtle. *Educational Leadership, 69*(1), 82–83.

Goodwin, B. (2013, April). A principal's success requires people skills. *Educational Leadership, 70*(7), 79–80.

Goodwin, D. K. (2005). *Team of rivals: The political genius of Abraham Lincoln.* New York. NY: Simon & Schuster.

Granada, J., & Vriesenga, M. (2008). Web-based walk throughs. *Principal Leadership, 8*(7), 24–27.

Gregorc, A. (1985). *Inside styles: Beyond the basics.* Maynard, MA: Gabriel Systems.

Gregory, A., Cornell, D., & Fan, X. (2011, August). The relationship of school structure and support to suspension rates for black and white high school students. *American Educational Research Journal, 48*(4), 904–934.

Gregory, A., Skiba, R., & Noguera, P. (2010, January/February). The achievement gap and the discipline gap: Two sides of the same coin? *Educational Researcher, 39*(1), 59–68.

Grimmett, P., Rostad, O., & Ford, B. (1992). The transition of supervision. In C. Glickman (Ed.), *Supervision in transition: 1992 ASCD Yearbook* (pp. 185–202). Alexandria, VA: ASCD.

Grissom, J. (2011). Can good principals keep teachers in disadvantaged schools: Linking principal effectiveness to teacher satisfaction and turnover in hard-to-staff environments. *Teachers College Record, 113*(11), 2552–2585.

Grissom, J. A., & Loeb, S. (2009, November). *Triangulating principal effectiveness: How perspectives of parents, teachers, and assistant principals identify the central importance of management skills* (School Leadership Research Report No. 09–1). Stanford, CA: Stanford University, Institute for Research on Education Policy and Practice.

Grove, K. (2002). The invisible role of the central office. *Educational Leadership, 59*(8), 45–47.

Hall, G. E., George, A. A., & Rutherford, W. L. (1979). *Measuring stages of concern about the innovation: A manual for the use of the SoC questionnaire.* Austin: University of Texas, Research and Development Center for Teacher Education.

Hall, G., & Hord, S. (1987). *Change in schools: Facilitating the process.* Albany: State University of New York Press.

Hall, G., & Loucks, S. (1978, April). *Innovation configurations analyzing the adaptation of innovations.* Paper presented at the annual meeting of the American Educational Research Association, Toronto, Ontario, Canada.

Hanna, R. (2013, July). *Common strategies for uncommon achievement: How districts enable and support high-performing schools.* Washington, DC: Center for American Progress.

Hargreaves, A., & Fullan, M. (2012). *Professional capital: Transforming teaching in every school.* New York, NY: Teachers College Press.

Hargreaves, A., & Dawe, R. (1989). *Coaching as unreflective practice.* Paper presented at the annual meeting of the American Educational Research Association, San Francisco, CA.

Harkavy, I., & Blank, M. (2002, April 17). Community schools: A vision of learning that goes beyond testing. *Education Week,* 38, 52.

Harris, S., Petrie, G., & Willoughby, W. (2002). Bullying among ninth graders: An exploratory study. *NASSP Bulletin, 86*(630), 3–14.

Harrison, C., & Killion, J. (2007). Ten roles for teacher leaders. *Educational Leadership, 65*(1), 74–77.

Hattie, J. (2009). *Visible learning: A synthesis of over 800 meta-analysis related to achievement.* New York, NY: Routledge.

Hattie, J. (2012a). Know thy impact. *Educational Leadership, 70*(1), 18–23.

Hattie, J. (2012b). *Visible learning for teachers.* London and New York, NY: Routledge.

Healy, J. M. (1990). *Endangered minds: Why children don't think and what we can do about it.* New York, NY: Touchstone.

Heifetz, R., & Linsky, M. (2002). *Leadership on the line.* Boston, MA: Harvard Business School Press.

Henke, L. (2011, May). Connecting with parents at home. *Educational Leadership, 68*(8), 38–41.

Hernandez, J. (2013, August 7). Under new standards, students see sharp decline in test scores. *New York Times.* Retrieved from http://www.nytimes.com/2013/08/08/nyregion/under-new-standards-students-see-sharp-decline-in-test-scores.html.

Hess, F. (2011, November). How to steer the tough budget road ahead: Accelerate your performance. *Phi Delta Kappan, 93*(3), 57–61.

Hess, F. (2013, April). Be a cage-buster. *Educational Leadership, 70*(7), 30–33.

Hess, R., & Robbins, P. (2012). *The data toolkit: Ten tools for supporting schools.* Thousand Oaks, CA: Corwin.

Heward, W. (2013). *Exceptional children* (10th ed.). Boston, MA: Pearson.

Hirsh, S. (1995/1996, December/January). Approaches to improving schools start with developing a shared vision. *School Team Innovator.*

Honig, M. (2012, April). District central office leadership as teaching: How central office administrators support principals' development as instructional leaders. *Educational Administration Quarterly, 48*(4), 733–774.

Honig, M., Copland, M., Rainey, L., Lorton, J. A., & Newton, M. (2010, April). *Central office transformation for district-wide teaching and learning improvement.* Seattle: Center for the Study of Teaching and Policy, University of Washington.

Hord, S., Rutherford, W., Huling-Austin, L., & Hall, G. (1987). *Taking charge of change.* Alexandria, VA: ASCD.

Houston, P. (2002). From tragedy emerge positive lessons for leaders. *School Administrator, 3*(59), 46.

Isaacson, W. (2011). *Steve Jobs.* New York, NY: Simon & Schuster.

Ishimaru, A. (2012, June). From heroes to organizers: Principals and education organizing in urban school reform. *Educational Administration Quarterly, 49*(1), 3–51.

Jacobson, R., Hodges, R., & Blank, M. (2011, October). Mutual support. *Principal Leadership, 12*(2), 18–22.

Jenkins, J., & Pfeifer, S. (2012, January). The principal as curriculum leader. *Principal Leadership, 12*(5), 31–34.

Johnson, J. (2008, September). The principal's priority 1. *Educational Leadership, 66*(1), 72–75.

Johnson, J. (2013, April). The human factor. *Educational Leadership, 70*(7), 17–21.

Johnson, P., & Chrispeels, J. (2010, December). Linking the central office and its schools for reform. *Educational Administration Quarterly, 46*(5), 738–775.

Johnson, S. M. (2012, Spring). Having it both ways: Building the capacity of individual teachers and their schools. *Harvard Educational Review, 82*(1), 107–122, 167.

Johnson, S. M., & Fiarman, S. (2012, November). The potential of peer review. *Educational Leadership, 70*(3), 20–25.

Johnston, R. C. (2001, March 7). Central office is critical bridge to help schools. *Education Week,* 18–20.

Joyce, B., & Showers, B. (1981). Improving inservice training: The message of research. *Educational Leadership, 37,* 379–385.

Joyce, B., & Weil, M. (1972). *Models of teaching.* Englewood Cliffs, NJ: Prentice Hall.

Kanter, R. M. (1997). *On the frontiers of management.* Boston: Harvard Business School Press.

Kelehear, Z. (2004). Reflection helps good leaders find inner balance. *Journal of Staff Development, 25*(2), 72.

Khalifa, M. (2012, August). A re-new-ed paradigm in successful urban school leadership: Principal as community leader. *Educational Administration Quarterly, 48*(3), 424–467.

Kipp, G. (2012, Spring). The proliferation of the peripatetic principal. *The Principal News, 41*(3), 38.

Kirn, W. (2007). The autumn of the multitaskers. *Atlantic Monthly, 300*(4), 72–76.

Kise, J. A. G., & Russell, B. (2008). *Differentiated school leadership: Effective collaboration, communication, and change through personality type.* Thousand Oaks, CA: Corwin.

Knapp, M., Copland, M., Honig, M., Plecki, M., & Portin, B. (2010, April). Urban renewal. *JSD.*

Kohn, A. (1996). *Beyond discipline: From compliance to community.* Alexandria, VA: ASCD.

Kouzes, J. M., & Posner, B. (2002). *The leadership challenge.* San Francisco, CA: Jossey-Bass.

Kouzes, J. M., & Posner, B. A. (2006). *The encouraging the heart workbook.* San Francisco, CA: Jossey-Bass.

Kriegel, R. (1991). *If it ain't broke . . . break it!* New York, NY: Warner.

Kruse, S. D., & Seashore Louis, K. (2009). *Building strong school cultures: A guide to leading change.* Thousand Oaks, CA: Corwin.

Lachat, M., Williams, M., & Smith, S. (2006). Making sense of all your data. *Principal Leadership, 7*(2), 16–21.

Lawton, W. (2002, April 2). Expert gives lesson in crisis communication. *The Oregonian,* p. C5.

Learning Forward. (2013). *Standards for professional learning.* Retrieved from www .learningforward.org/publications.

Lederman, J. (2013, February 15). Presidential Citizens Award bestowed to 6 teachers killed in Sandy Hook Elementary School shooting. *Huffington Post.* Retrieved from http://www.huffingtonpost.com/2013/02/15/presidential-citizens-medal-newtown_n_2696015.html.

Lee, V. E., Smith, J. B., Perry, T. E., & Smylie, M. A. (1999). *Social support, academic press, and student achievement: A view from the middle grades in Chicago.* Chicago, IL: Consortium on Chicago School Reform.

Lehmuller, P., & Switzer, A. (2002). September 11: An elementary school at ground zero. *Principal, 81*(4), 52–54.

Leithwood, K., & Jantzi, D. (2008, October). Linking leadership to student learning: The contributions of leader efficacy. *Educational Administration Quarterly, 44*(4), 496–528.

Lerman, B. (2010, September). Addressing bullying: Policy and practice. *Principal Leadership, 11*(1), 34–37.

Lerner, M., Volpe, J., & Lindell, B. (2003). *A practical guide for crisis response in our schools.* New York, NY: American Academy of Experts in Traumatic Stress.

Lewin, K. (1951). In D. Cartwright (Ed.), *Field theory in social science: Selected theoretical papers.* New York, NY: Harper.

Lewis, C. (2002). Everywhere I looked: Levers and pendulums. *Journal of Staff Development, 23*(3), 59–65.

Lewis, T., Amini F., & Lannon, R. (2000). *A general theory of love.* New York, NY: Random House.

Little, J. W. (1982, May). Keynote address to Napa mentor teachers. Napa, CA.

Long, C. (2008, May). Silencing cyberbullies. *NEA Today,* 28–29.

Louis, K. S., Leithwood, K., Wahlstrom, K., & Anderson, S. (2010). *Learning from leadership: Investigating the links to improved student learning: Final report of research to The Wallace Foundation.* Minneapolis: University of Minnesota and Toronto: University of Toronto.

Maeroff, G. (1993). *Team building for school change.* New York, NY: Teachers College Press.

Manobianco, M. (2002). Guiding practices for using data to improve student learning. *The Principal News: A Journal of the Association of Washington School Principals, 31*(1), 16–17.

Markle, B., & Van Koevering, S. (2013, May). Reviving Ed Bell. *Phi Delta Kappan, 94*(8), 8–12.

Marrs-Morford, L. & Marshall, R. (2012, September). Financial crisis 101. *Principal Leadership, 13*(1), 36–40.

Marshall, K. (2012a, November). Fine tuning teacher evaluation. *Educational Leadership, 70*(3), 50–53.

Marshall, K. (2012b, November). Let's cancel the dog-and-pony show. *Phi Delta Kappan, 94*(3), 19–23.

Marzano, R. (2009, September). Setting the record straight on "high-yield" strategies. *Phi Delta Kappan, 91*(1), 30–37.

Marzano, R., & Waters, T. (2007, March). *Balanced leadership framework: School leadership that works.* Presentation at the annual conference of the Association for Supervision and Curriculum Development, Chicago, IL.

Marzano, R., Frontier, R., & Livingston, D. (2011). *Effective supervision.* Alexandria, VA: ASCD.

Marzano, R., Pickering, D., & Pollock, J. (2001). *Classroom instruction that works.* Alexandria, VA: Association for Supervision and Curriculum Development.

Marzano, R. J., Waters, T., & McNulty, B. A. (2005). *School leadership that works: From research to results.* Alexandria, VA: ASCD.

Maxwell, L. (2006, October 11). School shootings in policy spotlight. *Education Week,* pp. 1, 16–17.

McFarlan, D., & Harrison, R. (2010, Fall). Synopsis of the CCSS initiative. *Curriculum in Context, 38*(2), 9–10.

McKenzie, K., Christman, D., Hernandez, F., Fierro, E., Capper, C., Dantley, M., et al. (2008). From the field: A proposal for educating leaders for social justice. *Educational Administration Quarterly, 44,* 111–138.

McNulty, R. J. (2009). *It's not us against them: Creating the schools we need,* Rexford, NY: International Center for Leadership in Education.

McShane, M. (2013, August 1). Common core not-so craziness. *Teachers College Record.* Retrieved from http://www.tcrecord.org.

McTighe, J., & Wiggins, G. (2012). *From common core standards to curriculum: Five big ideas.* Retrieved from http://grantwiggins.files.wordpress.com/2012/09/mctighe_wiggins_final_common_core_standards.pdf.

Medina, J. (2009). *Brain rules: 12 principles for surviving and thriving at work, home, and school,* Seattle, WA: Pear Press.

Meier, D. (1995). How our schools could be. *Phi Delta Kappan, 76,* 369–373.

Mellard, D., Prewett, S., & Deshler. (2012, April). Strong leadership for RTI success. *Principal Leadership, 12*(8), 29–32.

Mendels, P., & Mitgang, L. (2013, April). Creating strong principals. *Educational Leadership, 70*(7), 23–29.

Merton, R. (1957). *Social theory and social structure* (Rev. ed.). Glencoe, IL: Free Press.

MetLife. (2012). *The MetLife survey of the American teacher: Teachers, parents, and the economy.* New York, NY: Author.

MetLife. (February, 2013). *The MetLife survey of the American teacher.* Retrieved from https://www.metlife.com/metlife-foundation/what-we-do/student-achievement/survey-american-teacher.html.

Miller, G. (2007). Individuals with disabilities education act (IDEA) overview. Washington, DC: Committee on Education and Labor, U.S. House of Representatives.

Miller, L. H., & Smith, A. D. (1993). *The stress solution: An action plan to manage stress in your life.* New York, NY: Simon & Schuster.

Mintzberg, H. (1973). *The nature of managerial work.* New York, NY: HarperCollins.

Morrison, G. (2009). *Teaching in America* (5th ed.). Boston, MA: Allyn & Bacon.

Murawski, W., Lockwood, J., Khalili, A., & Johnston, A. (2009/2010, December/January). A bully-free school *Educational Leadership, 67*(4), 75–78.

Murphy, J., & Tobin, K. (2011, November). Homelessness comes to school. *Phi Delta Kappan, 93*(3), 32–37.

Nair, K. (1997). *A higher standard of leadership: Lessons from the life of Gandhi.* San Francisco, CA: Berrett-Koehler.

NASSP & NAESP. (2013). *Leadership matters: What research says about the importance of principal leadership.* Reston, VA: Authors.

National Association for the Education of Homeless Youth. (2013). *Homeless education 101: Facts and resources.* Retrieved from http://www.naehcy.org.

National Association of Elementary School Principals. (2001). *Leading learning communities: Standards for what principals should know and be able to do.* Alexandria, VA: Author.

National Association of Elementary School Principals. (2008). *Leading learning communities: Standards for what principals should know and be able to do, Executive summary.* Alexandria, VA: Author.

National Association of Secondary School Principals. (2004). *Breaking ranks II: Strategies for leading high school reform.* Reston, VA: Author.

National Association of Secondary School Principals. (2008). *NASSP leadership skills assessment.* Retrieved from http://www.principals.org/s_nassp/sec_inside.asp?CID=39&DID=39.

National Governors Association Center for Best Practices, Council of Chief State School Officers. (2010). *Common Core State Standards.* Washington, DC: National Governors Association Center for Best Practices, Council of Chief State School Officers.

National Mental Health Association. (2006). *Coping with the war and terrorism: Tips for college students.* Retrieved from http://www.nmha.org/reassurance/collegetips.cfm.

National School Public Relations Association. (1996). *NSPRA's complete crisis communication management manual for schools.* Rockville, MD: Author.

National School Safety Center. (2010, July 15). *Schools and readiness.* Retrieved from http://www.schoolsafety.us/free-resources/schools-and-readiness.

National Staff Development Council. (2001). *NSDC standards for staff development.* Oxford, OH: Author. Retrieved from http://www.nsdc.org/standards/index.cfm.

Neumerski, C. (2012, August). Rethinking instructional leadership, a review: What do we know about principal, teacher, and coach instructional leadership, and where should we go from here. *Educational Administration Quarterly, 49*(2), 310–347.

Newell, C. (1978). *Human behavior in educational administration.* Englewood Cliffs, NJ: Prentice Hall.

Newmann, F., & Wehlage, G. (1995). *Successful school restructuring.* Madison: University of Wisconsin.

Nidus, G., & Sadder, M. (2011, October). The principal as formative coach. *Educational Leadership, 69*(2), 30–35.

Noguera, P. (2011, November). A broader and bolder approach uses education to break the cycle of poverty. *Phi Delta Kappan, 93*(3), 8–13.

Noguera, P. (2012, February). Saving black and Latino boys. *Phi Delta Kappan, 93*(5), 8–12.

O'Neill, J., & Conzemius, A. (2002). Four keys to a smooth flight. *Journal of Staff Development, 23*(2), 14–18.

Oates, S. (1994). *With malice toward none.* New York, NY: Harper & Row.

Odden, A. (2012, September). Can we pay for current education reform? *Principal Leadership, 13*(1), 65–68.

Odden, A., & Archibald, S. (2009). *Doubling student performance . . . and finding the resources to do it.* San Francisco, CA: Corwin.

Olson, L. (2008, January 16). Assessment to rate principal leadership to be field-tested. *Education Week, 1,* 11.

Ornstein, A., & Levine, D. (2003). *Foundations of education* (8th ed.). Boston, MA: Houghton Mifflin.

Osher, D., Bear, G., Sprague, J., & Doyle, W. (2010, January/February). How can we improve school discipline? *Educational Researcher, 39*(1), 48–58.

Page, S. (2007). *The difference: How the power of diversity creates better groups, firms, schools, and societies.* Princeton, NJ: Princeton University Press.

Parker-Roerden, L., Rudewick, D., & Gorton, D. (2007). *Direct from the field: A guide to bullying prevention.* Retrieved from http://www.mass.gov/Eeohhs2/docs/dph/com_health/violence/bullying_prevent_guide.pdf.

Parsley, D., Dean, C., & Miller, K. (2006). Selecting the right data. *Principal Leadership, 7*(2), 38–42.

Patterson, K., Grenny, J., McMillan, R., & Switzler, A. (2002). *Crucial conversations.* New York, NY: McGraw-Hill.

PBIS.org. (2013). *Response to intervention (RTI) & (PBIS).* Retrieved from http://www.pbis.org/school/rti.aspx.

Peters, T., & Austin, N. (1985). *A passion for excellence.* New York, NY: Warner.

Peterson, D. (2013, April). Drafted! An urban principal's tale. *Educational Leadership, 70*(7), 74–77.

Peterson, K. (1982). Making sense of principals' work. *Australian Administrator, 3*(3), 1–4.

Peterson, K. D., & Deal, T. E. (2002). *Shaping school culture fieldbook.* San Francisco, CA: Wiley.

Peterson, K. D., & Deal, T. E. (2009). *Shaping school culture fieldbook.* San Francisco, CA: Wiley.

Pink, D. (2009). *Drive.* New York, NY: Riverhead Books.

Popham, W. J. (2008, September). Formative assessment. *Principal Leadership, 9*(1), 16–20.

Popham, W. J. (2013, January 9). Formative assessment's 'advocate moment.' *Education Week, 32*(16), 29.

Portin, B., Knapp, M., Dareff, S., Feldman, S., Russell, F. A., Samuelson, C., & Ling Yeh, T. (2009). *Leadership for learning improvement in urban schools.* Seattle: University of Washington.

Portin, B., Schneider, P., DeArmond, M., & Gundlach, L. (2003). *Making sense of leading Schools: A study of the school principalship.* Seattle: University of Washington.

Price, H. (2012, February). Principal-teacher interactions: How affective relationships shape principal and teacher attitudes. *Educational Administration Quarterly, 48*(1), 39–85.

PTA. (2009). *PTA National standards for family-school partnerships: an implementation guide.* Alexandria, VA: Author.

Quinn, J. (2002). Must principals "go it alone"? *Education Week, 21*(36), 40.

Ravitch, D. (2010). *The death and life of the great American school system.* New York, NY: Basic Books.

Rebora, A. (2013, March, 13). Interview with Charlotte Danielson on teaching and the common core. *Education Week Teacher.* Retrieved from http://www.edweek.org/tm/articles/2013/03/13/ccio_danielson_teaching.html.

Reeves, D. B. (2008). *Reframing teacher leadership to improve your school.* Alexandria, VA: ASCD.

Richie, J. (2013, May). The effective and reflective principal. *Phi Delta Kappan, 94*(8), 18–21.

Robbins, P. (1991a). *The development of a collaborative workplace: A case study of Wells Junior High.* Unpublished doctoral dissertation, University of California, Berkeley.

Robbins, P. (1991b). *How to plan and implement a peer coaching program.* Alexandria, VA: ASCD.

Robbins, P., & Alvy, H. (2004). *The new principal's fieldbook.* Alexandria, VA: ASCD.

Robbins, P., Gregory, G., & Herndon, L. (2000). *Thinking inside the block: Strategies for teaching in extended periods of time.* Thousand Oaks, CA: Corwin.

Robelen, E. (2013, May 15). Capacity issues confront implementation of standards. *Educational Week, 32*(31), 1, 12–13.

Robinson, J., & Espelage, D. (2011, October). Inequities in educational and psychological outcomes between LGBTQ and straight students in middle and high school. *Educational Researcher, 40*(7), 315–330.

Rodkin, P. (2011, September). Bullying—and the power of peers. *Educational Leadership, 69*(1), 10–15.

Rooney, J. (2013, Summer). For principals: Planning the first year. *Educational Leadership, 70,* 73–76. Retrieved from http://www.ascd.org/publications/educational-leadership/jun13/vol70/num09/For-Principals@-Planning-the-First-Year.aspx.

Rorrer, A., Skrla, L., & Scheurich, J. (August, 2008). Districts as institutional actors in educational reform. *Educational Administration Quarterly, 44*(3), 307–358.

Rose, M. (2009/2010, December/January). Standards, teaching, and learning. *Phi Delta Kappan, 91*(4), 21–27.

Rosen, M. (2013, September). *AARP Bulletin, 54*(7), 12–13.

Rosenholtz, S. (1989). *Teachers' workplace.* New York, NY: Longman.

Ross, A. (1981). *Child behavior therapy.* New York, NY: Wiley.

Rotherham, A. (2008, December, 15). 21st century skills are not a new education trend but could be a fad. *U. S. News and World Report.* Retrieved from http://www.usnews.com/opinion/articles/2008/12/15/21st-century-skills-are-not-a-new-education-trend-but-could-be-a-fad.

Rotherham, A., & Willingham, D. (2009, September). 21st century skills: The challenges ahead. *Educational Leadership, 67*(1), 16–21.

Rothman, R. (2011, September/October). Five myths about the common core state standards. *Harvard Education Letter, 27*(5), 1–2. Retrieved from http://hepg.org/hel/printarticle/513.

Rothman, R. (2012a, July/August). Nine ways the common core will change classroom practice. *Harvard Education Letter, 28*(4), 1–2. Retrieved from http://hepg.org/hel/printarticle/543.

Rothman, R. (2012b, November). Laying a common foundation for success. *Phi Delta Kappan, 94*(3), 57–61.

Sadler, D. R. (2008). Beyond feedback: Developing student capability in complex appraisal. *Assessment and Evaluation in Higher Education, 35*(5), 535–550.

Samuels, C. (2008, April 30). Principals at the center. *Education Week,* 26–28.

Sarason, S. (1982). *The culture of the school and the problem of change* (2nd ed.). Boston, MA: Allyn & Bacon.

Schein, E. (1985). *Organizational culture and leadership.* San Francisco, CA: Jossey-Bass.

Scherer, M. (2001). How and why standards can improve student achievement: A conversation with Robert J. Marzano. *Educational Leadership, 59*(1), 14–18.

Schlechty, P. (2001). *Shaking up the schoolhouse: How to support and sustain educational innovation.* San Francisco, CA: Jossey-Bass.

Schmoker, M. (2004). Tipping point: From feckless reform to substantive instructional improvement. *Phi Delta Kappan, 85,* 424–432.

Schmoker, M. (2011a, November). Curriculum no. *Phi Delta Kappan, 93*(3), 70–71.

Schmoker, M. (2011b). *Focus.* Alexandria, VA: ASCD.

Schmoker, M. (2011c, October). Turnaround: A tale of two schools. *Phi Delta Kappan, 93*(2), 70–71.

Schmoker, M. (2012, March). Refocus professional development. *Phi Delta Kappan, 93*(6), 68–69.

Schön, D. (1983). *The reflective practitioner.* New York, NY: Basic Books.

Schultz, H., & Yang, D. J. (1997). *Pour your heart into it: How Starbucks built a company one cup at a time.* New York, NY: Hyperion.

Scott, S., & Ganderton, D. (2012, April). Collaborative culture: A willingness to speak the truth serves as a call to action and an important 1st step, *JSD The Learning Forward Journal, 33*(2).

Scott, S., & McLain, B. (2011, April). Collaborative culture: Conflict is normal but learning to deal with conflict skillfully takes practice, *JSD The Learning Forward Journal, 32*(2).

Scott, S., & Moussavi-Bock, D. (2012, June). Collaborative culture: A shift in our perspective can change our attitudes and our outcomes, *JSD The Learning Forward Journal, 33*(3).

Scott, S., & Totten, R. (2013, June). Collaborative culture: Keeping the focus on student learning requires confrontational conversations, *JSD The Learning Forward Journal, 34*(3).

Scott, S., & Turner, J. S. (2010, October). Collaborative culture: Confrontation model of conversation provides tools to discuss and resolve tough issues, *JSD The Learning Forward Journal, 31*(5).

Seashore Louis, K., & Wahlstrom, K. (2011, February). Principals as cultural leaders. *Phi Delta Kappan, 92*(5), 52–56.

Senge, P. (1990). *The fifth discipline.* London: Century Business.

Shah, N. (2013, January 16). Fla. Data link suspension to lower graduation rates. *Education Week, 32*(17), 6–7.

Silver, S., & Hanson, J. R. (1996). *Learning styles and strategies.* Ho-Ho-Kus, NJ: The Thoughtful Press.

Singer, J. (2013, June). Seven super strategies for success over stress. *Educational Leadership, 70*(9), 24–28.

Skretta, J. (2007). Using walkthroughs to gather data for school improvement. *Principal Leadership, 7*(9), 16–23.

Sloan, W. (2008). Collaborating over coffee: Creating a successful school-business partnership. *Education Update, 50*(5), 1–7.

Smith, D. W. (2013, April 25). Who is today's principal? *The Whole Child Blog.* Retrieved from http://www.wholechildeducation.org/blog/who-is-todays-principal.

Soder, R. (2001). *The language of leadership.* San Francisco, CA: Jossey-Bass.

Sparks, D. (1993). The professional development of principals: A conversation with Roland Barth. *Journal of Staff Development, 14*(1), 18–21.

Sparks, D. (1999). Try on strategies to get a good fit: An interview with Susan Loucks-Horsley. *Journal of Staff Development, 20*(3), 56–60.

Sparks, D. (2007). *Leading for results,* Thousand Oaks, CA: Corwin Press.

Sparks, D. (2013, April). Strong teams, strong schools. *JSD The Learning Forward Journal, 34*(2).

Starratt, R. J. (2004). *Ethical leadership.* San Francisco, CA: Jossey-Bass.

Stewart, M. (2006, June). The management myth [Electronic version]. *The Atlantic Monthly.* Retrieved from http://www.theatlantic.com/doc/200606/stewart-business.

Stiggins, R. (2005). Assessment for learning: Building a culture of confident learners. In R. DuFour, R. Eaker, & R. DuFour (Eds.), *On common ground: The power of professional learning communities* (pp. 65–83). Bloomington, IN: National Educational Services.

Stronge, J. (2013, April). Principal evaluation from the ground up. *Educational Leadership, 70*(7), 60–65.

Stumbo, C., & McWalters, P. (2010/2011, December/January). Measuring effectiveness: What will it take? *Educational Leadership, 68*(4), 10–15.

Supovitz, J., Sirinides, P., & May, H. (2010, February). How principals and peers influence teaching and learning. *Educational Administration Quarterly, 46*(1), 31–56.

Swanson, C., & Lloyd, S. (2013, June 6). Graduation rate approaching milestone. *Education Week, 32*(34), 22–24.

Swearer, S., Espelage, D., Vaillancourt, T., & Hymel, S. (2010, January/February). What can be done about school bullying? Linking research to educational practice. *Educational Researcher, 39*(1), 38–47.

Sylwester, R. (1995). *A celebration of neurons: An educator's guide to the brain.* Alexandria, VA: ASCD.

Teeter, A. (1995). Learning about teaching. *Phi Delta Kappan, 76,* 360–364.

The Wallace Foundation. (2012). *The school principal as leader: Guiding schools to better teaching and learning.* New York, NY: Author.

The Wallace Foundation. (2013, January). *The school principal as leader: Guiding schools to better teaching and learning.* Retrieved from http://www.wallacefoundation.org/knowledge-center/school-leadership/effective-principal-leadership/Pages/The-School-Principal-as-Leader-Guiding-Schools-to-Better-Teaching-and-Learning.aspx.

Tierney, J. (2013). The coming revolution in public education. *Atlantic Mobile.* Retrieved from http://m.theatlantic.com/national/archive/2013/04/the-coming-revolution-in-public-education/275163/.

Tierney, R., Carter, M., & Desai, L. (1991). *Portfolio assessment in the reading-writing classroom.* Norwood, MA: Christopher-Gordon.

Tomlinson, C. A. (2012, November). The evaluation of my dreams. *Educational Leadership, 70*(3), 89.

Tovani, C. (2012, September). Feedback is a two-way street. *Educational Leadership, 70*(1), 48–51.

Tschannen-Moran, M. (2004). *Trust matters: Leadership for successful schools.* San Francisco, CA: Jossey-Bass.

Tucker, P. (2001). Helping struggling teachers. *Educational Leadership, 58*(5), 52–55.

Tyler, R. (1949). *Basic principles of curriculum and instruction:* Chicago, IL: University of Chicago Press.

Uebbing, S., & Ford, M. (2011). *The life cycle of leadership.* Oxford, OH: Learning Forward.

Umphrey, J. (2006). IDEA: A tool for students. *Principal Leadership, 6*(9), 6.

U.S. Department of Education, Office of Elementary and Secondary Education, Office of Safe and Healthy Students. (2013). *Guide for developing high-quality school emergency operations plans.* Washington, DC: Author.

Varlas, L. (Ed.) (2013, August). A closer look at principal evaluation. *Education Update, 55*(8), 5.

von Frank, V. (2010, Fall). Trust matters—for educators, parents, and students. *Tools for Schools, 14*(1).

von Frank, V. (2011, Fall). Leadership teams set the course for school improvement. *The Learning Principal, 7*(1), 1-1-5.

von Frank, V. (2013, September). Group smarts. *The Learning System, 8*(4). Retrieved from http://learningforward.org/docs/default-source/learning-system/ls-sum13-group-smarts.pdf.

Waller, W. (1932). *The sociology of teaching.* New York, NY: Wiley.

Warner, C. (2000). *Promoting your school: Going beyond PR* (2nd ed.). Thousand Oaks, CA: Corwin.

Wayne, L., & Kaufman, L. (2001, September 16). Leadership, put to a new test. *New York Times* (Money & Business Section 3), pp. 1, 4.

Weissbourd, R., & Jones, S. (2012, October). Joining hands against bullying. *Educational Leadership, 70*(2), 26–31.

Wheatley, M. (1992). *Leadership and the new science.* San Francisco, CA: Berrett-Koehler.

Wieder, B. (2013, March 5). *States tackle school safety after Sandy Hook shootings.* Retrieved from http://www.pewstates.org/projects/stateline/headlines/states-tackle-school-safety-after-sandy-hook-shootings-85899456250.

Wiggins, G. (2012, September). Seven keys to effective feedback. *Educational Leadership, 70*(1), 10–16.

Wiggins, G., & McTighe, J. (1998). *Understanding by design guide to creating high-quality units.* Alexandria, VA: ASCD.

Wiliam, D. (2012, September). Feedback part of a system. *Educational Leadership, 70*(1), 31–34.

Willard, N. (2005). *Educator's guide to cyberbullying and cyberthreats.* Retrieved from http://csriu.org/cyberbully/docs/cbcteducator.pdf.

Wolfe, P. (2001). *Brain matters: Translating research into classroom practice.* Alexandria, VA: ASCD.

Wood, F., Thompson, S., & Russell, F. (1981). Designing effective staff development programs. In B. Dillon-Peterson (Ed.), *Staff development/organizational development* (pp. 59–91). Alexandria, VA: ASCD.

Worden, J., Hinton, C., & Fischer, K. W. (2011, May). What does the brain have to do with learning? *Phi Delta Kappan, 92*(8), 8–13.

Yetter, N. (2012, November 14). Addressing bullying. *Education Week, 32*(12), 25.

Young, A. L. (2011, October). LGBT students want educators to speak up for them. *Phi Delta Kappan, 93*(2), 35–37.

Zenger, J., & Folkman, J. (2002). *The extraordinary leader.* New York, NY: McGraw-Hill.

Zhao, Y. (2009). *Catching up or leading the way.* Alexandria, VA: ASCD.

ADDITIONAL READINGS

Alvy, H. (2005). Preventing the loss of wisdom in our schools: Respecting and retaining successful veteran teachers. *Phi Delta Kappan, 86,* 764–766, 771.

ASCD. (2010). *Curriculum 21: Essential education for a changing world.* (Jacob, H. H., Ed.). Alexandria, VA: Author.

Bracey, G. (2009/2010, December/January). Our eternal (and futile?) quest for high standards. *Phi Delta Kappan, 91*(4), 75–76.

Burlingame, M. (2008). *Abraham Lincoln: A life.* (Vol. 1–2). Baltimore, MD: Johns Hopkins University Press.

Fullan, M. (1997). *What's worth fighting for in the principalship.* New York, NY: Teachers College Press.

Gardner, J. W. (1990). *On leadership.* New York, NY: Free Press.

Gawande, A. (2009). *The checklist manifesto.* New York, NY: Picador.

Greenleaf, R. (1991). *Servant leadership.* Mahwah, NJ: Paulist Press.

Hersh, R. (2009, September). A well-rounded education for a flat world. *Educational Leadership, 67*(1), 51–53.

Izzo, J. (2008). *The five secrets you must discover before you die.* San Francisco, CA: Berrett-Koehler.

Kendall, F. (2006). *Understanding white privilege.* New York, NY: Routledge.

Marzano, R. (2003). *What works in schools.* Alexandria, VA: ASCD.

Moss, C., & Brookhart, S. (2013, April). A new view of walk-throughs. *Educational Leadership, 70*(7), 42–45.

Murphy, J. (2005). Unpacking the foundations of ISLLC standards and addressing concerns in the academic community. *Educational Administration Quarterly, 41,* 154–191.

Sparks, D., & Loucks-Horsley, S. (1990). Models of staff development. In R. Houston (Ed.), *Handbook of research on teacher education* (pp. 234–250). New York, NY: Macmillan.

Index

Note: In page references, f indicates figures.

CORWIN

A SAGE Company